NOTES OF A TOUR
IN
NORTHERN ITALY

1.—NORTH PORCH, STA. MARIA MAGGIORE, BERGAMO.

Frontispiece.

NOTES OF A TOUR
IN
NORTHERN ITALY

GEORGE E. STREET

WATERSTONE · LONDON
HIPPOCRENE BOOKS · NEW YORK

Waterstone and Co. Limited
49 Hay's Mews
London W1X 7RT
Hippocrene Books, Inc.
171 Madison Ave.
New York, NY 10016

First published in London by
John Murray in 1855

This edition first published by
Waterstone and Co. Limited © 1986

UK ISBN 0 947752 42 0
US ISBN 0 87052 301 5

Front Cover: Seventeenth-century Italian brocade chasuble
Reproduced by kind permission of the Board of Trustees
of the Victoria and Albert Museum

Cover design by Michael Head

Printed and bound in Great Britain by
Richard Clay (The Chaucer Press) Ltd., Bungay, Suffolk

To the Memory

OF

THE RIGHT REV. SAMUEL WILBERFORCE,

LORD BISHOP OF WINCHESTER,

ETC. ETC.,

IN TOKEN OF THE AUTHOR'S MOST SINCERE AFFECTION,

AND

IN GRATITUDE FOR NUMBERLESS BENEFITS RECEIVED FROM HIM,

THIS VOLUME,

ORIGINALLY DEDICATED TO HIM IN 1855,

IS NOW INSCRIBED.

PREFACE TO THE SECOND EDITION.

THE First Edition of this volume has been so long out of print that I had almost ceased to regard myself as responsible for all that it contains. It was the rapid and fresh summary of a happy journey undertaken in the early years of my artistic career. There were, I knew, many details in which it could easily be improved, and many journeys taken over the same ground might have enabled me to go far more into detail than I was able to do when I published it. I find, however, on reading again what I wrote so long ago, that age and greater knowledge of the subject have generally confirmed my old ideas, and that, as far as regards the principles of my book, I still believe them to be true and just. In revising what I wrote, however, I have found myself obliged to make many alterations and additions, sometimes in relation to towns not visited on my first journey, sometimes in reference to buildings either not described at all or at best insufficiently described before. In doing this I have endeavoured not to increase too much the bulk of the volume, and as far as possible not to interfere with the general character or tone of its contents, though in the process of revision the larger portion of the book has had to be re-written.

I hope, if other occupations admit of it, before long to add to this volume a second, containing notes of tours in the

centre and south of Italy, undertaken with the same object
of studying and describing the too little appreciated art of
Italy in the Middle Ages, which seems to me to be almost
equally full of interest in all parts of the Peninsula.

The materials which I have accumulated for this purpose
are only too considerable, and the very richness of the subject
has made me shy of approaching it; but the necessity of
publishing another edition of this volume has revived my
resolution to complete as soon as possible the work which
I originally proposed to myself, and of which I have never
lost sight. But whether I accomplish this or not, the
volume which I now republish may, I hope, give a tolerably
complete view of Italian Gothic architecture north of the
Apennines.

Those who wish for further archæological details as to
the age and history of buildings, will not find great difficulty in supplementing what I have written. For myself I
confess at once that I have not had time or opportunity
for examining the documentary history of the buildings I
have described, and that the dates where I have given them
are generally obtained at second-hand, though never given
save where they accord with the architectural character of
the work. It was never for merely archæological purposes
that I made my many journeys in Italy. Before I first
travelled there I had made myself well acquainted with all the
best remains of the Middle Ages in England : I had travelled,
sketch-book in hand, through France and Germany, and I
knew, therefore, something of the art of our fathers in most
districts north of the Alps. But so far I had found no time
or opportunity for the study of those early Italian buildings
which give the key to the history and style of ours, or of
those later works in which, with more or less distinctness,
the architects north of the Alps repaid the debt they had
previously incurred to the South.

I felt then, as I do now, that no study of architecture was complete which did not proceed exhaustively with the study of all European varieties, and above all of that of Italy. Moreover, there was something in the practice and tendencies of our own day which gave special interest and fascination to such a study. We had gone on in our old paths, studying the works of our own country, which in some respects were deficient in their teaching. We wished to combine the best architecture, the best painting, and the best sculpture in our works. The world seemed to respond to our aspirations, and it is south and not north of the Alps that examples of such a combination have to be looked for. So again it was desirable at any rate to meet the demand which was naturally arising for colour in construction, and here again it was in Italy only that numerous ancient examples of such a combination were to be found. These were the special inducements to me in my earliest journey to Italy, and their influence is as strong as ever upon me. I feel, indeed, even more now than then, the importance of such study to the English architect of to-day. The more men educate themselves by the study of ancient examples, the more is their work likely to become refined and scholarly, whilst at the same time there is no real risk of its becoming less original.

It is quite possible, and one wishes above everything to see it usual, for architects to design all their work without special reference to, or really copying from, any old work. But before doing this they ought at least to put themselves in the same position as to knowledge of what had been done before as that in which their forefathers were. Unless they do so, the desire for originality will only be satisfied by the production of excesses and monstrosities, whose only claim is that they are new—one which, in spite of those who demand a new style, I venture to declare to be their sufficient condemnation.

It remains only to say, that since I first visited Italy two works have been published which add infinitely to our knowledge of the sister arts of painting and sculpture, and enable the artist to travel with a full certainty that he will not lose anything by reason of the ignorance or carelessness of his guide. I need hardly say that I refer to Messrs. Crowe and Cavalcaselle's 'History of Painting in Northern Italy,' and to Mr. C. C. Perkins's admirable volumes on 'Italian' and 'Tuscan Sculptors.' To the latter, indeed, I owe I know not how many acknowledgments for the information I have derived from him. He has done that for the History of Mediæval and post-Mediæval sculpture in Italy which had before hardly even so much as been attempted, and his facts and conclusions are almost always so stated as to command the assent of his readers.

PREFACE TO THE FIRST EDITION.

In these days of railways and rapid travelling there is scarcely any excuse for ignorance of Continental art. The most busy man finds some short holiday in the course of the year, and, if wise as well as busy, spends it not in quiet sojourn at home, but in active search of the picturesque, the beautiful, or the old, in nature or in art, either in his own country or abroad.

And as the holidays of busy men are short, and therefore to be made as much of as possible, I conceive that I shall be rendering some service, and providing myself with a fair excuse for my presumption, if I venture to shew, by a simple narrative of a tour undertaken in the course of the year before last, how much it is possible to accomplish with pleasure, and, when one has some definite object in view, with profit of no common kind, even in a short holiday.

There are many classes of travellers, and each doubtless flatters itself that its own is the very best of all modes of travelling; and sorry should I be to attempt to disabuse any one of so pleasant a self-deceit. But the more I think of it, the more certain it appears that the reasons and objects which always take me away from home are precisely such as make up the sum of happiness and pleasure to a traveller.

Indeed, without some definite object before him, beyond

the mere desire of relaxation and pleasure, few travellers know that thorough joy of heart which an architect feels as he begins the journey which bears him away from home on some ecclesiological or architectural ramble.

Such an one, hard-worked for more than five-sixths of the year, may, if he will, press into the short remainder left to him for a holiday as much both of profit and of pleasure as it is possible to conceive. He goes, sketch-book in hand, with some ancient town or thrice noble cathedral set before him as his goal; and, passing along smiling valleys, or over noble mountains, drinks in all that he sees, not the less gratefully or delightedly in that he views it as the preface only to his more intense enjoyment in the study and pursuit of his own well-beloved art.

If such be my case—and such it is—wonder not, gentle reader, that I desire to shew how much enjoyment may be snatched from time in little more than one short month, nor that I am anxious to put on paper the thoughts that have been uppermost in my mind as I travelled, and looked at and drew the old builders' works in the north of Italy, the more as they seem to bear with much force upon questions debated with more and more eagerness and anxiety every day, by very many of those who take the most lively interest in the progress of Christian art.

In past years I had travelled—rapidly, it is true, but not without learning much, very much, of what was useful—by the noble cities of Belgium, up the church-besprinkled banks of the fair Rhine, over the plains of Bavaria, and through much that was most noble and interesting in different parts of France and Germany; I had dreamt of old times and old men in the antique streets of Bruges and Nuremberg, and under the shade of the still more ancient walls of Regensburg, in the solemn naves of Amiens, of Köln, of Freiburg, of Strasburg and Chartres, and of many more most noble piles; I had paced the ruins of old abbeys, and studied, so far as I could, in all of them the science and the art of my forefathers; but so far all my time had been devoted to the study of Northern art, and I had found no time and no opportunity for the study of that modification of the pointed style which distinguishes the cities and the churches of the north of Italy. No wonder then that, with a prospect at last of a first sight of Italy and Italian architecture before me, I looked forward long and anxiously for the end of summer, for that happy autumn which brings ease and relaxation to so many a wearied heart; and that when at last, at the latter end of August, I found myself absolutely on my way, I was in no common degree disposed for the thorough enjoyment of all that I met with.

It is well here to observe, by the way, that there is much in the present position of architects and the world which may give to these few remarks upon the pointed architecture of the north of Italy—slight and sketchy though they may be—a degree of value beyond what they would have had only a short time since.

It is impossible not to feel that the great and general interest in art, created by the revival of true principles within the last few years, is a subject of the greatest congratulation to all true artists. It is not only in architecture, but happily in painting also, that first principles are now studied with some determination by men who command the respect of a world educated hitherto to admire and believe in the falsest and weakest schools of art. It was, therefore, with the desire to see how far these first principles were worked out by the architects of the Middle Ages in Italy, how far moreover they were developed in directions unattempted by their brethren in the North, and how far they have succeeded in leaving us really noble works for our study and admiration, that I undertook my journey.

Let me say, too, at the same time, that I started without either the intention or the desire to examine at all carefully the works of the Renaissance architects. For this there were many reasons—among others my own unfitness by predilection and education for the task, the shortness of my time, and the fact that, as it appears to me, their works have already received as much both in the way of illustration and of description as they deserve.

I should wish also, I must confess, in all my studies of foreign architecture, to confine myself to those buildings in which there appear to me to be the germs at least of an art true and beautiful in itself, and of service to us in our attempts to improve our own work. It does not appear to me that the works of the Italian Renaissance architects really contain this. I see no reason whatever for doubting that if we wish for a purer school of art we must either entirely forget their works, or remember them so far only as to take warning by their faults and failures. I see no reason for allowing that they have succeeded in carrying out true principles, either of construction or ornamentation, to any greater extent than their imitators in England. The same falseness of construction, and heaviness, coarseness, and bad grotesqueness of ornamentation, seem ever to attend their works, together with the same contempt of simplicity, repose, and delicacy which we are so accustomed to connect with them. In short, I see but little reason to differ from the estimate which Mr. Ruskin has given of their merits in the 'Stones of Venice,' and what he has so well said I need not attempt to enlarge upon.

My own feeling is, that as in the pointed arch we have not only the most beautiful, but at the same time incomparably the most convenient feature in construction which has ever been, or which, I firmly believe, ever can be invented, we should not be true artists if we neglected to use it.

I hold firmly the doctrine that no architect can properly neglect to avail himself of every improvement in construction which the growing intelligence of this mechanical age can afford him; but this doctrine in no way hinders the constant employment of the pointed arch; on the contrary, it makes it necessary, because it is at once the most beautiful and the most economical way of doing the work that has to be done.

There are, I well know, advocates for the round arch, whose theory appears to be that we ought to go back for some ages, to throw ourselves as it were into the position of men who knew only the round arch, and from this to attempt to develope in some new direction: this is Mr. Petit's theory, and it is, as appears to me, one which it is not difficult to meet.

Its supporters assert that pointed architecture is so essentially the effort of a particular age, and marked by certain peculiarities so decided, as to be filled, even in its most noble works, with a kind of spirit which in this age it is vain to attempt again to evoke. The old Gothic spirit is, they say, dead; and, glorious as it was, its flight was but meteor-like, and, having passed across the horizon of the world in its rapid course, it has sunk beyond all possibility of revival.

It appears to me that those who so argue confound the accidents with the elements of the true Gothic architecture of the Middle Ages, and mistake altogether the object which, I trust, most architects would propose to themselves in striving for its revival. The elements are the adoption of the best principles of construction, and the ornamentation naturally and properly, and without concealment, of the construction; the accidents are, as it appears to me, the particular character which individual minds may have given to their work, the savageness, or the grotesqueness as it

has been called, which is mainly to be discovered in the
elaboration of particular features by some particular sculptor
or architect, and which in the noblest works—and, indeed, I
might say, in most works—one sees no trace of.   The true
Gothic architects of the Middle Ages had, in short, an intense
love of nature grafted on an equally intense love of reality
and truth, and to this it is that we owe the true nobility
and abiding beauty of their works; nor need we in this age
despond, for if we be really earnest in our work, there is
nothing in this which we need fear to miss, nothing which
we may not ourselves possess if we will, and nothing therefore to prevent our working in the same spirit, and with the
same results, as our forefathers.

The mediæval architecture of Italy presents, however,
one further practical argument against this theory of the
lovers of the round arch which they cannot, I think, meet.

It will be found in the following pages that in Italy
there did not exist that distinction between the use of round
and pointed arches which did exist for three centuries north
of the Alps.   They were content there to use whichever
was most convenient, and whichever appeared to them to be
most effective in its intended position.   We therefore find,
in most Italian mediæval buildings, round and pointed arches
used in the same work, the former generally for ornament,
the latter for construction; and the effect of this is in some
degree to make us lessen the rigidity with which a study of
Northern art might otherwise affect our views on this point.
But I think no argument can be used by the lovers of the
round arch which would ever go farther than to leave us open
to the choice of both round and pointed arches, just as in
these old Italian buildings: they have no right to say,
"You may not use the pointed arch at all," but they perhaps
may be allowed to ask, "Why exclude for ever the round
arch?" and then I should refer them to Italy for a proof

that as a rule the mixture of the two is neither harmonious nor satisfactory; whilst at the same time I should go on to shew them that, when they talk of the virtues of Roman and Romanesque architecture, of the repose and the simplicity which distinguish them, of their grandeur and their general breadth and nobility of effect—in all these things they do but sing the praises of the best Italian architecture of the thirteenth and fourteenth centuries, and that in studying the style we may well be guided by it in what we do, not to the forgetfulness of the glories of our own land, but to the development in a forward direction of what we inherit from our forefathers of that architecture which, after a lapse of three centuries, we now see on all sides reviving with fresh vigour from its temporary grave, and which requires only prudence and skill on the part of its professors to make even more perfect than before.

My object therefore in the following pages will be mainly to shew the peculiarities of the development of pointed architecture in Italy, and specially to shew in what way the materials so commonly used there—brick and marble—were introduced both in decoration and in construction.   All these points are of the very greatest importance to us, for I am persuaded that not only will some reference to Italian models do somewhat towards the improvement of our art, but that in no matter is information more needed, and improvement more easy, than in the use of brick in architecture; whilst working in marble has been as yet so little practised among us, that we may almost regard it as at present unattempted, though, as I hope to shew, there is no longer any reason why this should be the case.

It is impossible to conclude this Preface without mention of the obligations which not only all who travel in Italy, but all who are interested in good architecture, owe to Mr. Ruskin. No man need or can profess his acquiescence in every one of the opinions which he has propounded, but as an architect I feel strongly that a great debt of gratitude is owing to him for his brilliant advocacy of many laws and truths in which every honest architect ought gladly to acquiesce. He may be well content to bear the opposition which he has evoked, satisfied that all that he has written is in the main most certainly for the benefit and exaltation of art of all kinds.

Nor less is a debt of gratitude to be acknowledged by every traveller to my friend Mr. Webb for his most excellent and trusty work on 'Continental Ecclesiology:' it is certainly the most absolutely correct guide-book ever drawn up for ecclesiologists anywhere; and in travelling over the same ground, as I have done in this tour, my excuse for giving what I have in the way of descriptions of the same buildings is, that what I have written has been all with a view, beyond that of merely describing the churches, of shewing the principles upon which their builders worked, and giving, so far as the limits of such a work will allow, drawings of the buildings I have described.

It will depend on circumstances whether I am able at some future day to continue my inquiries among the churches and domestic buildings of Central Italy, a tract at least as rich as that over which the tour described in the following pages took me.

It remains only to say that all the illustrations which I have given are engraved from my own drawings on the wood from my sketches made on the spot, and that I have endeavoured as much as possible to avoid giving subjects which have been before published. It would have been easy to add largely to them, especially from my sketches in Venice, but it seemed to me that, as this could only be accomplished by adding also to the cost of the book, it was much better to omit them. I have avoided therefore giving drawings of any buildings already drawn by Mr. Gally Knight, to whose work I must refer my readers for representations of several of the buildings described, and for illustrations of Venice I must refer to Mr. Ruskin's engravings and to the photographs which have rendered her features so well known to almost all students of architecture.

In conclusion, I cannot speak too highly of the assistance afforded to the architectural student by Murray's Handbook of Northern Italy: it is almost invariably correct, and gives just what one wants to know of nearly all buildings of any interest or importance.

Oxford, 1855.

(xx)

CONTENTS.

CONTENTS.

CHAPTER XI.

CHAPTER XII.

CHAPTER XIII.

CHAPTER XIV.

APPENDIX.

BRICK AND MARBLE

MIDDLE AGES.

—◦—

CHAPTER I.

" Yet waft me from the harbour-mouth,
Wild wind!   I seek a warmer sky,
And I will see before I die
The palms and temples of the South."
Tennyson.

Routes to Italy—Paris—Strasburg—Rouffach—Basel.

An architectural tour in Italy seems to afford about as
much prospect of pleasure and information combined as any
which it is possible for an English student to take.   He
may see, if time allows, so much on his road, that whether
one thinks of the journey or the end of it all is, at any rate
in the perspective, charming.   And in these days when, what
with railways, through-tickets, and Cook's and other guides
for timid tourists, the journey from one end of Europe to
the other is made so quickly and so cheaply as to be
within most educated men's reach, it is no wonder if most
of us in our turn make the venture.

Many are the ways by which one may reach the North
of Italy, but one or two only of them seem now to be
commonly used, to the exclusion of all others, and with
great loss of pleasure to all travellers who make the journey
more than once.   The natural, because the quickest, road is
now by the Mont Cenis tunnel to Turin, and for the country

described in these pages nothing can be more convenient. But when my first journey was made, it was more easy to take one of the passes leading to Milan, and so I went by the Splügen. Since those days I have found my way to and from Italy by other roads which I recommend strongly to others. I pass by such a well-known road as that by railway over the Brenner, in order to suggest three other roads, either of which brings the traveller down upon Venetia in the happiest possible frame of mind if he is at all capable of being moved to pleasure by the sight of exquisite scenery, pleasant and religious people, and roads and country not too much crowded with tourists.

The first of these is by the Lake of Constance, the Vorarlberg, and the Vintschgau to Botzen; the next by the Brenner pass as far as Franzensfeste, and thence by the Ampezzo pass through Cortina and Cadore—Titian's country —to Conegliano, and so by railway to Venice, a road lighted up by the wild beauty of the Dolomite mountains and now unaccountably neglected by English tourists; the third, and perhaps the most charming, though somewhat indirect, and requiring more time, again by the Brenner as far as Franzensfeste, thence by railway to Lienz—stopping to see the fine church and Dolomite mountains at Innichen on the way—and then by country carriages from the Pusterthal into the Gailthal where there is the most charming combination I know of pastoral and picturesque scenery, seasoned by interesting old churches; and thence to Ober Tarvis and by the stern and magnificent Predil pass to the head of the Adriatic at Gorizia, whence—after seeing Aquileja and Grado —the traveller may, with halts at Udine and Pordenone, reach his goal at Venice by railway.

But in this my first journey to Italy, I was sufficiently happy in finding the Splügen prescribed for me as on the whole the most convenient mode of reaching in succession

all the spots which had most special interest for me. My
scheme was to make myself fairly well acquainted with
some of the most interesting Italian cities north of the
Apennines, and for this purpose to descend from the Splügen
on Bergamo, and from thence to go on to Venice, halting as
often as necessary by the way, and then to return by Mantua,
Cremona, and Pavia, or by Ferrara, Bologna, Parma, and
Piacenza to Milan, and so home. And railways, if they have
made the journey somewhat more easy than it was, and
have deprived it now and then of the charm which always
attends the recollection of impediments and difficulties on
the road, have not in any way altered the advantages of such
a route for those whose tastes are at all akin to those which
I carried abroad with me in those days, and carry still with
undiminished strength. Whether, however, one enters Italy
by one pass or another, the first part of one's journey is by
the well-worn road to Paris, which, by reason, I suppose, of
its being the prelude to nearly every holiday tour that I
make, never seems to be stale, old, or too well-known.

There is something very novel, and it strikes me more
every time it is seen, in the aspect of everything directly you
have crossed the Channel; indeed, there is no country in
Europe so much as France, and no city, perhaps, so much
as Paris, which strikes an Englishman as being foreign in
its aspect, and new in all its customs and proceedings.
The dress of every one, the arrangements of the railways,
the harnessing and character of the horses, the mode of life
in hotels, and the ordinary habits and pleasant traits of the
middle classes are all quite fresh to the English eye. Nor
is the aspect of the country less so : fields cut up into small
strips of a dozen kinds of crops ; unprosperous-looking cows,
each feeding discontentedly and drearily, tethered to a man
or woman on a small patch of grass ; corn cut and then
stacked in small cocks for a month or two of exposure to the

pleasant changes of the atmosphere; and the entire absence
of hedge-rows and other trees than poplars, all go to
make up a thoroughly un-English picture.

After skirting the coast and its dreary expanse of
sandhills, reminding one very much of those singular
sands on the north coast of Cornwall, which are so often
shifting about, covering up new churches, or uncovering
the old oratory of some early British saint, we reach the
banks of the Somme, and then travel along a poor peaty
tract of country until the famous west front and short
but lofty nave of Abbeville come in view. Thence by a
valley (rather more rich than is common in good churches)
we continue our race for Amiens. Among these churches
I may instance the hipped saddle-back roofed steeples of
Picquigny, Hangest, and Pont Rémy, as very valuable
examples of their order; that of Picquigny, indeed, surmounting a central steeple, and finished at the top with
some delicate open ironwork, is about as graceful a specimen
as I know.

At Longpré is another church with a steeple of some
pretension, but not satisfactory. It has a perforated spire
of stone much too small for the size of the tower, and
ungraceful in the extreme.

At Amiens one always longs to stop again and again
to feast one's eyes upon its glorious cathedral, perhaps after
Chartres and the Parthenon the noblest and most mascu-
line piece of architecture in the world. But with us this
was impossible; our destiny was—come what might—
to endeavour at any rate to discharge ourselves in Paris
within the shortest possible number of hours from London;
and the dusk of the early autumn evening prevented our
having more than the very slightest glimpse of the Minster.

The refreshment-room at Amiens is one of the best I
have ever been in—reasonable, clean, and good—and placed

just at that happy distance from the sea at which the poor wretches who have been in the depths of woe on the passage begin to recover their presence of mind, and with it, of course—as good Englishmen—their appetites; what wonder then if the Buffet at Amiens prospers!

The rest of our journey to Paris was all performed in the dark, relieved only by the sight of the then long-expected comet, and it was almost midnight ere we found ourselves settled at our hotel.

I am never sorry to have a day in Paris. In spite of alterations and reconstructions which have converted an interesting old city into the most spick-and-span place in the world, there are even to the present day parts which are untouched by the improver, and full of a pleasant national character which seems to be little to the liking of the rulers of the French. There is, too, in spite of the changes which a great and rich city must always undergo, a great deal which is interesting to the architect. We may look at old engravings, and wish ourselves back in those old times when the walls surrounded the city where now the Boulevards run round its heart, when the Temple and a number of other important buildings, now wholly destroyed, adorned the country just outside the walls; but the city which has still, among other architectural treasures, such churches as Notre Dame, S. Germain des Près, the Sainte Chapelle, S. Martin des Champs, and a host of lesser lights, and the Chapel of Vincennes, and S. Denis within a short drive, is in quite a different category from such a city as London, and is indeed hardly second to any other in Europe in architectural interest.

To come to much later times and very different work, it is always pleasant to be able to walk down the Boulevard des Italiens to the Madeleine, and for a few minutes to gaze at a church which certainly presents one

very grand idea—that of space—clothed in very gorgeous
dress.   One always feels a certain sympathy for a church
in which so many people are ever praying; and I have
never yet been into this church without being able to count
them by scores.   The last time I was at Paris I remember
being struck by seeing for the first time a peripteral
building made really useful.   The walls within the columns
were hung with rich draperies, and a long procession coming
out marched round the circuit of the church between the
columns and the walls, and in again at the west door ; the
effect was, as may be imagined, very striking.

From the Madeleine we found our way to the new church
of S. Clothilde, a large cruciform church, and the last erected
in Paris in the Gothic style.   Its design is intended to be
of early character, but in reality is quite late in its effect;
nor do I know when I have seen anything much less successful than the two western steeples rising but a short distance
above the nave roof, and looking mean and weak to a
degree.   In plan the church is not badly arranged; there is
just such a choir as might easily be properly used, and a
large space for congregational purposes.

How much we want churches, in this respect at least,
somewhat like S. Clothilde, in our large cities in England!

There are here a great many windows filled with stained
glass, executed, I believe, by Mons. Marischal. His windows
are illustrations of a truth which men are very slow to receive
and act upon, viz. that in decorating a transparent material,
one whose transparency moreover is the sole cause of its use,
we have no right to shade it with dark colours so far as
to destroy its brilliancy.   These windows were elaborately
shaded, and, as a necessary consequence, were heavy and
dismal in their effect; besides which, most unpleasant
mixtures of green, yellow, and ruby, and of ruby and blue
—-very glaring and very bad—abounded.

The carving of the capitals is, as is usually the case in recent foreign works, all derived from natural types of foliage, and is fairly well done : but the carving of rather elaborate sculptures of the " Stations " did not please me, having none of the severity of ancient examples. When shall we see a school of sculptors rise able really to satisfy the requirements of the times ? I confess I despair more on this point than on any other ; for I have as yet seen no fair attempt made to recover the style, or work upon the principles, of the best mediæval sculptors. The work of our modern sculptors is nearly all foreign and unreal, and almost always involves the assumption that they are representing the proceedings of the Greeks or Romans, and not of the English : it is impossible therefore that such a school can be healthy, strong, or successful. We lack men who will give us (clothed with as much anatomical correctness as they like, so that they do not leave them lifeless and academical) representations of subjects from English history and national life, illustrations of the Scriptures which we still believe, of the faith which we still profess, conceived in something of the architectonic and yet really dramatic and romantic spirit which marks the best sculpture of the middle ages. The strange thing is that with works near at hand which few living men could rival, they absolutely refuse to study them at all, and I believe if we were to summon all the most eminent sculptors to a conclave and put them to the question, not one in four of them would confess to having ever been to Chartres or Bourges, and four out of five would assert that it would have done them no good if they had. If they would give us anything at all comparable to the great works of the best Greeks the case would be altogether different, but to be served with a réchauffé of the antique when one is crying out for something suitable to the present, is cause enough for the apathy of the English public about sculptors' work. We ask for English history or Bible story, and are treated to nymphs combing their hair; and for figures of our Lord and St. Peter, and get nothing but Musidoras and Clyties. No sculptor would lose much by the study of the best mediæval examples of drapery—and there are among the gothic statues which deck the doors and porches of the churches I have named, some of the most admirable description, such as warrant any one, who is at all troubled with feeling for his art, in using strong language about those who neglect them. In Italy we shall find the same careful shutting of men's eyes to what is good, simply because it belongs to the thirteenth or fourteenth centuries. Orvieto is left on one side in order to spend time over work not possessed of a tithe of the beauty of that on its cathedral façade; and, indeed, just as the French examples, they appear only too often never even to have been so much as heard of!

The study of ancient sculpture in England is not quite so easy, because our old buildings are not so rich in it as are the French; but if one is told—as one is too often—that the art of sculpture in the middle ages was unknown or rude in comparison with its state now, one may fairly refer to some of the modern attempts at its imitation for a proof that this was not the case, as e.g. to the recumbent effigy of Archbishop Howley at Canterbury, or to another, of some more humble individual, in the south transept of Chichester Cathedral; a glance only at which, and a comparison with some of the noble mediæval effigies lying in all the stateliness of their repose by their sides, will at once show any one that it is not merely necessary to put an effigy upon its back with its hands in prayer in order to vie with the effigies of the thirteenth and fourteenth centuries. The position is something, but not all, and requires very much more skill in its treatment than of late years we have had to bestow.

From S. Clothilde we went first to the pleasant gardens
of the Luxembourg—gardens which always make one envious
for London—and thence to Notre Dame. Here I always
feel no slight pride in the success which its architect has
achieved. Six hundred years have passed over Paris, one
effort after another has been made, vast sums of money have
been spent, and still this great work stands supreme and
separated by a vast distance from all competition, and
greatest beyond comparison of all Parisian buildings, not
only in its general scheme, but equally in the admirable
design and execution of every detail. There is much to
be seen and learnt here in every way. The west doors are
superb. The planning and construction are very fine, and
the series of sculptures behind the stalls full of interest
and well worthy of study.

From Notre Dame one goes, of course, to the Sainte
Chapelle. When this journey was undertaken everything
about this chef-d'œuvre was gradually growing to perfection :
the flêche was being put up on the roof, the painting on
the walls was nearly finished, and the altar was in progress.
Since then it has escaped, as it were by a special providence
(and why not?), from the incendiary fire which destroyed
almost the whole of the surrounding Palais de Justice, and
it still rises uninjured among the ruins. Of all the chapels
of the same kind it is certainly the most beautiful—and
whether one names our own St. Stephen's, or thinks of
others, such as the Chapel at S. Germer and the other
at Riom, the Paris chapel is certainly by far the finest—
being in truth a real work of inspired genius.

Altogether, I cannot help thinking that the effect upon
the mind of what one sees in Paris is very unsatisfactory ;
the revival of Christian art seems, as it were, to be only
skin-deep ; there seems to be no enthusiasm for it. What
is done is done in the same way as other public works, as

the business of the state, not by the will of the people. The scaffolding, which was just being removed from the avenue leading from the Tuileries to the Barrière de l'Etoile, after having assisted at the fête of Napoleon, was an illustration sufficiently apt of the work which seems to engage too many of the artists of Paris; Parisian fête composers and decorators really appear to be the architects of the day, and of course this fact must militate very much against real art in every branch, as its tendency is to make people accustomed to temporary exhibitions, the shortcomings of which are pardoned on the score of their temporary character, and so the artist is lowered in his tone by assisting in the production of works which are not intended—as all great works ought to be intended—to last for ages.

A day in Paris is generally a long and tiring one; and so we found it; but nevertheless we pushed on without delay, and leaving our hotel before the table-d'hôte was much more than half over, we drove to the station of the Strasburg Railway, and in a few minutes we were *en route*. If any one doubts the possibility of really resting one's body in a railway carriage, let him take the same precaution that we took, and he need not despair: a day of sight-seeing in Paris is certainly the best possible recipe for sound sleep in a railway carriage, and I believe that when we arrived at Strasburg, at about eight the next morning, we were very fairly rested. I confess, however, that I did feel a twinge of horror when I found that the train by which we were anxious to reach Basel left again in about half an hour—too long to wait, but not long enough for either breakfast or dressing. There seemed, however, to be no alternative, and so on we went, comforting ourselves as best we might with some sour grapes and bad dry bread—the sole edibles procurable at the Strasburg buffet !

The Railway from Strasburg to Basel is much more

enjoyable than iron-ways generally are. There is scarce a cutting during the whole extent of the journey, and the views of the chain of the Vosges are—before one has gazed on real mountains in Switzerland—very delightful.

The railway runs up the broad valley of the Rhine, and within a few miles of Strasburg approaches very near to the mountainous district. The outlines of the hills are bold, picturesque, and well varied; and, as they rise rather precipitously from the valley, are often crowned with ruined castles, and have on their lower slopes large and populous-looking villages, they are at any rate very pleasing neighbours for a railway journey.

A few architectural notes of such churches as are passed on this route (which I travelled not for the first time) will not be out of place, though, with one exception, there is not anything of great value.

At Schlestadt there is a large tower of late date to the principal church, which is rather fine in its effect. It has its two upper stages nearly similar, which is rarer at home than abroad. Another church has an early spire; and there is a smaller church with a good open turret. Opposite Schlestadt the chain of the Vosges is very striking, and some of the picturesque outlines of hills capped with ruined castles remind one of the more famous banks of the lower portion of the Rhine. Beyond Schlestadt we reach Colmar, the cathedral of which is large, and has a late tower capped with an ugly bulbous roof. Another church in Colmar has a good open-work and very light turret rising from the middle of the length of its roof. The effect of this kind of turret, of which we in England have no examples, is always very satisfactory.

But the best church in the whole extent of this journey is that of Rouffach, one on whose merits 'Murray'—whose services all travellers must gratefully acknowledge — is

silent. It is of early date, cruciform in its plan, and the
crossing surmounted by a good early tower and spire of
octangular form. Each side of the tower has a good
window, above which a string-course forms the base to a
gable on each side. The angles of the spire spring from the
bases of these eight gables, and the whole design reminded
me somewhat of the only example of the same type in England
—the beautiful steeple of Lostwithiel. Rouffach has a good
choir terminating in an apse, and a south-western steeple,
surmounted by a slender spire too small for the tower.
Altogether, the general effect of the church is very fine.
Beyond this point there are no features of interest; the
Vosges retreat into the distance, and nothing is to be seen
but a dead flat of field and wood, relieved occasionally by a
village or town, remarkable mainly for the ugliness of
its church. The busy manufacturing town of Mulhausen is
passed, the number of stations is carefully reckoned,
and long before you catch the first view of Basel you are
heartily sick of the slow pace at which the Strasburg and
Basel Railway Company always arrange to carry their
passengers.

Those who know the Hotel of the Three Kings at Basel will
understand how grateful was the information given to us, as
we mounted its steps, that the table-d'hôte was to be ready
in half an hour. Refreshing enough at any time, such an
announcement was doubly so to travellers just arrived from
a journey from Paris without a stoppage; and in no bad
spirit did we enter the salle à manger, whose windows,
opening into balconies which absolutely overhang the
great and glorious Rhine, flowing strong and quick for
ever in the same unceasing current, make it about the
pleasantest room of the kind that I know.

There are few things in the world so fine as a mighty
river, few rivers so fine as the Rhine, and few spots so

favourable for its contemplation as the balcony at Basel. As
you look at the deep colour of the water, you think of all
the wonders which on its way it has seen. You remember
your own exploits and pleasant walks in past times along the
lovely valley of the Aar, and over the barren and stony
waste of the Grimsel, to the source of this beautiful feeder
of the Rhine; or you think of Lake Constance and Schaffhausen, and of the beautiful valley of the Upper Rhine, and
of the lakes of Wallenstadt, Lucerne, Brienz, and Thun—
every one of which seems to the mind's eye to be represented and brought near by each wave that dashes madly
along before your gaze. And then, whither do they all so
swiftly wend their way? Down by minsters and by castles,
along broad plains, through narrow water-worn chasms, and
again through great, dreary, but many-peopled flats, into
the sea, there to mix themselves and all their recollections
in the great, glorious, but tradition-despising depth of Old
Ocean.

CHAPTER II.

" For pallid autumn once again
Hath swell'd each torrent of the hill;
Her clouds collect, her shadows sail,
And watery winds that sweep the vale
Grow loud and louder still."
Campbell.

Churches of Basel — Storks — Rheinfelden — Frick — Baden — Zurich: the
Cathedral — Fondness of the Swiss for Bright Colours — Lake of Zurich —
Rapperswyl — Linth Canal — A Wayside Inn — Wesen.

AT Basel we engaged a voiturier to take us to Baden, whence
the only Swiss railway was to have the privilege of conveying
us to Zurich. Our scheme for reaching Italy was to pass
by the lakes of Zurich and Wallenstadt, and then, following
the valley of the Rhine, to cross over the pass of the
Splügen to Chiavenna, and so to reach Lake Como.

We left Basel at two o'clock in the afternoon, hoping
to reach Baden by about nine; the weather looked threaten-
ing, but we took a cheerful view of this, as of everything
else, as all good travellers should, and comforted ourselves
with the thought that at any rate we could better afford to
have a wet day between Basel and Baden than between
Zurich and the Splügen.

The view of the city as you leave it is certainly very
striking; the cathedral spires are picturesque in their
outline, and the number of churches with turrets and steep
roofs combine with them to produce a most ecclesiastical-

looking town. Nor need any one interested in architecture
despair of finding much pleasure in a more careful inspection
of its buildings. They are full of interest, though generally
passed too rapidly by people in a hurry to get on to enjoy
the pleasures which await them beyond.

The roofing of the cathedral is worthy of notice as being
composed of variously coloured tiles, arranged in diamond
patterns over the surface of the roof, and giving a degree of
richness to the colouring of this generally heavy part of the
building which is very admirable.

In another fine church of the early part of the fourteenth century here, I remember being amused to see how
quietly the storks possess themselves of all kinds of places
for their nests, and think even the ridge of the steep
roof of a church a proper place for their abode. The
good people at Basel build their chimneys with flat tops
for the express benefit of their long-legged friends ; who,
from their elevated and well-warmed abodes, look down
sedately, and with a well-satisfied air upon their unfledged
brethren below.

Why the people here love storks, the people of Venice
pigeons, and the people of Berne bears, I leave to more
industrious inquirers to decide, satisfied only to notice
the fact that it is so, as each of these fancies adds one
to the list of local peculiarities so valuable in the recollections of a journey.

The road from Basel to Baden is for the first half of the way
very pretty ; we came in, unfortunately, for rather drenching
rain, and so lost all beyond the suggestion of some striking
views. The towns through which we passed were not o´´ much
interest, though there were many picturesque and pleasant-
looking subjects for the pencil. The most striking place on
the road was Rheinfelden, a largish village (or perhaps
I ought to say small town, as it rejoices in a Rath-haus

of some pretension), surrounded by very high walls, and entered by tall stone gate-towers, pierced with pointed

arches, and surmounted by upper stages of timber, with tiled roofs of quaint and effective character; and here and at Stein and Baden I noticed that almost all the houses were old and very little altered. I observed particularly the old shop-windows of very simple design, closed with folding shutters, and taking one back to old times most decidedly in their design.

SHOP-WINDOW, RHEINFELDEN.

Beyond Rheinfelden the road, which so far has skirted the Rhine rather closely, leaves it again for a few miles until it touches it for the last time at the small town of Stein.

From Stein we saw an imposing-looking church on the other side of the river at Sekingen. It has a great western front with two bulbous-topped steeples, and is of very considerable length. The division between choir and nave is marked by a delicate turret, and the whole church, as far as one can judge by a distant view, looks as though it would well repay a visit. There are six bays in the nave, five and an apse in the choir. The former has very simple windows, whilst in the latter they are rather elaborate. There is no aisle to the choir and no transept.

The rain continued incessantly until we reached the long straggling village of Frick, a quaint and antique-looking place, where our voiturier stopped for an hour to bait his horses, who, however, at Rheinfelden had enjoyed a treat in the shape of a loaf of very brown bread, a kind of food second only, in the estimation of foreign steeds, to the precious *morceaux* of lump sugar with which Swiss voituriers are so fond of encouraging and petting them.

We were nothing loth to stretch our legs; and finding that the church was worthless—one of those unhappy bulbous-spired and bulbous-roofed erections so common in some parts of the Continent, and the roof of even the eastern apse of which was twisted into a most ingenious and ugly compound curve—we took up our quarters in the respectable hostelry and "Bierbrauerei" of the Angel, and devoted ourselves to the consumption of coffee and beer of no bad quality. Our host wished sadly to see us located under his roof for the night, but we were resolute in our determination to reach Baden that night, and so persisted in going, though to our subsequent regret.

It was soon dark, and the new moon, which shone cheerfully upon us, gave us just a glimpse occasionally of the scenery, which about Brugg, where we crossed the Aar, and again at Königsfelden, seemed to be remarkably good.

At last, at about half-past ten o'clock, we reached what we fondly hoped was to be our resting-place. But Baden chose not to take us in, and to our horror, as we drove up to the chief and only available inn, we were met with the dismal announcement from the mouth of the civil landlord, that all the rooms were full.

However, we dismounted, and found that there was no other inn in Baden proper, but that at the Baths there were several; at them our landlord assured us that he knew we should find no room, and so we thought it useless to return and try. Our only course seemed to be to feed our horses again and then go on to Zurich; and as Swiss drivers and Swiss horses never seem to tire of trotting on slowly and drowsily along the road, there was no difficulty in at once coming to an arrangement with our coachman.

Accordingly, at midnight we started again, hoping at some early hour in the morning to reach Zurich. It was sufficiently provoking to be toiling on slowly and sleepily for nearly four hours almost alongside of a railroad which would have taken us early the next morning in three-quarters of an hour; but there was no help for it, and so we did the best we could, by sleeping whenever we were able, to pass the weary hours away.

At last, just as the day began to dawn, we came in sight of Zurich and its lake, and last, not least, we reached the great hotel. Here we pulled up, knocked desperately, awoke the slumbering porter—but, alas! only to hear again the unwelcome sounds which had greeted our ears at Baden! He suggested, however, that at the Hôtel Belle Vue we should probably find beds, and so on we drove, rather in despair at our prospects, though, happily, unnecessarily so, for the Belle Vue gladly opened its arms for our reception, and ere long we were, oblivious of all our toil, comfortably ensconced in bed. From our windows we had a pleasant view of our quarters; it was broad daylight, and the prospect was—as from such a position, looking up a lake, it always is —very fair and charming.

We were up again soon after eight, and were glad to find the morning fine, though the clouds were low, and we saw, consequently, nothing of the distant view of mountains which lends its greatest charms to Zurich. The town is, however, pretty and striking. The picturesque houses, with wooded hills on all sides beyond them, and very charming views of the lake, if they do not make its attractions first-rate, at any rate make them very considerable.

The main feature of interest for me was the cathedral, a fine Romanesque church, very fairly perfect, but mutilated in its interior arrangements by the Calvinists, in whose hands it now is. In plan, it has a nave with aisles of six bays, a

2.—CLOISTER, ZURICH CATHEDRAL.

short choir, and east of this a square-ended sanctuary, the
aisles having apses, roofed with semi-domes. In the nave
two of the aisle-arches make one groining bay. The transverse groining-ribs are of a simple square section, the diagonal
ribs having in addition a large round member. The triforium
is very large and fine, and is made use of for congregational
purposes, being fitted up with seats, which, curiously enough,
are all made to turn up as misereres. There are no transepts.
The sanctuary arch is loftier than the choir arch, and seems
to have been intended to be very distinctly marked. In the
clerestory there are two simple round-headed lights in each
bay ; the choir is arcaded all round internally, and for frigid-
ity of effect cannot be surpassed; the internal fittings com-
prise an immense pulpit, but, so far as I could see, not even
an apology for an altar.

The exterior has two western steeples,[1] and a north
doorway, each jamb of which has three detached shafts,
standing considerably in advance of the wall, which is entirely
covered with diapers. The arch itself is semi-circular, and
very simple in its moulding; but this simplicity rather adds
to than detracts from its general grandeur of effect. The
whole is inserted in an additional thickness of wall, set on,
as it were, against the original wall, and the extreme width
of the doorway itself is no less than eighteen feet nine inches.
The cloisters were remarkable, and very good of their kind ;
the arches rested on detached shafts, the capitals of which
were elaborately carved in a very peculiar manner, but very
effectively. The whole design was unlike any Northern
Romanesque, and bore much more similarity to the best
Lombard work. Unfortunately, the whole of this cloister

---

[1] In a view of Zurich, published A.D. 1654, these steeples are shown with
octagonal spires rising above the gabled sides of the towers ; the belfry stages
and cupolas now existing must therefore be of a date subsequent to the
publication of this view.

was rebuilt in 1851, the carving having been re-worked, or renewed throughout in imitation of the original. It will be seen, however, that, in spite of alterations, this is a very fine church, of a very early type, and peculiarly valuable in a country which, like Switzerland, has comparatively little left that is really good in the way of architectural examples.

There are other churches in Zurich, but I believe not old, and at any rate I had no time to examine them. One of them is appropriated to the use of the Roman Catholics ; and there is one desecrated, rising from the edge of the lake, and forming a prominent object in the general view of the town as you leave by the steamer ; this is of good outline, but has no details remaining of any value. The point chiefly to be noticed in the churches of Zurich appears to be the way in which their spires are all painted red, looking in the full sunshine very bright and picturesque.

The Swiss have a great feeling for bright colour, and on our way from Basel to Baden we noticed one of the many instances of this in several turrets covered with brightly-coloured glazed tiles. A light green seems to be the favourite colour, and is commonly used without mixture with any other. They look best with their lower side rounded, and when of small size ; and are constantly used in turrets rising out of roofs which are entirely covered with plain tiles. I remember, two years before, noticing with extreme pleasure the beauty of some dark green tiles used at Schaffhausen ; and I have already had occasion to mention those on the cathedral at Basel with equal commendation. Unhappily, we have to lament that English people, in their insane hatred of bright colours, if they saw such tiles used in England, would be horrified at such a violation of the correct sim-plicity and uniformity of colour to which the cheapness of slate has made them accustomed. Some modern attempts,

however, at introducing coloured tiles have not been so successful as could be wished; and of all, perhaps the least so
is the roof of the new Maria Hilf church at Munich, on
which tiles of light blue colour are used in such large masses,
that at first sight it seems that half the roof is stripped, and
that the pale blue sky is seen instead of roof.

At ten o'clock we left our hotel by the steamer for
Schmerikon at the head of the Lake of Zurich. The weather
still looked doubtful, though much better than on the previous day, and our host of the Belle Vue, taking a good view
of this, as is a landlord's duty, conducted us to the boat
with smiling anticipations of fine days to come.

The shores of the lake are, for the greater part of its
length, literally fringed with houses all painted white, and
contrasting violently with the trees, vineyards, and green
hills by which they are backed. On the north the shore is
low and gradually shelving down to the water; on the south
it is rather more precipitous, but after all not very striking.
At the head of the lake heavy dark round clouds hung upon
the hills, and left us in pleasant doubt as to whether or no we
had fine mountains to discover when they cleared away; a
doubt, as it happened, not settled, as far as we were concerned,
save by certain lively and not too trustworthy representations which we afterwards met with, in the shape of ad-
vertisements of the Zurich hotels, and which showed a line
of snow mountains as the ordinary horizon of their visitors

The churches on the lake are very numerous and very
similar. The steeples are almost always gabled, and from
these gables rise spires painted red, and very thin and taper
in their form. The gabled sides of the towers are generally
made useful rather than ornamental by the introduction of
enormous clock-dials. The only decidedly mediæval church
which I saw between Zurich and Rapperswyl was at one
of the villages on the north shore of the lake, I think at

Meilen, but I am rather uncertain as to the name. Its design is both novel and very good ; the pinnacles on the gable being unusual in saddle-backed steeples, and giving considerable picturesqueness of outline. The accompanying woodcut will show the general character of the design, and

CHURCH ON THE LAKE OF ZURICH.

it will be seen that the tower is on the north side of the choir. The steeple roof is covered with greyish-red tiles, with a pattern marked on them with yellow tiles.

The steamers on this, as on most Swiss lakes, are somewhat tedious in their journeys, as they take a most zigzag course, first calling on one side of the lake and then on the other, until one doubts whether one will ever reach the journey's end.

At Horgen of course we discharged a large proportion of our
English passengers, who were all bound for the Rigi, but
their places were soon occupied by the umbrella-loving
natives, who flocked in and out of the boat in great numbers
at every station, and by the time we reached Rapperswyl we
had no more fellow-countrymen in the boat, and perhaps,
like many Englishmen, to say the truth, we then first
thoroughly realised that we were abroad.   Much as one
loves one's country, certainly one source of pleasure when
abroad is the not hearing too much English spoken or
seeing too many English faces.

At Rapperswyl, famous for having the longest bridge in
the world, there is a most conspicuous group of buildings on
rising ground above the lake, very picturesquely thrown
together; it consists of a church and a castle; the latter
has several towers capped with pyramidal and saddle-backed
roofs, and the former has two towers in the position of
transepts, with saddle-back roofs gabled north and south,
the southern tower being considerably the larger of the two.
Altogether, the group is one of uncommon variety and
picturesqueness of outline.   Below, in the town, is a small
church, with a most happily-conceived though very simple
bell-turret rising out of the roof, square in its plan, but
capped with an octagonal spirelet.   This is a not uncommon
plan in this part of Switzerland, and is always most agreeable in its effect.   The views from the terrace by the side of
this castle are of singular beauty.   It is high enough above
the lake to command a good view of its whole expanse, and to
secure a not too distant view of some of the mountain peaks
of Glarus.   Rapperswyl is a good point to stop at, for the
sake of a visit to the famous pilgrimage church at Einsiedeln,
certainly one of the spots in Switzerland most curious and
interesting, though its buildings have no claims to our
regard on the score of architectural beauty.

Passing under, or rather through, the bridge, we found that it was very narrow and had no side railing of any kind, so that it appears to be far from a pleasant contrivance for crossing the mile or two of shallow water which here scarce serves to keep up the appearance even of a lake; and perhaps it is upon the score of the absence of real danger of drowning if one fell over that they dispense with any protection. At Schmerikon, which we reached in four hours from Zurich, we left our steamer, and immediately embarked on a barge in order to go by the Linth canal to Wesen; but we found that, however expeditious this might be in descending, it was a kind of conveyance not to be recommended highly to any one wishing to ascend the canal, inasmuch as—unlike ordinary canals—this is neither more nor less than the glacier-torrent of the Linth bringing down the melting snow from the Glärnitsch and Todi glaciers, and rushing along at a really tremendous pace; to those, however, who have time, it may be commended as affording magnificent views of the mountains of Glarus and of those which rise so grandly above the Lake of Wallenstadt.

As we entered the canal from the lake we were amused by the unsuccessful attempts of our crew to secure some wild-fowl, two of which they succeeded in shooting, and then, without any kind of regard for the feelings of passengers panting to arrive at Wesen in the promised two hours and a half, they deliberately proceeded—of course in vain— to chase the unhappy birds, which, though wounded, were quite able to dive much deeper than their enemies could reach, and so the only consequence of the chase was a hearty laugh at the expense of the baffled sportsmen, half an hour's delay, and much lost ground to be made up.

The entrance to the canal was very striking; a low hill covered with larch and birch rose from the water's edge, and above this, the mountains, gradually shelving upwards, were terminated in a line of rocky ridges of very grand and rugged character. Whilst we were admiring the view a slight shower passed over us, and the sun suddenly breaking out, produced one of those lovely effects of colour so peculiar to mountain scenery; a rainbow seemed exactly to fill up one of the great basins formed by the undulations of the mountains, and, after bathing a great sweep of mountain-side in the richest and most distinctly marked colours, gradually died away.

The canal, which at first looks more like a river, soon takes a bend to the S.W., and then, passing under a quaint wooden bridge, over which passes the road to Uznach, we found ourselves in what certainly looked sufficiently canal-like. The stream is so rapid that the walls built up on either side are preserved from being washed away by stone groins running out into the stream, and acting as so many breakwaters to keep the water in the centre. Slowly and steadily our horses pulled us up, whilst we, mounted on the top of the cabin, were able to see over the walled sides of the canal, and to enjoy the glorious prospect before us.

Before long our captain blandly informed us that he was going to stop for dinner at a wayside house, so we, anxious to make the same good use of our time, attempted to follow his example. Unfortunately the landlord, though very jolly-looking, had a very badly stocked larder, and we had to satisfy ourselves with bread, honey, and wine. It is true, indeed, that our host did produce some cold meat—portion, as I imagined, of a goat dressed some ten days back—but this was not eatable, and was valuable only as furnishing an opportunity to him of showing his perfect power of making the best of a bad thing. To season the goat he brought in vinegar and oil, and, putting them upon the table, exclaimed with some *empressement*, " Voilà, monsieur ; mais le vinaigre n'est pas bon !" just as if this was the strongest recom-

mendation he could give us! We laughed heartily, avoided
the vinegar, and parted good friends with our host, thanking
him from our hearts for having saved us the painful operation of making the discovery about its quality for ourselves!

Our not very satisfying repast finished, we embarked
again upon our barge, and in the occasional intervals, when
sudden and heavy storms of rain obliged us to seek shelter
in the cabin, we were much amused in watching the proceedings of some men belonging to the boat, who spent
the whole of the five hours consumed in the journey in an
unceasing game of cards; I must do them the justice to say
that they played very good-humouredly, and laughed without
ceasing. Under no circumstances could we have seen the
scenery more gloriously; occasional bright gleams of sunshine broke in upon and followed clouds of the most inky
hue, and then came pelting down heavy showers, accompanied by howling wind and darkness; and as we reached
the opening of the valley, looking up beyond Glarus to the
great mountains which close in its upper end, I think the
effect was really more grand and terrific than anything I
have ever seen. The mountains are of very fine outline,
and of great height, as we saw by the more than occasional
glimpses which we had of snow about their summits. By
the time we reached Wesen the wind was so violent that we
found it difficult to keep our places upon the top of the
cabin; and we disembarked just before dark, in time to see
the fine mountains on each side of the Lake of Wallenstadt
here and there through the storm-clouds, and its waters
beaten by the wind into not insignificant waves. We had to
walk through the entire length of the village—a picturesque,
quaint little place, sheltered under the almost overhanging
rocks at the side of the water—and arrived at last at the
capital and thoroughly Swiss inn, the Hôtel de l'Epée,
where we were to sleep.

Travellers now speed very differently along this country, and, I fear, see less than they ought of its beauties. Steamboats no longer attempt to pass beyond Rapperswyl, and the railway hurries one along by the beautiful Lake of Wallenstadt to the valley of the Rhine, only earning one's gratitude when one is in violent haste, and because by a branch line it makes a détour to Glarus and Stachelberg much more possible than it was when first I made the journey. On the whole I fear, where railways pass through beautiful scenery, the tourist loses more than he can possibly gain, not only in the views of the country, but equally in the incidents of travel, which are becoming only too monotonous and similar everywhere.

CHAPTER III.

"Where the mountains
Lift, through perpetual snows, their lofty and luminous summits."
Evangeline.

Wallenstadt — Sargans — Gorge of the Tamina — Ragatz — Chur — Ems —
Reichenau — Thusis — Zillis — Andeer — Splügen — The Splügen Pass —
The Custom-house — Cascade of the Medessimo — Campo Dolcino.

THE storm of the evening gave no kind augury of sunshine
on the morrow, and with rather anxious thoughts we listened
as it roared among the mountains which overhung our
hostelry. But it seemed that we had suffered enough, and
when we woke we found that, though the clouds had not yet
cleared off from the sides of the mountains, there was
nevertheless every prospect of a fine day.

We were obliged to leave by an inexorably early steamer
at half-past five for Wallenstadt, and so lost all but the
suggestion only of the magnificence of the mountains which
tower up so grandly over the north shore of the lake. Like
Goethe on his way into Italy, we might exclaim, "What do
we not pass over, both on the right hand and on the left, in
order to carry out the one thought which has become almost
too old for the soul!" But our time was limited, and our
chief anxiety to spend as much of our short holiday as we
could in Italy; and so, sad though we were to miss what
was doubtless so well worthy of being seen, on we were
bound to go without delay.

Before we started I had secured a voiturier whose carriage was at Wallenstadt to take us on to Chur, so that on this score I had no trouble before me. Our voyage was only too soon made. Unlike the Lake of Zurich, where the traveller rather hopes that each place at which he stops may be the last, on this lake, as the tiny steamer ploughs its way rapidly over its surface, with its goal always in view, and with not a place to stop at on its road, he ceases not to long that his pleasure may be prolonged!

By seven o'clock we were in our carriage, and *en route*. The sun began to shine, and every minute the clouds rose higher and higher; so that, before we finally lost—by turning into the valley of the Rhine—the last view of the valley of the lake, we could see the peaks of the mountains which we so wished to have seen before, the Sieben-Churfürsten, which tower so grandly over the lake.

Wallenstadt is but a poor place, its situation being unwholesome, and its inns not much to be commended. It has a church of modern character, with an old-looking tower in the position of a transept, with a saddle-back roof, gabled north and south. On the lower part of the south side of this tower are paintings of the Crucifixion and some other subjects, apparently of some antiquity. Just above the town, on the right, we passed the ruins of an old castle; and at a slight rise in the road had a beautiful view of the calm waters of the lake, looking blue, but very much smaller than it really is. This, no doubt, is owing to the great height of the precipitous rocks on its north side, which we now saw for the first time, the clouds having at last risen and disclosed some of the beauties which they had been concealing from us.

The valley from Wallenstadt to Sargans, just beyond which our route, after crossing the very low watershed, joined the valley of the Rhine, was strikingly beautiful.

Its ecclesiological features were not, however, remarkable, if I except the constant repetition of what I have often noticed in the Catholic cantons of Switzerland and in Tyrol—the occurrence, namely, of grated openings on either side of the western door-way, commanding the interior and protected by an open porch, through which passers-by, though not able to enter, might still see the altar. On our journey from Basel to Zurich we passed a church the altar of which was lighted up, and the doors behind these gratings left open very late at night. It was in a lonely place, and when I passed there was no one in or near the church. I never see this arrangement without wishing to introduce it in England. There are so many of our Churches which cannot conveniently be left always open, and where such a provision might suggest to passers-by, as it does here, the propriety of using a church at other times than those of public service.

The cultivation of this valley is not so uninteresting as its ecclesiology. Here we first found the vines trained about in the horizontal Italian fashion, whilst under them great gourds and pumpkins developed themselves to a prodigious size.

Sargans is a very picturesque old town, and has some capital examples of good Swiss carpentry in its houses; in addition to which there is a picturesque and antique-looking castle, rising high above the houses on a rock, guarding the eastern entrance to the town, and commanding the junction of our road with that of the valley of the Rhine leading to the Lake of Constance.

Our coachman was under a bond to travel as fast as a diligence which lumbered on slowly in advance of us, and as far as Ragatz was quite true to his word; there, however, we determined to pause for a few hours, not willing to pass anything so famous as the baths of Pfeffers

without a visit. Leaving our carriage, we mounted a
light car, and were soon ascending the beautiful gorge of
the Tamina to the baths. The road is capitally made, and
follows the windings of the mountain torrent so closely as
to require some nerve in those who drive rapidly along
on their road to or from the baths. The ascent is
steep, but in rather less than an hour we found ourselves at the baths. The rocks rise nearly perpendicularly behind the ledge of rock on which they stand, and
the only mode of access to the upper and more wonderful part of the chasm was by passing through the long
corridors, which betokened the once religious object of the
building. These passed, and in charge of a guide, we
crossed the torrent by a rude bridge, and then by a rather
precarious path made our way, as it seemed, almost into the
bowels of the mountain. The gorge is so very narrow that
in many parts the light of the sky is no longer visible, the
rocks overhanging each other above the head. All the
while the torrent is roaring by our sides, and we feel that
we are indeed enjoying an excursion into the very heart of
the rocky earth. At last we reach the end of the path, are
compelled by our guide to ensconce ourselves, one by one, in
a small kind of box formed round the source of the spring—
to pronounce it very hot and very nasty (its two most
eminent qualities)—and then, still admiring the matchless
grandeur of the rocky way, we regain our car, and are soon
again whirled down the hill to Ragatz.

Our driver is a cheerful, pleasant fellow, talks German
much better than the man we brought from Wesen, is
communicative, moreover, and seems to enjoy a laugh and
a joke uncommonly. Of course we become friends, and
with no trouble on our parts, though with some little on
his, it is arranged that our old driver shall remain where
he is, and that our new friend, proud in the possession of

the then very necessary Austrian passport, shall take us on as far at any rate as Chiavenna. A hurried Swiss luncheon—wine, honey, bread and butter—is soon despatched, and again we are on our way under the auspices of our new voiturier.

But we must not leave Ragatz without noticing its church, remarkable for its exceedingly good octagonal wooden spire springing in an unusual manner out of a square wooden belfry stage, and another church at (I think) Vilters, close to Ragatz, which has a lofty tower finished on each side with a sharp gable, and a thin octagonal spire rising from the intersection of the cross-gabled roof; both these steeples are in a position which for some reason is very popular in this district—the south side of the chancel.

WOODEN SPIRE—RAGATZ.

From Ragatz to Chur the churches are all very similar; they have tall towers generally in the same position as those near Ragatz, and capped with bulbous roofs, or sharp spires covered with metal. The road is not quite the most agreeable we have travelled; some of the views, it is true, are most lovely, and the mountains — among which towers pre-eminent the grand outline of the Falkniss — are very noble; but, despite all this, the valley is too wide, and the Rhine, by periodical inundations, manages to secure so nearly its whole extent to itself, that there is a waste, desolate, and pestilential look in the foreground which is not prepossessing. We arrived at Chur at about half-past

3.—CATHEDRAL, CHUR·

one, and, not sorry that our horses required rest, betook
ourselves to the inspection of this very curious town.

It is entered by old gateways, and many of the streets
are still full of ancient houses. The curious feature of the
place is however its complete division into two quarters—
the Protestant and the Catholic—the latter walled off, and
entered by its own gates.[1] It occupies the upper part of
the town, and contains in the cathedral church of S. Lucius
an attraction for architects which has unusual merit and
interest. Its plan consists of a nave of three bays, a choir of
one bay raised by twelve steps above the nave, and a sanctuary
much narrower than the nave and choir, and also of one bay.
The steps from the nave to the choir are narrow and on each
side, and between them is a very flat wide arch, under which
access is obtained to the crypt, the floor of which is a few steps
below the nave, and extends under the choir and sanctuary.
The plan is, it will be seen, not unlike that of the Cathedral at
Zurich, save that here there are no apsidal terminations at all.

A sketch of the interior of so singular a church cannot
be uninteresting, and it will be seen from this that the
whole is of the very earliest pointed work, and good of its
kind; the crypt is supported in the centre by a column
resting upon a grotesque animal. Two of the altars have
fine shrines of metal of the thirteenth century, and two other

---

[1] This division is seen clearly in one of the curious prints by Me-
rian, which illustrate a most valuable and interesting book, entitled 'Topo-
graphia Helvetiæ,' published at Frankfort-am-Main, A.D. 1654, and full
of most picturesque and exact views of Swiss towns; they are valuable,
as proving beyond all question their state in the beginning of the seventeenth century, and as being executed with very much artistic feeling. That
of Chur gives the whole town in the most complete manner; the castle, the
churches, the walls, and the many watch-towers, with the magnificent
mountains behind them, making one of the most picturesque *ensembles* con-
ceivable. Many of these views of Swiss towns are remarkable, as proving how
very regularly the mediæval towns were planned whenever there was the
opportunity, the streets all at right angles, and the great church and market-
place in the centre of the whole.

altars have ancient pricket candlesticks, and there are some
fine brass standard candlesticks also; the choir stalls are old,
and there is a late triptych behind the high altar, and a
very fine Sakramentshaus with metal doors just below the
northern flight of steps to the choir, which reminded me of
the very fine example in a similar position in the cathedral
at Ulm. The altar is of stone of the thirteenth century,
with five detached shafts in front, supporting the slab or
mensa. The whole church is groined. It is worthy of
notice that the choir makes a great bend out of the straight
line towards the north—so much, indeed, that it is impossible to avoid noticing it as one enters the church. The
steps from the nave to the choir lack dignity. But it is
true that if they had been in the centre, and the entrances
to the crypt on each side, the crypt would not have been
seen, as it now is, from the nave, and a striking effect would
have been lost. The west end has a fine round-arched doorway with several shafts in each jamb, above this a large
window of the same character, and in the gable a small
middle-pointed window. About ten feet in advance of the
west doorway is a curious remnant of a gateway with piers
and shafts resting upon monsters, looking, however, very
much as though it had been removed from elsewhere.

Service commenced just as I was obliged to think of
leaving the church; the priests wore red cassocks and
tippets, and very short surplices edged with lace, and
looked unclean and untidy; there was no one in the body
of the church, and the sacristan, after the service had
commenced, walked backwards and forwards about the
choir, down the steps into the nave, and then—after a
little attention bestowed on some matter there—out of the
church. On a subsequent visit to this church (in 1872) I
found repairs in progress, which bade fair to destroy some
of its great archæological interest.

Descending from the melancholy and squalid-looking Catholic quarter, we soon came upon the Protestant church, dedicated in honour of S. Martin, which is now somewhat remarkable. It is old, but it has been plastered, whitewashed, and then painted by some original artist over its whole exterior, in an extraordinary imitation of all kinds of inconsistent architectural devices; pilasters, cornices, mouldings, tracery, and the like, are all boldly represented with black paint, and in such style that we all stopped the moment we saw it, struck by the conviction that it must be a scene from some play, so utterly absurd, flat, and out of all perspective did the whole look.

The situation of Chur is very lovely, placed as it is just at the point where the Schalfiker Thal joins the valley of the Rhine, and upon the steep and rugged bottom slope of the mountains.

The weather was every moment becoming more glorious, and just as we left Chur, along the road which leads to Reichenau, we had one of the most lovely views we had enjoyed. It is not always the case, however beautiful may be the scenery, or however lovely the weather, that one finds everything group together perfectly; here, however, it did, and I commend the subject to the pencils of those who follow me on this route.

We soon reached Ems, whose church, situated upon a green knoll above the village, has the peculiarity of a small apsidal building east of the chancel apse. The key was not to be found, so that I could not go in to examine what this building was. This church had an octangular steeple, whilst another church in the same village had one of the bulbous coverings of which I have before complained. At Reichenau it is proper to go to see the house in which Louis Philippe acted in 1793 as schoolmaster under a Monsieur Jost, and I fear we fell rather in the good opinion

of our driver when we neglected so proper and regular a
custom; but so it was. The garden of the inn is charming,
and from its edge you obtain the best view of the junction
of the Vorder and Hinter Rhine, and having enjoyed this
thoroughly, we passed rapidly through Reichenau, across its
two quaint covered wooden bridges, and by the beautiful
meeting of the waters, until we found ourselves following the
course of the Hinter Rhine and fairly on the Splügen road.

We only wished to reach Thusis by sunset, and so our
time was ample for enjoyment; we walked much of the way,
detecting eagerly every here and there patches of snow on
the mountains in the distance, each of which is hailed as a
discovery by every fresh traveller, who feels himself trans-
ported with delight by the distant view of the pure white
against the sky.

Castles are here as numerous as ever upon the Rhine,
and at least a dozen, I should think, might be reckoned
perched on every favourable spot between Reichenau and
Thusis. As the road advances the valley widens out into a
kind of basin, into which flow two streams, the one through
the as yet unperceived gorge of the Via Mala rather to the
right, the other through an opening in the mountains
directly in front of us, which allows us a charming view
of the snowy heights above the Julier Pass, drinking
in the last red rays of the setting sun, long since passed
away from the ground on which we stand; then there is a
long ascent, and, passing peasants coming in from hay-
making, merrily laughing and singing, we drive up the
straight ugly street of Thusis to the Via Mala Hotel. But
the evening is too glorious to lose, and in five minutes we
are out again on foot to explore the commencement of the
black defile; and until we are absolutely turning into it,
so narrow is the gorge that it is not seen, but when seen,
and by such a light, how grand and beautiful it is! We

ascended some distance and then stood and admired. Above
us tremendous rocks towered high into the air, riven in two
for the narrow chasm in which we stood, at whose bottom
we heard the distant roar of the Rhine, and down below
and beyond, framed as it were between the grand outline of
rocky crag and pine-covered mountain, lay the valley of
Domleschg, still retaining, by contrast with the gloom
around us, some light upon its fields, and castles, and
villages. Rest was well earned after such a pleasant and
actively spent day, and, if we were late in starting in the
morning, it was as much the fault of our coachman as of
ourselves. However, though not so early as we intended,
we left soon after six, and in a few minutes were again in
the Via Mala. And now by daylight I doubt whether
we were not all disappointed; there is so much in a
name that one expects something *very* terrific from such
a name, and this it scarcely is. It is seldom fair to
compare one piece of scenery with another, but still I feel
that this was certainly not the most savage I had ever seen,
and therefore not justly *my* Via Mala. But beautiful in the
extreme it was, and I believe we all regretted that we so
soon found ourselves again in the more open valley on the
road to Zillis. Here we found a church with a lofty tower,
in the same position, and with a spire of the same design, as
that at Ragatz; the nave low and ugly, the chancel lofty,
with a steep pitched roof and apse; the windows pointed
but modernized; the belfry windows of the steeple of three
lights, with circular arches, and divided by shafts, which
were continued on in blank panels on each side of the
windows, so as to form an arcade of five arches on each side.
And this I believe was the last noticeable church we saw
before we reached Chiavenna, and in its arcaded belfry I
fancied that I saw something of an Italian influence at work,
which might well have been the fact.

We soon reached Andeer, where we waited but a short time, and then commenced a steep ascent. The lovely scenery, the mountains closing in round us, and the roar of the falls of the Rofla making music in our ears, made our way very enjoyable. There was but little chance, however, of rapid progress, as from Andeer to Splügen the road is almost always on the ascent, sometimes gradually, at others in steep zigzags up the shoulder of some obstructive hill, and constantly overhanging or crossing the rapid, white, foaming mountain-stream, sole representative here of the noble river whose broad waters have been admired at Basel. The air of desolation becomes more decided as one reaches Splügen. Trees and shrubs more scarce, and often blasted by the fierce rush of the wintry wind, or the keen sharp blow of the fallen rock, or the swift sweep of the avalanche, aid in making up the desolate picture. Vegetation has well-nigh ceased, and the eye, though deceived at first by the intensely red colour perceived every here and there on the hill-sides and on the rocks, discovers presently that not to flowers or plants, but to lichen or other such desolate vegetation, is it owing.

By the time we caught the first sight of Splügen the sky was overclouded, the wind rose, and a sudden heavy storm of rain gave us a lesson in the customs of the weather in these regions, to which our driver's quiet assurance that we should probably have a snowstorm on the pass added the few remaining drops required to make up the draught which we saw ourselves doomed to swallow.

Splügen, however, was repnted to have an inn which would give us enviable shelter for a couple of hours, and we entered at once, hoping, if we waited, again to see the blue sky before we crossed the boundary between the North and the South—between Switzerland and Italy.

The table-d'hôte was just about to commence, and in

came a diligence from Milan, and out came the passengers:
another carriage, which had pursued us relentlessly all the
way from Andeer, came in at the same moment, and down
we sat, about fifteen English people, not one of whom had
been in the house ten minutes before, not one of them
stopping for more than their own and their horses' dinners,
and all proceeding in different directions, either on their
way home satiated with travel, or just about to dive like
ourselves in full quest of pleasure and excitement, into a
new country.   These meetings are always curious, generally
amusing, and to the quiet and attentive observer of character not a little edifying.   On this occasion there was
subject-matter enough, and we found an old gentleman,
travelling sorely against his will, under the care of an active
and thoroughly vulgar wife, some literary old maids of
another party, and the enthusiastic damsel of a third, each
in their way amusing, and not the less so in that it was
necessary to inspect them and part with them so rapidly.

Splügen, in a soaking rain, is not a pleasant place; and
as I employed myself in sketching from the inn window the
very picturesque old bridge, which gives[1] all its architectural
character to the village, I conceive that I accomplished all
that was necessary; and when we got into our carriage
again, and, crossing by the bridge, left the Bernardin road
to the right, and finally plunged really into the Splügen
route, it seemed like a reward for my industry to find the
rain cease and the sun again occasionally shine out.

The ascent begins with a series of zigzags, which
rapidly carry the road high above the valley of the Rhine,
and then, passing through one of the long covered. galleries
for which this route is famous, it emerges in an upland

---

[1] I grieve to say it does so no longer. When I last crossed the Splügen,
in 1869, this bridge had disappeared, and one of iron had been erected in its
place. It was a capital example of the skilful carpentry of the old Swiss
bridge-builders.

valley or dip between two mountains, up which it takes a
steady course along a road macadamized, by-the-by, mainly
with the white marble which abounds here, until, just below
the summit, it comes again upon a steep mountain-side, to be
surmounted only by a patient unravelling as it were of the
intricacies of an endless zigzaging, which at last brings us
to the Swiss guard-house and the entrance to the great
gallery. The clouds are low and gathering; but still as we
see below us white patches of snow every here and there,
and above us the blue edge of a great glacier marked with
lines of crevasses and fringed with a white edge of snow,
we feel that we have really at last achieved the summit.
Noisily we trot through the arched gallery, and then, after
another slight ascent for a few minutes, we stop and put on
the drag, and then down we go rapidly and cheerily, backwards and forwards, occasionally giving a merry tap to some
corner post at the turns of the road, in order to let it be
known that we, our driver, and our horses, are all of us
heartily glad that we are at last on the south side of the
pass—no longer the German Splügen, but, as we learn from
divers notices along the road, the Italian Spluga. A short
drive takes us to the custom-house—not looked forward to
cheerfully by those who have met, as we had at Splügen, a
man turned back by mistake, and after two days' delay again
retracing his steps—but happily, in our case, passed easily
enough, and with an exhibition of the greatest courtesy and
civility from the Austrian officer, the mention of whom
reminds me of the great change which has taken place in
the political status of this country since first I made acquaintance with it. It is a change of no little importance to
the traveller, who now goes without let or hindrance almost
everywhere, instead of being worried out of his life by
troubles about passports which even Austrian courtesy could
not make tolerable.

We are soon off again across a drear and peaty-looking plain, with no view of the neighbouring mountains, and accompanied along the road by a troop of wild smuggler-like fellows, in broad-brimmed steeple-crowned hats, loose jackets, knee breeches, and coarse stockings, riding wildly along on rough horses, without saddles or bridles, but every one of them handsome grand-looking fellows, showing, as they smiled, teeth of the purest white, and more nearly coming up to one's idea of real Italians than any with whom, later in our journey and more in Italy, we happened to meet. Before long, however, we again commenced the descent, and then, after passing through two or three galleries of prodigious length, at last came out upon one of those spots, the view from which, as much perhaps by reason of its associations as for its intrinsic beauty, rests on the mind for ever after, as one of the most lovely ever seen. On our right a steep mountain track slopes rapidly and almost perpendicularly down to a narrow valley, whose opposite and no less precipitous side we are about to descend; below us, far down, we see the village roofs of Isola, with its church and Italian campanile; beyond—and this is indeed the great charm of the prospect—down the valley, where the atmosphere seems redolent of the South, we see a grandly formed mountain, and again to its right another but more distant; between these two dim and distant shades lies the lake of Como—beyond them the broad rich plain of Lombardy; the sun shines forth, and we dream henceforward of that valley, looked down upon from the gallery on the Splügen, as one of the brightest prospects of our lives!

We had not gone far beyond the last gallery before our voiturier made good a boast which he had often repeated, of showing us a real waterfall on a grand scale before we parted company, and, pulling up his horses, made us—not unwilling—dismount to look *down* the cascade of the Medessimo. A passage has been formed from the road to a point which just overhangs the fall, and here, securely parapeted round, you look down over a grand sheer fall of some eight hundred feet, in the course of which the torrent which goes to feed the threadlike Lira down below us in the valley, and just now roaring in bold volume underneath our road, loses itself in soft, delicate, and fairy-like spray, and ere it reaches the rock below, seems like some delicate mist falling from the sky for ever in endless and exquisite change of form. Just beyond the cascade the most wonderful part of the descent in an engineering point of view commences, and the road seems really to descend the perpendicular face of the rock, surpassing in boldness most other roads that I know, and affording very fine and varied views of the cascade on the descent. We soon reached Campo Dolcino, a miserable and most dirty-looking village; and were, sorely against our will, obliged to wait for our horses to bait; and then on we went, the sun some time set, and the night dark and cloudy. Presently a storm arose; and without lights, and travelling along a road turning sharp angles every minute, and never losing the music in our ears of the roaring Lira, our lot seemed more wild than enviable; at last we came to a house and tried unsuccessfully to borrow a light, but presently at another house we succeeded, and then guided by a lantern we pursued our way safely enough. I have seldom been out in so grand a storm; the lightning was vivid beyond all that I could conceive; and as at one minute it played about on the foaming water beneath us, and at another lighted up the whole mountain-side beyond with pale and intensely lovely light, flickering, playing, and dancing about in the wildest fashion, I believe we felt half sad when house after house appeared, and at last we entered the long, narrow, and thoroughly Italian streets of Chiavenna.

Another journey took me to Chiavenna at the same time in the evening, on my way north from Como. It was the night of the 8th September, the Nativity of the Blessed Virgin, and every peasant in his solitary châlet on the mountain-side was burning a bonfire in her honour. There seemed to me to be something very touching in this flaming burst of distant greeting from mountain to mountain, and few circumstances have ever brought home more vividly to me the isolation of these mountaineers, than the compensating power of a sympathetic faith which made them thus bid each other welcome by their flaring fires.

CHAPTER IV.

"But now 'tis pass'd,
That turbulent chaos; and the promised land
Lies at my feet in all its loveliness!
To him who starts up from a terrible dream,
And lo, the sun is shining and the lark
Singing aloud for joy, to him is not
Such sudden ravishment as now I feel,
At the first glimpses of fair Italy."

Rogers.

Chiavenna—Lake of Riva—Colico—Gravidona—Lake of Como—Varenna—
Stelvio Pass—Lecco—Bergamo: Broletto—Churches—Castle of Malpaga.

THE situation of Chiavenna is eminently beautiful: in a deep valley surrounded on all sides by mountains whose slopes are covered with soft and luxuriant foliage of oak and chestnut, and where every available open space is devoted to trellised vineyards, it contrasts strongly with the pine-covered hills so lately passed on the northern slopes of the Alps; placed, too, at the confluence of two streams—the Meira and the Lira—it rejoices in the constant rushing sound of many waters.

It was only necessary to move out of the shade of our hotel into the melancholy piazza in which it stands, to discover that an Italian sun lighted up the deep blue sky; and a walk to the principal church, dedicated in honour of S. Lawrence, a stroll through the narrow streets, and a rather toilsome ascent through a vineyard formed upon a rock which towers up behind a kind of ruined castle, and from which a capital view is obtained of the singular and beautiful cul-de-sac in which the town is planted, sufficiently convinced us of its power.

The church of S. Lawrence is entered from a large oblong cloister, in one angle of the space enclosed by which rises a tall campanile, its simple form, and its arcaded belfry full of musical bells, contrasting well with the outline of the hills which overhang and hem it in. On the east side of the cloister are the church, an octagonal baptistery, and a bone-house, all ranged side by side and opening into it, and the latter curious as an example of the extent to which the people of Chiavenna amuse themselves by arranging sculls and arm-bones into all kinds of religious and heraldic devices, and with labels to mark the names of their former owners. The *tout ensemble* is picturesque in its effect, and the cool pleasant shade of the cloister, with the view of the church and its tall campanile, and irregularly grouped buildings looking brilliantly white in the clear sunshine, was very pleasing.[1]

Italian beggars, persevering, and, at any rate in appearance, very devout, did their best to annoy us here and everywhere when we ventured to stop to examine or admire anything; and Italian beggars are certainly both in pertinacity and in filth about the most unpleasant of their class.

My voiturier gave me a lesson worth learning, and not perhaps unworthy of note for other unsuspicious travellers.

[1] Probably most travellers who pass by Chiavenna are now on their way to or from the Engadin by the beautiful Maloja pass. They will do well before they reach the top of the pass to notice on their left the ruined remains of a Gothic chapel of the fifteenth century, which may, I suppose, aspire to the honour of being at a greater height above the sea than any other Gothic church in Europe. Its architectural merit is not great, but still it has a certain value, as showing how well a simple little Gothic church looks among the wildest mountain scenery.

We had a written contract to Chiavenna, and thence to
Colico he had agreed verbally to take us for a certain sum ;
before we started I found, however, that he intended to
charge us three times as much as we had agreed upon, and,
as very luckily we found a diligence on the point of starting,
we secured places in the cabriolet at its back, from which
we had the best possible position for seeing the views, and
so left him in the lurch, with divers admonitions to behave
himself more honestly for the future.

At ten we left, and had a very enjoyable ride to Colico.
The valley, however, bore sad traces of the havoc made by
the inundations of the Meira, and of the storm of the
previous night. We soon reached the shores of the little
Lake of Riva, along whose banks our road took us sometimes
in tunnels, sometimes on causeways built out into the water,
until at last we reached the valley up which runs the Stelvio
road, and then, after passing along the whole length of
a straight road lined on each side with a wearisome and
endless row of poplars, we were at Colico. Here we
prudently availed ourselves of the opportunity of an hour's
delay in the departure of the boat for an early dinner, and,
then embarking, waited patiently the pleasure of our
captain.

The scenery of Lake Como has been so often extravagantly
praised that I was quite prepared to be disappointed ; but for
the whole distance from Colico to Lecco it is certainly on
the whole more striking than any lake scenery I have seen.
The mountains at its head are extremely irregular and
picturesque, and throughout its whole length there is great
change and variety. In this respect it contrasts favourably
with most other lakes, and I certainly think that not even
in the Lake of Lucerne is there any one view so grand as that
which one has looking up from within a short distance of
the head of Como over the Lake of Riva to the mountains

closing in the Stelvio, and rising nobly above the sources of the Meira and the Lira.

Somewhat, too, may be said of the innumerable villages and white villas with which the banks of the lake are studded; they give a sunny, inhabited, and cheerful feeling to the whole scene; and, reflected in the deep blue lake in those long-drawn lines of flakey white which are seen in no other water to such perfection, add certainly some beauty to the general view.

One of these villages—Gravidona—within half an hour's sail of Colico, ought not to be left unvisited by any one who cares about architecture.

Close to its little harbour stand two churches side by side, one an oblong basilica, the other a baptistery of, as it seems to me, such great interest that I give illustrations both of its plan and of its exterior. It will be seen that the dimensions are small, the total internal width being less than forty feet, whilst the design of the east end is most ingeniously contrived so as to give no less than five eastern apsidal recesses. There are two stair-turrets in the wall on each side of the western tower which lead up to a sort of triforium-passage which is formed behind an arcade in the side wall of the church, and one of them leads also to the first floor of the tower. The triforium consists of an arcade of seven arches in each side wall. The three small apses at the east have each their own semi-dome, and the chancel as well as all the other apsidal recesses are similarly roofed. All the walls retain more or less traces of old paintings, the Coronation of the Blessed Virgin occupying the principal apse, and the Last Judgment the west wall. The whole church is built in white marble and black lime-stone used in courses, or stripes, with extremely good effect.

The roof of this Baptistery is of wood. The exterior is best explained by reference to my drawing of the west

front. It stands on a charming site with a background of
lake and mountain, such as one seldom enjoys. There is
a contrast here, which strikes one very much, between the ingenious skill of the planning of such a building as this
and the rudeness of the execution of the details. I know

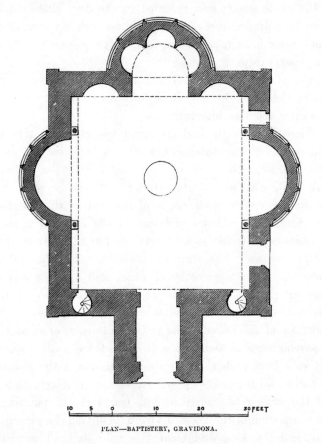

PLAN—BAPTISTERY, GRAVIDONA.

nothing as to the history of Gravidona; but it looks as though
the plan came from the hands of men who knew something
of the Church of San Vitale at Ravenna, whilst its execution
was left to the rustic skill of the masons of the country.

4. BAPTISTERY. GRAVIDONA.

The Baptistery is dedicated to S. John the Baptist. Close to it, as I have said, stands the Church of San Vincenzo, which though Romanesque in its foundation has been much modernized, and is now mainly interesting on account of the exquisite examples of late fifteenth century silversmiths' work which still enrich its sacristy. Conspicuous among these is a silver processional cross. This cross is nearly two feet across the arms by three feet in height from the top of the staff. There is a crucifix on one side and a sitting figure of Our Lord on the other; figures of SS. George, Vincent, Sebastian, Christopher, and Victor, and Our Lord on the base or knop; and half-figures of the Evangelists on the arms of the cross. The ornaments consist of crockets bent and twisted, of blue enamels, filigree-work, nielli, and turquoises set in the centre of dark-blue enamels. It is, in short, a piece of metal work which might well make a modern silversmith run down swiftly into the lake and drown himself in despair at the apparent impossibility in these days of rivalling such a piece of artistic and cunning workmanship, in spite of all our boasted progress!

Not much less splendid is a chalice of about the same age. It is ten and three-quarter inches high, has a plain bowl, but knop, stem, and foot all most richly wrought with figures, niches and canopies, and the flat surfaces filled in with fine blue and white Limoges enamels. The paten belonging to this chalice is very large—nearly ten inches across, and quite plain.

Half the passengers on the steamboat were, of course, Austrian soldiers and officers, the other half English or Americans, either resident at or going to Como. We, however, stopped on the way, and, leaving the steamboat in the middle of the lake, after a row of about twenty minutes found ourselves at Varenna, a village exquisitely placed just

where the three arms of the lake—the Como, the Lecco, and
the Colico branches—separate, affording, whether seen from
here, from Bellagio, or from Cadenabbia, the most lovely
lake views it has ever been my good fortune to see.

Here we had what seemed likely to be an endless
discussion upon the relative merits of a four-oared boat and
a carriage as a means of conveyance to Lecco. We inclined
to the latter; but, leaving the matter in the hands of an
active waiter, we busied ourselves with eating delicious
fruit, admiring the tall cypresses growing everywhere about
the shores of the lake, and watching the exquisite beauty of
the reflections of Bellagio and the opposite mountains on the
smooth bosom of the water.

We were soon off again, and well satisfied to find ourselves trotting rapidly along the well kept Stelvio Road,
instead of dragging heavily and slowly along as one always
does with a Swiss voiturier; soon, however, we were to find
that our driver was an exception to the Italian rule, and
that he who wishes to travel fast must not expect to do so
with vetturini.

The churches which we passed were in no way remarkable; they all had campanili, with the bells hung in
the Italian fashion in the belfry windows, with their wheels
projecting far beyond the line of the wall; but they all
seemed alike uninteresting in their architecture, so that we
were in no way sorry to pass them rapidly on our way to
Lecco. This eastern arm of the lake, though of course
much less travelled than the rest of its course, is very beautiful, and its uninhabited and less cultivated looking shores,
with bold cliffs here and there rising precipitously from
the water, were seen to great advantage, with the calm
unrippled surface of the lake below, and the sky just tinged
with the bright light of the sun before it set above.

Lecco contains nothing to interest a traveller; we had

an hour to spend there before we could get fresh horses to take us on to Bergamo, and wandered about the quaint-looking streets, which were full of people—some idly enjoying themselves, others selling luscious-looking fruit. We went into a large church not yet quite completed; it was Renaissance in style, almost of course, and on the old· plan, with aisles, but very ugly notwithstanding. In the nave was a coffin covered with a pall of black and gold; six large candles stood by it, three on either side, and two larger than the others on each side of a crucifix at the west end. The whole church revelled in compo inside and out. and there was external access to a wretched bone-house in a crypt.

Leaving Lecco, we had a long drive in the dark to Bergamo; the night was very dark, but the air was absolutely teeming with life and sounds of life; myriads of *cicale* seemed to surround us, each giving vent to its pleasure in its own particular note and voice with the greatest possible determination; and had I not heard them, I could scarcely have believed it possible that such sounds could be made by insects, however numerous they might be. We changed horses at a village on the road, and went on rapidly. The old town of Ponte San Pietro was passed, having been taken at first to be Bergamo, and remembered by the sound of a troop of men singing well together as they passed us in the dark in one of its narrow streets, awakening with their voices all the echoes of the place, which till then had seemed to us to be supernaturally silent. It was eleven o'clock before we reached Bergamo, and tired with our long day's work, we were soon in bed.

A prodigious noise in the streets before five o'clock the next morning gave us the first warning that the great fair of Bergamo was in full swing; sleep was impossible, and so we were soon out, enjoying the busy throng which crowded the streets of the Borgo, in a before-breakfast walk; the

crowd of women selling fruit, the bright colours of their
dresses, the rich tints of stuff hung out for sale, the display
of hair-pins and other ornaments in the innumerable silversmiths' shops, and the noisy, laughing. talking people who
animated the whole scene, made the narrow arcaded streets
of the busy place most amusing.

After breakfast we started at once for the Città, as the
old city of Bergamo is called.   It stands on a lofty hill over-
looking the Borgo San Leonardo, within whose precincts
we had slept, quite distinct from it and enclosed within its
own walls. The ascent was both steep and hot, but the
view at the entrance gateway of the Città over the flat
Lombard country was very striking, and well repaid the
labour of the ascent.   This vast plain of bluish-green
colour, intersected in all directions by rows of mulberry-
trees and poplars, diversified only by the tall white lines
of the campanili which mark every village in this part
of Lombardy, and stretching away in the same endless
level as far as the eye could reach, was grand if only on
account of its simplicity, and had for us all the charm of
novelty.

Through narrow and rather dirty streets, which do little
credit to the cleanly habits of the Bergamask nobility, to
whom it seems that the Città is sacred, and whose palaces
are, many of them, large and important buildings, we reached
at last the Piazza Vecchia, around which is gathered almost
all that in my eyes gives interest to Bergamo.

Across the upper end of the Piazza stretches the Broletto, or town-hall, supported on open arches, through
which pleasant glimpses are obtained of the cathedral and
church of Sta. Maria Maggiore, which last is the great
architectural feature of the city.

But we must examine the Broletto before we go farther.
And first of all, its very position teaches a lesson.   Forming

on one side the boundary of a spacious Piazza, on the other
it faces, within a few feet only, the church of Sta. Maria
Maggiore, and abuts at one end upon the west front of the
Duomo. It is to this singularly close—even huddled—
grouping that much of the exquisite beauty of the whole
is owing. No doubt Sta. Maria and the original cathedral
were built first, and then the architect of the Broletto, not
fearing—as one would fear now—to damage what has been
done before, boldly throws his work across in front of them,
but upon lofty open arches, through which glimpses just
obtained of the beauties in store beyond make the gazer
even more delighted with the churches when he reaches
them, than he would have been had they been all seen from
the first. It is, in fact, a notable example of the difference
between ancient grouping and modern, and one instance
only out of hundreds that might be adduced from our own
country and from the Continent of the principle upon which
old architects worked; and yet people, ignorant of real
principles in art, talk as though somewhat would be gained
if we could pull down S. Margaret's in order to let Westminster Abbey be seen; whereas, in truth, the certain
result would be, in the first place, a great loss of scale in
the Abbey seen without another building to compare it with
and measure it by; and in the next, the loss of that kind
of intricacy and mystery which is one of the chief evidences
of the Gothic spirit. Let us learn from such examples as
this at Bergamo that buildings do not always require a large
open space in front of them, so that they may be all seen
and taken in at one view, in order to give them real
dignity.

The whole design of the Broletto is so very simple as
to be almost chargeable with rudeness of character. The
ground on which it stands is divided by columns and piers,
the spaces between them being all arched and groined.

Towards the Piazza three of these arches, springing from
rather wide piers, support the main building, and another
supports an additional building to the west of it. Above
the three main arches are three windows, of which that
in the centre, though very much altered, still retains a
partially old balcony in front, and was evidently the
Ringhiera, from which the people standing in the Piazza
were wont to be addressed by their magistrates. The
windows on either side are very similar in their design and
detail ; their tracery is of fair middle-pointed character ; and
the main points in which they strike one as being different
from English work are the marble shafts with square capitals
in place of monials, a certain degree of squareness and
flatness in the mouldings, and the very pronounced effect
of the sills, which have a course of foliage and moulding,
and below this of trefoiled arcaded ornament, which in one
shape or another is to meet the traveller everywhere in
Northern Italy ; either, as here, hanging on under the sills
of windows, or else running up the sides of gables, forming
string-courses and cornices, but always unsatisfactory, because unmeaning and unconstructional. The origin of this
sort of detail is to be found in the numerous brick buildings
not far distant, where the facility of repeating the patterns
of moulded bricks led (as it did in other countries also)
to this rather unsatisfactory kind of enrichment. The
detail of the arcades supporting the upper part of the
building is throughout bold and simple, and I should say
of the thirteenth century ; the bases are quite northern
in their section, the caps rather less deep in their cutting,
but still in their general design, and in the grouping of tufts
of drooping foliage regularly one above the other, reminding
one much of Early French work, though they are certainly
not nearly so good as that generally is. There is a flatness
about the carving, too, which gives the impression of a

5.—BROLETTO, BERGAMO.

struggle, in the hand of the carver, between the Classic and Gothic principles, in which the latter never quite asserted the mastery. The lesson to be learnt from such a building as this Broletto appears to me to be the excessive value of simplicity and regularity of parts carefully and constructionally treated; for there are no breaks or buttresses in the design, and all its elements are most simple, yet nevertheless the result is beautiful.

To the west of the Broletto is a good open staircase (much like that in the Piazza dei Signori at Verona),[1] forming a portion of one side of the Piazza, and leading to the upper part of the buildings, and, I think, to the great clock-tower, which, gaunt and severe in its outline, undecorated and apparently uncared for, rears its great height of rough stone wall boldly against the sky, and groups picturesquely with the irregular buildings around it. I have omitted to notice that the whole of the Broletto, with the exception of the window-shafts, is executed in stone, and without any introduction of coloured material, so that it in no way competes with the exquisite piece of coloured construction which we have next to examine, immediately behind it.

A few steps will take us under the open-arched and cool space beneath the Broletto, to the face of the north porch and baptistery of Sta. Maria Maggiore. This is a very fine early Romanesque[2] church, but with many additions and alterations on the outside, and so much modernized inside as to be quite uninteresting to any one who thinks good forms and good details necessary to good effect. The plan is cruciform, with apses to the choir, on the east and west sides of the south transept, on the east of the north transept, and at the west end of an additional

---

[1] See illustration no. 13.
[2] The church was built in A.D. 1131 by Maestro Fedro.

north aisle; in all no less than five apsidal ends. The nave
is of three bays with aisles, and to each transept have been
added, in the fourteenth century, porches, thoroughly Italian
in their whole idea, and novel to a degree in their effect
upon an English eye.

A domed chapel, erected as a sepulchral chapel by
Bartolomeo Colleoni in the Renaissance style, on the north
side of the nave, is most elaborately constructed of coloured
marbles. The effect is too bizarre to be good; there is an
entire absence of any true style in its design, and there is
nothing which makes it necessary to criticize it with much
minuteness.

The best and most striking feature in the whole church
is the north porch,[1] a most elaborate structure of red, grey,
and white marble, to which a drawing without colour can
hardly do justice. It is supported upon detached marble
shafts, whose bases rest upon the backs of rather grand-
looking lions, curiously grouped with children and cubs.
Above the arches which rest upon these shafts, and which,
though circular, are elaborately cusped, is another stage
divided by columns and trefoiled arches into three spaces,
the centre of which is occupied by a noble figure of a certain
Duke Lupus on horseback, with a saint on either side in the
other divisions. All the shafts except those in the upper
division are of red marble; the highest stage of all is entirely of grey marble; in the middle stage all the moulded
parts are of red, and the trefoiled arches and their spandrels
of grey marble; the space at the back of the open divisions
and the wall over the main arches of the porch are built
in courses of red and white marble. All the groining is
divided into diamond-shaped panels, composed alternately
of black, red, and white marble, all carved in the same kind
of pattern. In the great arch of the porch the outer

---

[1] For a view of this porch, see the frontispiece of this volume.

moulding is of red marble, and all the cusping of grey. The construction of the whole is obviously very weak, and depends altogether for its stability upon iron ties in every direction.

The approach to the porch, by seven steps formed alternately of black and white marble, increases the impressiveness of the grand doorway, in front of which it is built, the whole of which is of white marble, whose carved surfaces and richly moulded and traceried work have obtained a soft yellow colour by their exposure to the changing atmosphere, and are relieved by one—the central—shaft being executed in the purest red marble. There are three shafts in each jamb, carved, twisted, or moulded very beautifully. These shafts are set in square recesses, ornamented, not with mouldings, but with elaborate flat carvings, in one place of saints, in another of animals, and with foliage very flat in its character, and mainly founded on the acanthus.

To an English eye these columns in the doorways are some of the most charming features of Italian architecture; but they must be always looked at as simply ornamental, and not as constructional features; and perhaps in all doorways the shafts, being really incapable of supporting any considerable weight, would be better if, by their twisting and moulding, it were clearly shown that their architect meant them to be simply ornamental. In the Bergamo doorway the spaces between the shafts are so strong in their effect, though carved all over their surface, that any lightness in the columns themselves is amply atoned for. Such a work as this northern porch at Bergamo is indeed a great treat to an English architect, teeming as it does with fresh and new ideas, and in a small compass showing so many of the radical points of difference between northern and southern Gothic, and at the same time offering so beautiful a study of

constructional colouring, that it is impossible to tire of
gazing at it.

The porch to the south transept is of a simpler but
somewhat similar design.   Both are placed against the
western half of the gable against which they are built, with
a pleasant ignorance of those new-fangled views of regularity
of plan which are the curse of modern architects.   This
southern porch is round-arched, and fitted exactly to the
doorway which it shields.   Its outer arch is carried on
detached shafts resting on the backs of monsters, and it is
mainly constructed of black and white marble.   It is of only
one stage in height, and has a deep cornice enriched with
a series of niches with figures.   An inscription below the
cornice gives the date as 1360.[1]   Above the porch, but independent of it, is a lofty monumental pinnacle corbelled out
from the wall, and richly sculptured with crocketed pinnacles
and gablets.   When the church is entered, the reason for
the apparently eccentric position of the porches is seen.
They were so placed to give more space for the altars to the
east of the transepts, and their successful effect is good
evidence that no artist need ever distress himself about a
want of regularity, if it is the result of a little common
sense attention to convenience in the arrangement of his
plan.

The southern side of the church gives a very fair idea of
what the general character of the original building of 1134
was.   The windows were very plain, the walls lofty, the
roof flat, and ornamented with corbel-tables up the gables
and under the eaves, and pilasters were used at intervals
instead of buttresses.   There is a central octagonal lantern

---

[1] "✠ MCCCLX · MAGISTER · JOHANES · FILIUS · C · DN̅I ·
VGI · DE · CAMPILIO · FÉCIT · HOC · OPUS." This Giovanni da
Campione was one of a family of architects of much celebrity. See their
genealogical tree in ' Italian Sculptors,' p. 106.

which may be old, but which is entirely modernized. The
most interesting remains are the various apses already
mentioned. They are of two divisions in height, the lower
adorned with very lofty, boldly-moulded arcades, above
which is an elaborate cornice, and above this again a low
arcade on detached shafts, behind
which the walls are considerably recessed to form galleries which produce
a very deep shadow. The capitals are
elaborately carved, and the upper
cornice is again very rich. Altogether,
little as remains unaltered of the old
fabric, it is enough to give an idea of
a very noble and interesting phase of
art. Near a doorway into the north
chancel-aisle the external walls have
traces, faint and rapidly decaying, of
some very exquisite frescoes or, more
probably, tempera paintings.

The steeple is in a most unusual
position—east, namely, of the south
transept—not less, I believe, than some
three hundred feet in height, of good
and very simple pointed character,
without any approach to buttressing,
and remarkable as having an elaborately arcaded string-course a few feet
below the belfry windows, which have
geometrical traceries enclosed within
semi-circular arches, affording, like the

CAMPANILE—BERGAMO.

south transept porch, a curious illustration of the indifference
of Italian architects to the use of the pointed arch where
strength was not of consequence.

Italian campanili have quite a character of their own,

so distinct from and utterly unlike the steeples of Northern
Europe, that this, the first Gothic example I had seen,
interested me exceedingly. Perhaps its detail was almost
too little peculiar, if I may venture to say so; for certainly
it has left no such impression of individuality on my mind
as has the beautiful campanile to whose grace so much of
the charm of Verona is due.

The cathedral at Bergamo, which is close to the Broletto
and Sta. Maria, may be dismissed in a word. It has been
rebuilt within the last two hundred years, and appeared
to be in no way deserving of notice. In a courtyard on its
north side is a small detached polygonal baptistery, founded
in 1275, which must have been very interesting. It is
all built of marble, and richly adorned with shafts; but
so far as I could see every portion of it has been renewed
within a few years. Beside Sta. Maria Maggiore and the
Broletto we found little to see. Two churches—one in the
Città, and another, desecrated, in the Borgo—have very good
simple pointed doorways, with square-headed openings and
carved tympana; but beyond these we saw scarcely any
trace of pointed work. We had a luxuriously hot day in
Bergamo, and, as we sat and sketched the Broletto, a crowd,
thoroughly Italian in its composition and proceedings,
gathered round us and gave us a first lesson in the penance
which all sketchers must be content to undergo in Italy.
Before long I found that my only plan was to start an
umbrella as a defence both against the sun and the crowd,
and this, though not entirely successful, still effected a great
improvement.

The walk down the hill to the Borgo was more pleasant
than the climb up, and we were soon at our inn again; and
then, after a most delicious luncheon of exquisite fruit and
coolest lemonade, concluded by a very necessary dispute
with our landlord about the amount of his bill, ending, as

such disputes generally do in Italy, with a considerable
reduction in the charge and the strongest expressions of
regard and good wishes for our welfare on our way, we
mounted our carriage, and were soon on the road towards
Brescia.

Not far from this road and within about eight miles
of Bergamo lies one of the most interesting of the many
castles of which one so frequently sees remains in the North
of Italy. This is the Castle of Malpaga, which was inhabited by the famous Condottiere Bartolomeo Colleoni, of
whom we have already heard at Bergamo, and of whom we
shall see something again at Venice. It belongs now to a
nobleman who lives in the Città of Bergamo, and leaves this
old and stately pile to the keeping of his hinds, who tend
his silk-worms, gather his grapes, make his wines, look after
his corn and cattle, and do as much as in them lies to gather
the fruits which mother earth yields in these parts with
such ungrudging profusion, but trouble themselves little
about the preservation of the old castle or its belongings,
seeing that they seem to give scant pleasure to their lord.

The castle as originally built was a square building
enclosing a courtyard built of brick externally, and adorned
with a forked battlement, which is common everywhere in
old buildings between this and Vicenza, and with four
square corner towers, of which one larger than the others
has a very bold and fine overhanging machicolated parapet.
In the centre of the south front the drawbridge still remains
in use, and was lowered for our exit from the castle. Outside the square castle was a space, and then a low wall again
furnished with the forked battlement. This must have been
a very picturesque arrangement; but unfortunately its real
character is now only intelligible to the skilled eye. For the
great Colleoni, finding himself in possession of a castle which
gave him insufficient space for his magnificence, built up

walls on the top of the old battlemented outer wall, and created his state rooms in the space between this new wall and the old external wall of the castle. These rooms of his have much damaged the effect of the outside of the castle; but internally they are still interesting, owing to the sumptuous character of the painted decorations with which he had them adorned. These were executed at about the time of the visit of Christian II. of Denmark to Colleoni, and are interesting if not great works of art. The old courtyard though small is very fine in its effect. The upper walls are carried on pointed arches and are covered with fresco or distemper paintings, said to have been executed by Giovanni Cariani of Bergamo, or by Girolamo Romanino of Brescia, extremely striking and attractive in their general style of colour and drawing. The most picturesque incidents are illustrations of Colleoni's career—the Doge of Venice giving Colleoni his bâton in the presence of the Pope, and a fine battle subject.

A squalid area for rubbish, children, pigs, cats, and what not, is left all round the moat, and beyond this are all the farm buildings and labourers' residences, which go to make up the *tout ensemble* of a great Lombard farmyard. The surroundings are not clean nor very picturesque, but the castle itself has so great an interest, that no one who visits Bergamo should pass it by unseen.

---

[1] The round church of San Tommaso in Limine, described by Mr. Gally Knight as similar in plan to San Vitale, at Ravenna, is only eight miles to the north of Bergamo, and ought, equally with Malpaga Castle, to be seen. I regret that I have never yet visited it.

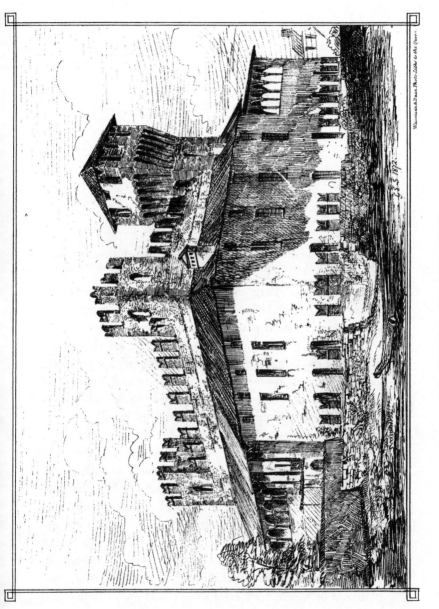

6. CASTLE OF MALPAGA.

CHAPTER V.

"Am I in Italy ?   Is this the Mincius ?
. Are those the distant turrets of Verona?
 And shall I sup where Juliet at the masque
 Saw her loved Montague, and now sleeps by him ?"

                                        Rogers.

Palazzuolo—Coccaglio—Brescia : new and old Cathedrals, Broletto—Churches
  — Donato — Desenzano — Lago di Garda — Riva — Trent —Verona.

OUR drive from Bergamo to Brescia was strikingly unlike what we had hitherto been so much enjoying. Mile
after mile of straight roads, between fields so closely planted
with fruit-trees that one never sees more than the merest
glimpse of anything beyond them, are certainly not pleasant ;
and the hot sun above us, and the thirsty and dry beds of
rivers which we crossed on our way, made us feel glad when
evening drew on, and we found ourselves rapidly nearing
Brescia.

I made notes at two or three places on the way. At
Palazzuolo is a great circular belfry, ornamented with a large
figure at the top and divers others about its base, built of
brick rusticated to look like stone, and altogether about as
base a piece of architecture as could well be found, but pardoned here because of the pure blue of the sky I saw behind
it, and partly on account of the view which it commands,
reaching, it is said, as far as Milan, and including the great
plain out of which, upon a slight hill, it rises. Palazzuolo is

nicely situated, and upon the first of the many rivers which
we had passed from Bergamo which had any water in its bed.
The houses, too, were almost all supported on arcades, giving
pleasant shelter from the sun.

Beyond this we came to Coccaglio, a small village with a
wretchedly bad modern church, glorying in a glaringly
sham front, and faced on the opposite side of the street by
the remains of a mediæval church—whose place it has taken
—and which is now shut up and rapidly going to ruin.   The
new church is built north and south—the old one orientat-
ing properly; but then the west front was the great feature
of the new church, and therefore it was necessary, of course,
to place it towards the road !

WINDOW—COCCAGLIO.

Coccaglio still has, however, some very valuable remains
of mediæval domestic work in its houses, of which I was able

7.—HOUSE AT COCCAGLIO.

to obtain some sketches. They were entirely executed
in brick and terra-cotta, except, of course, the capitals
and shafts of the windows, and appeared to be of the fourteenth century.

The upper portion of the house of which I give a sketch
remains very fairly perfect, though its lower story has been
entirely modernized. It will be seen that it is very uniform
in its design, the large and small windows alternating

DETAIL OF WINDOWS AND CORBELLING FOR CHIMNEYS—COCCAGLIO.

regularly; and that semi-circular arches are used in the
windows in connection with ogee trefoils. This is one of
the apparent inconsistencies which occur in almost all Italian
Gothic work; and might seem to give us ancient authority
for any amount of licence in our combination of the elements
of what we ordinarily consider to be thoroughly different
styles. The windows are marked by the same elaboration

of their sills which we noticed in the Broletto at Bergamo, and the detail of these, as also of the corbelling out from the wall of several chimney-breasts, is exceedingly good.

In a back street in the village I found a house the balconies around which were corbelled forward on finely moulded beams, which, judging by the moulding, could hardly be of later date than the commencement of the fourteenth century.

WOODEN BALCONY—COCCAGLIO.

Wooden mouldings of this kind are much rarer in Italy than they are in the North, and I particularly notice this little relic, therefore, which still remains to show how well the science of moulding was sometimes understood even there.

Such a village as Coccaglio is, as I found afterwards, a place to be made much of; for generally, except in public or important buildings in large towns, one sees very little trace of any mediæval domestic work beyond the perpetually

recurring arcading under the houses which is so general a
feature in all the towns in the North of Italy.

There is nothing further of any interest on the road, and
just after sunset we reached Brescia, too late to see anything of the general effect of the city.

Brescia is mainly famous, I believe, first for its connection with a story of the generosity of Bayard, the "chevalier
sans peur et sans reproche," and next for the large dis-
coveries of Roman remains which have from time to time
been made there. It is one of those towns, moreover, of
which guide-books, with an immense list of churches and
the pictures they contain, give perhaps too grand an idea
before they have been seen. It is, however, undoubtedly a
place of much interest, not only for the antiquary, but also
for the student of mediæval art, since, though its churches
are generally uninteresting, it has in the Broletto, sadly
mutilated and modernized as it is, the remains of one of
the most extensive and grand of these buildings, and to a
considerable extent executed in very excellent brickwork.

Our first visit in the morning was to the Piazza, in which
stand the two cathedrals—the old and the new—side by side,
and just beyond them the front of the Broletto, stretching its
great length up a slight hill and along a narrow lane beyond
the Piazza, whilst at its angle, towering up between it and
the cathedrals, stands a tall and rugged stone campanile,
without break or window until at the top, where, just as in
the corresponding tower at Bergamo, great rudely-arched
openings are left, through which appear the wheels and works
of the bells.

The new cathedral, approached by a flight of steps from
the Piazza, has a great sham front. It has, moreover, a large
dome, said to be inferior only in size to those of S. Peter's
and the cathedral at Florence, but not prepossessing in its
effect; nor did the church seem to contain any pictures of

value. By a descent of some twenty steps from the south
transept the old cathedral is reached. This is of very early
date, and constructed partly in stone and partly in brick.
The most remarkable feature is the nave, which is circular in
plan, with an aisle round it; the central portion, divided by
eight arches from the aisles, being carried up into a dome.
The choir and transepts are projected on the east side of the
dome, and the former is groined and has a five-sided apse. The
walls retain some fair mediæval monuments, and beneath the
church is a large crypt. The old stone altar in the choir is
a fine example of the thirteenth century. The mensa is, as
so often is the case, carried on shafts, no less than sixteen
in front and six at the ends, with carved capitals. The
stalls are in the apse, and a fine lectern stands behind the
altar.

The whole air of the Duomo Vecchio is chill and dismal
to a degree; it is neglected and dirty, and apparently shut
up except for occasional services, and left no pleasant impressions on our minds of our first Lombard cathedral; and yet
undoubtedly there is both here and at Aachen—where the
plan of the cathedral is so very similar—much to admire
in the idea of the plan, and I can quite imagine that a very
noble and useful church might in any age have been founded
upon this old Lombard type.[1]

Those who know anything of Spanish churches will be
reminded here of the two cathedrals at Salamanca, the relative
positions of which are just the same, a steep flight of steps
in either case, leading down from the south aisle of the new
cathedral into the old and deserted one.

From the cathedral we went at once to the Broletto, which

---

[1] S. Gereon, at Köln, is a magnificent example of a church upon the
same kind of plan; a grand choir projected from a decagonal nave, the effect
of which is cap'tal. No doubt such a nave. does much more than merely
suggest the possibility of adapting the dome to Gothic buildings.

S.—BROLETTO, BRESCIA.

stands in the same Piazza. The main portion of this immense
building appears to have been built rather early in the
thirteenth century. The arches throughout are both round
and pointed, used indifferently; but this mixture does not
betoken any diversity of date, as it would in England.

CLOISTER—BROLETTO, BRESCIA.

A large quadrangle is formed by the buildings, which has
a cloister on two sides, and traces of another cloister on a
third side now built up. The cloister still remaining on the
east side is ancient and on a large scale; it opens to the
quadrangle with simple pointed arches resting upon heavy
piers, and a row of piers running down the centre divides it
into two portions, so that it may be judged that its size is very

considerable. The groining has transverse and diagonal ribs,
the former being very remarkable, and, as not unfrequently
seen in good Italian work, slightly ogeed; not, that is to say,
regular ogee arches, but ordinary arches with the slightest
suggestion only of an ogee curve in the centre. Of the
external portion of the building the west front is the most
perfect, and must always have been the finest; it consists
of a building containing in the upper story five windows,
the centre being the largest, and possibly once the Rin-

DETAIL OF CIRCULAR WINDOW—BROLETTO, BRESCIA.

ghiera, to the south of which rises the great belfry of rough
stone, and beyond that a wide building with traces—but
no more—of many of the original windows; north of the
building with the five windows is a very beautiful composition
executed almost entirely in finely-moulded bricks; it has an
exquisite door with some traces of fresco in its tympanum,
executed mainly in stone, of which I give a drawing, and a
magnificent brick rose window, above which is a brick cornice,
which continues over the remainder of the west front and
along the whole of the north side.

The size of the building is prodigious, and certainly the
detail of all the parts (excepting perhaps the cornice, which

DOORWAY—BROLETTO, BRESCIA

BRICK CORNICE—BROLETTO, BRESCIA.

is of the common arcaded kind) is most beautiful and valu-

able. The brickwork is so good and characteristic that I
have given several sketches of it. All the arches have occasional voussoirs of stone, and the centre of the arch is always
marked by a key-stone, and these are sometimes slightly
carved to distinguish them from the other stone voussoirs.
The abaci are of brick, moulded and very varied. The
doorway given in the woodcut on the preceding page has
stone jambs, caps and bases, lintel and outer arch, the label
and cusps being of terra-cotta; above this the whole of this
portion of the front is of brick, and very admirably built.

SAN FRANCESCO—BRESCIA.

Of the churches of Brescia there seem to be but few of
any interest; that of San Francesco, of whose west front I
give a sketch, is the best, and, though not of uncommon
design, is worth notice; the mixture of white and black

marble and brick is very judicious; but I must protest once more against the arcaded eaves-cornices, which are very elaborate and heavy; nor can I bring myself to like the great flat gable, covering both nave and aisles, and divided only by pilaster strips, which characterizes so many mediæval Italian churches. In this west front of San Francesco the cornices and the mouldings of the small circular windows are all of brick, and the rest of the front of stone, the rose window having voussoirs of black and white marble. The only other part of the church which appeared to be of any interest was a campanile on the south side of the choir: this had stone belfry windows, well treated with simple plate tracery, and there is a singular and lofty lantern over one of the chapels on the north side of the church, all of rich brickwork dating from about 1480.

The sun was at its hottest as we wandered about the streets of Brescia; but there was so much pleasure in the examination of the busy people who thronged its narrow tortuous streets, that we enjoyed it very much. In Italian towns, too, there is not much difficulty in finding the way; we ask the road to some church, and forthwith, in place of a long and not very intelligible direction, in which we are sure entirely to confuse our right hand with our left, the person we ask turns round with us, walks by our side, shews us our object, and, politely taking off his hat and bowing, takes leave of us. It was by such aid as this that we found the church of the Carmine, which is another very late Gothic church. The west front is most fantastic and unpleasing, and the pinnacles composed of round bricks, disposed alternately over each other, and common in most Italian brick buildings, are very ugly; there is, however, a good simple cloister attached to the church on the north; it is of the same design as almost all in this part of the world, having simple round shafts with carved caps and circular arches. An inner

cloister which I remember of old as occupied by the ever
present Austrian soldiers, is now (1872) open to all the world,
and neither cared for nor used.　　Here the south side of the

CLOISTER OF THE CARMINE CONVENT—BRESCIA.

cloister is of two stories in height, the lower similar to the
one just mentioned, the upper having two arches to one arch
of that below, and the arches picturesquely shaped, being
cinquefoils, with the central division of ogee form, and with

moulded terminations to the cusps. There is a fair campanile here, with brick traceries and strings, but with a
modern belfry-stage.

A little bit of cloister, or gallery, on the north side of Sta.
Afra, has arcading of similar character in its upper gallery,
but the arches are trefoiled.

In the Contrada della Pace there remains a very bold fragment of a castle tower. It is built of very roughly-jointed
stone, and is perfectly plain till near the top, where it has
a bold machicolation with tall square angle-turrets, the whole
battlemented with a forked battlement. Out of the centre
of the tower a tall thin tower rises to some height above the
battlements.

One of the most picturesque spots in the city is the
Piazza, at the end of which stands the Palazzo della Loggia;
the effect on coming into it from the narrow streets in which
we had been wandering was very pleasant, the large open
space being surrounded with rather elaborate Renaissance
work with rich coloured sun-blinds projecting from the
windows over the sunny pavement, which in its turn was
thronged with people in picturesque attire selling fruit and
vegetables. The streets are all arcaded, and some of them
have very considerable remains of frescoes on the exterior,
giving much interest to the otherwise ugly walls; they
have, however, suffered very greatly from exposure, and
are only in places intelligible; still they give traces of
brilliant external colour, and are therefore much valued in my
recollections of Brescia.

Compared with Bergamo, Brescia has the air of a smart
and busy place; its streets are wider and better paved, and
the smells which still greeted us were not quite so bad as
there. The staple manufacture of the city seems to be that
of copper vessels; shop after shop, indeed street after street,
is full of coppersmiths' shops; the men all sitting at work,

and keeping up a ceaseless din of hammering, in open shops, so that all the world may see them. Nor is the copper-smiths' the only trade that loves publicity, for here as else-where the barbers' shops are very amusing, quite open in front, with perhaps a yellow curtain hanging down half way, affecting only to conceal the inviting interior, which however is always sufficiently visible, occupied in the centre by a chair, on which sits the customer gravely holding a soap-dish to his chin whilst the barber operates; and this going on all day makes one think that shaving is, after all, one of the great works of an Italian's time!

When we left Brescia the heat was intense; the road, too, was deep in dust to an extent not to be understood in England. There had been a drought of some weeks' dura-tion, and the much-travelled road from Milan to Verona, along which our way now lay, plainly told the tale which the dry, parched, cracked-looking earth on each side of our way, and the sad faces of every one as they talked about the failure of the vintage, amply confirmed. Unluckily for our-selves we had not taken the advice of our driver to have a close vehicle, but had insisted upon having an open carriage, the consequence of which piece of self-will was that we had hard work, even with the aid of umbrellas, to protect our-selves from *coups de soleil*. We now learnt that in hot weather in Italy it is not always the best plan to have as much of the sun as one can get. In England it always is, but he who acts on his English experience in Italy will surely repent his mistake.

We managed, however, to exist through the clouds of dust, relieved perhaps by the sight of a regiment of swarthy and unpleasant looking Austrian soldiers marching through the sun and dust, many of them with their knapsacks and arms, but all with great-coats on to preserve their white uniforms. When we saw them we could not help con-

trasting our relative lots, and then, feeling how much worse
off they were than ourselves, we went on a little more con-
tentedly than before. The road, too, became slightly more
interesting ; instead of miles upon miles of straight lines, we
had a more winding way, and after a time occasional beautiful
glimpses of the mountains which marked to us the situation
of the Lago di Garda.

We drove without stopping through Donato, a place of
no interest apparently save for the huge dome of its church,
and then passing under a very fine viaduct resting upon a
long range of pointed arches, (which carries the railway
which soon after our return was opened, and now whisks
only too many travellers from Milan to Venice and back
without a halt on the way,) we commenced the descent
towards the town of Desenzano, beyond and above whose
roofs stretched the beautiful expanse of fair Lago di Garda,
with its great calm surface, and fine group of distant mountains hemming in with picturesque and irregular outline, its
upper end.

We soon reached the poor and desolate streets of the
town, and diving into the dark court of the not over-clean
looking hotel, gave ourselves up for a time to the contemplation of the quiet loveliness of the scene. The contrast
between the flat shores of the lower part of the lake and
the mountains which crowd around its head is very
striking, and to this it is that Desenzano owes all that it
has of interest. We strolled out for a short time, looked at
washerwomen kneeling in small tubs on the edge of the lake,
and washing their linen upon the smooth face of the stones
which pave its shore, and then went on, as in duty bound, to
look into the church. This we found to be neither very old
nor very interesting, but curious as illustrating the extent
to which, in Italy, the practice is sometimes carried of
putting altars in every direction without reference to their

orientation.   Here the high altar and some others faced due south, whilst most of the remainder faced east, and I think scarcely one turned to the west.

The remains of an old castle rise picturesquely above the little harbour, from which steamboats sail for the tour of the lake, and bidding farewell for a time to dusty roads, let us embark on one of these for Riva at the head of the lake on our way to Trent, which is, artistically speaking, the northernmost really national city and cathedral in Italy.

Our steamboat kept to the west side of the lake, touching at a few villages and towns, and for the most part ploughing its way along beneath some of the highest and most precipitous rocks that I know.   We took a band on board on the way, and discharged them into a big barge under a cliff, on the top of which was being held a village festa, at which they were to perform; and we all looked with no little compassion upon the heavily weighted performers as we saw the people who had preceded them climbing the steep mountain sides above us.

The Lago di Garda seems to me to be in its upper reach one of the most beautiful of Italian lakes.   But it should always be taken in the way we went, for the contrast between the sublimity of the upper end and the tameness of the lower end is so great that nothing but disappointment would be felt by those who saw the head of the lake first.

One or two of the towns on the western shore have churches of some interest.   At Salo there is a Gothic church with windows which have a wide external splay and an enriched brick moulding or label all round them.   The windows are of one light, and have ogee-cusped heads. Another church, at (I think) Gargnano, is of much more importance.   It is cruciform, with a domical lantern at the crossing.   The nave has a simple clerestory and aisles, and the west end, built in black and white courses, has

one great arch which encloses the doorway, above this a
lancet window, and above this again a circular window
without tracery.

From Riva—one of the most pleasant resting-places on
the Italian lakes—a good road through fine scenery leads to
Trent, a journey of some six or eight hours. The descent upon
Trent is very fine. The town standing by itself well away
from the fine mountains which form the background to the
view, the old walls and towers around it, and the interest
of the cathedral and other buildings behind them, combine to
give a sense of the importance and grandeur of the city
which the facts of the case hardly justify. Perhaps, too,
there is something in the historical importance of the place
which, without one's knowledge, sways the judgment.

There is in fact only one building of great architectural
importance—the cathedral; but, as I shall shew, it has
the greatest interest, not only on account of its real merit,
but also because it is a startling example of the way in
which, in the thirteenth century,[1] the Lombard architects
adhered to their old lessons and habits in spite of all the
developments which were then universally accepted on the
northern side of the Alps.

The church is a round-arched building throughout, but
the mouldings and details everywhere show a knowledge of
thirteenth-century work, and have none of the character of
true Romanesque or Lombard art. Yet at the same time
there is in many respects a most close imitation of Lombard
features. There are arcades under the cornices of the aisles,
arcades under the eaves of the apses, open porches supported
on shafts whose bases rest on monsters, and other features

---

[1] I say this advisedly, though knowing very well that some German antiquaries assert this cathedral to have been built in the time of Bishop Ulrich II.,
A.D. 1022–1055. Those who say so must, I think, be entirely blind to all architectural detail.

which, looked at apart from the sections of mouldings and details of sculpture, might well warrant a much earlier date being fixed on for the execution of the work than I have named. An inscription which fixes the date of some works here in 1212 [1] may fairly, I think, be assumed to give the date of the greater part of the fabric, though some portions, as e. g. the western wheel window and the northern porch, are probably not so early by at least a hundred years. But I am not concerned to deal with the question only from an archæological point of view, and will at once therefore go on to give some description of the building.

The ground-plan is in the shape of a Latin cross—with an eastern apse, two small apses to the east of the transepts, and a nave and aisles of seven bays. There is an octagonal lantern over the crossing, and the whole church is groined. The doors are, two in the east walls of the transepts, one at the west end (of marble), and one with a projecting open porch over it near the east end of the north aisle. Two western towers were intended to be built, and the staircases to them are carried up in the western and southern aisle walls in a very unusual and picturesque fashion. They commence in the third bay east of the towers, and are carried up in a continuous rise, opening to the church with a series of arches stepping up to suit the level of the staircases. The western bay to which these stairs lead is groined at a lower level, as well as at the nave level, so as to form a very lofty gallery open to the church.

The clerestory consists of very small windows, and there is no triforium ; the main portion of the columns goes up to

---

[1] Anno Domini MCCXII. ultima die Februarii presidente venerabile Tridentino Episcopo Frederico de Vanga, et disponente hujus Ecclesie opus incepit et construxit magister Adam de Arognio Cumane Dioc. et circuitum ipse, sui filii, inde sui Aplatici cum appendiciis intrinsece et extrinsece istius ecclesie magisterio fabricarunt. Cujus et sue prolis hic subtus sepulcrum manet. Orate pro eis.

Whiteman & Bass. Photo Lith. to the Queen.

10. DUOMO. TRENT.

and carries the groining, and though the main arches are all
semi-circular, there is nevertheless an evident attempt—and
it is successful—to give an impression of height to the interior. The continuous arcades under the eaves are carried
also across the front of the transepts, and give a great effect of
richness to the external architecture. Of the two towers only
one is complete, and this was built in the sixteenth century.
The northern porch is the only place in which the pointed
arch appears, and it seemed to me to be of the fourteenth
century, though the doorway is of Lombard character, with
very quaint but poor carving in its tympanum, of Our Lord
with the four Evangelists. The whole church is built of stone,
and has a Classical want of life and vigour which one notices
only too often in the best Lombard work. Were it not for the
building attached to its north-east angle, I suspect the general
impression would be much less agreeable than it is. This is a
lofty erection with two square turrets and a small apse at the
east, parts of which seem to be earlier than the date I have
given to the cathedral. It is connected with the north-east
angle, but its axis is not parallel with that of the cathedral,
and there is consequently a good deal of picturesqueness in
the perspective, besides which it prevents the otherwise insipid outline of the whole building being perceived.

The porch on the east side of the south transept, of which
I give an illustration, is one of the most interesting portions
of detail in the building. Its front is supported on two
shafts, one of which is an octagon, resting on the back of a
lion, the other four shafts cut out of a single block and ingeniously knotted together in the centre, and resting on the
shoulders of four sitting figures—altogether about as strong
an illustration of mediæval love of change and variety as could
be found. It must have been the work of a sculptor who was
just a little savage with the somewhat tame uniformity of
the whole of the architectural scheme of the cathedral.

I found little else to see in Trent. Sta. Maria Maggiore has a Romanesque steeple, quite plain below, but with its two upper stages arcaded, the arcades resting in the lower stage on shafts coupled one behind the other, and in the upper tripled in the same way. I do not remember before to have seen this last arrangement. A tower in the walls between this church and the cathedral is a rhomboid in plan, and was, I suppose, built of this strange shape to suit some necessity arising out of the position of streets and walls. Considerable portions of the walls remain ; they are of stone, finished on the top with the forked Italian battlement, and having square projecting towers at short intervals.

Trent Cathedral and the fine church at Innichen in the Pusterthal, are quoted frequently as the two finest churches in Tyrol. That at Innichen has not the same entirely Italian character which marks that at Trent. In the latter I always feel that climate, people, and town are all in concert to make one suppose oneself in Italy, which certainly is not the case at Innichen. North of Trent the architecture of the Tyrol (as at Botzen and Meran) is entirely German, whilst in Trent itself, were it not for a steep roof here and there covered with bright glazed tiles, and a few such slight indications, no one would suspect the presence of any German influence whatever.

I have travelled so frequently from Trent to Verona by the railway that I always regard it as one of the most natural and obvious roads of approach to Italy for Englishmen. It takes its course through so fine a country that one does not easily tire of the journey, and finally, it sets travellers down in the city which, perhaps more than any other in northern Italy, charms the cultivated traveller by the beauty, interest, and grandeur of its buildings. Who that has taken this way to Verona does not remember with pleasure the last quarter of an hour of his journey, as the railway, making a circuit round two-thirds of the city, reveals first a mixed group of lofty steeples, presently the great church of San Zenone, then Sta. Anastasia, anon San Fermo, then crosses the swift-flowing Adige, and at last lands one at the station, full of anxiety to make the nearer acquaintance of the buildings of "Verona la degna," which from afar look so wondrous brave and fine?

CHAPTER VI.

"Come, go with me.   Go, sirrah, trudge about
Through fair Verona."
                    Romeo and Juliet, act i. scene 2.

———◆———

Verona: Campanile of the Palazzo dei Signori — Sta. Anastasia—Monuments
— Piazza dell' Erbe — The Duomo — The Baptistery — Sta. Maria l'Antica
— Cemetery and Palace of the Scaligers — Domestic Architecture — Piazza
di Brà—The Austrians — Ponte di Castel-Vecchio — San Zenone — San
Fermo Maggiore — Chapel near the Duomo — Romeo and Juliet — Dwarfs
—Wells.

WE reached Verona in the evening, and were up early on
the next morning, anxious to get a general idea of the city.
But I was no sooner out of my bed than I saw from my
window, over the roofs of the opposite buildings, the
campanile of the Palazzo dei Signori, a lofty, simple, and
almost unbroken piece of brickwork, rising, I suppose, at
least three hundred feet into the air, and pierced with
innumerable scaffold-holes, in and out of which, as I looked,
flew countless beautiful doves, whose choice of a home in the
walls of this tall Veronese tower will make me think kindly
of putlog-holes for the future.   Certainly, if the Italian and
English principles of tower-building are to be compared with
one another, the Italian need give no fairer example of its
power than this simple and grand erection.

It rises, as we found afterwards, out of a large pile of
buildings, and for a short distance above their roofs is built
in alternate courses of brick and a very warm-coloured stone,

11.—CAMPANILE, PALAZZO SCALIGERI, VERONA.

and then entirely with brick, pierced with only one or two
small openings, and terminating with a simple belfry-stage;
the belfry windows, with their arches formed without mouldings, and with the sharp edges only of brick and stone
used alternately, are divided into three lights by shafts of
shining marble; the shafts, being coupled one behind the
other, give strength with great lightness, and are very striking
in their effect. These windows have, too, remarkably large
balconies, but without balustrading of any kind. The upper
and octangular stage of the campanile is comparatively
modern, but rather improves the whole effect than otherwise.

I could hardly tear myself away from this noble work;
but much more was to be seen, so I dallied not long before I
set forth on a journey of discovery, giving myself up gladly
to sketching and ecclesiology.

The hotels in Verona are both of them near Sta. Anastasia, and at the eastern end of the long and at first narrow
and picturesque Corso. The Adige separates the city from
its eastern suburb, and from the hills crowned by the Castel
San Felice and the picturesquely stepped city walls. Its
yellow waves wash with an angry rush the foundations of
the houses which overhang it all along its course, but the
only views of it are to be obtained from the bridges, and from
the open space near the Castel Vecchio. At the extreme
north-western angle of the town stands the church of San
Zenone. One soon finds one's self constantly on the Corso, and
to the north of this lie the cathedral, Sta. Eufemia, the Castel
Vecchio, and San Zenone, whilst to the south of it are the
tombs of the Scaligers, San Fermo Maggiore, the Roman
Amphitheatre, and the Palazzo Publico. Without further
attempt to describe the map let us visit the buildings, of
which the list I have given, though by no means exhaustive,
includes the finest.

The Veronese architects in the Middle Ages were certainly

some of the best in Italy.   San Zenone is by very much the
finest church of its kind that I know ; Sta. Anastasia is on
the whole one of the best churches of a later date ; and
San Fermo Maggiore affords some of the best detail of brickwork, and the tombs of the Scaligers the best examples of
monuments in all Italy.

The first thing seen on turning out of the hotel is the
west front of the church of Sta. Anastasia, looking so beautiful at the end of the narrow street, whose dark shade contrasts with the bright sunshine which plays upon its lofty
arched marble doorway and frescoed tympanum, and lights up
by some kind of magic the rough brickwork with which the
unfinished church has been left so brightly, that, as you gaze,
thoughts pass across your mind of portions of some lovely
painting or some sweeter dream ; you feel as though Fra
Angelico might have painted such a door in a Paradise, and
as though it were too fair to be real.   There, however, it is,
rich and delicate in colour, shining with all the delicate tints
of the marbles of Verona, pure and simple in its softly-
shadowed mouldings, beautiful in its proportions, and on a
nearer approach revealing through the dark shade of its
opening, and over and beyond the people who early and late
throng in and out, the vague and misty forms of the solemn
interior.

Sta. Anastasia is one of the most complete and representative pointed churches in the North of Italy, and deserves,
therefore, a rather detailed description.   Its date is about
1260 to 1290.   The ground-plan is very simple—a nave of
six bays, then one which is the crossing of the transepts, a
very short choir of one bay finished with an apse and
two chapels on the east side of each transept.   The nave
aisles are narrow, and the whole design is characterized by
intense simplicity of detail and arrangement.   The width of
the nave, and the height of the columns and arches, give, on

entering, an idea of vast space and size. The columns are
very simple, cylindrical in section, and support arches built
of brick, and only chamfered at the edge; from the caps of
the columns flat pilasters run
up to the commencement of
the groining, and above the
nave arcades there are two
small circular openings, one
in the place of a triforium,
opening into the roof of the
aisle, the other above it and
larger, filled in with plate
tracery in stone, and forming
the clerestory.

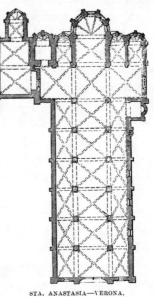

The arrangement of the
plan is in several respects unlike that of northern Gothic
buildings, and as most complete Gothic churches in Italy
are very much of the same
type, it is as well here to
point out the peculiarity.

STA. ANASTASIA—VERONA.

The most marked features
are first the shortness of the choir, and next, the fact that
whereas in northern Europe it is usually the aisle vaulting bay which is square, whilst the nave bay is oblong from
north to south, here the nave groining bay is square, and
the bays of the aisle oblong in the direction of east and west.
The difference of effect is great, simple as the statement
seems. In these Italian churches there is much greater
space between the columns of the nave arcades, the groining
is consequently divided into much larger bays, and the whole
interior has a largeness of treatment which is not common
in the North. On the other hand there is much less of
the complexity and intricacy which are so charming in

our interiors, and you see at a glance the whole of the
church.

In Sta. Anastasia the apses on each side of the choir have
an even number of sides, as has also the sacristy, which is a
room on a magnificent scale, to the north of the church.
This is a peculiar feature, producing as it does an angle in
the centre of the apse, which we shall see again at Venice and
Vicenza, and which is seldom seen out of Italy.[1]

The whole is so simple in design and construction that
it depends for its rich effect on the painting which covers
almost every part of it, and which harmonizes well with the
architectural lines. The decorations appear to have been
done, or at any rate commenced, within a short period of
the completion of the church, and are therefore very valuable.
The ground of the painting is white, many of the patterns
of borders being very elaborate compositions of flowers and
foliage. The main arches are painted to represent voussoirs
of red brick and stone, but I am inclined to think that they
are really entirely of brick; their soffeits, which are very
broad and flat, are all painted with large scroll patterns of
foliage. In the groining the diagonal ribs are painted at the
intersection with stripes of colour alternating with white,
and on each side of all the ribs a wide border of foliage is
painted, whilst in the centre of each groining-cell some
large device is painted in a medallion, some of these being
merely ornamental, others having figures. The detail of
much of the painting is cinquecento in its character, and
not valuable as an example to be literally copied,[2] but its
general effect is certainly very beautiful, and it is worthy of
all praise in respect of the strictness with which it is kept
subservient to the architecture, and in some respects, indeed,

---

[1] The church of the Capuchins, at Lugo, is a Spanish example of the same
arrangement.

[2] Admirable drawings of it have been published by Mr. Grüner.

even serves to atone for its deficiencies, as, e. g., in the broad
painted horizontal borders, which take the place, very
successfully, of brick or stone string-courses, which in the
construction are entirely omitted.

It surprised me, I confess, very much, to find a church
painted throughout without any use of gold, and yet with
good result; so it is, however; the effect is most solemn
and religious, and there is a very rich effect of colour; the
fact is, that the white ground answers the same purpose in
a degree, though of course not to the full extent, that gold
would.

But if the walls are beautiful in their colour, not less so
is the pavement, which, from one end of the church to the
other, remains to this day to all appearance just as it was
on the day that the church was finished. The nave and
transepts are all in one pattern; the spaces between the
columns in a variety of beautiful designs, and divided from
the nave and aisle pavements by a strip of white marble on
each side; and the aisles again are on the same scheme
throughout. The colours of the marble used are white, red,
and bluish grey, and the patterns very simple and generally
geometrical in outline, and there is a quiet richness of effect
in their arrangement which is exceedingly beautiful. Such
a pavement must unhappily be for ever Italian, and we in
England can scarce hope ever to attain to anything so
exquisite; but we do not well to forget that by the mixture
of a small quantity only of marble with our encaustic tiles
we should attain to much greater beauty of effect than we
can by the use of tiles alone, and there are many towns—as,
e.g., Plymouth—the very pavement of whose streets is of a
material which might most advantageously be introduced,
more often than it has yet been, inside the walls of our
sanctuaries, as well as under the feet of every passer along
the streets.

There are some monuments and paintings here quite worth looking at. The Pellegrini Chapel, next to the choir, has two fine trefoil-headed monuments in red marble with the background painted with subjects of about the same age (circa 1392); and in the Cavalli Chapel there is an admirably painted wall, against which has been put a monument which, though somewhat rude and coarse in its sculpture, nevertheless produces a very fine effect of colour and architecture combined.[1]

The window tracery of Sta. Anastasia is rather singular plate tracery, consisting of mere piercings through the

AISLE WINDOW—STA. ANASTASIA, VERONA.

stone with very little moulding; most of the windows are of two very lofty trefoiled lights with circles and trefoils

[1] An extremely careful chromo-lithograph of this wall and monument has been issued by the Arundel Society, accompanied with a notice of both, written by Mr. Ruskin.

pierced above, very simple and severe, and remarkable for the quaint way in which the cusping is arranged, not with some reference to vertical lines, as is ordinarily the case with us, but just as fancy or chance seems to have dictated. The clerestory windows are circular openings cusped.

There is a curious but not very happily treated arrangement inside—a step all round the inside walls, projecting some three or four feet from them, and panelled all round against the riser with a small trefoil arcading—the whole in red marble.

Externally the church is almost entirely built in red brick with rich cornices and rather ungainly buttresses and pinnacles of brick; the windows have brick jambs with stone tracery, and on the north side of the choir is a fine lofty campanile, finished at the top with a low, very plain, and octangular capping, and unpierced with openings, except in the belfry-stage. Of the west front only the doorway has been completed; this is in courses of red, grey, and white marble, and most effective; the rest of the front is left in brick, finished exceedingly roughly, with a view to leaving a key for the marbles with which, no doubt, it was intended to veneer the entire front. The wooden framework of this door, of which I give a detail, is very curious; it is of deal, coëval with the doorway, and the framework is external, not internal.

The west front of the church stands in a small piazza, on the north side of which is the little church of San Pietro Martire, between the east end of which and Sta. Anastasia is a wall dividing a small burial-ground from the Piazzetta; on the top of this wall, and supported upon corbels, is one of those monuments peculiarly associated with Verona, because so numerous there, though they are often met with elsewhere in Italy; they are either large pyramidal

canopies supported upon trefoiled arches resting on four
marble shafts, with a kind of sarcophagus or an effigy
beneath ; or else, when attached to a wall, they have two
detached shafts supporting the same kind of trefoiled arch
and surmounted by a flattish pediment. Their effect is
almost invariably beautiful in the extreme, and their only
defect is, that they all require to be held together by rods

DOOR-FRAME—STA. ANASTASIA.

of iron connecting the capitals of the columns. This,
however, is soon forgotten when one feels that there is no
pretence ever or anywhere at its concealment; and notwithstanding this slight defect, one cannot help loving and
admiring them ; for there is a grace and beauty about the
form and proportion of the Veronese trefoiled arch, such as
is never seen, I think, elsewhere, and the very flatness of
the carving and the absence of deep moulding seem all
adopted in order that nothing may interfere with the simple
beauty of the outline of the arch. In this case the monument is supported on a large slab of stone corbelled forward
and balanced upon the top of a thin wall over the archway

which leads into the churchyard of San Pietro. Four shafts
with sculptured capitals, resting on the angles of this slab,
support four trefoiled arches, (those at the ends narrower
than the others), which are almost destitute of moulding save
that the outer line of the arch has a broad band of delicate
sculpture all round it. The arch terminates in a small
cross, and above on each side is a very flat pediment,
moulded and finished on the under side with one of the
favourite Italian arcaded corbel-tables; the finish is a
heavy pyramidal mass of stone rising from behind the
pediments. The four bearing-shafts are of white marble,
all the rest of the monument of red. Within the four
supporting shafts stands a sarcophagus, supported on the
backs of couchant lions, very plain, but ornamented at
the angles in very Classic fashion, and bearing a recumbent
effigy.

The church of San Pietro has three or four smaller monuments enclosed within its small courtyard; two of them
are on the ground and have round arches on detached shafts
with an Agnus Dei carved in the centre. The third is
corbelled out from the wall, and the face of the monument
is covered with sculpture, that of the figures being very
inferior in style to that of the foliage enrichments. This
little group of monuments, varying in date from 1283 to
1392, is well worth study, and I found it more than usually
interesting owing to its entire unlikeness to any English
work. The church against which these monuments are built
is small but deserves notice; it is of brick with a stone canopy
on shafts corbelled out above the west door; the buttresses
are mere pilasters, and run up without any weathering till
they finish in an arcaded corbel-table at the eaves; the
windows have wide brick splays outside, and trefoil heads of
stone without any chamfer or moulding; on the south side,
the church—in point of size a mere chapel—is divided into

four bays, one of which has a monument corbelled out by
the side of the window. It is built entirely of red brick,
not relieved in any way, except that the window arches are
in alternate voussoirs of brick and stone. The wooden
framework of the west door deserves notice as being very
unlike the English mode of door-framing, and very good
in its effect. The accompanying sketch will best explain
it: and it must be understood that, instead of being internal, as such framing would usually be in England, in this

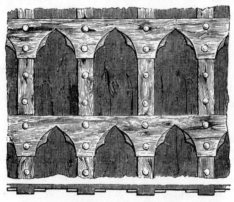

DOOR-FRAME—SAN PIETRO MARTIRE.

example it is external, just as in the somewhat similar
door of Sta. Anastasia, of which I have already made
mention.

Turning back from the Piazzetta of Sta. Anastasia, and
traversing again the narrow and gratefully shady street by
which we reached it, we soon found ourselves at the end of
the Piazza dell' Erbe, the most picturesque square in the
city, and at an early hour in the morning quite a sight to
be seen. The whole open space was as full as it could be
of dealers in vegetables and fruits, all of them protecting
themselves and their stores from the intense glare of the sun
under the shade of prodigious umbrellas, at least five times

as large as any of ordinary size, and certainly five times as
bright in their colours, the prevailing colour being a very
bright red.   Altogether it was a thoroughly foreign scene.
The houses, some ancient, but all picturesque and irregular,
surrounding the irregularly-shaped Piazza, the magnificent
campanile of the Scaligeri Palace rising proudly behind the
houses on the left, the fountain in the centre, and the great
column of red Veronese marble rising close to us, which at
one time bore the winged lion—mark of the dominion of the
Venetians—all combined to produce a very striking picture.
An hour or two later in the day when we passed, the people,
the umbrellas, and the fruit were all gone, and somewhat of
the charm of the place was gone with them.

From the Piazza dell' Erbe we went to the cathedral,
anxious to see and hear somewhat of a service which we
found was to take place.   There was a great throng of
people, and we had some difficulty in finding even standing
room among them ; we were not at all sorry, however, to
have gone, for we came in for a sermon most energetically
preached, and enforcing in very powerful language the necessity of repentance.   The pulpit was very large, and as
the preacher delivered his sermon he walked from side to
side, and often repeated again to those on his left the
substance of what he had already said to those on his
right.   The people, who crowded every available place
within hearing, were exceedingly silent and attentive ; and
at intervals the preacher stopped for a minute to cough
and use his handkerchief, which was a signal for an imme-
diate general blowing of noses and coughing all over the
church.   The "*Ebben infelici !*" with which he commenced
his sermon, was a good index to its whole tone, and makes
me remember with pleasure the vast crowd listening to
Christian doctrine in the grand nave of the Duomo.   Would
that we could see any prospect of the day when in England

our larger churches may be used in this way, when,
with pews and all their concomitant evils swept away, we
may see a vast crowd standing and sitting, leaving no
passage-way and no waste room, anxious only that they
may, by pressing near, join in the services at the altar, and
hear every word of warning and of advice! The nave of
Westminster, so thronged, would soon show how great has
been our mistake in leaving our large churches so long
unused.[1]

The Duomo is a really fine church, Romanesque in its
shell, but altered completely internally in the fourteenth
century. It has only five bays in length, but the dimensions
are so large that the nave and aisles alone measure about 225
feet × 97 feet inside. There are slightly recessed Romanesque
apses in the side walls, and a great tomb or shrine of S. Agatha,
which is worth looking at. The columns in the interior are
very lofty, of red marble, and, instead of being plain and
cylindrical, as at Sta. Anastasia, are moulded with very
good effect. Their capitals are, however, heavy, and the
carving of the foliage on them not at all satisfactory. The
whole interior is very solemn, and specially beautiful on
this bright September day, with almost all the light excluded by thick curtains—here and there a stray gleam of
the most intensely bright light finding its way through
some chink, lighting up with sudden brilliancy the deep
cool shade, and—reflected from the bright surface of some
great marble shaft—suggesting the grandeur which can
hardly really be seen.

The choir is divided from the nave by a screen of marble,
consisting of detached columns with Ionic capitals and a
continuous cornice, the whole screen semi-circular in plan,
and coming forward into the nave. This, the work of

---

[1] I leave this passage as it originally stood. It is pleasant to feel how
completely unnecessary it is now to use such language on the subject.

Sanmichele, is certainly about the most effective work of this kind and age that I have seen.

The west front of the Duomo is still in the main in its original state. It has a rich porch supported on shafts (whose bases rest on the backs of lions), and of two stages in height, a flat pediment surmounting the upper stage. Another flat pedimental cornice is carried over the whole front at the same level; but out of this a wall rises above the central portion the width of the nave and height of the clerestory, which is again surmounted by a third flat pediment—a confused and not very graceful arrangement, which found an imitator in Palladio, when he built that ugliest of fronts, the west end of San Giorgio Maggiore at Venice.

The windows at the ends of the aisles are very Italian in their character. They are insertions in the wall of two narrow lights within an enclosing arch, which is again surrounded by a square line of moulding. The effect of this not uncommon Italian arrangement is exceedingly unsatisfactory, as it appears to make the window with its arch and tracery quite independent, constructively, of the wall in which it is placed; it appears in fact to be merely veneered on to the face of the wall.

On the north side of the cathedral is a cloister of good detail, which was originally of two stages in height, but is now considerably altered in parts. It is exceedingly similar to the cloister of San Zenone, which we shall see presently, consisting of a long arcade of pointed arches carried on marble shafts; it is now in a very ruinous condition.

The Baptistery—San Giovanni in Fonte—is a detached church near the east end of the cathedral, which does not look as if it had been at first intended for its present use. It is a building of the twelfth century, with nave and aisles ending in three apses, lighted by a small clerestory, and with some columns which are probably Roman. The font, which stands

in the centre, is of enormous size, and is sculptured with eight
subjects beginning with the Annunciation and finishing with
the Baptism of Our Lord.　These sculptures are very rude.
The bason of the font is almost seven feet in diameter, and in
its centre is another smaller bason of graceful shape.　I do
not happen to have seen an explanation of these inner basons
in the fonts in Italian baptisteries.　They look as if they
were meant for the priest to stand in whilst he immersed the
catechumens around him.

And now that we have visited two of the great churches,
we must no longer delay our visit to the church of Sta.
Maria l'Antica, whose small burial-ground is fenced from the
busy thoroughfares, which on two sides bound it, by an iron
railing of most exquisite design, divided at intervals by
piers of stone on whose summits stand gazing upward as in
prayer, or downwards as in warning to those who pass below,
a beautiful series of saintly figures.　Within, a glorious
assemblage of monuments meets the eye—one over the
entrance doorway, the others either towering up in picturesque confusion above the railing which has been their
guardian from all damage for so many centuries, or meekly
hiding their humility behind the larger masses of their
companions.

The monuments are all to the members of one family
—the Scaligeri—who rose to power in the thirteenth
century, and held sway in Verona until almost the end of
the fourteenth.　In this space of time it was, therefore, that
these monuments were erected, and they are consequently of
singular interest, not only for the excessive beauty of the
group of marble and stone which, in the busiest highway of
the city, among tall houses and crowds of people, has made
this churchyard, for some five hundred years, the central
point of architectural interest, but because they give us
dated examples of the best pointed work during nearly the

whole time of its prevalence in Verona. In the monument of the first Duke we see the elements of that beauty which, after ascending to perfection in that of another, again descends surely and certainly in the monument of Can Signorio, the largest and most elaborate of all, and, therefore, I am afraid, the most commonly admired, but the one which shows most evidence of the rise of the Renaissance spirit, and the fall of true art. Nor is it, I think, to be forgotten, as an evidence of the kind of moral turpitude which so often precedes or accompanies the fall of art, that this Can Signorio first murdered his own brother Cangrande II. that he might obtain his inheritance, and then, before he died, erected his own monument, and adorned it with effigies of SS. Quirinus, Valentine, Martin, George, Sigismund, and Louis, together with allegorical figures of the Virtues with whom he of all men had least right to associate himself in death, when in life he had ever despised them. The inscription, which records the name of the architect on this monument, does but record the vanity of him who was content thus to pander to the wretched Can Signorio's desire to excuse the memory of his atrocious life by the sight of an immense cenotaph.[1]

The tomb of Cangrande I. forms the portal of the church as well as the monument of the first and greatest of the family. It is perhaps altogether the finest of all; the shafts which bear the pyramidal canopy are supported on corbels; between them is a simple sarcophagus sculptured with a bas-relief, and upon it lies Cangrande with his arms crossed in token of his resignation and faith. At the top of the pyramidal covering is the figure of the brave knight riding forth to war on his gaily caparisoned steed.

---

[1] It is not a little remarkable that this should be the monument a copy of which the late Duke of Brunswick desired in his will to have erected over his grave !

Next to this monument in date, as in merit, is that of Mastino II., wanting perhaps in some of the severe simplicity of the other, but even more striking, as it stands at the angle of the cemetery. It is a thoroughly grand and noble erection of two stages in height, the lower unimportant, and only serving as a means of raising the monument sufficiently high to be well seen from the exterior; upon this stand four shafts, between which, and supported upon four much smaller shafts, is the sarcophagus on which lies the recumbent effigy, at whose head stand angels with expanded wings [1] guarding the deceased. The sarcophagus is adorned with bas-reliefs—that on the west side being the Crucifixion—and has engaged angle-shafts. The four main bearing-shafts at the angles of the monument have finely carved caps with square abaci from which rise simple trefoiled arches with steep pediments on each side filled with sculpture in relief, and between these are exquisitely simple niches, each a miniature reproduction of the entire monument, and containing between their delicate detached shafts figures of saints. The whole is finished with a heavy pyramidal capping, crocketed at the angles with crockets so abominable in their shape and carving that they go far to spoil the entire work, and surmounted by the figure of the Capitano del Popolo, spear in hand, riding on his war-horse; the horse and horseman riding with their faces towards the setting sun, as all in life must ever ride; the effigy below lying so that at the last day the beams of the day-star in the East may first meet its view, and awaken him that sleepeth here in peace.

This contrary position of the figure in life and in death, observed also in others of these monuments, is an evidence of the care and thoughtfulness with which every detail of these noble works was wrought out.

---

[1] The wings of these angels are of metal, though the figures themselves are marble.

The monument of Can Signorio is not worthy of so long a description; it is octagonal in its plan, and in many respects below the idea shadowed out so beautifully in the others; the reduplication of niches and gables, far from improving, only perplexes the design: and when to this is added that the carving throughout, as well as the other details, show strong signs of a leaning towards Renaissance, one may see some reason why this, the most elaborate and complicated of all the monuments, is after all far from being the most successful.

Mastino II. died in the year 1351, and we may therefore, I think, look upon his monument as a fair enough example of Italian architecture just at the period at which in England it had reached its culminating point, and a careful examination of it cannot, therefore, be thrown away. In the first place, I must notice that the sculpture, which has the air of being rather sparingly used as too sacred a thing to be idly or profusely employed, is exceedingly good. The foliage is almost always very closely copied from natural forms, is very thin and delicate in its texture, and thus really present to the gazer that idealized petrifaction of nature which it ought always to be the sculptor's effort to give, and not, as is, I fear, sometimes the case, even in good English work, so profusely scattered over the whole surface as to give one a sense of its lack of great value. The worst part of the carving is, as I have before said, that of the crockets, which are as bad as the worst modern Gothic could be. The sculpture of the human figure is throughout very good; remarkable for simple, bold, deep folds in the draperies, quite Gothic in spirit, and much more akin to our best fourteenth-century work than to any Classic examples.

As an example of the science of moulding this work is however valueless; there is absolutely no moulding upon it ; and why should there be? Would it have been well that the lovely marble, whose brilliant white gloss was sure ere long to be stained with dark streaks of black by the beating of rain and the staining of age, whilst here and there the white would stand out more brilliantly than ever,—would it have been well, I say, that this should have been still further streaked with deep lines of many mouldings? Most assuredly not : the architect had to deal with a material which best takes its polish and exhibits its beauty and purity when used in flat surfaces and in shallow carving, and he did right therefore in not moulding it as he would have moulded stone.

There is a sharpness and hardness about the lines of the arches, however, which perhaps almost verges upon rudeness, and, though I can see that it may be fairly defended, I could yet wish that it might have been softened.

But the points in which such work is a grand example to us are, first, the value which it shows that we ought to place upon the simple detached circular shaft, and, next, the beauty and strength of effect which the cusping of a large arch in a proper manner gives. In these two points

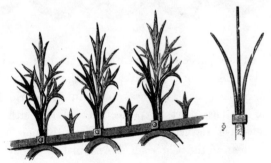

CREST OF METAL RAILING—VERONA.

this monument and most of its class teach us lessons which we ought not to be unwilling to learn, and which, if we at all

wish to develope beyond the point at which our own ancestors ever arrived, we must not fail to attend to in our
own work.

And now I must bid farewell to this lovely spot, the
most attractive certainly, to me, in Verona. The situation
of the monuments, rather huddled together, with the old
church behind them, the archway into the Piazza dei Signori
on the other side, and the beautiful iron grille[1] which
surrounds them, the number of saintly and warlike figures

METAL RAILING—VERONA.

and the confused mass of pinnacle and shaft, half obscured by
the railing, do, I verily believe, make the cemetery of Sta.
Maria l'Antica one of the best spots in the world for the
study of Christian art in perfection. What either Köln
or Regensburg Cathedral, or the Wiesen-Kirche at Söest
is to Germany, the Choir of Westminster Abbey or the

---

[1] This grille is worthy of especial notice. Instead of being hard and stiff,
it is all linked together, so that it is more like a piece of chain mail than of
iron railing. Its intricacy adds manifold to the effect of the group of tombs
which it half conceals.

Chapter-House at Southwell to England, Amiens Cathedral
or the Sainte Chapelle of Paris to France, such is the
Cemetery of the Scaligeri in Verona to Italy—the spot
where at a glance the whole essence of the system of a
school of artists may be comprehended, lavished on a small
but most stately effort of their genius.

Close to their burial-place stands also the Palace of the
Scaligers. The old portion of this fronts towards the Piazza
dei Signori, a small square used only by foot-passengers,
and surrounded by elaborate Renaissance work. The
buildings surround a quadrangle—the Mercato Vecchio—out
of one angle of which rises the immense campanile which I
have already noticed, and which is said to have been erected
by Can Signorio about A.D. 1368, though I should have
thought that a rather earlier date would have tallied better
with its style. Besides this the most striking feature is the
external staircase in the courtyard, whose treatment, of a
kind not uncommon in ancient Italian architecture, is very
beautiful, though I fear very weak and unstable, if I may
judge by the number of the iron bars by which it is held
together. There are many windows here of very good detail,
and an arcaded cornice all round the courtyard, and close
by and also facing the Piazza dei Signori there is another
fine lofty battlemented tower.

In a street close to the monuments of the Scaligers, whose
name I have forgotten, but in a line with the Viccolo
Cavaletto, I found a most valuable example of domestic work
in a very fairly perfect state. As far as I could make it out,
it consisted originally of three sides of a quadrangle, the
fourth side towards the street being enclosed by a wall and
arched gateway. The buildings all had arcades on the
ground-level, forming a kind of cloister, and the staircase to
the first floor was external, and built against the wall on the
road side. A great many alterations have been made in the

13.—COURT-YARD OF THE PALAZZO SCALIGERI, VERONA

house at various times, but in the sketch which I give I have shewn so much only of it as appeared to belong to the original foundation. In its construction pointed and round arches have been used quite indiscriminately, and in some of the arches the depth of the voussoirs increases towards the centre of the arch. This is a rather favourite Italian device, and I was always as much pleased as at the first

DOORWAY—OLD HOUSE, VERONA.

with the effect of strength and good proportion which it produces. Most of the arches are built with alternate voussoirs of brick and stone, but beyond the outside line of the brick and stone arch there is invariably a line of very thin bricks laid all round the arch, delicately defining without pretending to strengthen the main arch, just as a label does with us. I noticed too, generally, that this thin

brick was of a deeper, better colour than the other bricks,
which are seldom any better than the common English bricks,

WINDOWS—OLD HOUSE, VERONA.

and are always built with very coarse joints.   This house is
finished at the top with the quaint forked or swallow-tailed
Ghibelline battlement, so characteristic of Verona, and which,

BRICK BATTLEMENT—VICCOLO CAVALETTO, VERONA.

as we found afterwards, was in use at Mantua, Cremona,
and for some distance south of Verona, but which I first
met with in Verona.

I am not pretending to journalize regularly, but rather

14.—COURT-YARD OF OLD HOUSE, VERONA.

to note down the remarkable points of the various buildings
as they occur to me, and, before I forget that it was Sunday
when I was first looking at the Veronese churches, I must
mention that in the evening we found our way to the great
Piazza di Brà, surrounded by barracks and public buildings,
and containing the vast Roman amphitheatre for which
Verona is so celebrated. Its size is prodigious, and, except
in the outer circuit of wall, it is nearly perfect; indeed, it is
impossible to look upon such a vast structure without a
great admiration for the men who ventured to conceive and
carry it into execution.

It is difficult now to conceive how the audience could be
found who would fill so vast a space; and certainly the
modern efforts in this direction are mainly serviceable as
shewing the immensity of the theatre. When I was last in
Verona a theatre had been erected in the arena, and a
performance was in progress. The audience might have
been tolerably large in an enclosed theatre, but here it
seemed to be the merest handful; and when we stood on the
highest attainable part of the walls, we found ourselves so
far from the stage as to be unable to hear a single word that
was said. There is no need to describe here so well-known a
building as this; suffice it to say, that though the detail of
the architecture is poor, the general design and execution of
the structural arrangements, and the magnificence of the
whole scheme cannot fail to strike one with the same wonder
that one feels in the presence of many of these great Roman
works; and it is striking indeed, to see one of them so
perfect as to be still capable of use, and really used.

All the Austrian portion of the inhabitants of Verona
crowded the Piazza di Brà on Sunday evening to hear
an Austrian military band, and we enjoyed not a little a
stroll among a crowd of uniforms of all shapes, kinds, and
colours. Verona more than most towns, even in Austrian

Lombardy, seems to be sacrificed entirely to Austrian soldiery. It is quite melancholy to walk along a street of palaces, some of them converted into old-furniture stores, others going to ruin; and when suddenly you do come upon a flourishing and smart palace, if you look in you are sure to see an Austrian sentinel, and find that it is an officer's quarters; and equally when you meet a conveyance, if it is smart and dashing, with good horses and a stylish coachman, it is quite certain to be occupied by some dignified-looking military man. So, too, on the Monday evening, when we went to the French opera (a very pretty, tastefully got-up theatre by the way) there were absolutely none but Austrians in the house—in the boxes, officers and their wives, in the pit, subordinate officers and privates. Who can see this immense staff of foreigners in occupation of a city like Verona without feeling sadly for the people who live under such a rule, and for the ruler who is compelled to maintain such a force to keep his subjects in order? [1]

This, however, is a digression, and I must go on to describe the remaining architectural features of the old city.

On the way to San Zenone Maggiore, which is quite on the extreme western verge of the city, one passes the Castello Vecchio, a very grand pile of simple mediæval fortifications erected in the fourteenth century by Cangrande II. There are several towers and lofty walls, all topped with the forked Veronese battlement; and connected with it is the magnificent Ponte di Castel-Vecchio, a great bridge across the rushing Adige, built entirely of brick, the parapet of the regular Veronese type, and the piers between the arches rather large and angular, and finishing with battlements

---

[1] I need hardly say that all this is changed, and I hope changed for the better. The city looks more thriving than it did, and more of the old mansions are properly occupied than was the case in the time of the Austrians.

rather above those of the bridge. The main arch is of great size—it is said to be· not less than one hundred and sixty feet—and one of the most remarkable points in its appearance is, that, instead of being in the centre, it is on the side of the river next the castle, while the other two arches, descending rapidly to the north bank of the river, give the bridge an odd, irregular, and down-hill kind of look. The architectural features of this bridge are, however, not the only objects of interest on this spot; for just after passing the castle the road bends down to the side of the river, and presents an admirable view of the campanili, steeples, and spires, with the steep hills on the opposite bank of the stream, and the mountains in the distance, with the rapid, turgid, white-looking Adige flowing strongly at one's feet.

A longish walk through squalid suburbs leads us to the open space in front of the noble basilica of San Zenone; it is a desolate waste-looking space, and the poor, old, uncared-for church looks now as though its day was well-nigh past; as if neglect and apathy were all that men could give now where once they were wont to lavish so much of their treasure, and love, and art.

The church, as it now stands, seems to have been entirely rebuilt in the course of the eleventh or twelfth century, and its proportions are so very grand, and its detail generally so perfect, that I think it may certainly be regarded as on the whole the noblest example of its class; indeed, except the very best Gothic work of the best period, I doubt whether any work of the Middle Ages so much commands respect and admiration as this Lombard work. There is a breadth and simplicity about it, and an expression of such deep thought in the arrangement of materials and in the delicate sculpture, which with a sparing hand is introduced, that one cannot sufficiently admire the men who planned and executed it. Beyond this, the constructive science was so excellent and so careful, that with ordinary care such a church as San Zenone would seem still likely to last for ages.

The view of the west front is certainly very striking. The whole church has been singularly little modernized. By its side to the north is a fine simple red brick tower, I suppose originally belonging to the city walls; behind and near the east end of the church, but visible here, the tall and much-arcaded campanile; and on the other side the little church of San Procolo with a fourteenth-century painting of Our Lord under a gabled canopy overhanging the doorway. The west front of San Zenone is simple but dignified. The nave and aisles are finished with cornices following the flat pitch of the roofs. The walls are divided by many vertical lines of pilasters which rise from the plinth to the eaves-cornice. The main part of this front is stone, but a good deal of marble is used, e.g., the rose window has tracery of red marble enclosed within an order of white marble; the doorway and sculpture are in white marble, once much enriched with colour, and the arcaded band all across the front is of red marble. Add to this that the stone used is all of an extremely warm yellow colour, and an idea may be formed of the effort that was made here in the principal front (as often in Italian churches) to shew that God's house was the noblest that could be built.

The doorway well deserves a chapter to itself. Its lintel has illustrations of the labours of the twelve months, its jambs subjects on the right from the Old Testament, on the left from the New. In front of this door there are detached shafts standing on monsters and supporting a low canopy. An inscription on the façade " Salvet in eternum qui sculpsit ista Guglielmus," gives the name of the sculptor, the same man probably who about the middle of the twelfth century sculptured the western doorway of the cathedral at Modena.

No less worthy of study are the bronze doors of this doorway. Here, as is so often the case in mediæval Italian
works, we have the names of the artists employed—
Guglielmo and Nicola da Figarola—with the pious expression of hope that he who sculptured the work might be
saved eternally. The subjects are very rude in their detail ;
they illustrate subjects from the Old Testament, and are
executed in thin plates of bronze nailed on to the wooden
doors. A row of small windows, one in each of the many
divisions of the front, extends all across near the top of the
porch ; whilst above is a large circular window, filled in
with wheel tracery, and treated as was not uncommon as an
illustration of the Wheel of Fortune. Round this window is
an inscription explaining its symbolism.

We went first into the cloister on the north side of the
nave. The arches are very small, and of brick, supported
on coupled shafts of red Veronese marble, which have
marble caps and bases, and rest on a dwarf wall of stone
capped with a thin course of marble. The arch bricks are
of a rich red colour, and contrast well with the brickwork of
the ordinary kind above them ; they are used without any
kind of moulding or ornament—and yet I doubt whether I
have ever seen a more lovely cloister than this. The
arcades on the north and south sides have round arches ;
those on the east and west are pointed ; and on the north is
a projecting arcade of the same detail, which once formed
the lavatory. The whole of this cloister is in a very sad
state of filth, neglected and unused, and will, I fear, ere
long become ruinous.[1]

From the cloister you enter by a side door into the
north aisle of the choir ; much better, however, would it
always be to enter from the west, for it is there, when

---

[1] This cloister is said to have been built in 1123. This is, I think, at least
fifty years earlier than its real date.

standing at the top of the flight of ten or twelve steps
which leads down from the door to the floor of the nave,
looking down the great length of the church, scanning its
singular perspective of timber roofing, the great height and
simplicity of its walls, and the mysterious view down into
the crypt under the choir through the recently opened
arches, that one feels most deeply the great and religious
effect of the church.   To an eye used to northern Gothic
there is something very new in such a building.   Its shape,
its material, its arrangement, are all unlike what an English
eye is used to, but I cannot say that I paused for an instant
in doubt as to whether I might really admire or not; for I
felt at once how very good the work was, not only in its
general effect, but as much in the treatment of the details,
in its colour, and in its arrangement.

The general plan is very simple—a great parallelogram,
divided into a nave of vast width with northern and southern
aisles; the aisles terminated with square east ends, the
choir with an apse of five bays, which is, however, of later
date than the rest of the church.   The chief singularity in
the design is the division of the piers of the main arcades
into primary and secondary—the first being large heavy piers
supporting great arches spanning the nave and aisles, which
are finished in a line with the top of the walls; and the
latter more delicate circular marble columns of very Classical
character, with finely carved capitals, and looking almost
too slight to support the vast height of clerestory wall
which towers up above the arcade which they carry.   The
timber roof, or ceiling, is curious; the framing is all concealed, with the exception of the collar-beams, which connect
the points of the trefoil which forms the internal line
of ceiling.   This trefoil outline is all boarded, divided into
panels, and painted.   The effect of this great length of
panelled roofing, partly concealed by the great arches which

16. SAN ZENONE. VERONA.

Westerman & Bunt. Photo Litho. to the Queen.

15.5.1877

cross the nave, is certainly fine. The wooden roofs of the
aisles, too, are original, and their beams are painted very
much like the Austrian sentry-boxes, in zigzag lines of black
and buff. Much of this painting, however, did not appear
to me to be old.

At about two-thirds of the length of the church between
the west door and the apse it is cut in two, so to speak, by
that which perhaps is now the greatest charm of the interior
—the crypt. When I first visited San Zenone this crypt
existed, but its existence was not realized from the nave.
The only access to it was from the aisles, and even here the
arches were partially blocked up. A flight of steps across
the whole east end of the nave led up to the choir and
concealed the old entrance to it. This, it has lately been
found, was originally formed by three open arches from the
nave with a flight of steps descending under them to the level
of the crypt, whilst two arches on either side of these gave
access to it from the aisles. This is the old scheme, and the
only possible approach to the raised choir must originally have
been that which has now been restored, viz., two narrow flights
of steps against the side walls, so contrived as not to interfere
with or conceal any part of the sculpture or other decorations on the western face of the arches to the crypt. The
church as now restored yields to few with which I am
acquainted in the solemn effect which is the result of
mysterious light and shade, multiplied vistas of columns
and arches, and picturesque originality of design. It is
evidently rather a result of growth than of first intentions.
The crypt—like our own remarkable example at Wimborne
—seems to be an insertion. The columns and piers of the
choir pass on into the crypt, whose piers and vaults are
built against them. There is an obvious difference too in the
style of the church and of the crypt, showing that at least
a hundred years must have elapsed between the erection of

the former and the insertion of the latter. The choir now
occupies the three eastern arches of the old constructional
nave, and beyond this has a square bay and a five-sided apse,
the two last divisions being groined and decorated with a
good deal of colour. The apse is of the fourteenth century,
but all its windows have been modernized. The crypt follows
exactly the dimensions of the choir, but is divided into no
less than nine bays in width, and six bays in length, exclusive of the apse. The red marble columns which support its
groined roof are all monoliths, delicate in their proportions,
and many of them probably antique. The vaulting is quadripartite, and there are considerable remains of wall paintings,
which appear to be nearly cöeval with the crypt. In the
centre of this crypt is the shrine of San Zeno, half concealed
by the gloomy but effective lighting, and surrounded by
a metal railing made of quatrefoils, buckled or tied together, very much in the same style as the railings round
the Scaligeri monuments. The altar in this crypt is worth
notice on account of its sculptured front. This has in the
centre a small crucifix with SS. Mary and John, and on
either side, under arches, figures of the Evangelists. The
face towards the nave of the seven arches which form the
western part of the crypt is decorated with extreme care
and finish. They are admirable examples of the really
polished work of the Italian artists of the end of the
twelfth century. The arches from the north aisle deserve
special notice. They are carried on coupled shafts which, as
well as their capital, are of red Veronese marble, the archivolt
being of stone. The section of both shafts is circular, but
one of them is delicately twisted to a spiral curve on its
upward course. The refinement of this treatment of shafts is
very characteristic of the best Italian work, and this coupled
shaft, simple as its treatment is, and common as are the
elements of its design, is so beautiful that it makes a real

sunshine in a shady place. Not less are the arches above it worthy of admiration. The sculpture here, of a trailing branch of foliage, is very slightly relieved, but its outline is so graceful, its imitation of nature so close without being merely realistic, and its fitness for its position so complete, that I think I have never seen anything in its way more satisfactory, and certainly never anything really ornamental in the best sense, the elements of which were more severely simple.[1]

The colour of the whole interior is, to my mind, charming. It was first of all built in alternate and very irregularly divided courses of brick and stone. On this warm-coloured ground, one pious man after another came and painted what seemed to him best—a Madonna, a crucifixion, a saint, or a group of figures—with not much thought beyond that of making the particular work in which he was interested tell its own story well and produce its own effect. So little did he think of other men's previous work that the same subjects are not unfrequently repeated. The result is that the walls were here sober and there gorgeous, but everywhere coloured, and everywhere more or less interesting. Yet the materials of which they are built are just those which we see every day of our lives, and it was the skill of the workman, not the richness of his materials, which made his work so worthy of our admiration.

Only one portion of the church is decorated upon a regular system; this is the eastern part of the choir and the apse, which has part of its walls and its groining very elaborately painted, though with but little gold; the groining ribs are richly coloured, and on each side of them is a wide border, generally subdivided into regular geometrical figures, and the spaces between these borders are painted blue and powdered with gold stars. In the south aisle is an

---

[1] The sculptor of this work left his name—Adaminus— on the capital.

altar under a baldachin, supported at the angles by four
clustered shafts knotted together in mid height—a capricious
custom of which Italians seem to have been especially fond,
and the only excuse for which, so far as I can see, is that it
proves that all the shafts were cut out of one block, and
therefore of more value than four plain detached shafts cut
out of separate blocks could be. There is perhaps, also, a
relief to the mind, after looking at a long series of similar
shafts, to come at last upon some one or two marked by
capricious singularity such as this. Be this, however, as
it may, the eye certainly always feels inclined to admire
them, though the reason is never quite satisfied; and
perhaps some better excuse does exist for their use than I
have as yet been able to discover. It is probable that these
columns belonged originally to the baldachin over the
high altar. The canopy which they now support is not
old.

The vestry on the north side of the choir is worth a
visit, if only for the sake of its prettily panelled and painted
ceiling. Here the panels are very small, and left in the
natural colour of the pine, and the ribs are decorated
with white, red, and black. There is also in this room a very
good fourteenth-century marble cistern and lavatory under an
arch in the wall; and lastly, in the wardrobes, among many
things not worth seeing, a finely embroidered bishop's mitre
of the twelfth century, wrought in gold on linen. In front
is a figure of Our Lord, at the back one of the Blessed
Virgin, with emblems of two Evangelists on each, and a band
below with figures of the Apostles, the stoles also being
adorned with figures.

The arrangement of the choir shows the common Italian
plan of stalls round the apse behind the altar. They are of
early Renaissance character, with some relic of Gothic feeling
in the traceries of the backs and elbows. There is also a

good example of a square choir lectern, with a large base to contain books, and a revolving gabled desk.

Until the beginning of this century, there were only two altars in this church, one in the choir the other in the crypt. The verger told me that his father remembered the other altars being brought from a suppressed church, and erected here.

The campanile is well seen from the cloister, where it composes finely with the coursed walls of the church, and the many-shafted arcades of the cloister. It is a lofty square tower of several stages, with small pinnacles, and a low circular brick spire crowning it.

I must not leave San Zenone without mentioning the construction of the exterior, which—with the exception of the west end, which is of stone and marble—is entirely of red brick and very warm-coloured stone. The courses of stone are, as a general rule, of about the same height, whilst those of brick are very varied, some only of one course, others of four or five. The cornices at the tops of the walls, too, are very good, supported upon corbel-tables with round arches resting upon corbels, and much improved in their effect by the judicious introduction of thin deep-red bricks between the courses of carved stone, which are thus thrown out forcibly. It is in this use of red brick, and in the bold and successful way in which brick and stone are shown in the interior, that this church is so full of instruction to an English eye; and I could not see such a work without regretting bitterly the insane prejudice which some people indulge against anything but the cold, dreary, chilling respectability of our English plastered walls, which to me seems to be fit only for occupation by savages.

Every time I visit this noble church, I leave it with greater regret; its exceeding grandeur appears to deserve a

better fate than the spare use to which it seems now to be
abandoned.   To see all these painted or coloured walls,
all these marble piers, and all this vast expanse of wall and
roof waste and desolate, apparently not half used and never
filled with a throng of worshippers, reminds me too strongly
of the sad and similar fate of some of our own English
churches not to awaken a sigh as I look at it.   To some
men it is a comfort to find that their neighbours are no
better than themselves in these matters, but I confess that
to my mind a great church disused is a subject only for
mournful recollection, just as a noble church much used
and filled with crowds of worshippers is an object for
emulation and admiration.   Here, in good truth, I know not
where the worshippers are to come from, so decayed and
forlorn is the neighbourhood.

On the way back from San Zenone into the city a small
church is passed—the oratory of the same Saint—where
his body is said to have rested for a time before it was
taken to the Basilica.   The only architectural features are
of a long subsequent period, a very good circular window
in the west gable, and a doorway with a pointed canopy
supported on shafts above it, under which of old no doubt
there was a painting.

Beside San Zenone I think the only very grand church
as yet unmentioned is that of San Fermo Maggiore—a vast
Romanesque basilica without aisles, but with small transepts,
and a chancel and north and south chancel-aisles opening
into the nave by three arches, which exactly correspond with
its vast width; a not very beautiful arrangement, which we
shall meet with again in the church of the Eremitani at
Padua, and in others of the great churches of the preaching
orders of monks.

The fabric of the east end, and the eastern half of the
nave appears to be of very early date—I should be disposed

to say the end of the tenth, or beginning of the eleventh century. A lofty crypt is constructed under the whole of this part, all the columns of which are square; some of them mere masses of masonry, others slender monoliths. The mouldings here are rather Roman in character than Lombard. The groining is all of brick, and very extensive remains of paintings are still to be seen throughout, the large columns having single figures painted on them, one on each face. Access to the crypt is obtained (by the clergy) from the cloister, south of the church, and by the people through a very spacious staircase entered from the outside by a door just west of the north porch. So good indeed are the means of access, that no doubt the crypt was once extensively used by the laity, for whom these stairs were specially intended. It is now not used at all—just as is the case with old crypts all over Europe—but then it is fair to say that the church is no longer served by the Regular Clergy by whom it was built, and that their conventual buildings were when first I saw them occupied by Austrian soldiers, and are now still turned, I believe, to some equally secular use. I think we may fairly assume that in 1313, when the church was restored and in part reconstructed, the old crypt was retained partly on account of its associations, and partly because of its convenience for those who might at first not quite sympathize with the novel arrangements of the church above, a great unbroken area built and contrived for the use and convenience of an order of preachers, and not for receiving a number of altars.

A monument close to the entrance of the crypt is worth notice. It represents a professor with his pupils sitting each at a desk. The books have inscriptions on them. The professor's has "Vita brevis;" a pupil, "Ars longā;" another, "judicium difficile;" and another, "tēpus fugit."

In the interior of the nave we have, as has been observed,

a work which has been so much altered that it is in fact, as we now see it, a work of the fourteenth century. It is about fifty feet in width, and covered with a timber roof, constructed so as to form a ceiling of a number of cusps boarded and panelled on the under side, and tied with iron ties in place of collar-beams. Two vertical divisions of the panelling are arcaded, and filled with paintings of saints, and the whole roof is darkly stained, and richly painted. Beyond this the only very striking feature is the pulpit, which is corbelled out from the south wall about midway in its length. It is old and picturesque, and is surmounted by a delicately carved and lofty canopy—the whole in marble. It is surrounded by wall paintings of about the same age, and presents a fairly unchanged example of what such combined works of the painter and the architect were in the palmy days of the fourteenth century. These paintings are of much interest. Behind the pulpit are the four doctors and the four Evangelists seated, the ascent of Elisha in a chariot of fire, and twelve prophets with scrolls. Under the canopy is the Crucifixion.

Going to the exterior one finds on the north side two transepts, and north of the chancel a tower. East of the eastern transept and of the tower are small apsidal projections of Romanesque character, both of them in ruins and unused. The masonry here is different from that of the later work, being of alternate courses of single brick, and of stone.

The exterior of the principal apse is very remarkable, and belongs to the fourteenth century. Each side has a steep gable with elaborate cornices, mouldings, and pinnacles, partly of stone and partly of brick. The gables are built with circular bricks, and there is a cusped circular window in each gable. Seen from the bridge which crosses the Adige close to the church, this picturesque east end is one

17.—S, FERMO MAGGIORE, VERONA.

of the most picturesque things in Verona. Unfortunately
the campanile does not equal in importance the church to
which it belongs.

The west end will be best understood by the accompanying sketch. It is constructed entirely in red brick
and warm-coloured stone, and I confess that it impressed me
most pleasantly, as having in its four delicate lancet windows
some sort of affinity to our own English work. The north
porch is very fine of its kind, and the jambs of its doorway
are constructed of black, white, and red marble, used
alternately. The arcading against the walls is noticeable as
shewing the use of thin courses of red brick for the purpose
of defining the lines of the stonework.

The monuments on each side of the west door are good
simple examples of a favourite Italian type. They are, as
we shall see, of all dates, and even when developed to a great
size, are still corbelled in the same way out of the walls.
In the North of Europe, we have no analogous treatment
of monumental memorials, and this rather enhances their
value. The arch to the monument on the left of the west
doorway is painted in a charmingly simple Giottesque style,
and there is a painting also behind a modern statue in the
door-arch, of Our Lord surrounded by angels. In the arcades
above the monuments there were figures of saints painted,
with imitations of mosaic. All these details are worth
mentioning in order to give some idea to those who have not
seen Verona, of the extent to which everywhere the eye is
feasted with remains of early art. Indeed, one feasts un-
interruptedly there on all that can delight the eye in form
and in colour!

With the mention of one more church I believe I may
bring my notes in Verona to an end, and this is a small
chapel which stands just opposite the south side of the
Duomo, and whose name I could not learn. It is much like

San Pietro Martire in its general arrangement, but remarkable for the exquisite beauty of its windows, the arrangement of the bricks and stonework in which is beyond all
praise. These windows are constructed with trefoiled heads
of stone, enclosed within an arch of mixed stone and brick,
round whose outer edge runs a band of delicate terra-cotta
ornament. The spandrels of the trefoils are filled in with
refined sculpture, instead of being pierced with the dark eye
usually found in northern Gothic. There is, too, an entire
absence of mouldings, yet, notwithstanding this, the general
effect is one of combined delicacy and richness of no common
kind, so much does carefully-arranged and contrasted
colour do for architecture. A third window is entirely
of brick, save the trefoil head of the opening. The side
elevation of this little chapel is very singular in its whole
arrangement; there are three bays divided by pilasters,
which finish at the top in an arcaded cornice of brick; in
each of the two western bays is a lancet window, and the
centre bay has in addition a doorway, and a corbelled out
monument above it; in the eastern bay the window looks
just like one of those curious English low side windows, as
to the use of which we have had so many ingenious theories;
the east end has no trace of any window, and is finished with
a flat-pitched roof, and a brick corbel-table running up the
pediment. There is no stone used except in the window-
heads and arches.

There are many other churches in Verona on both sides
of the river, and into several of them we went, but without
finding any of equal merit to those which I have already
noticed. Santa Eufemia has a fair west front, of late pointed,
and we found one or two good cloisters just like those mentioned at Brescia. Other churches have fronts built, and
interiors remodelled, by Sanmichele and his successors, in a
style which by no means approved itself to me; others

there were which I did not succeed in reaching,[1] and there is one dedicated in honour of S. Thomas of Canterbury, which is not, however, otherwise of any interest; it has a very late Gothic west front, of poor character.

It is impossible to walk about Verona without meeting at every turn with windows whose design is similar to those so often seen in Venice, but the execution and arrangement are generally so inferior here to what they are

there, that I shall defer saying much about them until I am describing the palaces and ancient buildings of Venice. They are almost always finished with ogeed trefoils at the top, and are arranged singly, or in couples or more together, and one above the other, the same in each story of the house; their mouldings are thin and reedy, and the carving of tleir finials, when they have any, is very poor. Examples of these windows will be seen by most travellers in the rooms of the Albergo delle Due Torre.

DOMESTIC WINDOW—VERONA.

The views from the bridges across the Adige are very striking. The main part of the city is on the right bank, and the river describes nearly a semi-circle round it. The opposite bank is only partially built over, and has a largish suburb, upon rather rapidly rising ground; beyond this the walls of the city are seen with occasional towers, and marked

---

[1] The most important of these is the interesting church of San Stefano in the suburb on the opposite side of the Adige. It has been much modernized, but has still, I believe, an early crypt and an octagonal steeple over the crossing, of the same age as San Zenone.

all the way by their serrated battlements climbing the irregular outline of the hills in the boldest fashion. Then crossing over to the other side and turning round, you see the thickly-built city full of towers and churches rising far above the turmoil of the crowd below into the pure sky, and, by their number and size, making Verona one of the most striking old cities I know.

Of course no one goes to Verona without thinking of Romeo and Juliet. I fear, however, that when I was shown the Casa de' Cappelletti, a small inn in a narrow street, and asked to connect it in any way for the future with the creation of Shakespeare's brain, my fancy refused to be sufficiently lively to perform the required feat. The simple fact is that, real relics not existing, the good people of Verona have wisely met the demand which Shakespeare has created, and have discovered a tomb for Juliet, and other reminiscences of the fair Veronese, which I dare say satisfy very well the majority of travellers.

At Verona, as in the other towns through which we passed in Italy, we were quite astonished at the number of misshapen dwarfs that we saw; we could not account for this at first, but I suppose it is because children, until they can walk, are tied up in rolls of linen so stiffly as to deprive them of all power of motion. The only wonder is how any of these unfortunate children ever manage to walk at all.

In the courts of the houses at Verona there are generally wells, with ingeniously contrived arrangements for enabling the occupants of the various surrounding houses and balconies to let down their buckets for water without themselves going down to the wells. There are guide-ropes to the well from each angle of the courts round which the houses are usually built, along which the buckets run, suspended by rings and held by ropes from the balconies, until they reach the iron-work over the well, and then fall perpendicularly down to the water.

I have visited Verona many times, and each visit seems to me to give greater pleasure than the last. I fear I have given but a faint idea of the indescribable charm which it has to all who are fond of early art. There is little which one can compare with the situation and surroundings of such cities as Venice and Florence, and yet I suppose most travellers would agree with me in reckoning the interest of these three towns as not far from equal, and greater in very many ways than that of any other Italian cities.

On this first journey we were driven away by bad weather which, when it sets in, generally continues for several days, and we left, inwardly resolving that no long time should elapse before we returned—a resolution which has been abundantly and often fulfilled—and as the waiter at our hotel honestly told us that we should be very likely to find fine weather at Padua, whither we were next to journey, we took his advice, and then, getting into an omnibus contrived to hold thirty persons, and I should say at least twenty feet long, with four horses harnessed with long drawn-out traces to increase the already prodigious length, we were soon at the terminus of the Verona and Venice railway.

CHAPTER VII.

" ' And whither journeying ?—' To the holy shrine
Of Saint Antonio in the city of Padua.' "

Rogers.

———◆———

Neighbourhood of Verona — Vicenza : Cathedral — San Lorenzo — Santa
Corona — Pallazzo della Ragione — Gothic Palaces — Palladio's works —
Teatro Olympico — Padua : Giotto's Chapel — The Eremitani — Sant' An-
tonio — The Duomo.

MANY of the villages near Verona are remarkable for the
remains of castles of the middle ages. I have never, however,
been able to find time for the examination of any of them,
and, judging from hurried views which I have had of three
or four castles south of Verona, I suspect that they would
scarcely repay a long *détour ;* they seem generally to be more
remarkable for their general contour, and their quaint forked
battlements, than for any of that delicate detail and appliance
to ordinary wants which it was especially my object to see
and study.

The railroad from Verona to Vicenza and Padua is not
interesting ; the country is beautiful and luxuriant in detail,
but rather tame, flat, and over-green in the general view.
The Veronese mountains, however, are in view on the north,
and as one approaches Vicenza the hills throw out their
spurs into the flat country, covered with vineyards, orchards,
and fruit trees ; village follows close upon village, each with
its white church and white campanile, contrasting strangely

with the rich colour above and around, and at last the towers and roofs of Vicenza are descried on our left.

And is it possible, my readers will exclaim, that you, an architect, can have dared to pass within sight of Vicenza without making long sojourn there to drink in the lessons which the works of your great master Palladio are there to instil! Even so, reader; for in this world there are unhappily two views of art, two schools of artists—armies of men fighting against each other; the one numerous, working with the traditions and rules of their masters in the art, exclusive in their views, narrow in their practice, and conventional in all their proceedings, to the most painful forgetfulness of reality either in construction or in ornament; the other young and earnest, fighting for truth, small in numbers, disciples of nature, revivers of an art to all appearance but now all but defunct, yet already rising gloriously above the traditional rules of three centuries. The one class representing no new idea, breathing no new thought, faithful to no religious rule; the other rapidly endeavouring to strike out paths for themselves as yet untrodden, gathering thoughts from nature, life from an intense desire for reality and practical character, faithful moreover to a religious belief, whose propagation will be for ever the great touchstone of their work. The one class, the disciples of Palladio, journeying towards Vicenza with a shew of reverence to learn how he built palaces of compo with cornices of lath and plaster, already in two short centuries falling to decay, wretched and ruinous! the other stopping long at Verona, dreaming over the everlasting art of the monuments of the Scaligers, and of the nave of Sta. Anastasia, still, though five centuries have passed with all their storms about their heads, fresh and beautiful as ever, fit objects of veneration for the artist in all ages!

A disciple, therefore, of the last of these two schools,

I stayed not longer at Vicenza than was necessary to satisfy myself of the truth of the charges against Palladio's work there, and to note the few, but interesting, mediæval remains. The situation of the city is beautiful. Near it to the north are mountain ranges, and where these descend into the plains there are smaller hills covered everywhere with luxurious vegetation. The first view of it is also very fine. In front is the old brick tower at the Porta di Castello, with its deep brick machicoulis sloping boldly outwards, and finished with a square battlement under a flat roof. Beyond this are seen the steeples of the city, and highest among them the Torre dell' Orologio, a tall slender brick tower in the Piazza dei Signori, in the centre of the town. The most important Gothic churches are the Cathedral, San Lorenzo, and Santa Corona. They seem all to be in very much the same style—one derived no doubt from Venice, as we shall see when we arrive there. The plans usually are of this kind. The bays of the nave are square in plan, those of the aisles oblong in the direction of the length of the church, the choirs apsidal, and the chapels on each side of them also apsidal, but with an equal number of sides so that there is an angle in the centre. The transepts are square-ended, the sacristy at the end of one of them, and the tower at the side of the chancel aisles. The Cathedral departs from the type of plan just mentioned, but is, I think, the only exception to the rule. It has a very wide nave without aisles some 55 or 60 feet in the clear, but it has been so much repaired and altered that it is now very uninteresting. Good effect is obtained by the very great elevation of the altar which is raised above a crypt, the entrance to which is by flights of steps on each side of the steps which lead up to the choir. The exterior is mainly of brick save at the west end, which has an arcade of stone with a doorway in the centre division.

GES. 1867

Whiteman & Bass. Photo Lith[...]

19. PORTA DI CASTELLO. VICENZA.

This kind of west front is repeated in the more interesting church of San Lorenzo, which is finished with one vast gable in front of nave and aisles, and has for its lower stage an arcade of seven divisions, with a fine pointed doorway occupying the three central arches. This part of the front is mainly of stone, with enriched members round the arches in brick, and it is divided from the upper stage by a corbel-table. The gable is of brick with a large stone circular window in the centre, and five smaller circular windows following the line of the flat gable which crowns the whole. I was not much impressed by this design, the only virtue of which is a certain amount of simplicity and breadth.

The interior of San Lorenzo is lofty and spacious. The nave and aisles alone measure about 150 feet by 90, and there are spacious transepts, choir, and chapels. The columns are circular, and have capitals so badly carved that it is somewhat difficult to say whether they have shells or tufts of foliage for enrichment. Very small circular windows in the clerestory, and a groined roof, complete the design. The best portion of the exterior is, I think, the elevation of the bays of the nave aisles. Here there are two simple trefoiled lancets with a shallow buttress between them, and a circular window above in each bay. This design is refreshingly pure and simple. The steeple is on the east side of the north transept. It is of six stages in height, the stages being marked by slightly sunk panels, and corbel-tables under string-courses, which are formed by a pattern in the bricks, not by any projecting moulding, so that the straight outline of the steeple is not broken. The result is not particularly good.

Santa Corona has, like the other churches, a single gable in front of the nave and aisles, with a western doorway and a large circular window above. I have a recollection of it as of one of the most ungainly of fronts. The campanile here is much like that of San Lorenzo, but has a low octagonal belfry-stage finished with a small circular brick spire.

Santa Corona may well be more visited, for a picture by John Bellini than for its own merits. This is a picture over one of the altars in the north aisle representing the Baptism of Our Lord—one so quiet and beautiful in colour, so dignified and solemn in its design, that it is impossible to admire it too much. Behind the group of angels who hold Our Lord's garments, is a mountain landscape such as one sees from Vicenza. It is a sublime work. The marble reredos is coeval with the picture : it is furnished with two low screen walls right and left of the altar, a common and proper arrangement for its protection when, as here, the altar stands in the aisle itself and not in a chapel.

I did not find any other church worth noticing, and soon made my way to the Palazzo della Ragione. The great feature of this building is the enormous hall, no less than 72 feet wide inside, and covered with a great arched timber roof boarded on the under side, and divided into vertical panels by bold ribs painted black and white. This roof is held together by two tiers of iron ties, and being arched and boarded at the end as well as at the sides, has somewhat the look of the inverted hull of a great ship. The effect is imposing, though at the same time it is somewhat gloomy, owing to the absence of all high light.

This great hall was Gothic inside and out until Palladio cased the front with open arcades, standing out from the walls and entirely concealing from below the old windows. These were large single lights with moulded jambs, but not of very good style. The original staircase remains with good marble shafted balustrades. The old work here is said to have been done before the year 1444, the hall having been burnt in 1389. This date is of some importance, as the walls of the upper portion are faced like the upper stage

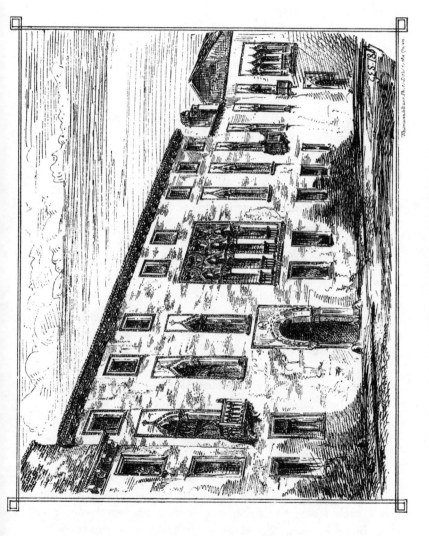

20. CONTRADA PORTO. VICENZA.

of the Ducal Palace at Venice, with marble arranged in a diaper.

The slender and lofty tower of brick which rises at one end of the building, the two Venetian columns (Vicenza became subject to Venice in 1404), and the Palazzo itself, in spite of its small architectural merit, combine to make a charming picture, rendered more beautiful when I saw it, by the animated crowd of peasants who filled the Piazza. The streets here are very picturesque, rather in spite of Palladio and Scamozzi than in consequence of what they did. Some of them are arcaded, and the Gothic houses are still very numerous. They are all, however, of late date— at least I saw none earlier than about 1350. They are of the same design as some of the well-known Venetian palaces, only here they rise out of narrow streets, instead of as they do there from the water. The usual arrangement is to have on the ground floor a single doorway, not necessarily central, and on the *piano nobile* a fine traceried window with balconies in the centre, single windows also with balconies near the angles, and intermediate windows of the same design but without balconies. These are always treated in the same way with small shafts, and with animals seated on their angles, and are supported on bold corbels. All the carving that I saw was weak and confused in outline, and poor in detail, and the capitals are generally too large for the arch mouldings which rest on them—a common fault in Italian Gothic work.

I give a view in the Contrada Porto which illustrates two of the best of these houses. Almost the whole of this street happens to consist of houses of the same age, and one of them has on one side of its internal courtyard open arcades on each story, the upper one having its balustrades re-- maining between the columns, similar in design to those in window-balconies.

In their original state most of these houses seem to have been left in red brick, the windows being of stone, with thin white marble slabs fitted into the spandrels above the arches. Projecting balls of marble are often fixed in front of this marble lining. Some houses seem, however, to have been plastered almost from the first with a view to painting, and I can hardly say a word against such a plan, with the recollection of the glowing—in spite of their being faded— tints which one still sees at Brescia, Genoa, and elsewhere in Italy. But where the house has architectural features, which are at all good of their kind, the painter is very apt to ignore them entirely in his work, so that what was meant to be a good piece of architectural work, becomes in the end a badly cut-up ground for a painting. Where there is no architectural detail to be spoilt, any amount of painting may be lavished on an external wall; and I know few examples which better show with how much good effect it may be done than the great house of the Fugger family in Augsburg, which many Italian tourists now-a-days may see and admire on their way to or from Italy. The other objection to external painting is its evanescent character; but good colour is beautiful even in its decay, and I suppose the best artist will paint what will do most good to his own generation, and trust to his successors for doing as much for their own times!

One of the most fanciful houses in Vicenza is the Casa Rigafetta, below the Palazzo Pubblico. The ornaments are not pure, and there is too much straining to make the most of an opportunity by putting everything possible into a small space, but still the whole is decidedly pretty. The balconies here are in plan half a quatrefoil. Near this house is one with carved angle-shafts, a feature which I do not remember to have seen in Venice.

Palladio's works are supposed now to be the glory of

Vicenza. I cannot forgive the artist who did not care to give solidity to his work, and the power of executing a vast amount of enrichment in the cheapest way, and with the commonest materials, is about the greatest snare into which an architect can allow himself to fall. I am well aware that Palladio was not the inventor of trumpery modes of construction. His admirers might quote the architects of Pompeii fifteen hundred years before him, as offenders in the same way, and the curious preservation of their works as the justification of their offence; but Palladio followed after men of his own kind and craft who for centuries had studiously endeavoured to do their work honestly, and he deserves, therefore, all the hostile criticism of those who object to a revival of bad practices which in our own day and country have done more real damage to architecture than anything else that can be named.

One only of Palladio's works interested me, and this rather as a curious experiment than as a work of art. This is the Teatro Olimpico, a famous open-air theatre. There is first of all a semi-circular auditorium open to the sky, and only remarkable for a mean arrangement of pilasters at the back. The great object of interest is the stage, on which a permanent scene has been constructed by Palladio. In order to make this look much larger than it really is, the streets, palaces, and temples which are represented are built in perspective. To accomplish this the stage rises very rapidly, the buildings are squeezed up, and built in sharp perspective, so that in the end a triumphal arch, which is really forty feet from the front, looks as if it were four hundred. Should an actor by any chance so far forget himself as to walk into what looks like a practicable street, in a minute he would find himself able to shake hands with the statue on the top of the arch, the illusion would be entirely destroyed, and the scenery would all look like a collection of dolls' houses. As an ingenious deception from one point of view, and under certain conditions, the scheme is successful, and probably this is as much as Palladio himself would have claimed for it.

We had now seen all that we cared to see in Vicenza, and gladly found ourselves again *en route*. There was nothing to see on the road, and we were not sorry when our engine gave token by its whistle of our approach to Padua. The omnibus discharged us in a few minutes at the hospitable doors of the Stella d'Oro, and we were soon out again with the view of making the most of our time.

Padua, when I first saw it, seemed to me to be a most melancholy city; grass grew in the streets, the footways were all formed under dark and dismal arcades, and not only the externals of the half-occupied palaces, but those even of all the houses, looked squalid, dirty, and miserable; nor was there any relief when one got into the more open spaces, for the large piazze on either side of the Palazzo della Ragione, or townhall, looked as squalid and uncared-for, as dirty and unprepossessing, as they well could; nor was this universal squalor rendered at all less remarkable by the fact that Padua rejoices in a caffè, which is said to surpass any other even in Italy, for its smartness; and the array of well-dressed gentlemen who frequented it, certainly made the neighbourhood look more wretched by contrast than it otherwise would.

The Caffè Pedrocchi was however soon passed, and our first object was the Palazzo della Ragione, whose vast and singular hall, about two hundred and fifty feet long by ninety feet wide, is one of the greatest architectural curiosities in the city. Its exterior has been modernized, so that now it is only remarkable for its long expanse of roof, but the interior is still in its original state. The access to the Hall, which in this and other respects much resembles that at Vicenza, is from external arcades on the first floor, to which

four staircases lead from below.   The walls are low, and
covered with paintings arranged in arcaded panels ; some of
these are said to be by Giotto, and the whole of them, I believe, were at any rate painted in his time, but have probably
been repaired and retouched extensively long since.   The
windows are small, low down in the walls, and admit scarcely
more than sufficient light for the lower part of the hall.
The roof shews in section a vast pointed arch of timber,
boarded and divided into panels by a succession of heavy
vertical ribs scarcely at all moulded.   The construction is
obviously so weak as, from the very first, to have made the
iron ties which hold it all together absolutely necessary.
A curious feature in the design is, that instead of having
gable walls the roof is hipped, and shews therefore at
the end just the same section as at the sides.   What
little light finds its way into the dark obscurity of the roof
is admitted through some small dormers high up in its
framework.   The effect of the hall is gloomy, and, compared
to our own great halls, certainly shows some lack of knowledge of construction on the part of its architect, and its bald
heaviness makes it absurd to compare it to our own noble
Westminster hall, though their very similar dimensions might
naturally tempt us to do so.   It dates from about the beginning of the fourteenth century, and the story runs that it
was designed by a certain Frate Giovanni, who, travelling in
India, saw the roof of a great palace the construction of which
so pleased him that he brought back drawings of it with him,
and erected its fellow here in Padua.   How much truth
there is in this tradition I cannot say, but this much
seems clear, that in some way Padua has, if not a very
beautiful, at any rate a very remarkable Sala, and one which
is quite unlike any other room in Europe, with the single
exception of the corresponding room at Vicenza, which was
no doubt copied from it.

It has been burnt and damaged in one way and another
repeatedly since it was first built, and in the course of the
restorations the paintings on the walls have been excessively
damaged, in many parts repainted, and in some obliterated
altogether. The work was commenced at any rate, if not
completed, just at the time that Dante and Giotto were
together in this part of Italy. The walls are all divided
into four panels in height by borders, with painted pilasters
for vertical divisions, and the panels are generally arched
and cusped. The paintings include the apostles, the signs
of the zodiac, representations of the months, the planets, and
the constellations. The whole scheme is far too complex to
be intelligible without a key. This fortunately is accessible
in the very careful and complete account of all the subjects
of the paintings on the walls which was prepared in 1858
by Mr. W. Burges, and printed in the 'Annales Archéologiques.' With infinite pains he made out the meaning of
the whole of the figures—no light task, as the walls being
divided by painted borders and arcades into several stages
in height and an almost interminable number in length,
spaces are provided for some four hundred subjects.[1]

At one end of the hall was the chapel of San Prodoscimo,
formed I presume by screens. The judges sat round the
hall, forming so many courts in one room. At the opposite
end was a cage or prison, so that here, under one roof, with
walls covered with illustrations, sat all the courts of Padua,
without any of those ingenious divisions and subdivisions
which are now necessary for the administration of the very
smallest sort of justice, and it may be hoped with as much
honesty as there certainly was simplicity.

Now-a-days the hall is quite unused save as a receptacle
for lumber, of which the most remarkable example is the

---

[1] See also ' Pietro Brandolese, Scultura, Pittura, &c., di Padova.' Padova, 1795.

remnant of a gigantic horse made by Donatello to travel on
rollers in some old Paduan pageant.

From the Palazzo della Ragione, we found our way to
what must, so long as it lasts, be the great glory, as it is
the chief charm, of Padua—Giotto's Chapel , founded in 1303.

This stands in private grounds and on one side of a desolate green walk which leads up to a private house to which it

ARENA CHAPEL—PADUA.

now forms an appendage. From the first it was a little private
chapel, and in no respect remarkable for size or costliness of
material or design. The plan is a simple oblong nave with
an apsidal chancel, and a sacristy on the north side, and
nothing can be simpler than the exterior. The walls are of
brick, divided into bays by narrow pilasters. The west door
is round arched, as are also the windows. The interior is
even more simple ; the whole nave has not a moulding, the

walls are continued on into the semicircular ceiling without
any cornice, and all the ornament is added in colour.

The windows all have a deep splay outside, very simple
stone traceries, and glass fitted to wooden frames placed inside against the stonework. There seem also to have been
shutters outside, for which the hooks still remain. A sort of
penthouse, or perhaps a cloister-roof was carried along in
front of the chapel, but of this nought remains but the
corbels which carried it. There is no more to be said about
the exterior than that it is simple and good of its kind—
the kind being very humble.

Let us go inside, and we shall pass a very different
verdict. Giotto is to many of us not only a person singularly gifted in a great age, but in some sort the embodiment
of an idea. The idea is that of an artist, pure, simple, and
direct in his work, who should excel equally in all the arts,
and show—even though his work be an exception to all rules
—the consummate success of such a course. The man was
fortunate in his day and in his friends. Here, where we
stand to admire, he painted, whilst probably Dante looked
on. For merely human and artistic interest there is, therefore, no room which more rightly deserves to be the object
of endless pilgrimages; and there is none in which one will
find the artist more faithful to his calling, more full of recollection and self-restraint than in this.

I know, therefore, no one building, of such very small
size and cost, which can claim the same degree of interest
as this small Chapel of the Arena. It is, indeed, one of the
glories of art that the works of its great masters cannot
diminish in value, or even be competed with by subsequent
masters: when once done, they are done for ever; and so
the Pietà of Giotto, in this little chapel at Padua, is now—
as it was when first painted in the commencement of the
fourteenth century, and as it will continue to be so long as

the neglect with which it is now treated allows it to exist—
one of the great paintings of the world, one of those fountains from which school after school and age after age of
artists may drink instruction and knowledge, and never fail
to gain more, the more they study its many excellences, and
its intensity of feeling and conception.

The architectural portion of the interior may be first of
all described. The apse is simply a sanctuary, and the
chancel is formed by marble screens on each side of the nave,
leaving a broad entrance-way between them, and enclosing
about one-third of its length. Against the west side of these
screens are altars, each with a small carved marble reredos ;
whilst on the east of them are steps leading to the two ambons ; that on the north being a book-rest, carved in marble,
and fixed with its face to the east ; that on the south of iron,
and turning upon a pivot. Between these screens and the
sanctuary arch are modern stalls on each side. The sanctuary has seats all round the apse (except in the eastern

bay), each with a delicate
white marble canopy.
The sacristy is groined,
and has a thirteenth-cen-
tury press of wood of a
design rather curious
than beautiful, but very
rich in its detail. In the
nave, as I have already
said, the walls have nei-
ther cornices nor string-
courses to break their
even surfaces, and their
face is continued on in a

SIDE WINDOW—ARENA CHAPEL.

semicircular waggon vault. There are six lancet windows
on the south, none at all on the north, and a three-light

window very high up in the gable at the west end above the
doorway.

The architectural merit of the building is simply, I think,
that it performs satisfactorily the office of giving ample
unbroken surfaces of wall for paintings.

The arrangement of these is very regular. The vault is
divided into two parts by wide coloured borders, the space
between which is painted blue, powdered with gilt stars, and
in each bay there are five small medallions with figures on a
gold ground. The side walls are divided by borders into
three divisions in height; the upper division containing
subjects from the life of the Blessed Virgin; the central,
those illustrative of the life of Our Blessed Lord; whilst
those nearest to the ground are representations of the
Virtues and Vices opposed to each other; the last division
tinted only in one colour, the others richly painted in
bright colours upon a field of blue.

The borders which divide the paintings are very well designed, their patterns being always very clearly defined with
white leading lines, and a line of red on either side always
accompanying each line of white. The paintings themselves
are very wonderful; there is an earnestness of purpose and
expression about them such as one rarely meets with; each
subject is treated with a severe conscientiousness, not always
conventionally where a departure from strict rule is for any
reason necessary, but still, generally speaking, in accordance
no doubt with the ancient traditional treatment. This,
illuminated as it is by the thought and love and earnest
intensity of feeling which Giotto lavished on all that he
did, makes his work here the most perfect example of a
series of religious paintings that I have ever seen. Of
course in such a large series of subjects there must be
great variety of excellence, and I am content to agree
with the rest of the world in awarding the palm of

excellence to the Pietà, in which the expression of intense feeling in the face of the mourners over the body of Our Lord is certainly beyond anything of the kind that I know.

The series is very complete, and, beginning with the history of Joachim before the birth of the Blessed Virgin (the seventh subject), is continued down through the leading acts of Our Lord's life to the descent of the Holy Ghost on the day of Pentecost;[1] whilst the west wall is occupied by a Last Judgment; and throughout the subjects Our Lord, the Blessed Virgin, and the apostles are always represented in vestments of the same colour.

Most of these paintings are in very perfect condition, and the *tout ensemble* is nearly as charming as it was when first painted. I was sorry, however, to notice some of the paintings lined all over by a recent copyist, and much damage has been·done by damp, especially in the Last Judgment on the west wall. I do not care very much for the painting on the lower part of the walls. The figures of Virtues and Vices are very finely designed, but the imitations of marbles and mouldings painted in perspective were, I hope—being the last work to be finished—done after Giotto had completed his work.

Close to Giotto's Chapel stands the great, and to an English eye, singular church of the Eremitani. It has a very broad nave of immense length, unbroken by aisles, and roofed with

---

[1] Since this was written the whole of these subjects have been published by the Arundel Society, and Mr. Ruskin's notice of them has also been given to us: they are very valuable as exemplifying, as well perhaps as colourless engravings can do, the exceeding value and originality of this series of paintings. It is to be wished that they may produce some effect upon the minds of our modern artists, who much require to take home to themselves the lesson of sincerity and earnestness of purpose, combined with the highest kind of subject, which Giotto so eminently exhibits in all his works. An extremely good series of photographs of the whole of these paintings may now also be obtained in Venice.

one of the cusped roofs already noticed at Verona, in which
the real construction is (with the exception of the tie-beams)
entirely concealed by boarding on the under side; this
boarding being generally arranged in a succession of large
cusps or curves; the effect here is, I think, very heavy and
unsatisfactory, but we must bear in mind that the span is
prodigious, and the pitch of the roof very flat. The chancel
and an aisle on either side of it open into the east end of the
nave with three arches, and look so small as to be more like
mere recesses than important integral parts of the plan.
There are in this church a great many frescoes and paintings
of much interest—among which are some by Mantegna in a
chapel on the south side of the nave which are worthy of
careful study as being, probably beyond almost any other wall
paintings which exist, an evidence of the fact that interest
in treatment of subject, drawing and design of consummate
excellence, perspective and decorative colouring of the walls,
may all be included in a fresco without interference with
the wall surface, or indulgence in tricks of chiaroscuro,
without which no painter now seems willing to do his work.
Yet if Mantegna cheerfully accepted such rules for his
wall-painting, would it be beneath modern painters to do
the same for theirs, and could they ask for a better teacher
or guide than this consummate artist?

Less interesting to the artist than these works of
Mantegna are the paintings in the apse executed by
Guarienti in the middle of the fourteenth century. Here are
figures of the planets: the Sun, Moon, Venus, Mercury, Mars,
Saturn, and Jupiter, each with allegorical figures, male and
female, of the Seven Ages of Man influenced by the planets.[1]

At the west end of the nave is a great painted Rood, one

---

[1] The order of the planets attached to the seven ages is as follows:—I. The
Moon. II. Mercury. III. Venus. IV. The Sun. V. Mars. VI. Jupiter.
VII. Saturn.

of those curiously shaped crosses meant to receive a painting of the Crucifixion instead of a carved figure, and cut round with quaintly carved and cusped indentations, of which so many examples remain, though they are generally found now in picture galleries. This no doubt stood originally on a Rood beam, where one sees such a Rood represented in one of the wall paintings in the upper church of S. Francis at Assisi.

When I was last at Padua the west front of this church was being repaired—a very dangerous and terrible operation in Italy, where, so far as I have seen, there is less feeling for, or knowledge of, Gothic architecture than in any other part of Europe. The interior, too, has been ruined by the way in which the old ceiling has been painted, in blue and shaded white. In a building whose characteristic feature is a certain grand simplicity and austerity, it is especially disgusting to see light and tawdry colouring introduced, seeing how completely out of harmony with the whole idea of the church it is.

At the west end are some fine monuments of stone and marble boldly corbelled out from the wall, adorned with good carving of foliage, and angels looking out from circles.

The east end is less altered than any part of the exterior of the building. The immense gable of the nave is divided into four parts, the outer of which have lancet windows, whilst in the centre is an insignificant apse, which is almost exactly repeated on the east side of the south transept. The large sacristy on the north side, and a campanile of not much interest on the same side redeem to some extent what would otherwise have been a most uninteresting elevation. The windows here have a wide external splay, semi-circular arches, and stone trefoil heads inserted rather clumsily under the arches.

What a grand idea it was on the part of the preaching orders to build these enormous naves for their congregations !

Here, when enthusiasm for preaching was new born and
general, a congregation, numbered rather by thousands than
by hundreds, may have gathered round the preacher, all
within sight of him, and, with the aid, probably, of an awning
stretched across the church over the pulpit, all within sound
of his voice.

From the Eremitani we found our way with some
difficulty through miserable streets to the church of Sant'
Antonio, probably the most remarkable architectural work in
many respects in this part of Italy.

It seems that about A.D. 1231 it was determined to erect
a great church in honour of S. Antony, the patron of Padua,
and Nicola Pisano, then one of the most eminent men of
his day, was sent for to undertake the work.[1] The view of
the exterior which I give, will best serve to shew in how
singular and original a manner he accomplished his work.
S. Mark's at Venice must have been in his eye when he
designed his church, and the crowd of cupolas which form its
roof remind one forcibly of its most distinguishing feature.

On first sight Sant' Antonio certainly does not prepossess
the beholder in favour of such a bold departure from every-
day rules of art. It is built almost entirely of a light red
brick, not much better than the common London brick in
colour—a poor material wherewith to attempt the construction of a noble church. Stone is used very sparingly in
the voussoirs of the arches and elsewhere. The cupolas are
heavy in their effect, but relieved by that over the intersection
of the nave and transepts, which rises higher than the others,
and is certainly striking in its design and outline, which is,
for the main portion of its height, that of a simple cone.

[1] This is the tradition, but it is one which is not, I think, supported either
by documentary evidence or by the style of the building. Nicola left Padua
four years before the church was commenced; and Fra. Carello is mentioned
in the archives of the convent as one of the architects, of whom no doubt there
were several before the work was finished.

Round and pointed arches are used indiscriminately, and the walls are divided everywhere by pilasters, and surmounted by arcaded corbel-tables, in all these respects giving the building the appearance of being much earlier than it is. The west front is very peculiar, and recalls the fronts of the churches in Vicenza which I have described, and is entirely un-

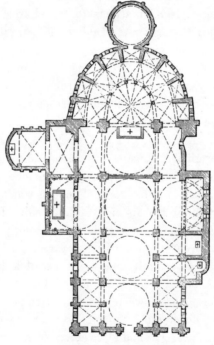

GROUND PLAN—SANT' ANTONIO, PADUA.

like any of the churches of Pisa, which would hardly have been the case had it really been designed by Nicola Pisano. One great flat gable with an arcaded eaves-cornice finishes the whole, and out of its apex rises a tall polygonal turret, almost as high as the dome in front of which it stands. The lower part of the west front has a central entrance of mean character, and on either side two unequal arches of construction, the walls within which are pierced with windows. Above these, and just beneath the great pediment-like gable, is a long arcade of simple pointed arches, behind which are a passage and three windows opening into the church. This front is a sham front, and not excusable on account of its grandeur or its beauty. Indeed, had it followed the outline of the fabric, it would have been neither ungainly nor heavy, both of which it most assuredly is now.

The interior is striking from its height, but cold in the extreme in effect; the domes are all whitewashed in the brightest and freshest manner. The plan gives three domes to the nave, one and an apse of seven bays to the choir, and one to the transept. The aisles open into the nave with pointed arches—two to each dome. The choir aisle is continued all round the choir, and a chapel is thrown out to the east of this, which is again crowned with a dome.

The north transept contains the chapel of the patron saint, full of gorgeous ornaments of all kinds, but not very ancient. Opposite it, in the south transept, is a curious groined chapel, divided from the church by five pointed and trefoiled arches of yellow marble, resting upon Classical-looking columns, and all very richly painted and inlaid. Above the arches are five statues in niches, and the intermediate wall-surface is inlaid with white and red marble in a regular pattern, such as we have seen in the pavement of Sta. Anastasia at Verona, with very good effect.

The cloister on the south side of the church is very large and good, and some fine arches occur in it, composed of black and yellow marble with bricks of varied colour introduced. On its east side three open arches, filled in with a double iron grille, open into what was, no doubt, the chapter-house. Going from this into a second cloister to the east of it, no one can fail to be struck by the extreme picturesqueness and novelty of the view. In the foreground is the simple

21. SANT' ANTONIO. PADUA.

pointed-arched and open arcade of the cloister; above this
rise the gable of the south transept and the eastern apse
with its surrounding aisle, and two lofty octagonal brick
turrets, on each side of the apse, which look like minarets
from Cairo, and combined with the collections of domes on
the roof give a completely Eastern effect to the whole view.
If, however, the detail of this striking building is examined,
one can hardly be satisfied. There is throughout, as there so
often is in Italy, a sad want of skill and neatness in the
adjustment of details as compared to what is common in
northern Gothic buildings. This indeed is a feature of all
the works of the Pisani, and gives them the character—so
common and so fatal in modern works—of being to a great
extent the work of assistants and not of the master.
Nothing can be much more clumsy than the provision for the
steps leading to the turrets, nor weaker than the rectangular
tracery inserted in the circular window of the transept. This,
however, is a work of the middle of the fourteenth century,
and Nicola Pisano, even if he were the first architect of the
church, would not be responsible for it. I cannot say that
I was at all satisfied either with the internal or external
effect of the church—though it must be confessed that,
when seen from a distance, there is excessive grandeur in
the grouping of the multitude of domes, with the steep cone
rising in the centre, and giving point and emphasis to the
whole.[1] The arrangement of the windows and arches round
the apse, for instance, is confused and weak to a degree; and
I do not feel that Nicola Pisano has fairly settled the question
of the adaptation of the dome to pointed buildings by his
treatment of the domes here. The question is still, I think,
an open one; and though it may be doubted whether with

[1] The eastern chapel and dome are comparatively modern, and the coverings of the other domes appear to be also modern; but I suppose they follow
the old outline.

our present opportunities it will soon be satisfactorily answered, I still feel that it would not be difficult to answer it
far more successfully than has been done here.

In the evening we heard some very fine music of ancient
character in Sant' Antonio, after which there was a sermon;
and though it was a week-day, there was a large congregation, very attentive and quiet.

The Duomo is a cold, unattractive church—said, however, to have been designed by Michael Angelo—and rather
bold in the treatment of the pendentives under its dome.
By its side stands a Lombard baptistery, the interior of
which I did not succeed in getting a sight of; and I believe
that I missed some valuable examples of fresco-painting with
which its walls and domed roof are covered.

We wandered about the melancholy streets of Padua,
searching in vain for objects of any interest to our antiquarian eyes. It is true that the columns and arcades which
support the houses are, many of them, ancient; but they are
of a character very common throughout the north of Italy,
and were not sufficiently novel or striking to draw off our
attention from the melancholy and dilapidated look of the
houses and shops which they half concealed and half supported. We saw also one or two old monuments at the
corners of streets—one of them called the tomb of Antenor
—similar in their idea to those which are so frequent in
Verona.

The next morning, therefore, saw us making our way to
the railway station for Venice, sad only in leaving Padua
that we could not spend more time there for the study, more
quietly and carefully, of the lovely little Arena Chapel and
the paintings of Giotto.

CHAPTER VIII.

"Break, break, break,
   On thy cold gray stones, O sea !
But the tender grace of a day that is dead
   Will never come back to me."
                              Tennyson.

Padua and Venice Railway — Venice : Piazza and Church of S. Mark — Torcello — The Lagoon — Murano — Sta. Maria dei Frari — SS. Giovanni e Paolo — Sta. Maria dell' Orto — Other Churches — Domestic Architecture — Fondaco de' Turchi — Other Byzantine Palaces — The Ducal Palace — Foscari Palace — Ca' d'Oro — Other Gothic Palaces — Balconies — Venetian Architecture — A Festival — Paintings.

LITTLE is to be seen as one leaves Padua to distinguish the city at all vividly, save the oriental-looking cupolas of Sant' Antonio, and the great roof of the Sala della Ragione, looking like the inverted hull of some great ship, with its convex sides towering up above the otherwise not remarkable-looking city.

And now our destination was Venice, and anxiously we looked out ever and anon, impatient, long before the time, to see the tall outline of S. Mark's campanile against the horizon. The view was too contracted to be really beautiful ; on each side of the railway rank and luxuriant hedges of acacia sprouted their tall branches above the carriages, and beyond them might be seen plantations of maize, flax, and other crops, all remarkable for their prodigious growth and size, and watered by countless small canals, and here and there with

turgid, muddy-looking streams rushing on from the mountains to discharge themselves into the Adriatic, and gliding
between great artificial banks which gave them the appearance rather of large canals than rivers.   Nothing breaks the
dead monotony of the scene, for it is misty, and the Tyrolese
Alps, which ought to show their jagged peaks to the north,
are invisible.   The stations follow each other in quick succession, and at each stands some diligence or carriage whose
ingrained panoply of white dust, added to that which rises
here and there white and cloud-like in the dry glare of the
Italian sun which beams overhead, makes one feel grateful
that—however unpoetical such a mode of approach may be—
a railroad carries us to Venice.   Nor is such a country as
this along which one passes from Padua to Venice without
its moral.   I suppose there is nothing more certain than that,
ordinarily, the appreciation of high art, and success in its
practice, have never been so marked in countries whose natural
features are lovely as in those in which the devoutest student
of nature's beauties can see nothing to admire or love.   So
Venice, surrounded by waters, and then by a country which
would be entirely tame and uninteresting, were it not for the
exquisite distant views of the Friulan Alps, fell back on her
own resources, and provided herself with that substitute for
the loveliness of nature which—alone of man's works—the
loveliness of beautiful art can be.   And perhaps, it is better
for the traveller, that no interest should be felt save in
the end of the journey, where the journey has so brave an
end !

At last, however, the broad watery level of the Lagoon
is reached; Venice rises out of the water at a distance of
some two miles; and then across an almost endless bridge
the railway takes us into the outskirts of the city; a confused
idea of steeples and domes is all that is obtained, and one
finds oneself going through that most painful of processes to

an excitable man, the usual examination of luggage; at last, however, we are outside the station, the Grand Canal lies before us, and we are vehemently urged to get at once into an omnibus-gondola. But no, this is too absurd a bathos for our first act on entering Venice, and we step therefore into a private gondola, and, propelled rapidly and lightly over the still, unruffled water, sink at once into that dreamy kind of happiness which of all conveyances in the world the gondola is best calculated to encourage. A short reach of the Grand Canal is soon passed, and then, with the picturesque cry of warning, "Ah, stalì!" we turn sharply into a narrow canal to the right, and, shooting down the tortuous street of water, presently cross the Grand Canal again midway between the Rialto and the Foscari palace, dive into another canal still narrower than the former, and at last, after frequent glimpses of mediæval houses and palaces, find ourselves safely housed at our hotel close to the Grand Canal, and within two or three minutes' walk of the Piazza San Marco.

We stopped but a short time here, so impatient were we to obtain our first glimpse of the church and palace of S. Mark, to which Venice owes so much of her fame. We passed along some narrow winding alleys, lined on either side with open shops, on the counters of which lie exposed for sale not over dainty-looking edibles, and in whose dim interiors little light of day seems ever to enter to help the busy workmen who may always be seen there plying their trade; and then, going under an archway crowded with busy folk in rather noisy consultation, we found ourselves, in four or five minutes, standing under the arcade at the upper end of the great Piazza San Marco. Long lines of regular architecture, arcaded below, heavy with cornices and elaborated windows above, carry the eye not unpleasantly down to the lower end of the piazza, at the right-hand angle of which towers up into the air a vast campanile, simple and unbroken in its outline, without visible window or any buttress-like projection, until its upper stage, where it has a very simple open arcaded belfry, capped with a pyramidal roof; and then across nearly the whole width of the piazza, and partly concealed by the curiously irregular position of its campanile, stretches the low singular and Eastern-looking church of S. Mark. Before it rise the masts from which of yore hung waving in the wind the banners of the old Venetian state, and crowds of pigeons, fed here by civic liberality, cover the pavement with their pleasant fluttering presence. The charm of the west front is certainly most indescribable; and I confess to feeling a doubt, as I looked at it, whether it was not more akin to some fairy-like vision, such as one might see in dreams, than to any real and substantial erection of stone and mortar; for, indeed, to a mind educated in and accustomed to the traditions of northern Gothic, there is something so very *outré* in the whole idea, something so startling in its novelty, that it is hard at first to know whether to admire or not. It is far from imposing in size, but yet, as it is looked at more and more carefully, it grows much and rapidly on one's love, and at last imprints itself on the mind as a real work of art of a very beautiful and unusual kind, wrought out with an abundance of beautiful detail, but in such a way as to prevent its being possible that it could ever be absolutely reproduced or taken as a model.

As you pace down the broad level space of the Piazza, the feeling of the strangeness of the whole scene increases. There are of course no horses, and no vehicles of any kind; it is a large square in which all the space is footpath, and on which, in addition to the many men who pace it rapidly with busy brow, or idly lounge whilst enjoying the weather and the place, hundreds of pigeons are constantly fluttering or walking about in quiet confidence, sure that they will not be

molested by any one.   And then, as one draws near to the
church, it is easy to understand rather better than at first in
what its real charm lies; this is no doubt before anything else
in its beautiful colour; the whole front is shafted to a greater
extent than almost any building I know, the shafts all rather
heavy, but of marble of the richest kind; the groining of the
seven entrance arches is filled with mosaics, and the walls
are encrusted everywhere with marble.   Instead of ordinary
gables masking the roof, the front is finished with great ogee
gables most extravagantly crocketed, and obviously a modern
alteration of the original Romanesque finish; behind these a
cluster of fourteenth-century cupolas completes the view.
Of the seven arches which compose the façade, four have
doorways; the outer arches on either side are very narrow,
and answer in width to the kind of cloister which masks the
church on the south, west, and north sides; and the central
arch is much wider and loftier than the others, rising indeed
so high as to break through the line of balustrading which
runs across the front just above the other arches.

Within this central arch is a grand doorway, the stilted
semicircular arch of which is of three orders, the central
plain, the others covered with carvings.   The piers supporting the main arches have tiers of shafts in two heights; the
lower tier corresponding in height with those of the doors
pierced within the arches, and the others, which are smaller
in diameter, and more numerous than those which support
them, rising to the springing-line of the main arches.   The
side doorways have very Eastern-looking arches, the semicircular line being carried on nearly to the centre, and then
turned up into an ogee.   These and some other portions as,
e.g., the windows over two of the doors, and the pinnacles
between the gables, belong to the fourteenth century, whilst
the finish of the gables themselves—great ogee crocketed
gables with figures at the apex of each—is probably of the

fifteenth century. All these archways open into the cloister,
or narthex already mentioned. Here, where the roofs still
glow with the most precious early mosaics, and the walls
with marble, either used as inlays or for shafts, one gets a
first and not unworthy hint of the beauty which awaits one
in the interior.

And then, on entering the nave, the deep tones of an
organ are heard reverberating through the old building;
many people kneel devoutly at their prayers around us; the
hot glare of the sun has gone, and in its place a cool, quiet,
dim light reveals the whole magnificence of the design. It
is quite in vain to describe this in formal architectural terms.
The colour is so magnificent that one troubles oneself but little
about the architecture, and thinks only of gazing upon the
expanse of gold and deep richly-tinted mosaic all harmonized
together into one glorious whole. The mosaics commence
throughout the church at the level of the crown of the main
arches dividing the nave from the aisles, and are continued
up the remainder of the wall and into the domes; even the
angles or arrises of the walls and arches are covered with
gold mosaic; so that all architectural lines of moulding are
entirely lost, and nothing but a soft swelling and undulating
sea of colour is perceived. There is nothing violent or garish
in all this profuse decoration. The gold mosaic, used as it
always is in early works, set irregularly in, and surrounded
by a white line or joint of plaster, is never conspicuously
bright; the drawing of the figures and subjects may be
criticized, but at any rate it is always direct, simple, and
intelligible, and the colours of the draperies bright and
harmonious, whilst the arcading and wall-lining which fills
the lower part of the walls is all of marble, which has now a
rich, warm, but quiet tint, singularly suitable as a base to
the more gorgeous colouring of the upper part of the walls
and domes.

Altogether this is a church beyond most others suggestive of worship. Other churches sometimes suggest the same feeling either by enormous size or vast height. At Köln or Milan man feels so small and so contemptible in comparison with the vastness of his own work that he is subdued in spite of himself. In countless other great Gothic minsters the same feeling is produced. But at S. Mark's it is produced in an intensified degree, and by a building the scale of which is in every way small, if not almost insignificant. There is no long vista of arches, no complicated perspective, and no vast height to awe the beholder, yet the mystery of colour does for it even more than the mystery of size does for Köln or Beauvais, Milan, Toledo, or Bourges. It is, therefore, emphatically a church for worship, one in which even the most careless treads with hushed footstep and bated breath, and where, in spite of crowds, an aweful silence seems always to reign supreme save when it is broken by the religious sound of the services of the church.

The ground plan is no doubt known to most of my readers. It is a typical example of the Greek or Eastern church as distinguished from the Romanesque, a cross whose arms are not far from equal, covered by a series of cupolas, one in the centre, one to each of the three eastern arms, and two to the western—with aisles to the nave and choir, and a cloister round the north, west, and south sides of the nave, of which the two former are the porches, and the latter the baptistery of the church.[1]

Under the eastern limb of the cross is a crypt, which has in recent years been opened and drained, and is now always open to inspection. This is divided under the choir into

---

[1] The dimensions are worth giving to show how little this church owes to mere size. It is 245 feet long, 201 feet across the transept, and 170 feet across the west front. The height of the central cupola is 90 feet, and that of the west front 72 feet.

five aisles in width by a multitude of small shafts carrying
quadripartite vaults, and in the centre of which just under
the choir altar, is the shrine of S. Mark. Another apse is

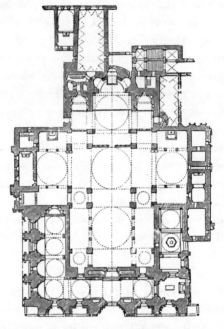

GROUND PLAN—S. MARK, VENICE.

formed under the south aisle of the choir, and under the
north aisle is a corresponding crypt save that there is no
apse to it. Much modernized as this has been in the course of
repair, and entirely devoid of all colour or decoration as it is,
it is still full of character, and adds largely to the interest
of the church.

If we return to the nave, we shall find that it is not
only in general effect it is so very worthy of admiration; it
still retains much of its old furniture, and in spite of a few
modern mosaics, and one or two more modern altars, is less
altered in its general effect since the fourteenth century

than any great church that I have ever seen. The screen
between the nave and choir with the ambons on either side
of it first deserve notice. The screen is mainly a work of
A. D. 1394.[1] It consists of a series of columns carrying a
flat lintel or cornice on the top of which is a row of
extremely good statues of the apostles. They have that
grand sweep of the figure which one knows so well in early
fourteenth century work in France, and are free from the
somewhat heavy and clumsy treatment which marks so much
of the work of the Pisani. The screen has been raised on the
base of the older Byzantine screen, which consisted of a simple
continuous arcade now nearly hidden by the more modern
steps to the choir. The ambons are probably of the same age
as this older screen; the gospel ambon being of two stages in
height, with a good staircase to it from the choir aisle, that
for the epistle being comparatively low and simple, but still
large enough to contain two or three modern pulpits. The
screens to the choir aisles are of the same sort as the main
screen, but are placed one bay to the east of it. They are
all three interesting as showing that a Gothic architect could
use with good effect a common Classic arrangement, and
indeed lend fresh grace to it by the detail of the sculpture
and inlaying with which he adorned it.

Dimly seen from the nave through the Rood-screen, but
far more interesting than even it, is the great baldacchin
or canopy over the altar in the choir. Here we have the
simplest form—four columns carrying round arches and the
wall above them finished with a plain horizontal capping.
The arches may be modern; though if they are so, they are
copied from the old, as is evidenced by the painting at the
back of the Pala d'Oro, which shows the placing of the shrine
of S. Mark under a similar baldacchin; but the groining is

---

[1] The inscription on the screen, which gives the date and the name of the
Doge Antonio Venerio, gives also the names of the sculptors.

old, and the alabaster columns are of extreme interest, being
covered all over with most elaborate sculptures of Scripture
subjects.   The subjects in the north-east column give the
history of Joachim and Anna, and the birth of the Blessed
Virgin Mary; the north-west has the nativity of Our Lord,
the marriage in Cana, &c.; the south-west subjects from the
Passion; and the south-east the miracles of Our Lord.   Few
modes of decorating an altar are altogether so fitting and
beautiful as this, and I hope the day is not far distant when
we shall see many of our English altars standing under
canopies of the same sort.   St. Paul's cathedral may well prepare the way for us in this, by reviving what was usually
accepted as the best kind of reredos by our English church-
builders in the eighteenth century.

Here, too, is a brass eagle so like one of our own, that
one might almost give it credit for coming from an English
smith or founder.

Returning to the nave, one finds nothing more worthy of
admiration than another smaller baldachin over an altar
between it and the north aisle.   This is hexagonal, carried
on shafts with stilted arches and roofed with a steep roof.
Its dimensions render a small altar a necessity—a matter of
common occurrence in old examples.   Another reredos and
altar in a chapel at the north end of the north transept,
dating from 1430, may also be noticed.   Here the altar is
panelled in front and carved with two angels censing a cross,
and low open screens with arcades carried on shafts are
placed a few inches from the ends of the altar.   The foot-
pace is not carried round the altar, so that it can only be
approached from the front.

Of another sort of furniture—monuments of the dead—
S. Mark's has, as might be expected, a good many examples.
The earliest are the probably Roman sarcophagi,[1] which lie

---

[1] The tomb of Vitale Faliero and another.

in the outer aisle or cloister right and left of the entrance ;
the next, near them,[1] where the sarcophagus is still retained,
but adorned with Christian emblems and sculpture; and of
considerably later date, and much more artistic interest, are
the tombs of the Doge Andrea Dandolo, and of Sant' Isidoro.
Here the sarcophagus is surmounted by a canopy, reverent
angels stand on either side drawing back partially the curtains
from the front of the effigy, and in the centre of the tomb
is a bas-relief of the Madonna, and at the ends the Annunciation, S. Gabriel on one side, the B. V. Mary at the other.
This is the type of monumental memorial on which so much
of the time of Venetian sculptors seems to have been spent.
Here, indeed, and on the very similar figures of the Virgin
on so many of the tympana of doorways throughout the
city, we have to study the sculptor's art from the time of the
Byzantine carvers who wrought the still numerous early
capitals, until the artist of the Ducal Palace came to revive
the art with his original and splendid series of capitals.

But of all the features of this grand church, that which
next to the gorgeous colour of the walls most attracted me
was the wild beauty of the pavement. I know not what
other word to use which quite describes the effect it produces. It is throughout arranged in the patterns common
in most Opus Alexandrinum, but instead of being laid level
and even, it swells up and down as though its surface were
the petrified waves of the sea, on which those who embark
in the ship of the church may kneel in prayer with safety,
the undulating surface serving only to remind them of the
stormy sea of life, and of the sea actually washing the walls
of the streets and houses throughout their city. It cannot
be supposed that this undulation is accidental, for had it been
the consequence of a settlement of the ground we should see
some marks of it in the crypt and in the walls, and some

---

[1] The tomb of the Doge Marino Morosini.

tokens of disruption in the pavement itself. And the corresponding example of Sta. Sofia, Constantinople, where we have it on record that there was an intentional symbolism in just such a floor, is conclusive as to the intention of its imitators here.

Of the mosaics with which the church is richly adorned I cannot pretend to give a complete account. They deserve a volume to themselves. As regards choice of subjects, it is noticeable that the most prominent figure is that of Our Lord, who is seated and surrounded by prophets. Below are the emblems of the four Evangelists, and the four rivers of Paradise. Whilst again in the west dome He is surrounded by the apostles and the Evangelists, and everywhere the general scheme is a lesson to those who now-a-days too often forget the relative importance or the proper order and arrangement of the divine story in the schemes they adopt for stained glass and mural decoration. As regards colour, I need not repeat what I have already said; but it may be observed that wherever modern mosaics have taken the place of old ones there at once we see a complete collapse, and a loss of all good effect. This is mainly owing, beyond doubt, to the attempt which their designers made to produce the effect of pictures, instead of thinking first and mainly of the decorative effect of their work on the building. But at the same time it is obvious that their eyes had lost all feeling for good colour, and that in attempting to draw with a certain amount of academical accuracy, they had equally lost all sense of the prime necessity in such works of simplicity of arrangement, and directness in the telling of their story. There is no part of the church in which some of the best of this sort of decoration can be studied with more ease and advantage than in the cloister on the north side of the nave. Here the mosaics are so near the eye, and the details of design and colour so fine that one is never tired of admiring them.

I never leave S. Mark's without taking one look at least
at the four bronze horses, which, placed as they are on
columns high above the ground, add so much to the strange
character of the west front, and are in themselves such
exquisite examples of their kind. Strange ornaments these
for the façade of the chief church of a city where horses' feet
have hardly ever trod! Equally strange, if you are to have
horses in such a position at all, is the way in which these are
supported. They stand balancing themselves nicely on the
caps of small columns. Extremes meet; and I am not so
sure but that this extraordinary arrangement is not better
than that which is usually adopted. If horses are to be
supported above the ground, they may almost as well be
so in this way as on the ordinary pedestal, which looks
equally unsafe if the bronze is instinct with life. These
horses were brought from Constantinople after the fourth
Crusade, circa 1203. They are of admirable character, and
are probably of Greek workmanship. With every other
moveable thing worth moving, they were taken to Paris, and
returned after the Peace in 1815.

There is a picture in the Accademia by Gentile Bellini,
which ought to be looked at after a visit to S. Mark's.
In it we see the church much as it is at present; but an
enormous procession which winds its tortuous way about the
piazza, defiles before houses every one of which seems to be
ancient, and I never look at the now uninteresting lines of
houses which surround it without wishing for the resuscitation of the buildings which G. Bellini saw and drew.

We went into the treasury to see the treasures and plate
belonging to the church, but I was much disappointed to find
that, in an artistic point of view, there was really very little
to admire, or else what was admirable was not shewn. The
treasury is a dark room lighted up by a few wax candles, but
so badly that it was difficult to see at all satisfactorily.

I was unable to obtain a sight of the Pala d'Oro, as the altar-piece behind the high altar is called; it is only un-covered on feast days, and I have never happened to be in Venice when it was visible. I was very anxious to have seen it, as it is a most magnificent piece of workmanship in gold and enamel. It was executed in Constantinople, and brought to Venice in 1102. Some Italian writers have claimed it for their forefathers as an Italian work; but the documentary evidence of its Eastern origin is supported by the details of the design and execution of the earliest portions of the work. M. Durand has published a very careful description of it in the 'Annales Archéologiques,' vol. xx. He gives a list of no less than one hundred and sixty-nine panels or figures, in a considerable number of which the accompanying in-scriptions are in Greek characters. The Pala was "restored" in the thirteenth century and again in the fourteenth, when no doubt considerable additions were made to it. The painting at the back has fourteen subjects on a gold ground, and is dated 1345.

Over and over again when at Venice must one go into S. Mark's, not to criticize but to admire; and if ever in any building in which the main object is the study of art, assuredly here one must go for worship also. I think I never saw an interior so thoroughly religious and religion-inspiring as this, and it is well, therefore, not lightly to pass it by as useless for our general purposes. It seems to shew, as strongly as any one example can, how much awefulness and grandeur of character even a small building may attain to by the lavish expenditure of art and precious materials throughout its fabric; for it is to this that S. Mark's owes its grandeur, and to this only. There is nothing imposing either in its size or in its architecture; on the contrary, they appear to me to be both moderate, and the former rather mean; and yet this grand display of mosaics upon a gold ground makes the

building appear to be both larger and better than it is, and
fully atones for all other defects. Could we but place one of
our cold, bare places of worship by the side of S. Mark's,
and let the development of Christian art in the construction
of the fabric be ten times as great in our Northern church as
in the Venetian, we may yet rest assured that every religious
mind would turn at once to the latter, and scarce deign to
think of the former as a place of worship at all. If this is
so, does it not point most forcibly to the absolute necessity
for the introduction of more colour in the interior of our
buildings, either in their construction, or afterwards by the
hand of the painter? And architects must remember that
this ought all to be within their province as directors or
designers, and therefore that they must not, as now, venture to design cold shells which may or may not afterwards
receive these necessary and indispensable decorations, but
from the very first must view them as part and parcel of
the work in which they are personally concerned; and then,
but not till then, shall we see a satisfactory school of architects in England.

The interest of S. Mark's is not, however, only religious
and artistic; on other grounds it is certainly one of the
buildings most worthy of study in all Europe. Its architecture is purely Byzantine; and whether its design was derived
from Constantinople or from Alexandria, it presents us with
an almost unique example of the architecture of the Eastern
church transplanted almost without alteration to the domains
of the Western. Nor is this all. It played no small part in
modifying the distinctly Roman influence by which otherwise the whole of Northern Europe would have been affected.
When we see a church so far from S. Mark's as that of S.
Front at Périgueux modelled after it, and in its turn influ-
encing a vast number of churches in that and the neighbouring districts, we may realize what S. Mark's did towards the

development of Romanesque into new forms and combinations, and may then value properly every portion of its fabric. Byzantine architecture was the development of Greek art in the hands of the then vigorous and active Eastern Church. It is not a direct reproduction therefore of Classic art which is to be seen in S. Mark's, but one stage of a development the influence of which—partly owing to the effect of commerce, partly to her isolation—was largely felt, down to the very last days of active Venetian artistic life. This has been well condensed in a short sentence by Mr. Ruskin. "All European architecture," he says, "good and bad, old and new, is derived from Greece through Rome, and coloured and perfected from the East. The Doric and Corinthian orders are the roots, the one of all Romanesque buildings—Norman, Lombard, Byzantine; the other of all Gothic—Early English, French, German, and Tuscan. The old Greeks gave the shaft, Rome gave the arch. The Arabs pointed and foliated the arch." But in the colouring and perfecting the church of S. Mark had the lion's share, just as in the ground-plan it is to Venice and the East that we owe the cruciform arrangement of so many of our buildings, instead of the basilican form to which we might otherwise have been condemned.

There is another respect in which S. Mark's is extremely Eastern. This is in the almost entire absence of figure-sculpture in its original construction. The subjects and figures on the columns of the baldachin are too delicate to be noticed from a distance, and it was not until A.D. 1394 that the choir-screen was introduced, with figures of the Apostles on either side of the rood, erected no doubt to supply a want which had been long felt before it was gratified. At the same time figures were added in niches between the gables of the exterior, but even now they form a small and inconsiderable part of the decoration of the church.

I have lingered on paper as I did in reality about S.

Mark's; but if we wish to see Venice we must tear ourselves
away from it.   We will go out by the baptistery, and here
we are at once on the Piazzetta, the noble façade of the
Ducal Palace on one side, and a great work of Sansovino's
—the library of S. Mark—on the other; at the end of the
Piazzetta are two monolithic granite columns, one of which
bears the lion of S. Mark, the other the figure of the ancient
patron saint of Venice, S. Theodore; between them is seen
the dark-blue line of the sea rippled into a thousand twinkling
waves, and beyond this the Isola San Giorgio, remarkable for
one of Palladio's churches—a building, as I think, irredeem-
ably ugly, but, nevertheless, much admired by many. If you
walk down to the strand, where a hundred gondolas wait for
hire—some black and funereal-like, others dressed up with
gay awnings, and all of them proud and swan-like with their
bright steel prows rising lightly and high out of the water—
and then, turning round, look first down the Riva dei Schiavoni,
towards the sea, taking in the long sea-front of the Ducal
Palace, then the narrow gap bridged by the famous Bridge
of Sighs, and on again, noting bridge after bridge, and the
Gothic palace now turned into the Hôtel Danieli, and then
on to the promontory running out towards the Adriatic,
occupied by the Public Gardens and planted with the only
trees that Venice boasts—how lovely is the scene! or if,
looking back up the Piazzetta to S. Mark's, noting the tall
campanile and the quaint clock and clock-tower beyond, and
the domes and turrets, niches and figures, which crown the
church, how much more vividly does it not impress the mind!

   Venice is full to excess of striking pictures, and it would
be endless to say in how very many respects it has a character
of its own which can never be forgotten. The strange silence
of its watery streets, broken only by the cry of the gondolier
or the delicate plash of his oar in the water, is not the least
impressive thing to the stranger; and when, after trying

in vain to thread on foot the labyrinth of passages which confuse him irrecoverably in a few minutes, he commits himself to the dark recesses of a gondola, how delightful is the quiet, smooth, and yet rapid way in which, without more labour than is necessary in looking about, he finds himself now following the narrow winding of some small canal, awakening the echoes between the high walls of palaces or warehouses on either side of the way, or anon, upon turning with a graceful sweep into the smooth broad reach of the Grand Canal, making his gondolier move gently and slowly, as one by one the great palaces which grace its banks and form its retaining walls are carefully scanned, whilst the various and ever-changing perspective of the whole is dwelt upon, to be remembered afterwards with such intense pleasure !

From S. Mark's I remember trying to find my way to San Stefano; and, taking a map of Venice, and calculating upon the orientation of the churches being fairly correct, I flattered myself that I might without difficulty make my way: the result was simply that for half an hour I was threading the mazes of all the passages around the church, and at last reached it only by chance; and I found afterwards that it would not at all do to take the churches as marking the cardinal points of the compass, for, as may be seen from the campanile of S. Mark, there are scarcely two churches in the city exactly alike in their orientation.

But pleasant as it is to recall one's recollections of highways and byways in Venice, I think, if we wish to understand her architecture thoroughly, we shall do well first of all to make a pilgrimage to Torcello, that sad and weird cathedral, standing forlorn and deserted on a wretched island in the lagoon, wherein we see the handiwork of the earliest Venetians, and the prototype of much of the later work in Venice itself. The story of Torcello has been told often—by no one with more feeling or more pathos than by

Mr. Ruskin, and I need not attempt to repeat it. Suffice it
to say that about A.D. 641 the church was first built, whilst
in 864 it was restored, and being nearly decayed by age, was
again most studiously repaired in 1008;[1] whilst in 1361,
according to the testimony of Cornaro,[2] there were still
standing on the same island divers churches (forty-two in
number) adorned with columns of pietra dura, and with
mosaics. Strange indeed is the difference here between
then and now!

My first visit to Torcello was sad and sombre enough to
begin with. We started early from Venice in a thick mist,
making our way first to the cemetery, where there is a good
tall campanile, then to Murano, and through its shabby
water streets, passing the end of San Donato (which shall
be described later), and then on through long canals edged
on either side by miles of green mud, and thronged with
market boats and noisy boatmen. Here and there across
the lagoon we saw a tall campanile marking the position
of each settlement or island in this waste of sea and mud,
and, last of all, that of the cathedral of Torcello, some five
minutes' walk among decaying walls and unmown grass from
the half-ruined landing-place to which our gondolier tied his
boat. All that remains of the city is before us in small
compass. On the left a fourteenth-century building, said to
have been the Palazzo Publico; in front a stone seat or throne
in the centre of what was once the market-place; on the right,
the Byzantine church of Sta. Fosca; and beyond, and connected with Sta. Fosca by a cloister, the modernized-looking
cathedral, plain, bare, and uninteresting on the outside, with
a detached campanile near the east end. This is all Torcello
has to shew; but, forlorn and decayed as everything in the
place is, it is precious in the highest degree to the architect

---

[1] 'Sagornino Chronicon,' p. 119.
[2] 'Il Palazzo Ducale di Venezia,' per Francesco Zanotto, i. p. 9.

who cares about the growth of his art. The cathedral is full
of interest, though much damaged by extensive repairs,
carried on in a reckless mood by the Austrians, not long
before they lost Venetia, when new roofs were put on, and the
mosaics were so much damaged that I remember collecting a
handful of fragments from a barrow of rubbish before it was
shot into the canal ; at the same time a scaffold was erected
for a proposed restoration of the great western mosaic which,
though threatened and indeed commenced in 1857, had not
in 1872 been proceeded with. The exterior has been completely modernized. In plan the cathedral consists of three
parallel naves of ten bays, all finished with apses. The
columns dividing the nave from the aisles are of veined
marble, with capitals of exquisite workmanship, founded,
indeed, on Corinthian examples, but modified by Byzantine
influence and by study of nature. The arches are stilted
and high ; above them is a small clerestory of very simple
windows. The central apse retains its raised rows of seats,
though their brickwork alone is left ; the throne for the
bishop is placed in the centre, and retains some of its marble
inlay. Under this raised east end a descending passage is
formed, connecting the two smaller apses, and with a small
apse formed in the thickness of the east wall opening into
it. Three bays of the church are given to the choir, which
is fenced round with richly sculptured marble screens. On
the west the screen has marble columns carrying a flat
entablature, and below them is a solid portion some four feet
high covered with panels of flat sculpture, one having two
peacocks drinking out of the same vase, another two lions
at the foot of a branching tree, and another a complicated
interlacing pattern of foliage. Such a screen is the obvious
prototype of that in S. Mark's, and the sculptures with
which it is adorned are evidently the work of some early
Byzantine workman—whether brought from Aquileja from

22. DUOMO. TORCELLO.

the ruins created by Attila's invasion, or wrought on the
spot, I cannot say, but of a character which we still see
in some of the nearly corresponding screens in the existing
cathedral of Aquileja. North-west of this rood-screen stands
the marble ambon—a pulpit of two divisions, one (circular)
facing south, the other (square) facing west. This and the
staircase leading to it are full of delicate and good carved
work. The arrangement has an absurd likeness to many a
modern English scheme of pulpit and reading pew, and
there is certainly force in an observation which Mr. Webb
makes,[1] that such an arrangement would never have been
thought of, unless the Gospel was to be understood by the
people. Now they do not understand it, it is no longer said
from an ambon, and ambons seem to be much less useful to
Romans than rood-screens are to us!

The screens north and south of the choir do not seem to
be so old as the other, and are simple low screens.

In the mosaics of the apse and western wall we have,
perhaps, the finest examples of Venetian mosaics. The apse
is lined with slabs of veined marble below, and has above a
mosaic of the Blessed Virgin Mary with Our Lord and the
twelve Apostles, and the patron of the church, S. Heliodorus.
The whole west wall is covered with a grand mosaic of the
Crucifixion at the top, the Descent into Hell under it, and a
Last Judgment at the base, which is carried down on each side
of the west door, in the tympanum of which is a half figure
of Our Lady. A mosaic at the end of the south aisle has
Our Lord with SS. Michael and Gabriel, and below them S.
Gregory, S. Martin, S. Ambrose, and S. Austin.[2] Save where

---

[1] 'Continental Ecclesiology,' p. 306.

[2] The mosaics here, as in Venice, are wholly of glass. The gold is covered
with a thin film of glass, and the other colours used are dead white, black,
dark and light blue, green and red. The very smallness of the palette was
here, just at it was with the old painters on glass, a distinct advantage, saving
them from the bizarre and confused effect produced in such works by the use
of too many colours or shades of colours.

these mosaics occur, the walls have been persistently white-washed, so that the appearance of the church is now far from attractive. It is not the less of great interest, as an example of a very early church founded on a Roman basilica, but with Byzantine influence most conspicuous in the sculpture of its ornaments. Here, as in S. Mark's, the floor is paved with Opus Alexandrinum, of which, in spite of damage done during the late repairs, it is a fine example. There is nothing to admire on the exterior, though the large stone shutters to the windows—single slabs of stone about four inches thick, working on stone pivots—have a most primitive air. The campanile has not much to distinguish it from others, but the top affords an interesting view of the lagoon and the sea with Venice in the distance, and the Alps of Friuli far away to the north.

A few yards through the cloister bring us to the church of Sta. Fosca. Here by the side of the Romanesque we have a capital example of a Byzantine plan, which seems to me to be of the greatest value in connection with the whole of the round-arched palaces of Venice of which so many remains still exist. Sta. Fosca is a square church with small projections on the north, south, and west sides, and a deeper projection for the altar on the east. There are three eastern apses, and the western side is screened by an open cloister, which is octagonal in plan. The square centre is domed on very simple pendentives, and the capitals are similar in character to those in the cathedral. The best detail is to be seen outside the east end, where there is some good arcading and an enriched band of chevron ornament, formed by recessing the brickwork, and a mixture of red and buff brickwork, which is very effective.

The last time I was here, I found myself, in the middle of making a sketch of the west front of Sta. Fosca, suddenly struck by the strange likeness of its octagonal cloister to the

most typical elevations of the Byzantine palaces in Venice.
These always have a centre and wings divided by piers; and
whilst the arches in the centre are of ordinary proportions,

EAST END—STA. FOSCA, TORCELLO.

those in the wings are narrow and considerably stilted.   In
Sta. Fosca precisely the same effect is produced by the
elevation of the three sides of the octagonal cloister, two of
them being reduced in width and seeming to have narrow
stilted arches, owing to their being canted and not seen in
true elevation.   I confess I could hardly help thinking that
here I saw the accidental germ of an arrangement which,
commenced in Romanesque or Byzantine buildings, was
imitated in many of the finest of the Gothic palaces, and was
revived with invariable persistency in the Renaissance.

The return to Venice was more pleasant than the journey
out had been.   The water had risen enough to cover the

mud everywhere, and now a vast expanse of apparent sea
was lighted up by the hot sun, and in the far-off distance
the horizon was lined with the long picturesque range of the
Alps, tender and transparent in hue, and sweet reminders to
the dwellers on this monotonous lagoon of the world which
lay outside their boundaries in the far north. On the road
we stopped at Mazzorbo, where there is a dated example of
a Gothic doorway. This has a square-headed opening, and
above this an ogee canopy or label over a figure of Our Lord,
and some kneeling figures. The date inscribed on it is
A.D. 1368.

Farther on Murano is passed, and a halt made for a visit
to the church of San Donato—once a building of the highest
interest and well known to all readers of Mr. Ruskin's books.
Unfortunately my first visit to this church was after it had
been in part " restored," in the largest and worst sense of
the word. The old brickwork was being renewed, plastered,
and painted up, till most of its interest had vanished; and
now, I fear, only those who saw San Donato some ten years
ago can have any idea of its architectural value and interest.
This was chiefly centred in the east front, where there is
a central apse with a lean-to end to the aisle on either side.
The wall is divided into two stages, by a bold string-course
and double line of chevrons formed by recessing the brickwork
and inserting panels of coloured and carved white marble.
The lower stage is arcaded mainly in red brick, whilst the
upper has a wall deeply recessed behind arcades under the
eaves, with delicate balustrades between the columns which
carry the arcades. This upper part of the building is mainly
of buff-coloured bricks, with thin lines of red to mark the
pattern of arches, and it is curious that the light bricks are
much larger than the red.[1] The pavements here are very

---

[1] The red bricks are $2\frac{1}{4}$ thick × $9\frac{1}{2}$ in. long, whilst the yellow bricks are
$3\frac{1}{4}$ thick × 12 in. long.

fine examples of Opus Alexandrinum, with a more than usual
proportion of black marble, and there is a grand mosaic in
the apse, of the B. V. Mary and Our Lord on a gold ground.

One or two Gothic houses in semi-ruinous condition, and
a very fine fragment of late Byzantine work quite in ruins—
the Palazzo da Mula—remain in Murano, but of these there
is such good store in Venice itself that we may pass them by.

Most visitors, I suppose, go to Murano in order to visit
Dr. Salviati's glass and mosaic manufactory. He has succeeded in reproducing a material quite equal to that used
in the old mosaics. Still more difficult feat—he has succeeded also in making glass so like the old Venetian glass
in colour, texture, and design, as to puzzle all ordinary
judges. I cannot sufficiently admire or praise the singular
power which Dr. Salviati has shewn in the education of his
men. A party of six or eight made for me before my eyes,
in a few minutes, a tall, delicate, and richly adorned goblet,
in which every part was done by eye and fancy; no modern
accuracy was attempted, and the result was a thoroughly
beautiful and artistic work. All artists know how difficult
it is to get a workman nowadays out of the hard mechanical
groove of dull uniformity, and Dr. Salviati's success is an
encouragement to all of us when we are tempted to despair
of making the attempt.

From Murano a few minutes take us again into the
watery streets of Venice. We have now seen the two buildings which ought first of all to be studied—Torcello and
S. Mark's, and in them we have the key to everything that
follows. The Venetians commenced in their earliest buildings
with works which shewed but little original invention or
power. It was their fortune to have, by reason of their situation and their commerce, a great connection with the East.
They received, therefore, a great impetus at the first from
Byzantine art. Nowhere in Europe was so great an influence

of the kind exerted; and to us, whose early architecture was almost entirely Romanesque in its origin, it has a special interest and novelty. But if the early Venetians copied Byzantine models, employed Byzantine workmen, and thought rather more of the beautiful colours for which their Eastern acquaintances gave them a taste than did their neighbours on the mainland, it must be frankly conceded that in later times they developed a very original form of Gothic out of these very materials, and owed comparatively little to any external aid in their great works of the fourteenth and fifteenth centuries.

The first business of a tourist in Venice is to secure a gondolier with intelligence enough to understand his proclivities, and patience enough to humour them. I have more than once or twice had to thank my gondolier for shewing me old work which otherwise I should never have seen, and I am grateful accordingly. I am grateful, too, whenever I think of a gondola, for the most luxurious machine for sketching from which has ever been constructed; and the more so, when I recollect how for an hour at a time I have been persecuted in most Italian towns by all the idlest, dirtiest, and worst-behaved people of the place whilst I have made my sketches of their buildings. In a gondola in Venice one knows no such troubles, and the sketcher's life, as long as he can work in it, is as happy and undisturbedly serene as is possible. But no artist must suppose that everything worth seeing can be seen from the water: a few walks will convince him that, in the narrow *calli* as well as on the water-side, much that is interesting is to be found; and when he has studied Venice both by boat and by pavement, he will find, as I do, that the subject is too large for a chapter, and requires rather a volume for its thorough elucidation.

The buildings of Venice divide themselves into two great classes—the churches and the civil buildings; of these the

former is the smaller and the less interesting class. But as
we have already seen at S. Mark's and Torcello the earliest
examples of the churches, it will be best to say all that has
to be said about them here, and to take the palaces and
houses by themselves afterwards.

We have seen that S. Mark's was built in the eleventh
and twelfth, and largely altered in the fourteenth century.
Between these two periods little if anything was done in
church-building in Venice; or if it was, it has disappeared.
Just as in Germany, the thirteenth century seems hardly to
have existed for Venice, and we go at a bound from the simple
nervous round-arched work of S. Mark's to the here somewhat poor and tasteless churches of the fourteenth century.
One or two small campanili—San Polo, San Samuele, and
San Barnaba are the best—remain to show what the size and
character of the earlier work were. They have plain arcades
in the walls, rising from the ground to the belfry, and this
has generally windows of two or three lights carried on
shafts. At San Barnaba [1] a spire with parapets and pinnacles
was added to such a steeple in the fourteenth century, the spire
being circular in plan and built of round-ended bricks. San
Paterniano has an hexagonal brick tower with two light belfry
windows, also of Romanesque character. The whole of these
works are of brick, and usually the walls batter outward
towards the base. In this respect, as in the general design,
the great tower of S. Mark's follows those early examples, as
also in its means of access to the top, which is a continuous
slope in the thickness of the wall in place of the newel staircase in use all over the North of Europe. Finally, all these
older works are very small and modest in scale and design.

Let us now give up all thought of early works, and see

---

[1] The twelfth-century bricks here measure seven inches by two inches,
and are built with a half inch mortar joint; they are of red and yellow colour,
used indiscriminately, and, though good and lasting, extremely rough in their
make.

what the fourteenth and fifteenth centuries did for Venice
in the way of churches. Taking them in their order of
merit, we will go first to the Frari, the church of the Fran-
ciscans, thence to SS. Giovanni e Paolo, that of the Domini-
cans, to the Madonna dell' Orto, San Stefano, the desecrated
church of the Convent of La Carità, now forming part of the
Accademia, San Gregorio, Santa Zaccaria, San Giacomo del
Rialto, and some smaller fragments.

I must confess that on the whole, in spite of the grand
size of some of them, I was rather disappointed on first
seeing these buildings. One cannot but be impressed
with the magnificent size of such a church as the Frari,
with its many interesting details, and its monuments and
woodwork. But in spite of all this, there is something
wanting. I had not expected larger churches, but I had
imagined that their style would be more pure, and at the
same time more unlike what I was accustomed to elsewhere.
The impression they left on my mind was decidedly that
they were very inferior in almost every respect to churches
of the same size and degree of ornament in the North of
Europe, whilst in scarcely any point did they seem to me
to have features which could with any advantage be imitated
by us. I had allowed myself to expect a very different
result, and was proportionately disappointed. There is no
church in Venice—(in what I am now saying I mean always
to except S. Mark's)—comparable either to Sta. Anastasia
or to the cathedral at Verona in the interior; and the
exteriors, though fine as examples of the bold use of brick,
are nevertheless not first-rate, nor at all superior to what
one sees elsewhere.

Sta. Maria Gloriosa dei Frari ought first to be described,
as being certainly the finest of its class. The first stone is
said to have been laid on April 3rd, 1250, Nicola Pisano
being the architect. The campanile was begun in 1361

23.—INTERIOR OF STA. MARIA GLORIOSA DEI FRARI, VENICE.

under Jacopo Collega, and completed in 1396 by Pietro Paolo his son.

The first impression of the church on landing from the gondola on the desolate-looking piece of pavement which here, as in many of the Venetian churches, forms a court between the canal and the west front, is not pleasing. The design of the west front is nothing short of being positively ugly; it is finished with a great sham gable, with a curved outline, somewhat akin to the degraded taste of our worst Jacobæan art, and entirely without any beauty or even picturesqueness of appearance; the doorways, too, are particularly poor, consisting of a succession of twisted and reedy mouldings, thin and shadowless, like so many cords stretched from cap to base and round the arch, without any proper distinction of jamb and archivolt.

The internal effect of the church is much finer than its west front would lead one to expect. The plan is simple; a nave and aisles of six bays, transepts with three eastern chapels to each, and a choir of one bay with an apse of four bays projecting beyond the others. The tower is in the angle between the north transept and the nave, and a large sacristy with an eastern apse is built against the south transept. The nave and aisles measure about 230 feet by 104, and the transept 160 feet by 48,—magnificent dimensions undoubtedly. The columns are simple, cylindrical, and very lofty, their capitals carved with foliage, which looks late and poor in its execution, though grouped in the old way in regular tufts or balls of foliage. The arrangement of the wall above the main arcade is very similar to that of the Veronese, and, indeed, to that of most Italian Gothic churches; a plain wall being carried up to the groining, relieved only by a small clerestory window at the highest point. One is apt to compare this arrangement with the artistic arrangement of clerestory and triforium in our own churches; but herein we do not act quite fairly to Nicola Pisano, who is said to have designed the Frari, and his brethren. They had to work in a country where light must be admitted very sparingly, and where therefore it is impossible for architects to revel in the rich traceries which fill the bays of the churches of the North; they lived among a nation of painters, and deemed, perhaps, that these plain surfaces of wall would one day glow with colour and with Scripture story. For these reasons, then, I defend them for the bareness and over-great plainness which are certainly at first felt to be so remarkable in their work. The real beauty of these interiors is owing, more than to anything else, I believe, to the simplicity and purity of the quadripartite groining which covers them in, and which, even where other features would seem to tell of debasement and absence of pure feeling, invariably recalls us to a proper recollection of the infinite value of simplicity in this important feature—a point lost sight of in England after the thirteenth century, to the incalculable detriment of the beauty of some of our greatest churches. It is not difficult to prove that this must be the case, for I take it for granted that we all feel that ornament for its own sake is valueless; and equally, that doing in a troublesome, and therefore costly way, that which may be done as well and as strongly in a simpler manner, is unpleasant and distasteful as an exhibition of the wasteful expenditure of human skill and energy; and therefore, as simple quadripartite groining with diagonal and transverse ribs, and no lierne or intermediate ribs, is quite sufficient for the construction, and as the vaults are in no degree whatever strengthened by the multiplication and ramification of perplexing ribs, such as we see in later days in fan tracery and other contemporary modes of vaulting, that it is the truest and most agreeable system of roofing in stone.

The simple groining of the Frari is entirely executed in

brick, and springs in the aisles from pilasters corbelled out of the walls midway in height, just as in Sta. Anastasia at Verona, and in the nave and choir from clusters of shafts rising from the caps of the columns.

The apse is the noblest feature of the whole church ; its windows, with their singular and not quite pleasing transome of tracery, are refreshing because they have tracery, though indeed it is of a rude and heavy kind.

There is something impressive about the arrangement of the church. The choir is prolonged by the length of about one bay and a half into the nave, and fenced off to the west by a great screen, surmounted by figures of the Apostles, with a crucifix rising in the centre. The nave is, of course, quite free from any fixed seats ; and this, with the great area of the transept and the fine perspective of the long range of seven apsidal chapels on its east side, gives a grand air of spaciousness to the whole interior. There are some fine monuments here, quite worth notice as very characteristic of Italian art. They are generally high tombs corbelled out from the walls, with arched canopies over them, inclosing paintings. Here the south transept wall over the door to the vestry contains a group of such monuments, which is extremely picturesque. The monument of "Beatus Pacificus" (A.D. 1437) has a graceful painting of the Annunciation over its arch, and sculptures under it of the Baptism, and, on the tomb, of the Resurrection and the Descent into Hell.[1] Another monument has a life-size figure on horseback, and all have so much freshness to an English eye, and yet so much identity in principle with our own old monuments, that they are well worthy of study. Last, but not least, are two immense monuments facing each other, near the west

---

[1] The crockets on the monument of A.D. 1437 are exactly similar to those on the western gables of S. Mark's, and prove that these are of about the same date.

end of the nave, to Canova and Titian, preposterous in size, heavy, ugly, and cold in character, quite unsuitable to a church, and, so far at least as I could judge, entirely devoid of merit as works of religious art. There is, too, a painting by Giovanni Bellini of the Madonna and Saints, which ought to be visited, in the grand and well-used sacristy—a room such as one never seems to see save in Italy. It is still in its old frame over the sacristy altar. Both in artistic interest and in religious effect it is perfectly fine; the sub-ject—a Madonna and Child, such as Gian Bellini alone could paint. Angels playing instruments, sweet and pretty in character, and saints full of reverence and awe for Our Lord, all treated with a colour of exquisite depth and rich-ness throughout, make this as worshipful a picture as I know. There is also in the north transept a most elaborately framed Gothic triptych, with figures well drawn and rich in colour.

The stalls in the Frari are all placed in the nave west of the transept, as in Westminster Abbey. They are of very rich Renaissance character, but with some late Gothic features. In the north transept is some elaborate Gothic panelling—very German in character—which looks as if it had come from the back of the old choir stalls. Here, too, is a crucifix, probably the original rood. Some fragments of stained glass are still visible; they are coarse and rude in detail, but extremely fine in colour; and one must picture the church full of rich glass in order to do justice to the scheme of the mediæval architect.

To the south of the nave are large uninteresting cloisters, and it is only at the east end that the exterior at all repays the ecclesiologist for the pains he must take to get all round it. The view which I give will best illustrate its general character. The windows are all transomed, the tracery and portions of the arches being executed in stone, the rest of the wall being entirely of brick or terra-cotta with some

24—STA. MARIA GLORIOSA DEI FRARI, VENICE.

red marble in the eaves-arcading; the bricks are not particularly good, and the terra-cotta borders, cornices, and
ornaments are poor and meagre in their design. The most
observable point about the detail is the great and ugly splay
on the exterior of the windows, and the facts that the window
mouldings are returned round the sills and that all the
apsidal terminations in the church finish with an angle in
the centre—a peculiarity which is very seldom met with, but
very much to be commended as a variety.

There is a degree of clumsiness about the way in which
the arches of the windows are set upon the jambs which is
very characteristic of Italian Gothic; but this, and other
points open to criticism, do not prevent the east end of this
church from being a very noble conception, broad and grand,
unbroken with the lines of buttresses which generally too
much confuse apsidal terminations, and yet very vertical in
its effect. There is no petty attempt at relieving or orna-
menting plain wall where it occurs, but it is left in the
native rudeness of the rather rough-looking red brick,
which is in no respect better than the bricks one may get
anywhere in England. The cornices are very marked, and
those in the clerestory have the common and ungraceful corbelled arcading in brick, to which I have a special antipathy.
The clerestory windows of the transepts and choir are, I
need hardly say, quite modern, and of a kind, unfortunately,
most popular throughout the north of Italy. North of the
choir is a tall brick campanile, leaning rather dangerously
to the North, finished with an octagonal upper stage, and,
though not very remarkable, making a conspicuous feature
in most of the views of this part of Venice, and at any
rate to be admired for its simplicity and the absence of effort
in its design.

Next in order of merit to this church are those of SS.
Giovanni e Paolo and of the Madonna dell' Orto, both of

them savouring most strongly of the influence of the Pisani, and in very many points remarkably like the church of the Frari.

We will take SS. Giovanni e Paolo first.   The plan is of the same sort as that of the Frari—nave with aisles, and transepts with two chapels opening on each side of them. These are all apsidal, but planned in the usual way and not as at the Frari.   The east end is a fine composition, having an apse of seven sides, and is the only part of the exterior to which much praise can be given.   It is divided into two stages by an elaborate brick cornice and a good balustraded passage in front of the upper windows.   The traceries are all unskilfully designed, and set back from the face of the wall with a bald plain splay of brickwork round them; the lower windows here have two transoms, and the upper a single band of heavy tracery which performs the part of a transom in an ungainly fashion, though not so badly as in the great south-transept window in the same church.   Here, just as at the Frari, it is obvious that the absence of buttresses to these many-sided apses is the secret of the largeness and breadth which mark them; and, to say the truth, not only are large buttresses to an apse often detrimental to its effect, but at the same time they are very often not wanted for strength. The interior is remarkable on account of the fine scale on which it is built, and for the large number of interesting monuments corbelled out from its walls.   Many of them are mediæval and rich in sculpture of figures, not only on the tombs themselves, but again in the face of the wall, around their canopies.   The effigy of the deceased is almost always placed on the top of the high tomb or sarcophagus, which, in order that it may be visible from below, is made with a slope towards the spectator, the effect of which is most distressing.   Much more beautiful generally is the curtained tester often put above the figure, on either side of which guardian angels, holding back the folds of the draperies, allow us to join them in looking at the figure on the tomb. There is here a very fine lectern—a double-headed eagle standing on a scorpion —with a rich mediæval stand and base.

There are small two-light windows just over the arches in the nave which take the place of a triforium, and which look almost as if they were the clerestory windows of an earlier church whose arches were much less lofty than those which now exist.

In the small piazza in front of the church stands one of the glories of Venice—the monument of Bartolomeo Colleoni. As is the case with too many equestrian statues the base seems dangerously small for the steed, slow and stately as his movement is. What a grand air of valiant determination this old warrior wears! what a serious purpose the artist had in his work, and how carefully he has rendered every detail of trapping and armour on both man and horse! We have already heard of this famous condottiere in his chapel at Bergamo and in his castle of Malpaga. His statue was the work of Andrea Verocchio, but was completed by Alessandro Leopardi, between 1479 and 1488. Colleoni had left his whole fortune to the republic of Venice on condition that his statue should be placed in the Piazza of S. Mark. This being contrary to the laws, an ingenious loophole for escape was discovered; the bequest was secured by the erection of the statue in front of the Scuola di San Marco, whose strange Renaissance front (built with coloured marble in a horrible sort of perspective, which is the lowest depth to which architecture ever reached) stands at right angles to the front of SS. Giovanni e Paolo. For any one who wished to be remembered near S. Mark's church, the catastrophe would be as great, if he cared about art, to find himself connected, instead, with such an abortion as the Scuola of that ilk, as it would be to Bartolomeo Colleoni to find himself

here in the suburbs when he stipulated so carefully for a
place in the very centre of the city!

Next in order of merit to SS. Giovanni e Paolo I should
place the church of Sta. Maria dell' Orto. This church is in
a very bad state, and so far ruinous as to require to be
supported in its interior by a forest of shores and scaffold-
poles, which makes it quite impossible to get a good idea of
the general effect. It has fair pointed arcades resting upon
very Classic-looking columns, with capitals of poorly grouped
and executed foliage. It is decidedly inferior to the two
churches just described, in every respect save the treatment
of its west front, which, poor as it is, sins less against all
acknowledged rules than do theirs; its character is of a kind
of pseudo-pointed, very flat, hard, and awkward. The cornice, with the open Italian pinnacles above it, over the central
portion, is better in its effect than the singular row of niches
which stands in lieu of cornice for the ends of the aisles; but
it is worth while, nevertheless, to observe how simple is the
design of these niches, taken separately, and how far this
simplicity and the genuine beauty of their cusping and arching go towards redeeming the want of taste which is shown
in the choice of their location. The doorway and rose window in the west front are of red and white marble, and in
the side windows the tracery and monials are of white marble,
and the jambs alternately red and white. The rest of the
wall is brick, but has been plastered and washed with
pink. The windows at the end of the aisles are remarkable
for transoms of tracery supported upon two heights of delicate marble shafts, and entirely independent of the glazing
which is fixed in frames within them. This kind of arrangement, incongruous and unsatisfactory as it is here, is worth
recollecting, as being suggestive of an obvious opening for
the use of traceried windows in domestic work; and it is a
plan of most frequent occurrence in the best Italian eccle-

siastical architecture.   Many of the windows of Sta. Anastasia at Verona are constructed in this way, showing on the
outside elaborately cusped and pierced plates of stone, against
which on the inside the glazing is fixed, surrounded only
with a plain circle of stone.

San Stefano is another really striking Gothic church.
Its interior, notwithstanding the gaudy red damask with
which the Venetians here and elsewhere delight to clothe
the columns of their churches, is very fine and unlike what is
common in the North of Europe.   The dimensions are very
large.   The nave is about forty-eight feet wide, and the
whole length about one hundred and seventy feet.   There are
a cloister and a chapter-house north of the nave, and a
campanile detached at some distance to the east.   The arcades of six pointed arches dividing the nave from either
aisle are very light, and supported on delicate marble columns,
whose capitals, with square abaci and foliage of Classical
character, hardly look like Gothic work.   The masonry and
mouldings of the arches are not arranged in a succession of
orders, as is the case in almost all good pointed work, but
have a broad, plain soffeit, with a small and shallow moulding
at the edge, finished with a dentil or billet ornament, which,
originally used by the architect of S. Mark's in order to
form the lines of constructional stonework within which
his encrusted marbles were held, was afterwards, down to
the very decline of pointed architecture, used everywhere in
Venice—not only in its original position, but, as at San
Stefano, in place of a label round the arch.   Its effect is
much like that of the English dog-tooth ornament—a succession of sharp hard lights and shades, useful as giving
value and force to a very small piece of stonework, and
therefore exceedingly valuable when used as it is at S. Mark's,
and equally contemptible, I am bound to say, when used, as
it is in later work at Venice, simply as an ornament; for this

it is not and cannot be, as it is the result of no skill or taste on the part of the workman, but just such an enrichment as might be rather better done by machine than by hand. The roof of the nave is a painted timber roof, boarded in a series of cusped lines on the under side of the constructional framework, so as to hide it. I must not forget to add that the interior of San Stefano requires to be held together by iron ties in every direction—a sin to which, in Italy, the eye soon has to become accustomed.

The whole of the exterior is very carefully executed in brick, the moulded work being well done, though very late in date and not good in effect. The western doorway is of a favourite Venetian type. It is square-headed, enriched with mouldings and carving, and above it is an arched canopy with pinnacles on each side and with an ogee arched label carrying enormous crockets. The finial is a three-quarter

figure, and an angel occupies the spandrel between the arch and the label. Above the door is a large circular window, unadorned with tracery or filling-in of any kind. The window from the east end of the church, of which I give an engraving, is a very character istic example, of great width, and utterly unlike any example out of Venice.

WINDOW—SAN STEFANO.

Perhaps the very worst traceries in Venice—which is saying a good deal—are in the windows of the apse here, where the traceried arches of the head are repeated over the transom, but inverted and standing on their points. More worthy of admiration is a fine tomb corbelled out from the cloister wall to Andreas Contarina, "MCCCLVII. Dux creatus

Whiteman & Bass, Photo-Litho to the Queen.

25. SAN GIACOMO DEL RIALTO. VENICE.

MCCCLXXXII. in cœlum sublatus;" the arched bridge under
the choir (which is carried over a canal) should also be noted,
as well as the very fine campanile, which, though not boasting
of any Gothic detail, is full of the spirit which made the
earlier campanili so effective. But if we wish to see the best
campanile in Venice, I think we must go back to the Rialto,
and there, not far from the Grand Canal, we shall see in that
of San Giacomo a perfectly fine example.[1] It is almost entirely of brick, and the fine long lines of its arcades give a
great effect of height, whilst the details are all good and
quite Gothic in their character.

The other churches in Venice are of less importance than
those which I have described, but the number of remains, of
which only too many are desecrated, is very large. The
Accademia has attached to it the desecrated church of the
convent of La Carità. This has three parallel aisles ended
with apses, the usual traceries and cornices, and the unusual
(I am glad to say) feature of three western gables with
arched outlines[2] filled in with much small tracery in brick
and terra-cotta. Another desecrated church near this—that
of San Gregorio—is more interesting. It is of the same
general design as La Carità, and, like it, is built of yellowish
bricks. The window traceries are of white marble. The
most interesting feature here is the cloister, entered by a
remarkable doorway from the Grand Canal. The doorway is
square-headed, with an ogee trefoiled archway or window on
either side, and a sitting figure of a bishop under a slight
canopy over the doorway. The cloister has five bays on each
side, divided by columns which rest on a marble and brick
base, and carry a wooden framework enriched with very good
mouldings.

---

[1] I refer here to San Giacomo del Rialto. Its neighbour, San Giacomo del
Olio, has also a brick campanile, but of inferior merit.

[2] A view in the 'Nuremberg Chronicle' shews these three gables just as
they now are.

Another desecrated church is that "dei Servi," which has a fine lofty brick front with a large rose window.

In the Campo Sta. Zaccaria is a portal much like that of San Stefano, save that it has in the tympanum a good figure of the Blessed Virgin with Our Lord with a saint on each side—the two Saints John, I think. The Virgin is seated on a Gothic throne carved in very low relief, and the whole composition is decidedly fine; comparing it with the door-way at Mazzorbo, I should say this must be a work of A.D. 1380. The church of Sta. Zaccaria is an early Renaissance building, with many of its arches pointed. It has an aisle and chapels round the choir, an unusual plan in Venice, but otherwise it has no interest.

The church of l'Abbazia has some fair detail in its cornices, with pinnacles at its west end of the same type as those in the Madonna dell' Orto, and has poor ogee-headed pointed windows; near it is another of the canopied doorways—the gate of the Corte Vecchia—with an outer arched canopy, within which under an ogee-shaped label stands the Blessed Virgin with Our Lord in an aureole on her breast. Two saints stand at her side, and groups of little figures kneel at her feet, whilst from the upper finial Our Lord gives His blessing. This bears the date of 1505.

I think I have now said enough about these late Gothic churches. I have never been able to interest myself much about them. The work of which they are specimens is so exceedingly poor, cold, and distasteful to me, that I feel much inclined when I attempt to sketch them to give up ecclesiology in despair. The truth is that, S. Mark's excepted—and of course it is a very wonderful exception—the churches in Venice do not come up to the expectations of any one who has ever experienced the delight of visiting the churches of much smaller cities in France, Germany, and England. True, indeed, there are much interest and a great breadth and dignity about the general effect of such a church as that of the Frari; but for all those lovely points of detail which in every direction amaze us by the art they display and the rich array of beauty with which they clothe the walls of Northern cathedrals, there is here no kind of equivalent.

When I had thoroughly come to this conclusion, and settled in my own mind by repeated inspection that my judgment was not harsh or unfair, I confess I felt a weight off my mind. I was now free to indulge myself to the full in the search for what Venice really has in greater abundance, perhaps, than any other city in Christendom—remains, namely, of mediæval domestic work. Nothing can be conceived more delightful than such a search. You seldom go a hundred yards—often it is much less—without coming upon some remains, or perhaps some nearly perfect example, of an old Venetian palace; and then, with the gondola fastened to one of the great posts which line all the canals, the well-satisfied gondolier lying stretched on his back behind the awning, your friends laughing and talking within its dark recess, you sit most luxuriously, and make your notes and sketches with a degree of quiet comfort which is not a little conducive to accurate and careful sketching, and to diligence in its pursuit.

Venetian palaces divide themselves naturally into two great classes—the Byzantine and the Gothic; and it surprized me very much to find remains so perfect and so extensive of the former class even on the banks of the Grand Canal itself, where change has been ever so frequent and so rife. Indeed, it is singular that nearly all the Byzantine palaces are situated on its banks.

Of these palaces, certainly the most striking by far are the Ca' Loredan, the Ca' Farsetti, and the Fondaco de' Turchi. They all agree singularly in the general idea of their design, and consist of a grand scheme of arcading over

the entire front.   Divided generally into two stories in
height, they are again divided in a marked manner in width
into a centre and wings.   This division is effected solely by
a great difference in the spans of the arches forming the
arcades, which in the wings are much narrower than in the
central division. In the upper arcade the spaces between the
columns, and indeed the whole arrangement, are often studiously unlike those in the lower range; but, at the same time,
there is so very much similarity in the detail of the whole,
that this variety, far from being perceived as an irregularity
or a fault, does in truth just suffice to give force and vitality
to what might otherwise appear to be monotonous and too
often repeated, and recalls to mind not a little the very
similar kind of difference between the upper and lower order
of shafts already described in the west front of S. Mark's.

We cannot do better than take, as an example of the
finest type of a Byzantine palace, the magnificent, though
now desolate, decaying, and ruined façade of the Fondaco de'
Turchi, once the palace of the Dukes of Ferrara.   The whole
front of this was originally cased with a thin facing of marble,
like the coeval works at S. Mark's—a kind of decoration
which, neglected as this fine relic has been for years, we
cannot be surprized to find almost altogether destroyed;
small fragments do, however, still here and there remain to
tell of the original magnificence of the work.   The lower
stage of the Fondaco consists of a continuous arcade of ten
open arches, with three narrower arches at either end,
forming the wings, so to speak; the upper stage has eighteen
arches in the centre, and four in each wing.   In the wings
the piers supporting the arches are, I think, all moulded
pilasters; in the centre all the arches rest upon columns;
and throughout the whole building the arches, which are
all semicircular, are considerably stilted.   The entire building is constructed in brick, which was originally, as I have

before said, covered all over with a thin veneer of marble;
in the spandrels of all the arches this is relieved by small
circular medallions delicately carved, and over the upper
stage is a string-course, above which there would seem to
have been a long series of slightly sunk panels with round-
arched heads, filled in with delicately arranged and beautifully sculptured patterns in marble. These panels are
immediately below the eaves of the roof. Many of the abaci
and string-courses, and all the thin pieces of marble which
form the soffeits of the arches, have their projections finished
either with a nail-head or dentil moulding, and between the
shafts of the upper stage there are traces of balconies.[1]

A very noticeable point in the general effect of the façade
of the Fondaco de' Turchi is that, from the peculiar shape
and great projection of the capitals of the shafts and the
narrow span of the arches, the whole of the arcading has, at
a small distance, almost the effect of a series of trefoils, and
so seems to pave the way for the continuous traceries of the
Ducal Palace and other later buildings.

There is a ruined fragment of a house of the same age
as the Fondaco de' Turchi in a canal behind the Foscari
Palace. Here the centre arch is very wide, has four stilted
arches on the sides, the archivolts are all delicately carved,
and small sculptured medallions are introduced in the spandrels. Here, I think, the red brick of the walls was always
intended to be seen. Of very similar character is a much
larger fragment on the right of the Grand Canal after passing
under the Rialto. Here there are two stories still remaining.
The round-arched doorway has two open and stilted arches
on each side, and then a space of blank wall; and the upper
stage has a group of seven arches in the centre, and a single

---

[1] I leave this description as it stood in 1855. Since then the whole of
this interesting building has been so elaborately restored, that I doubt whether
an old stone remains. It has lost all its charm, and this was once intense.

arch at each end over the blank wall below. The labels of
these upper arches are turned up at the point into an ogee
shape, which, strange as it may seem, must be original, as
the detail is early, and they are surmounted by a collection
of carved medallions and a carved string-course of early
style.[1]

The Ca' Loredan has two stages in height, above which all
is modern—but all the Byzantine arrangements of these two
stages are perfect. There are five open arches in the centre,
and an arcaded pier on each side; and in the next stage,
though the division of centre and wings is preserved, the
arches are increased in number, and consequently the
columns of this stage do not come above those of the lower
stage. The string-courses are formed with a billet mould;
the capitals are some of them genuine Byzantine, and some
copies of Corinthian. The wall-faces were all inlaid, but
they were in part altered in the fourteenth century, when
some coats-of-arms and figures were added. Those at the
extreme angles are of David and Goliath, and on each side
of the centre sitting figures of Justice and Force.

Next to the Ca' Loredan is the Ca' Farsetti (now the
Municipio), which is, I think, slightly the older building of
the two. Here there are three arches resting on shafts in
the centre, and an equal number resting on piers on each
side, and a continuous arcade of fifteen arches on the upper
stage resting on coupled shafts.

The Palazzo Businetto on the Grand Canal opposite the
Ca' Grimani, has remains of Byzantine work in its two lower
stages. Here the caps are Byzantine in character, the
archivolts flat inlays, with a billet mould on each side, and
a carved string-course of running foliage inclosed between
two lines of notched or billet mould.

This short notice of some of the more important Roman-

---

[1] This house is in the Sestiere di Cannaregio, Parrochia San Canciano.

26 BYZANTINE WELL. VENICE.

esque and Byzantine remains enables me to make a few general deductions: (1.) These buildings were always of two stages in height. (2.) They had the entrance in the centre, and had generally a distinction between the centre and the wings. (3.) The capitals were generally Byzantine in character, but often copied from Corinthian. (4.) They were of brick, but generally veneered with thin slabs of marble. (5.) They were enriched with circular, square, and arched medallions inclosing carving of foliage and animals, and frequently of coupled birds or animals regarding each other,—a device always indicative of an early date and an Eastern origin; and (6.) The string-courses were generally carved either with continuous running foliage, or with leaves arranged in threes; the centre turning over, the side leaves extended flatwise, and upward. This last string-course is exactly copied from Sta. Fosca, Torcello, and is carved all round S. Mark's inside; whilst the former, though it is Byzantine in origin, is carried round the wall of the Ducal Palace between the south-east angle and the Bridge of Sighs. The illustration of a Byzantine cistern from the centre of a courtyard which I give, is useful as shewing very clearly the character of the carved foliage which adorns the string-courses and panels of these Byzantine buildings. This is always effectively carved with deep cuttings, which produce bright and sparkling effects of light and shade.

One especial fault of the Venetians seems to have been their proneness to repeat the same architectural idea an infinite number of times; and there is something in this so characteristic of the place and the people, that the reason for it is worthy of some consideration. Venice, surrounded by water, and cut off from that kind of emulation which in other places always has the effect of producing life and change very rapidly in the phases of art, seems to have contented herself, when once she had well done, with the

conviction that improvement was either impossible or
unnecessary, and so, whilst changes were going on in the
mainland, to have rested satisfied with a slight alteration
only, and that one of detail always, for centuries ; and it
is thus that I account for the singular sameness which
characterized all the efforts of her Gothic artists. The
façade of the Ducal Palace is really precisely the same in its
idea as that of the Fondaco de' Turchi or the Ca' Loredan,
altered only in detail—its very beautiful traceries taking
the place of, but doing the same work as, the simple encrusted arcades of ·its predecessors. And again, in the
fronts of other and much smaller palaces—indeed, in all the
fronts of the Gothic period—it is singular how exactly the
same idea in the general arrangement is always preserved.
Let me describe an ordinary palace. It is divided into three
or four stories in height, the several stages being generally
separated by string-courses. The lower story opens, by an
arched doorway in the centre, to the water ; and on either
side of this doorway a few small windows serve to light the
basement. The second stage has a grand window of some
five or six lights, divided by shafts of marble, and rich with
tracery, in the centre ; and on either side, one or two single
lights, with tracery corresponding with—and often, as it
were, cut out in a slice from—the traceries of the central
window. The third stage is nearly a reproduction of the
second, though sometimes slightly less important ; and the
upper stage is either again a repetition of the others, or else
consists of a few small windows placed over the others, and
very unimportant and unpretending. The whole is crowned
by a slightly projecting eaves-cornice, generally very meagre
in its character, and with a line of genuine dog-tooth ornament on its lower edge. Above this, probably—for only one
or two examples remain at all in their original state—was a
parapet like those which still in part remain on the Ca' d'Oro,

at the back of the Ca' Foscari, and on the Ducal Palace, light and fantastic to a degree, and almost masking the flat roof behind.

Such, as will be seen by the views with which, I doubt not, almost all my readers must be familiar, is the general idea of the Gothic palaces in Venice, and it admits of very slight modification. Occasionally, as in the Ca' d'Oro, the windows are inclosed within a square line of delicate moulding, the space within which is encrusted with marble, and entirely distinct from the string-courses, so as to give very much the impression of a plain wall veneered here and there with a window; or, again, sometimes the whole central division of the first and second stories is veneered on to a façade in which the other windows are treated construction-ally; but in all cases from first to last (except, as we shall see, in the Ducal Palace, and for this exception there is some explanation in its vast size and other reasons), the distinc-tion between the centre and the wings was never lost sight of, and never forgotten. This was the great idea of all these buildings, and most perseveringly was it reproduced down to the last, when, gradually losing even the life which beautiful detail had once lent, it sank through successive stages, until at last, easily and well-nigh imperceptibly, it succumbed, without a struggle, to the rise of the Renaissance feeling, giving only in revenge to its successor, the curse of an obligation still to go on building to the last, for whatever want or on whatever occasion, with the conviction that a centre and two wings must ever be necessary to a grand façade. It so happens that, in addition to the large and purely Byzantine palaces in which this arrangement is preserved,—in a delicate manner, it is true,—there still remains one remarkable example of the period of transition from Byzantine to Gothic, in a house which forms one side of the Corte del Remer (facing the Grand Canal just above the spot where it is spanned by the Rialto), which serves to shew clearly the first attempt at translation of this Byzantine idea into Gothic.

In the principal story of this house the central feature is the entrance doorway, whose finely ornamented arch of markedly horseshoe outline is very conspicuous. On either side of this, and connected with it in one group, are two windows divided by shafts and with arches of very singular shape; it is as though a stilted semicircular arch had been suddenly turned up in the centre, not with the graceful ogee curve of later days, but with simple, hard, straight lines. Beyond these windows, one of later date, but probably inserted in the place of the original window, completes the similarity which the arrangement of the openings in this house bears to that common in all the later Gothic palaces. The arches which support the staircase in front of this house are entirely executed in brick, and are probably later in date than the house itself, though it is noticeable that they are of a very early and pure type, and that here, as generally throughout the North of Italy, the pointed arch was first used in construction, and then, some time after its first introduction, and very generally in some modified form, for ornamentation also.

And now, having so far cleared the way, let me ask my readers to go with me to the Ducal Palace, and there undertake a somewhat careful examination of its very famous design.

I shall not enter into a general description of the entire building, because, as this has undergone prodigious alterations since its first erection, it is unnecessary to do much more than refer to the two fronts, which still retain, nearly without alteration, their mediæval design, and to those portions only of the interior and courtyard which have not been altered.

The whole building forms three sides of a hollow square :

27.—CORTE DEL REMER, VENICE.

one side rises out of the deep recesses of the Rio del Palazzo, spanned near its outlet by the famous Bridge of Sighs, and is entirely of Renaissance work; the next side, rising from the Riva dei Schiavoni, faces the Giudecca, and is of the purest Venetian Gothic; and the third, facing the Piazzetta di San Marco—the small square which connects S. Mark's with the water—is also Gothic, and of the same type. The back or north side of the palace abuts upon S. Mark's.

I cannot pretend to decide at all absolutely upon the vexed question of the dates of the mediæval portions, because, as the reader will find in an interesting discussion on the subject in the second volume of Mr. Ruskin's 'Stones of Venice,' it is a source of hot disputes. But the following appear to me to be the main points.

The Ducal Palace was burnt in 1105, restored in 1116, and rebuilt in 1173—1177. The two columns on the Piazzetta were brought to Venice in 1172, about which time the two Piazze were formed. Between this date and 1301, nothing is recorded to have been done to the palace. But even at this date it was a grand building, and is described in 1275 by Maestro Martino da Canale as "Grande e bellissimo a maraviglia."[1] He was equally enthusiastic about the church of "Monsignore San Marco," and of his campanile, "so great and so high that one cannot find its equal." Sivos in his chronicle (A.D. 1621) says that the Sala Grande was commenced in 1301, and completed in 1310, at which date the Grand Council consisted of nine hundred members; and one Pietro Baseggio is said to have been the architect between 1309 and 1361; he was succeeded or assisted by Filippo Calandario, and both of them, according to Zanotto, were described as being architects, sculptors, and navigators![2] Calandario had raised himself from the

---

[1] Zanotto, 'Il Palazzo Ducale di Venezia,' i. 39.
[2] Ibid., i. 52–60.

humble post of shipbuilder at Murano, to that of Capo
Maestro of the Ducal Palace, a man of great weight in the
city, but finally finished his career only too much in accordance with custom, being convicted as one of Marino Falieri's
fellow-conspirators, and hung from the balcony of the
Ducal Palace in A.D. 1355.

On the 28th of December, 1340, a decree was issued
ordering the construction of a staircase on the east side of the
palace to lead to the new rooms, which seems to establish the
fact that at this date a considerable portion at any rate of
the second stage was built. The plague visited Venice in
1359 and 1361, and stopped all work. In 1362, because the
unfinished work was going to ruin, the Council determined
to complete the new hall; and in 1365, this being done,
Guariento of Padua began to paint it, in the time of the
Doge Mario Cornaro.[1]

The capital next the south-west angle of the lower
stage bears a date which appears to some[2] to be 1344 (as to
which I have never been able to satisfy myself), and long
afterwards we find the date, 1404, on the large window
of the highest story of the sea-front. Finally, in 1419,
there was a great fire which damaged the old portion of
the building, so much that a decree was passed to rebuild it
in conformity with the rest, and this work was completed in
1423, when the council sat in their great council chamber for
the first time; and in 1439-41 the last Gothic work was added
to the palace by the Doge Foscari, viz. the Porta della Carta,
built (as appears by their contract) by Giovanni and Barto-

---

[1] "1362, die iv. Dec. Quia est magnus honor civitatis providere quod sala
magna majoris consilii nova non vadat in tantam desolationem in quantam
vadit cum notabili damno nostri communis: et sicut clare comprehendi potest,
leviter potest compleri, et reduci ad terminum, quod satis bene stabit cum non
magna quantitate pecuniæ; vadit pars quod dicta sala nova compleri debeat,"
&c. &c.—Decree in Zanotto, i. 72.

[2] Mr. Burges, in his account of the capitals, 'Annales Archéologiques,'
vol. xvii. pp. 74-88.

lomeo Bons, between the years 1438 and 1443, in the small
space which intervenes between the north-west angle of the
Ducal Palace and the south side of S. Mark's.   All these dates
are important, and I believe undisputed, the only question
being as to which parts of the building they refer to.

And now, before I say more about dates, let me describe
these two Gothic fronts—the sea-front and the Piazzetta-
front—and then we may perhaps see our way to some sort of
comprehension of the relative ages of the various portions of
the fabric.

The whole design is divided into three stages in height,
the upper nearly equal to the united height of the two
lower stages, and faced entirely with a delicate diaper of
marble cut in small oblong pieces, which look, save in their
texture and colour, only too much like bricks.   In this
marble-faced wall are pierced a number of windows with
pointed arches—the tracery of which has been taken out
—and in or near the centre of each façade a much larger
window and balcony, which look as though they had been
subsequently inserted.   The lowest stage consists of a long
and uniform arcade of very simple pointed arches resting
upon circular columns with elaborately carved caps; these
have been shortened by some twenty inches of their old
height, by the rise of the water, and the consequent elevation of the pavement of the Riva, to the great damage of
their effect.   The intermediate stage is a magnificent arcade,
supporting very vigorous tracery, too well known to everybody to require much description, and divided from the
stages above and below it by large and pronounced lines of
carved and moulded string-courses.

It is important to observe that up to the top of
the second string-course the whole of the architecture
is of the very best kind of Venetian pointed; the arches
of the lowest stage are well proportioned, and, though

very simply, still well moulded; and the detail of the whole of the second stage is, to say the least, not at all inferior. They form together, without exception, I believe, from all I have either seen myself or heard, the very best and truest specimen of Gothic architecture south of the Alps.

Above this noble work the third stage comes, and I confess, to my eye, with patent marks in every stone of which it is composed, that it was designed by some other hand than that which had been so successful below. There is something quite chilling in the great waste of plain unbroken wall coming above the extreme richness of the arcades which support it; and moreover, this placing of the richer work below and the plainer above is so contrary not only to all ordinary canons of architecture, but just as much to the ordinary practice of the Venetians, that I feel sure that the impression which I have had from my first acquaintance with drawings of it is substantially correct, viz. that the line at which alterations and additions have been made is to be looked for rather in a horizontal than in a vertical direction; that in all probability, consequently, the builder of A.D. 1301 commenced with some portion of the sea-façade and gradually carried on the greater part of the building to the height of the two stages as we now see them, leaving his building finished in precisely the same way as the corresponding halls at Padua and Vicenza—two stories in height, with arcades covering the outer walls of the upper as well as of the lower stage; and that when the Council Chamber was found to be too small, and larger rooms were required, another architect suggested the advantage of obtaining them by raising an immense story above the others, and, without destroying much of his predecessor's work, providing rooms on the most magnificent scale for the Doge and his Council.

The assumption that the Piazzetta-front has been copied from the sea-front involves a belief in a veneration for and exact imitation of older work which is (to say the least) extraordinarily rare, if not unique, in mediæval works.   It involves a belief also in the possibility of a spirited and successful copy being made of an old capital by a mediæval sculptor without fresh thought or any fresh invention of any kind.   This will be seen if we examine the capitals of the lower stage of the palace.   Here at first sight one is struck by what appears to be the astonishing variety of the capitals. They are nearly all adorned with figures or subjects as well as with foliage, and are certainly in both fronts of various degrees of merit; but on closer acquaintance it is perceived that the variety of capitals is not so great as it seems, for that several of those in each front are merely replicas of those in the other.   If any portion of the two lower stages had been built before the rest, it would have been the whole of the sea-front and six arches of the Piazzetta-front, for at the end of these there is a column equal in size to those at the angles, and which might therefore by possibility itself have been an angle column for a time.   But its larger size may also fairly be accounted for by the fact that it comes under the side wall of the large building above, and was in any case therefore a convenient arrangement if not quite a necessity ; but the real difficulty seems to me to be, that if there were any considerable difference in the date of these works, all experience would lead one to expect that the earlier works would be the most uniform and the best, whereas in point of fact this is far from being the case.   For instance, in the sea-front there are various capitals which are of poor execution.   These are, counting from the south-east angle, the third (large and coarse heads), the eighth (also coarse heads), the thirteenth (lions' heads), the fourteenth (beasts), and the fifteenth, which is certainly not so fine as the replica in the Piazzetta-front (the twenty-sixth capital, counting as before).[1]

The case for the contemporaneous erection of these two fronts becomes even stronger if we ascend to the open gallery on the first floor and examine the capitals there. They are all similar in general character; and though they become gradually better as one goes from the south-east to the north-west, they give the impression of all being of nearly one date, and moreover they all appear to be later in date than the whole of those in the lower stage.

On the other hand, there seem to be at least two points which make strongly in favour of the later date which has been given to the twelve northern arches of the Piazzetta-front. These are, first, that all the eight capitals which are replicas are in this northern part of the front, and none of them in the first six arches from the south-west angle; and, secondly, that the plate armour in the sculpture above the capital of the north-east angle (Judgment of Solomon) is later in date than the period which I assume for this work, and later than the chain mail shown in the third and eighth capitals of the sea-front. To the first objection a sufficient answer is that some of the best of the capitals to these twelve arches are of original design—not replicas; and in reply to the last objection (which is of much force) the only, but at the same time obvious reply is, that the Trajan capital, just under this late armour, is one of the most beautiful of the entire series, and that on the whole it is much more likely that some of the sculpture was left in block and finished later, than that no difference should be made in any of the mouldings or details of the

---

[1] The capitals which are replicas of each other are the 4th and 35th, the 7th and 28th, the 8th and 31st, the 9th and 29th, the 10th and 30th, the 11th and 34th, the 12th and 33rd, the 15th and 26th. The 25th, 27th, 32nd, and 36th (north-east angle) are original, though they are in the northern portion of the Piazzetta-front. See Appendix, with key-plan.

work of two periods.   There is indeed some, though not
very strong, evidence that the sculpture of this capital
is not earlier than about 1423.   There is, according to
Zanotto, an inscription on it, "+ Duo Soci Florentini incise,"
and he argues from the use of this last word, that the two
men were the same who made the monument to the Doge
Tommaso Mocenigo in 1423, in which, according to Sansovino, they used the same unusual term "inciserunt;" this
interpretation of the inscription is the more allowable in
that, as I have said, the details of armour in themselves
suggest a date not much earlier than this for the sculpture
connected with it on the angle just above the cap.   This
date of course brings this work to very nearly the same period
as that of the execution of the Porta della Carta, and it has
been assumed by some that these capitals were the work of
the Bons who built it.   Such an assertion is as wild as that
of M. Didron, who says something as to their belonging to
the thirteenth century, for the very shortest inspection of the
Porta della Carta would convince the most sceptical that no
part of the capitals could have been executed by any of the
men who wrought at it.   In comparing the merits of the
carvers of the earliest and the latest capitals, it is due to the
latter to say that one of the finest of the whole series is this
Trajan capital at the north-west angle, and there is no
internal evidence in it which could lead one to suppose it to
be the work of a man who would ever condescend to copy
another's work.

No one can examine the building without seeing that
there is not only in the detail, but equally in the general
design, a marked difference between the two lower stages
and the upper stage.   In place of the extreme boldness
which marks every part of the former, we see mouldings
reduced in the latter to the smallest and meanest section
possible ; the windows of the upper stage are badly designed,

whilst the traceries of the second stage are as fine as they
can possibly be ; the angle-shafts of the upper stage are of
the latest type, elaborately twisted and violently defined,
instead of being merely delicate roundings off of the hard
line of wall, as all the early Venetian angle-shafts are ; the
parapet, too, is not equal in its design to any of the lower
work, and crowns with an insignificant grotesqueness the
noble symmetry of the two lower arcades ; and finally,
the chequer-work of marble which forms the whole of the
upper wall is a mode of construction which I have not seen
in any early work, though it is seen in the Porta della
Carta (A.D. 1429), and in one other late work, the Palazzo
in the Campo Sta. Maria Mater Domini.[1]

Looking at all the circumstances of the case, I think the
fairest explanation of them is, that the whole sea front and
the six arches of the Piazzetta (columns 1 to 24 on the
plan) were first built, that the extension to the north
(columns 25 to 36 on plan) was then immediately undertaken
by the same artists, and finally that the whole upper story
was built and the sculpture of its capitals completed before
1423. The capitals of the lower arcade were probably
sculptured by degrees, and certainly not by one hand,
between the years 1310 and 1361.

There is a confirmation to some extent of this view in
a MS. in the Bodleian Library of the fourteenth century
(the Romance of Alexander), which contains a curious
contemporary view of Venice. This drawing has been engraved at p. 26 of the second volume of the ' Domestic Architecture of the Middle Ages ;'[2] here it will be seen, with the
usual amount of licence which characterizes most mediæval

---

[1] The similar marble facing at Vicenza was executed between 1400 and
1444. See p. 144.
[2] Published by Mr. Parker, of Oxford, to whose courtesy I owe the use of
this illustration.

28.—VENICE IN THE FOURTEENTH CENTURY.

From the Romance of Alexander.

representations of places or towns, that it has nevertheless been intended as an absolute representation of what its
draughtsman had seen. The columns with S. Theodore and
the lion of S. Mark on their capitals, the bronze horses and
the domes of S. Mark's, the position by the waterside, and
the representation of the Ponte di Paglia, are all proofs of
this; but the important point for my present purpose is, that
he drew the Ducal Palace as *a building of two stories in
height*—the first a simple arcade, the second an arcade with
tracery. In the distance behind this, his drawing shews a
picturesque assemblage of buildings, whilst figures are represented behind the upper arcade as though it were only a
kind of immense balcony. There can be no doubt whatever
that this old drawing tells in favour of the view that the
upper stage was not built until after a considerable interval;
for it is almost impossible—looking at the way in which the
rest of the drawing is made—to believe that all reference to
it would have been omitted, had it been in existence at the
time the artist saw it.

It will be seen that my supposition that the original
design of the Ducal Palace was of considerably less elevation
than the present building, would tend to make it very much
more like the Byzantine type than it is; but even now
no one can dispute the family likeness. The amount of
constructive art is as nearly as possible the same. The
weight is supported by a succession of shafts placed at very
short intervals from each other, and in neither is there any
approach to the system of pier, arch, and buttress, so distinc-
tive of Gothic art in the North of Europe. The pointed arch
is used, it is true, in the palace; but, after all, the mere
use of the pointed arch does not make thorough pointed
architecture, and therefore, interesting as it is as a variety
of the style, the Ducal Palace is, I think, not properly
to be placed in the first class of Gothic buildings. Indeed,

the second stage, whose exquisite beauty is the charm of the whole building, does not exhibit the pointed arch at all in a properly developed form, and is strong enough to support the great weight of wall above, only by reason of the massy character of its tracery, and not by the proper application of constructional arches. I have already said that there is no approach to buttressing; but the angles require some help, and this is given partly by increasing considerably the size of the shafts, and partly by iron ties at the springing of the arches running for some distance in each direction from the angles.

All the mouldings are very simple; they are generally composed of three-quarter beads, small fillets, and large flat hollows, constantly arranged in the same order. The label of the main arcade is a plain bead. In the string-courses boldly-carved flowers are repeated with a slight interval between each, and the upper string-course has a row of nail-heads in one of its members. The cusping of the tracery is quite square in its section, and the cusps finish with a square end, to which is attached—and with good effect—a small circular ball of red marble. The parapet is of the somewhat peculiar kind I have already mentioned, and I confess I have never been long enough in Venice to accustom myself to, or to admire, its extreme peculiarity of both outline and design.

And now before we leave this subject let me offer a remark, as every one who writes on it must, on the admirable story of these sculptures. I have never sat in front of one of them for any space of time without seeing some wayfarer stop to study the story of some one of the capitals. They are a book at which more thousands have looked with pleasure for some five hundred years than at any other single book in the world, with the one exception of the Bible. And the lesson to architects is obvious. Concentrate your labour and

your story on some one part of your building where all men
may read it ; tell some simple story and you will interest
your readers, if you will but tell it so simply that by good
chance they may be able to read it. Lay out a scheme so
well that if you die your successor may carry it on. Here,
as I believe, the architect completed his two stages of
arcades, whilst the sculptor was changed, but kept generally
to the scheme of subjects first of all laid down. At the three
exposed angles are the three archangels, below them the
moral lesson—as much wanted now as then—of the Drunkenness of Noah, and the Story of Tobit (with S. Raphael) ; at
another angle The Fall (under S. Michael) ; and at the last
the Judgment of Solomon (under S. Gabriel). In the lower
range of capitals the stories and catalogues of virtues and
vices ; the illustrations of fruits, animals, every-day life ; the
labours of the months, trades, sciences, and arts—are all
illustrated, and complete a cycle of subjects which, ill-treated,
would always have a certain value, and which, well treated
as most of them are here, have the very highest charm.

For a building which owes its general impressiveness
entirely to the uniform character of its architecture, it is
especially fortunate that there should be so much also in
the detail to attract and reward constant and minute examination. It is for this reason that the range of great
capitals to the columns of the lower arcade is of so much
importance. They are so large, so close to the eye, so
interesting in their story, and on the whole so carefully and
artistically executed, as to afford the greater pleasure the
more the building is known. The key-plan to these capitals
which I give[1] will be useful to shew what the general arrangement of the subjects is. I have already shewn that
there are repetitions of many of the subjects, but it is equally
worth notice that the foliage which forms the framework for

---

[1] See Appendix at the end of the volume.

the subjects is also repeated.   There are, I think, only four
varieties in its arrangement.   In the first the capitals are
arranged very simply—in some cases rudely—with tufts of
foliage or heads.   The capitals numbered 2, 3, 6, 13, 16, 20,
23, 27, and 34, are examples of this.   In the next the foliage
of the lower part grows up vertically, bending slightly out to
support the sculptured subjects.   These are generally the
most graceful of all, and infinitely richer in effect than the
first class.   The capitals numbered 1, 7, 9, 12, 18, 24, 26, 28,
33, and 36, are examples of these.   In the third class the
foliage is generally marked by the same feeling, but it rises
vertically to the angles, and curls over under the subject;
the 19th and 25th capitals are examples of this class.   In
the fourth class the foliage curves over downwards, both at
the angles and under the subject.   The neckings below the
capitals are wrought on the shaft itself. They are sometimes
moulded, sometimes corded, and sometimes delicately carved
with foliage; these last are by very much the more beautiful,
and generally accompany the best wrought of the capitals,
whilst the inferior capitals have, in all cases, the plainer
necking.

The capitals in the upper arcade have not so much story
as those below.   They have generally a head on each side in
the midst of foliage, and are square in plan, though the
lower caps are octagonal—a few only have their names
written over them; but on the ground-story most of the
capitals have, or have had, explanatory inscriptions.   Some
of the upper capitals close to the north-west angle are among
the best.   The curves of the foliage in the angles of the
capitals are admirably wrought, and may be compared, to
the damage of the latter, with some of the lower capitals in
the sea-front.   The upper range of capitals gradually de-
teriorates from the north-west angle as you go to the south-
east. These last are really very bad, having rude gross carving

of the human figure, and foliage feebly massed and treated ; but the upper capital of the south-west angle with the figures of the four winds, and the two or three capitals near it, must be excepted from this remark, being superb in design and execution.

The remains of original work in the quadrangle are much less important. The arcade on the first floor remains, but none of its details are good, and on the east side it is a poor Renaissance copy of the other sides. The whole of the lower arcade has been destroyed or altered. But in the upper walls, which are faced with brick, some of the original windows remain; they are small, but of the same sort of detail and character as the larger windows in the outer walls.

The building has lost much by the gradual raising of the pavement. This is now about twenty inches above the old base of the columns, and their proportions are so far altered for the worse. And it has lost immensely also by the destruction of the inlaid marble which once filled all the spandrels of the main arcade. Two panels only of these remain, and both in the sea-front. They are charmingly designed, inclosing circles which exactly touch the labels and strings.

Of the modern additions to this grand building I shall not say anything. They are not beautiful in themselves nor interesting by reason of their decorations, if I except those walls on which Tintoretto has lavished so much of his skill. The architects of the fourteenth and fifteenth centuries were artists in very deed, and it is with their work only that I can feel any real sympathy.

Such, then, is the Ducal Palace : a building certainly in some respects of almost unequalled beauty, but at the same time of unequal merit; its first and second stages quite perfect in their bold nervous character, and in the almost interminable succession of the same beautiful features in

shaft and arch and tracery, forming perhaps one of the
grandest proofs in the world of the exceeding value of perfect
regularity and of a repetition of good features in architecture,
when it is possible to obtain it on a very large scale.

Leaving the Piazzetta, and stepping into the gondola
which has been waiting for us hard by, let us now go
in search of other palaces ; but let us not imagine that we
are to see anything equal to the Ducal Palace.   There is, it
appears to me, a great gap between it and all other Venetian
buildings ; and yet all others seem to have been founded on
it, or on the buildings out of which it grew.   Their traceries,
seldom absolutely alike, have still so much general similarity
that at first one may well fancy that there is no variety at
all ; and, as I have before said, the general arrangement of
their windows and doors is so nearly identical, that this
impression is the more likely to grow upon the mind.

We will not attempt to take the buildings as they come ;
but rather as we think of them, and to some extent in the
order of their merit, let us note down a few of the glories of
the domestic work of Venice.   And first let us stop in this
narrow canal, for we have by our side one of the most
exquisite little pieces of detail in the whole city.   It is
an archway, simple and delicate in its proportions, lovely as
it is simple, and appropriately placed hard by the bridge
called " del Paradiso."   I trust that my sketch is clear
enough to shew how pure and good the work is.   The main
points to be noted are the characteristic flatness of the
details, and the line of dentil-moulding, which defines all
the leading architectural features, originally invented for
borders of incrustations at S. Mark's, and here, as everywhere in Venice, used for decoration afterwards.   The
incrusted circles of marble on each side of the figure give
great life to the spandrel beneath the arch, and the windows
seen behind shew us a late example of the not unfrequent

29.—ARCHWAY, PONTE DEL PARADISO, VENICE.

use of the semicircular and ogee arches together in the same
window.

Another precious fragment—the Palazzo San Giorgio,
I believe—is reached from the land side by passing under
an arch somewhat similar to that on the Ponte del Paradiso.
This arch is turned between the upper stories of two houses
at the end of a *calle* properly yclept " dell' arco detto bon,"
and is finished with a steep gable. Beyond it is seen a
fragment of wall veneered with marble, with the upper part
of an early two-light window, and two circular medallions;
and above this a piece of wall veneered in diamonds of red
and white marble—so far as I know, a unique example of
such a treatment. The window-head is of that earliest form
of ogee, a circle just turned up to a point in the centre,
which has so manifestly an Eastern origin, and which must
not be confounded in date with our English ogee arches.

In another, and rather desolate, canal in the outskirts of
the city, wider than usual, and with a footpath at the side
of the water, instead of having the walls of the houses
running down into it, and forming its boundary, is the
Palazzo Cicogna, which I remember gratefully because it
is one of the few exceptions to the general rule of regularity. The whole design of this building is very irregular :
a detached shaft at one angle supports a portion of the
house which overhangs and forms a sort of open passage-
way ; to the right of this opening is a four-light shafted
window, and then a plain wall pierced with two windows,
each of a single ogee trefoiled light. The upper story has
two single windows over the others, whilst over the larger
windows and the passage-way is a large window conspicuous
from its size and the peculiarity of its tracery. It is of six
lights divided by very good shafts, and properly arched with
pure and good trefoiled arches ; above these, and inclosed
within the perpetual indented or billeted string-course, is a

complicated system of intersecting circles pierced at regular
intervals with quatrefoils. The section of this upper part
is very much thinner than that of the arches beneath.
This window is in a most shaken and decayed state, and not
likely, I fear, to be long preserved. The whole elevation is
finished with a shallow cornice supported on corbels.

A doorway on the Ponte San Tomà is quite worthy of a
visit. It has the usual square opening of reddish marble,
and above this is a pointed arch of moulded brick; the
tympanum is filled in with a square carved centre panel,
and the ground beyond this with quatrefoils of brick or tile
very prettily disposed, and quite deserving of illustration.

And now let us go back to the Grand Canal; we
shall enter it by the side of the Palazzo Foscari, which,
with two other contiguous palaces, occupies quite the post
of honour at the bottom of the principal reach of the
canal, and commands the whole view of its noble and
ever-busy way to where the arch of the Rialto and another
bend in the canal close in the view. We will go a few
strokes only towards the Rialto, and then turn round to
look at the palaces we have just passed. They certainly
form a most magnificent group, and are in every way
worthy of their conspicuous position. The palace at the
junction of the two waters is that of the Foscari; the
others belonged, I believe, to two of the Giustiniani family;
and but a few yards up the canal, which runs by the side of
the former, is one of the smaller remnants of Byzantine
work already referred to. This group is so well known as
scarcely to need any description—suffice it to say, therefore, that throughout these palaces the windows are shafted,
and the glass is fixed in wooden frames behind the stonework. This is beyond all doubt what we ought to do; it is
the only sensible and rational mode of adapting the system
of traceried and shafted windows for domestic purposes, and

30 DOORWAY. PONTE S. TOMA. VENICE.

has here, as elsewhere, the prestige of ancient authority to
recommend it to the consideration of those amongst us who
will do nothing without it. I have enlarged on this point
elsewhere, and will, therefore, say no more upon it now,
save that in Venice such a thing as an English monial
ordinarily is, was never known. Windows were invariably
shafted from the earliest period to the latest, and so far
invariably of the highest order, inasmuch as they admitted
of the definite expression of the point at which the monial
terminated and the arch commenced, and inasmuch, too,
as the coloured surface of the detached marble shaft must
ever be far more lovely than the lines of tracery mouldings
carried down even to the sill.

The angle-shafts of the Palazzo Foscari have caps and
bases in each stage of the building ; those of the other
palaces continue up without interruption.

The date of the smaller palaces, and probably of the
large one also, is very early in the fifteenth century ; and
the latter had, in 1574, the honour of being the grandest
palace that the Venetians could find in which to lodge
Henry III. of France. They are all three very similar in
their design. Their water-gates are pointed, and the windows
in the water-stage small and unimportant. The second stage
is more important, and has cusped ogee window-heads and
balconies. The third stage is, however, the *piano nobile*, all
the windows having deep traceried heads and large balconies.
The fourth stage is very nearly like the first, save that
instead of balconies there is a delicate balustrading between
the shafts of the windows, which is very frequent in good
Venetian work, and always very pretty in its effect. All the
windows in these three palaces have ogee-heads generally
finished with carved finials, and inclosed within a square
outline formed by the small dentilled moulding, and giving
what I have before had to refer to—to some extent the

effect of a panel with a window pierced in it, veneered on the front. The Foscari Palace is the only one of these three that has any string-courses. The arrangement of the windows—large in the centre and smaller at the sides—is so nearly regular and of a sort of two-and-two kind of uniformity, that one scarcely notices that nevertheless, when internal arrangements make it necessary, a departure from this strict rule is allowed.

The back entrance to the Foscari Palace is on the side canal. It is of some interest as retaining, in a very perfect state, an example of a very picturesque treatment in brick of the Venetian battlement. This consists of a series of piers finished with a steep gabled outline, and pierced with trefoiled openings. A good example of this sort of battlement remained near the Fondaco de' Turchi, and deserves illustration. It is quite a Venetian invention, and errs on the side of quaintness.

BRICK BATTLEMENT—VENICE.

In a small courtyard, desolate and dreary, reached after crossing the Ponte di Paglia and one or two other bridges on the Riva dei Schiavoni, is the Palazzo Badoer, a fourteenth-century palace, the ogeed arches of the windows in which are more than usually good; whilst the beauty of the central window, inclosed within a square line of moulding, within which the wall is incrusted with marble relieved by medallions, is very great. The structure of this, as of most Venetian palaces, is brick which has been frescoed; but it is now in a very lamentable state of decay. The balconies of the lower windows are clearly modern, but there is a trace of the original balustrade between the shafts of the windows in the second stage; and in front of the side-lights to the upper window is a grille of iron-work taking the place of a balcony, and composed of a combination of quatrefoils. The arrangement of the windows in this front is not absolutely regular, but still the centre is very marked; and though it is of early date, the true use of the arch nowhere appears. The usual[1] dog-tooth cornice finishes the walls under the eaves. In the courtyard of this house are two of the wells which give so much character to all the courts in Venice. They appear generally to be of early date, and look, frequently, like the capitals of large columns, taken down and placed upon the ground. Those in front of the Palazzo Badoer are perhaps more like fonts.

Another palace, also said to belong to one of the Badoer family, placed at the junction of two canals very near the Scuola di San Giorgio and the Greek Church, is remarkable as being now one of the very few houses in which the red brick walls are still in their original state, and not defiled by compo, paint, or whitewash. This house has three fronts, with one old doorway on the canal, and two on the land. The back facing the Campo San Severo has an unusually fine and lofty entrance, a square doorway with a pointed arch above (which I suppose once held tracery), and a group of five windows with circles or disks of marble in their spandrels

---

[1] I say "usual," because it is really quite curious to see how repeatedly either the dog-tooth or the nail-head is used in this position. The commonest eaves-cornice consists of a simple chamfered stone—the chamfer covered with dog-tooth—supported on moulded corbels at short intervals.

above. Amongst other things it is remarkable as an instance
of the way in which windows were sometimes placed absolutely at the very angles of the building. Judging by the
similarity of its tracery to that above the Porta della Carta
in the Ducal Palace, this angle window must date from about
1400 to 1430. It has a very bold shaft at the angle, whilst the
jambs have pilasters ornamented at their angles by a twisted
cord-like moulding, which is frequently met with in the
later work. There is a small angle-shaft elaborately twisted
just above this window, and very much like the angle-shafts
of the Ducal Palace.

The composition of the main window in the front of this
house is, I think, very striking. The lower window of four
lights (one of which is larger and loftier than the others—a
curious instance of the junction of regularity with irregularity), and whose arches are ogee trefoils, is surmounted by
another window of four lights, with delicate balustrading
between the shafts; and on each side of this upper window,
and forming part of the composition, is a single light, with
projecting balcony. The effect of the whole arrangement is
pleasing, and is frequently repeated in other palaces. The
marble incrustation over this window is very much like that
in the other Palazzo Badoer; and from the centre of the
medallions of marble small balls of marble project, fixed with
metal, and giving great life and beauty to the medallions,
and I think without any sacrifice of truth. The main fabric
of this building must be of the latter part of the fourteenth
century—the arches of the principal window being of a very
excellent though simple type. Venetian balconies, of which
this palace affords such good examples, are very beautiful
and very characteristic. Nowhere else are they seen in
such perfection ; nowhere else, perhaps, were they ever so
absolutely necessary. The palaces rose out of the dark
water which washed against their foundations, and no ground

31.—ANGLE WINDOW, VENICE.

could be given up for shady arcades as in other Italian cities,
nor were there any paths to be strolled along; the only
resource was, therefore, to gain from the air that which the
land could not afford, and by projections in front of the
windows to obtain that power of enjoying the delicious
evening atmosphere, so cool and pleasant after the fatigues
of the too sultry day. These balconies are almost always
very similar, consisting of a number of delicate shafts with

BALCONY—VENICE.

carved capitals, supporting a piece of stone whose under side
is notched up in a series of trefoils (generally ogee), resting
upon the capitals of the shafts. These are divided occasionally by pilasters, under which are corbels jutting out
boldly to support their weight; and above which sit, generally,
quietly and placidly eyeing the gondolas as they shoot
silently by, small lions, dogs, or other animals—a quaint
finish which one soon learns to like; their angles are often
marked by corded mouldings, and the edges of their floors

and copings are almost always moulded and specked with the perpetual notchings of the nail-head, and their under sides or soffeits are frequently carved or panelled.

There was great variety in the planning of these balconies. In the Palazzo Persico, for instance, in which the central windows of the second and third stages form one great panel, the lower balcony is continuous across all four lights of the window, whilst the outer lights only of the upper window have balconies, the two middle lights having instead a balustrade between their shafts. In other cases the balconies extend to four lights only of a six-light window, whilst in most they are confined to the central windows, to which they give much additional dignity. The Ca' Fasan affords an almost solitary example [1] of tracery in a balcony; and the effect of this is so vastly inferior to the usual shafted balconies, that it seems scarcely necessary to pause to consider why it should be so. Obviously, however, it is not very convenient to have the fretful points of cusps and traceries set, as it were, to catch every projection or point of your dress whenever you lean over the edge of the balcony to inhale the fresh air or scan the busy scene below.

In the Casa Persico, to which reference has already been made, the central window is an elaborate composition of the same kind; but the lower one is of more importance, and has a continuous balcony; and here I may notice the finials with which the ogee arches of Venetian windows are so often finished. They appeared to me to be invariably tasteless and poor in execution, and very mean in their outline. I did not see one finial in Venice which was satisfying, even when found in conjunction with otherwise fine work; and I used to wish heartily, when I reached some palace not before seen, that

---

[1] There is another traceried balcony in the canal near the Bridge of Sighs. It is the only other example I know in Venice.

I might find its arches finished without them. There was some reason for the wish, too, in the fact that it is in the later work that these tasteless ornaments are commonest. I saw them first at Verona, and lamented over them there, but at Venice I was positively annoyed by the persevering and endless thrusting of their poverty and badness upon my wearied eyes.

And now let us go again into the Grand Canal, and we shall not have gone very far up the broad water above the Rialto before we shall find, on our right hand, one of the most striking groups of mediæval palaces and houses which can be seen anywhere, even in Venice; this is where the famous Ca' d'Oro unites with some three or four other houses, of rather earlier date, and gives a very fair idea of what the water-scenery of the ancient city once was. There is some difficulty in criticizing the Ca' d'Oro, because, in the first place, it has been restored to render it fit for the occupation of Mdlle. Taglioni; and, in the next place, much of the elaborate decoration from which it derived its name, has perished or been destroyed. As it is, however, it is still a very sumptuous example of the later fourteenth-century Gothic. Its whole face is inlaid with squares of red and white marble, and a great amount of carving is spread over the entire surface, round and between the windows. This is very flat, but good in its effect. The arcade on the water-story, and the traceried arcades above, all open into recessed courts—an arrangement peculiar, I think, among Gothic houses, and similar in its purpose to the arcades in the Byzantine palaces. Some of the balconies are good, and the carving of the capitals and moulding of the window-traceries are very characteristic of Venetian pointed. The whole design is one-sided, and gives the impression of a house to which an additional wing has been added. The water-stage consists of an open arcade of five arches, the

central arch round, the remainder pointed, and on one side
of these are two windows with a continuous balcony. The
second and third stages have, above the five open arches,
elaborately traceried windows, of no less than eight lights
in width, filling almost the entire front, the outside lights
having balconies, whilst the others have balustrading. Over
the two windows of the water-stage are single-light windows
in each stage. There are throughout this front many
medallions of dark marble, which, let into a field of light
marble, are most brilliant in their effect.

The most remarkable features in
the Ca' d'Oro are, however, the
triple and elaborately carved and
chevroned angle-shafts, which I have
nowhere else seen,[1] and the very
singular parapet. The height of
this is greater about the centre and
at the two ends than elsewhere;
but this appears to have been done
rather with the intention of carrying up to the very top the noticeable division in the building itself
than for any other reason. A very
small portion only of the parapet is

CAPITAL OF WINDOW-SHAFT—VENICE.   perfect, and this it is rather difficult
to get at. The small balls of marble affixed to the outer edge
of the trefoils are like those in the tracery of the Ducal Palace,
and in the centre of the medallions of marble everywhere
throughout the city. Their effect is certainly very piquant.

By the side of the Ca' d'Oro there are three ancient houses
of considerable interest, and the second from the Ca' d'Oro,

---

[1] They may be compared with the chevroned and spiral columns in the
archway, leading from the north aisle into the baptistery of the Frari, erected
between 1361 and 1396, which is probably about the date of the Ca' d'Oro.

W. Wilson del.

Whiteman del and Photo Litho to the Queen.

32. PALAZZO SEGREDO. VENICE.

the Palazzo Segredo, was a very good example indeed; it has unhappily, I believe, all been restored and painted, so that now few would believe that it could ever have been (as it was) one of the very best works in Venice of its age. It quite deserves illustration, on account of the extreme vigour and beauty of its great window, which has more of the flavour of the arcade in the Doge's Palace, than anything else in Venice. These three houses are all more than usually irregular in the arrangement of their windows.

Lower down the Grand Canal, and nearly opposite the Post-office, is the Palazzo Pisani-Moretta—a very late building, in which all the balconies are Renaissance, with ordinary balustrading; but this occurs so often in connection with the latest examples of Gothic work, that I am disposed to believe that they were possibly, after all, contemporary in their erection. This palace, too, is remarkable for its double entrance-doors, with ogee arches, and for the manner in which the central window is carried up in an uninterrupted way to the very cornice; the lower traceries being very fair, those in the upper story very weak and bad.

The Palazzo Falcanon (alla Riva Tonda) is another fine house. It has two water-gates; is four stories in height, the third being the principal floor; the angle shafts are all spiral, and the string-courses all ornamented with cable mouldings, which, as is usual, are twisted in reverse ways from the centre of the front.

The Palazzo Celsi, near the Frari, is, like the Badoer Palace, an example of a fine regularly designed house with its brickwork left in its natural state; and the Palazzo Orfei is an instance of the finest (and a very fine) front being turned towards a *campo* and not towards a canal. The long group of mediæval houses which formed one side of the Campo Sta. Maria Formosa was equally worthy of admiration, but has lately been modernized—a fate which is only too rapidly overtaking most of what one used to admire in this once fortunately neglected city !

The window of which I give an illustration, on the Ponte del Fornaro, is a rare but extremely good example of the combination of sculpture and tracery. Here the carvings are good examples of the emblems of the four Evangelists very ingeniously treated, and the whole window has more force than most of the traceried windows.

With notices of two more buildings, the Palazzi Cavalli and Barbaro, I shall conclude my remarks upon the existing examples of Venetian domestic work. Neither of them calls for much remark. The traceries of the Cavalli Palace are heavy and unsatisfactory, and contrast unfavourably with the greater simplicity of the windows in the Palazzo Barbaro. The two palaces stand, however, in a very fine position on the Grand Canal, commanding the view from the Foscari Palace in one direction to the church of the Salute and the mouth of the canal in the other. Nearly opposite them is a very striking house, the Ca' Dario, built, I imagine, about the commencement of the sixteenth century, before the revived Classic feeling had fully possessed the Venetians, and displaying some effective and beautiful arrangements of constructional decoration with coloured marbles. It is, in fact, an attempt to revive, to some extent, the art of incrustation, as practised at S. Mark's; and so successful is it, that I wonder much that more examples are not met with.

In the Grand Canal, and near this spot, are many other buildings, all worthy of illustration, but adding, I think, nothing to what we already know. The Ca' Fasan is the most unlike the other mediæval houses of any; but it pleased me so little that I could not bring myself to waste time by sketching it. It is only fair to say that in its traceried balconies it approaches more nearly to the latest

33. WINDOW. PONTE DEL FORNARO. VENICE.

GES. 1868

Whitman & Bass. Photo Litho to the Queen.

34. CASA GOLDONI. VENICE.

northern pointed than any other building in Venice, and
that it has perhaps at the same time less breadth and dignity
than any.

Two fine palaces [1] are now turned into hotels, and that
at which I stopped was full of remains of pointed windows;
indeed traces of pointed work are singularly plentiful, and
I might go on to an interminable length were I to attempt
to describe them all. The Arsenal is old, I believe, but has
been modernized. It may be visited now for the sake of the
grand and quaint old lions which sit before its entrance.

Of the interiors of these houses I cannot say very much.
They usually have a great hall in the centre of each floor,
into which the various rooms open; and the windows of
these halls are generally the most important in the elevation.   The frames of the windows were of wood, placed
behind the traceries, and the original ceilings were the
moulded beams of the floors. I have only seen one good
Gothic staircase in Venice. This is in the Casa Goldoni,
and has for its balustrade a series of shafts with piers at
intervals. Its detail in short is that of the balcony, but
sloped up to suit the rise of the steps. Pointed arches of
brick carry the steps. This house may well be visited by
other than architectural pilgrims, and will be found near the
Ponte San Tomà. A fine early Renaissance staircase remains
in the Palazzo Minelli, near San Paterniano. This is circular,
with continuous open arcades following the rise of the steps,
the usual shafted balustrade filling the lower part of the
openings between the columns. The chimneys of these
palaces are very singular. Not many old examples remain,
but they are still copied, and that some of them are really
old is proved by the extent to which they are shown in early
Venetian paintings, as e.g. in the works of Gentile Bellini
and Carpaccio. In my illustration the examples Figs. 2 and 3

[1] The Europa and Danieli's.

are copied from paintings, and Fig. 1 is from a palace near the Ponte Bernardo.

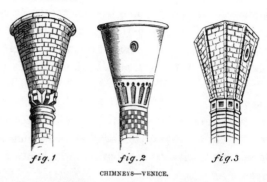

fig. 1   fig. 2   fig. 3

CHIMNEYS—VENICE.

And now that we have so far passed in review a series of the finest remains of mediæval architecture in Venice, it is time to inquire how much is to be learnt by what we have seen, and in what degree it differs from the developments of pointed architecture with which we are familiar in Northern Europe.

I think the very first point to be observed is that in Venice architecture was never essentially constructional in the sense in which it was in our own land. The pointed arch is rarely used except in churches, and in its place traceries, increased in size and scale to do their work, are made to carry the entire weight of walling above them, as is the case, to take the foremost example, in the second stage of the Ducal Palace. And it is remarkable that, when the arch was used, from a very early date it was the ogee arch, and not the arch formed by two simple curves; indeed it may almost be said that the pure pointed arch was never used, save where it would have been quite impossible with any other contrivance to bridge the necessary gap, or provide sufficiently for the weight to be supported. How striking a contrast this is to the way in which in England men worked with and exhibited the pointed arch, evidently as if, and because, they loved it!—using it not only as a sturdy servant to do heavy work, but as the friend of whose friendship they were ever the most anxious to boast. I do not complain of the flatness and lack of breaks or recesses in the masses of the great Venetian buildings, because this no doubt arose in part from the value of every foot of ground so hardly gathered from the sea, and the difficulty of throwing out buttresses into the narrow depths of the canals out of which they rise. And the same conditions which enforced this flatness are grateful because they involved the charming balconies which are so peculiarly Venetian, and gave a breadth and simplicity to the outline which has its own artistic charm.

In the science of moulding I cannot but think that it is quite useless to compare works executed for the sunny skies of Venice with those fitted for the gloomy sunlessness of a northern climate. The one kind are as properly soft, gentle in their alternations of light and shade, and delicate, as the other are piquant and sharp, rejoicing in the dark shade of deep hollows and endless intricacy of outline and arrangement. But I feel no doubt whatever that, unfair as it may be to compare one school with the other, seeing that each worked for its own wants, it is yet most clear that the Northern architects were developing a much deeper art, and working with much more consummate skill, than were the Venetian. The endless variety of the arrangement of capitals, and the necessary grouping of mouldings to fit their varying outlines, was carried to the extreme point of perfection by the one school, whilst in the other not only was there much less depth and relief, but also very much less variety. The abacus of the Italian capital was almost always square in plan, and, as an almost necessary consequence of this, mouldings retained very much the same arrangement and shape for the whole period of the prevalence of the pointed style, and generally rather leaned to the side

of heaviness than of delicacy. Venetian mouldings are composed of the constant combination of a three-quarter bead and
a shallow hollow, divided by small fillets, and so invariably
arranged in almost exactly the same order, that it requires
very great care to decide upon the date of buildings by
their mouldings with any sort of approach to certainty.

In addition to simple mouldings, there are also the
ever-recurring ornamented mouldings which are so peculiarly
characteristic of Venetian works of all dates. These consist
generally of sections which in England we should consider
Romanesque, but which in Venice appear to be much
more common in the latest works than in the earliest;
chevrons, cable-mouldings, billets, and the like, are seen
everywhere, and suggest the question whether this class of
ornamented mouldings, so largely used in the early days of
architecture in England and so little afterwards, might not
with some advantage be rescued from the contempt into
which it has fallen with modern builders. They have the
advantage of being within the power of any ordinary workman to execute, and do not, therefore, require the handiwork,
which is so rare and so precious, of thoroughly good carvers.
Add to this, that some features originally invented for use
in the way of holding together marble incrustations, were
afterwards used universally for their own sakes as ornamental
mouldings, for which office they were in no way fitted, and
I think nearly as much has been said as can be of Venetian
mouldings in stone. Those in brick are even less satisfactory; but they occur mainly about the churches, and, as I
do not recognize anything at all distinctively Venetian in
their design or arrangement, it will be better to say more
about them after we have seen the brickwork in other cities
in the North of Italy, compared with which that at Venice is
not of the first order.

In the practice of carving, as in that of moulding, I see

no reason for yielding the palm to the Venetian. It is true
indeed, that the Byzantine capitals—of which such magnificent examples exist at S. Mark's—are some of the most exquisite I have ever seen, true and precise in their sculpture,
revelling in the utmost delicacy of intricate work, and always
refined and elaborated with great evidence of care and
thoughtfulness; but, after the earliest school, and those later
examples in which they were copied and regarded as models,
there appears to me to be much less to admire. There is a
confusion and want of fixed purpose about many of those
which are commonly referred to as the best types of Gothic
sculpture, which is at best not satisfactory; and I confess
that I came away much more pleased with some of the
Byzantine capitals than with any others. They have some
notable points of difference from those to which we are used.
They are generally much larger in proportion to the shaft
than ours; and instead of having a regular neck-moulding,
they rise out of the shaft with a kind of swell, which, as
being less definite, is to me less satisfactory than our neck-
moulding. The capitals of all dates are very generally
similar in their outlines—this in part arising from the constant occurrence of circular columns with capitals whose
abaci are square, and in part from the imitation, more or less
closely, of Byzantine models. Indeed, it is impossible not
to see how great an influence the earliest remaining work—
that of the eleventh century—had in Venice until the end of
the fourteenth and far into the fifteenth century; the most
beautiful and striking arrangements of the former age are
reproduced and only slightly modified in the finest work of
the latter to a very remarkable extent: and so much more
decidedly and frequently than are the traces, in northern
pointed, of any hankering after the features of Romanesque
buildings, that I think but one conclusion can fairly be drawn
from the sculpture of Venice as well as from its architecture,

viz. that pointed architecture was never developed as purely
and thoroughly in Venice as in the North of Europe; and
that, though it retained its sway there nearly as long as it
did elsewhere, it never thoroughly understood or felt its own
strength, and worked and toiled tied down and encumbered
by Byzantine fetters and Classic sympathies. There is much,
notwithstanding this, to admire—and, above all else, the
greatest beauty of the style, wherein it so far left us behind,
the thorough appreciation and unsparing use of the shaft.
It is quite astonishing how very little this was ever used in
England. Occasionally, indeed, it was freely used in grand
buildings, and in some individual features it was frequently
seen in thirteenth-century buildings; but at the very period
when, if ever, architecture was in its perfection—in the early
part of the fourteenth century—it was almost entirely
forgotten and thrown aside. All honour, therefore, to the
men who so perseveringly and determinedly used it as did
the builders at Venice for three centuries! And all shame
to us if we do not attempt for the future so far at any rate
to follow in their steps! So rare are any but shafted windows
in Venice, that at present I hardly remember a single
instance of a window with monials formed by the continuous
mouldings of the tracery; and it is obvious that this gave
occasion, not only to the use of beautiful marbles—never so
well used as in shafts—but also to the constant use of carved
capitals. In domestic buildings, as I have before remarked,
this arrangement of shafted windows is very valuable,
because it suggests one obvious way in which we may unite
traceried windows with the very newest arrangement of
window-frames or sashes in the most comfortable nineteenth-
century houses; for in these Venetian palaces the glass was
always contained in a separate wooden frame set within
the marble shafts and tracery.[1]

---

[1] This arrangement is not by any means unknown in Northern Europe,

Besides the use of the shaft in the ordinary way, I must not forget to say that parapets frequently (or perhaps it were better to say balustrades)—as, e.g., at S. Mark's—and balconies everywhere, are composed of a vast number of very delicate shafts, set very close to each other, and surmounted by long pieces of stone cut out in imitation of arching, and not really to be regarded as a succession of arch-stones, but rather as coping-stones to hold the shafts together.   And, again, they are used very beautifully for the support of open pinnacles, one at each angle, inclosing a figure, just as in the monuments of the Scaligers at Verona. Examples of this are to be seen in the pinnacles which have been added between the gables of S. Mark's, which are exceedingly good in their effect; and again in the pinnacles which terminate the church of the Madonna dell' Orto.

One more point is worthy of remark—the treatment, namely, of the angles of buildings.   These were almost always marked either by a roll-moulding or by a succession of nook-shafts, sometimes extravagantly chevroned or otherwise ornamented.   This, when done simply, was always satisfactory, but, in its later and more elaborate form, was, I think, as unsatisfactory.   The delicate rounding off of the angles of walls was a point not unthought of in England. In the thirteenth century a nook-shaft was the common contrivance; in the fourteenth, a chamfer; and in the fifteenth men reverted entirely to the square form.   Here, however, there is a great and very interesting variety in this apparently simple feature.   The most satisfactory plan

---

though certainly uncommon as compared with Italy, where it was almost universal.   There is an example of the thirteenth century at Easby Abbey, Yorkshire, and another at Oakham Castle ; whilst in France the ancient houses at Cluny all have it; and at Ratisbon, one of the most interesting cities in Germany, a great number of houses of the twelfth and thirteenth centuries, of prodigious architectural interest, have it.

of all is where a quarter-circle forms the angle, and is
finished with a small incision in the form of a V on either
side, as it unites simplicity with strength of construction
and softness of contour, and does not force itself too pro-
minently upon our observation ; and, next to this, the most
satisfactory form is where, instead of the moulding being
round, it is pointed at the angle.   The twisted shafts of the
upper stage of the Ducal Palace, and the triple and
chevroned shafts of the Ca' d'Oro, are not improvements upon
the refinement of the earlier mode.

I have already spoken of the exquisite beauty of the
inlaid marbles in S. Mark's ; nothing can be better than
their effect, and nothing seems more wonderful than that
they should not have been used more frequently in later
buildings.   I was, perhaps, a little disappointed in not
finding, as I had expected, the marble arranged generally in
geometrical patterns ; but this is quite the exception ; and
one sees only, in a medallion here and there, the exquisite
beauty which their arrangement in this way may produce.
As a rule the walls are faced with thin slabs of marble, each
of the size in which it came to hand, sawn into as many
slices as its substance would allow, and then riveted to the
walls and held in place securely by projecting thin lines of
stonework built into the wall, and cut with indented or billet
ornaments along their edges.   There is, however, a degree
of real as well as apparent weakness which is not at all
satisfactory in this system of incrustation, and I thought
how much more noble such work might well become, were it
to be inlaid only where no strong work was required to be
done—as, e.g., in spandrels of arches,[1] or within arches—and
not as here to the concealment of every one of the necessary
constructional features.   It is to be observed, however, that
the slabs of marble are generally higher than they are wide,

---

[1] It was only so used in the Ducal Palace.

so as at once to destroy any thought of their being really constructional.

The south side of S. Mark's is, perhaps, the place above all others in Venice where this inlaid work may be seen to the greatest advantage. Some of the great arches which stand in place of gables are divided into four or five square-headed lights by shafts supporting semicircular arches, the tympana of which are filled in with delicate and perpetually varied filigree-work in marble, whilst above them a succession of panels or medallions shews all the resources of the rich materials which were to be exhibited. In another case, just over the entrance from the Piazzetta to the church, the tympanum of the arch is filled in with large medallions, one exquisitely carved, the others plain; whilst the arch of the window below the tympanum has its beautiful marble spandrels adorned on either side with medallions which, for exquisite arrangement of vari-coloured marbles in geometrical patterns, are perfectly admirable. There is enough, therefore, in the Venetian system of incrustation, though much unhappily be lost, to give ample food for our study and admiration; and its only weak point is, as I have said, its too frequent neglect or concealment of the constructional features of the buildings it adorns.

It is easy, however, to cavil at particular details, and scan with a critical eye the architectural beauties of Venice; but let it not be thought for an instant that all the wonderful pictures which every new turn or new point of view brings before the eyes are unappreciated. A few days spent there suffice almost to fill a lifetime with reminiscences of all that is novel, beautiful, and strange; and days such as I have spent, year after year, rejoicing in the daytime in the full brilliancy of a September sun, and at night in the calm loveliness of a Venetian night, have been just the most delightful in every way that could be passed.

We were at Venice on the festival of the Nativity of the Blessed Virgin—a great feast-day, which it had been my fortune to spend some two or three times before in Roman Catholic countries. I confess that here we were not edified. We came in, as we went from church to church, for rather more than the usual number of the *désagrémens* which always seem to attend the decoration of the churches, and especially the altars, for such festivities abroad. The strongest impression left on my mind was one of wonder at the paltry character of the long array of what by courtesy are called, I suppose, wreaths of flowers, manufactured of pink gauze, or some equally unnatural material. These, with vulgar draperies hung outside the church doors, and in additional quantity about the altars, with the most noisy and gladsome ringing of bells, completed the external demonstrations; all the shops were most studiously closed, and the churches and open places were thronged with people. At S. Mark's we heard[1] some abominably light opera-music, which sounded, as may be imagined, very discordant within its solemn walls.

One morning we devoted partly to the ascent of the campanile in the Piazza. The ascent is entirely by inclined planes; the outer walls of the tower are in fact double, and in the space between them these inclined planes are formed; and it is worth notice that to this day, in all buildings which we have seen in progress in this part of the world, inclined boards are used instead of ladders for obtaining access to scaffolding; and in one of the mosaics in the entrance-porch of S. Mark's, where the building of the Tower of Babel is depicted, precisely the same kind of arrangement is shewn. This is interesting, as shewing the tenacity with which old customs are adhered to. The view, when the top is reached, quite repays the labour of the

---

[1] I *have* heard a polka played by the organist in S. Mark's!

ascent, as it gives the best possible idea of what Venice
really is.   We get an impression of a very densely populated
town, hemmed in on all sides by water, and looking very
flat and low; in the distance small islands pave the way to
the mainland, or shelter us from the sea; these, where they
are more distant, look like mere black spots on the smooth,
unrippled expanse of water: and in the far horizon we see
to the west the purple outline of the mountains about
Vicenza; and to the north of these, and rising grandly into
the sky, the snowy peaks of the southern range of the
Friulan Alps.   Below and around are countless churches,
all placed confusedly without respect to orientation—a
neglect, if anywhere excusable, surely so here, where land is
the exception and water the rule.

The last day we spent in Venice was most enjoyable.
We had been all day in our gondola, now stopping to sketch
some Gothic palace, anon shooting into some narrow canal
to escape the bright heat of the sun, winding our way now
here, now there, just as the fancy of the moment seized us,
and realizing more than ever that "the longest summer's
day was all too short" for a last day in so fair a place.   In
the evening, just before sunset, we went out into the
Lagoon, and, rowing round the small island of Giudecca,
watched the gradually waning light reflected on the smooth,
calm water, which seemed too silent and too soft to be
disturbed by a word from any of us; and then at last,
turning back and coming suddenly through a short canal
into the main stream just opposite the Dogana, we moved
on gently till we came abreast of the Ducal Palace.   It was
just dark; the moon was rising behind us in all her beauty,
and in front, lamp after lamp was suddenly lit along the
Piazzetta, then along the palace-front, all along the Riva
dei Schiavoni, until at last, before we landed, as far as we
could see, the bright lights, reflected in a hundred gleaming,

flashing lines, were fitfully dancing in long streams of light upon the bosom of the waters.

We stepped on shore to find ourselves led on by the sound of military music, and to be tempted by the luxury of ices eaten *al fresco* in the Piazza ; and then, when the crowd gradually dispersed, we too, among the last, found our way to our hotel, charmed so much with our last night in Venice that it is impossible not to recollect that evening with the deepest pleasure.

It is not without purpose that I have held silence with regard to the churches and buildings generally of the Renaissance school in Venice. These have had in their time many more admirers than have the examples of architecture which it was alike my business and my delight particularly to examine ; and to the present day I doubt not that nine people out of ten, led by their valets-de-place, go to see what is worst in point of taste, and so reap the reward of allowing themselves to be made to see with another's eyes, instead of enjoying the intense pleasure of working out and exploring for themselves all the treasures of this mine and storehouse of ancient art. It is partly because I feel the greatest repugnance to the buildings themselves, and partly because I fear to make my notes, already lengthy, far too long for the patience of my readers, that I do not venture upon this additional field of study ; but not in the least degree because I doubt the result, for I believe firmly that, tried by the fair rules which must regulate merit in a constructive art, the Renaissance buildings of Venice would be no nearer perfection than those of any other city. Something perhaps there is in the gloomy grandeur of their vast masses rearing their rusticated walls and deeply recessed windows darkly above the comparatively cheerful and bright-looking walls of the neighbouring Gothic palaces, which may impress the minds of some, but they must be of a sombre temperament who really love them. Still more must they be of a tasteless temperament who can endure with patience the succession of eccentricities with which Palladio and his disciples have loaded their churches. I pretend not, however, to discuss the point. I had not time for everything, and preferred giving up the attempt to like what from my heart I have ever disliked, and what nothing that I saw in Venice would make me dislike at all less heartily.

Neither do I pretend to say anything about Venetian pictures; guides without number may be found of more service and more knowledge, and to their hands I leave their proper charge. A word only upon one point—their adaptation, namely, to the sacred edifices of which they are the most notable ornaments.

Now I must at once say that there is no church, so far as I saw, in Venice, with the single exception of S. Mark's, which is to be compared in this respect (in its effect, that is, as heightened by colour) with such buildings as the Arena Chapel at Padua or the church of Sta. Anastasia at Verona —the one an example of the very noblest art working under strict architectural limitations; the other, of simple decorative painting. The fact is, that the Venetian pictures give the impression that they might do elsewhere as well as in a church, and therefore entirely fail in identifying themselves with the walls on which they hang; whilst no one can ever think of the noble works of Giotto at Padua, without recalling to mind the religious order of his works and their identification with the building which contains them; and at Verona the result of the system adopted in the painting is marvellously to enhance the effect of the architecture without in any way concealing or damaging it. In Venice the case is quite different. The church of San Sebastiano. in which Paul Veronese is buried, and which internally is

almost entirely covered with his paintings, is an example of
what I suppose I must call the best Venetian treatment.
This consists, however, of immense oil-paintings covering
entire walls, and absolutely requiring, in order that they
may be at all properly appreciated, that the spectator should
stand in a particular spot—in some cases by the side of the
altar—and that the windows should first have blinds drawn
down, and then, when he goes to look at another painting,
have them drawn up again. This is all very unpleasant.
But besides this, there is no very sensible advantage to the
colour of the buildings from these decorations ; certainly
they are far behind mere decorative paintings as vehicles for
bringing out the architectural features ; and so they are
visited very much as pictures in a gallery, and without in
any case being identified with the churches in which they
are preserved. The mosaics at S. Mark's are, on the other
hand, some of the very grandest examples of the proper
mode of decorating interiors with representations of religious subjects, all conceived and arranged with some order and
relation to each other. But of the other Venetian churches
there does not seem to me to be any one whose artists at
all succeeded in equalling the example so early set them.

I do not pretend in these pages to speak at all of
paintings irrespective of architecture, or I might find much
to say upon the store of works, of a very noble school, in
which this great city is so rich. The immense rooms of the
Ducal Palace, covered as their walls and ceilings are with
the works of Tintoretto, Titian, and Paul Veronese, cannot
be forgotten ; still less can the many works of Giovanni
Bellini, and of other painters in the churches, and in the collection in the Accademia—rich among others in the works
of that great and interesting painter Carpaccio—be passed
over ; whilst the decorated walls of the various Scuole are in
many cases of hardly inferior interest. I am sorry that I

was obliged to take the great merits of some of the grandest works somewhat on faith; it was in vain to think of actually studying them in a short time, and, educated as I have been to love the works of an earlier date and another school more heartily than these, I must confess, barbarous as the confession may appear to be, that I was not thoroughly pleased with what I saw. The magnificence of the chiaroscuro and colouring of these great pictures scarcely atoned to me for the degree to which—owing generally to the immense array of figures and confusion of subject—I failed to carry away distinct conceptions of the story intended to be told. It may be said that this is the result of want of taste or education, but still the feeling is so different when for the first time pictures by Fra Angelico, Giotto, Raffaelle, Perugino, or Francia are looked at, that it is hard to avoid believing that, though their power over colour may have been somewhat less, their power of attaining to the highest point of the true painter's art—that of leaving indelible impressions on the minds of all beholders—was immeasurably higher. Thus much only by way of excuse for not saying more about what the world in general rightly conceives to be one of the great glories of Venice.

And now I must say farewell, and, doubtful though I may be as to the claims of Venetian art in the Middle Ages to be considered as at all equal to that of the same period in Northern Europe, I am very grateful for many new ideas gathered and much intense pleasure enjoyed in the examination of its treasures; and so, rather sadly laying myself down to sleep for the last time in Venice, I began to deem that my journey henceforward must be rather less interesting than it had been; with Venice a thing of the past, instead of, as it was on my outward course, full of all the beauties with which the liveliest fancy could crowd its walls and palaces by anticipation.

CHAPTER IX.

" A sea
Of glory streams along the Alpine height
Of blue Friuli's mountains."

Childe Harold.

———◆———

New Roads to Venice — The Pusterthal — Innichen — Dolomite Mountains— Heiligenblut — Kötschach — Kirchbach — Gail Thal — Hermagor — Ober Tarvis — Predil Pass — Gorizia — Aquileja — Grado — Udine — Pordenone.

To those who wish to find new roads to old haunts let me recommend the road to Venice described in this chapter. A more interesting way for any one who has already travelled through Lombardy to Venice cannot be desired. It affords a sight not only of charming scenery, primitive people, and churches of some interest, but gives an opportunity for a visit to Aquileja, Grado, and Udine, all of them places well worthy to be known by all lovers of architecture. Leaving the Brenner railway at Franzensfeste, we made our way first of all to Innichen. Here I found a very fine Romanesque church which, placed as it is not very far to the north of the distant mountains which one sees from Venice, and full as it is of Italian influence in its general design, may well be included in my notes. It is a cruciform church with a central raised lantern, three eastern apses, a lofty south-western tower, and a fifteenth-century narthex in front of the rest of the west end. The nave is divided from the aisles by columns which are, (1) ten-sided, (2) four half columns attached to a square, and (3) octagonal. The first and third are massive columns decreasing rapidly in size from the base to the capital. The central lantern has an octagonal vault upon very simple pendentives, and the apses have semi-dome roofs. A fine south doorway has the emblems of the four Evangelists, sculptured around Our Lord in the tympanum. Innichen is a small and unimportant village, but boasts, I think, of no less than five churches; and fine as is the mother-church, I suppose most travellers would agree with me in thinking the background of mountains to the south of it, the most delightful feature of the place. Truly I know few things more lovely than the evening view of the church and village, with the tall fantastic peaks of the Dolomite Drei Schuster behind, lighted up with the glowing brilliancy which is so characteristic a result of the Dolomite formation, by the last rays of the setting sun. Below all was gloomy, dark, and shaded; above the whole series of towering peaks seemed to be on fire, and most unearthly did they look. The attraction of such sights as I had seen before compelled me to give a day to an excursion southwards to the Kreuzberg pass, to have a glimpse, at any rate, of the Auronzo Dolomites, and I had no reason to repent the day so spent.

Leaving Innichen and going eastward, we went first to Lienz; then, after a *détour* to Heiligenblut, we crossed from the Pusterthal to the Gail Thal, and from thence across the Predil pass to the Adriatic at Gorizia. From Innichen till we reached the Italian sea-board, we saw and were much interested in a series of churches, generally of the fifteenth century, and all built apparently by the same school of German architects. They are small mountain churches, and are mainly remarkable for the complicated and ingenious character of their groined roofs. They have usually aisles, columns without capitals, and no distinct arches between

them, but only vaulting-ribs. The panels between the ribs
are often ornamented with slightly sunk quatrefoils, or in
some cases regularly filled with tracery.

One of the best of these churches is that at Heiligenblut, in Carinthia. Here, where the main object of every
one is the exploration of the mountains grouped around the
beautiful snow-peak of the Gross-Glockner, it is not a little
pleasant to find again, as at Innichen, a remarkable church
just opposite the inn-door. This was built as a pilgrimage
church to contain a phial of the sacred blood, and is extremely interesting architecturally as a church, built with a
regular system of stone constructional galleries round the
north, south, and west sides of the nave. The aisles are
narrow and divided into two stages in height—both groined
—and the upper no doubt intended for a throng of people to
stand in, and see the functions below. Now, however, just
as in most modern galleries, raised tiers of seats are formed
in them, and their effect is destroyed. A pretty Retable at
the end of the north gallery suggests that originally perhaps
they were built in part to make room for side altars, but
this was clearly not the primary object. The fronts of the
galleries are covered with paintings of no merit, which illustrate the beautiful legend of S. Briccius, who is said to have
brought the phial of blood from the East, and to have
perished with it in the snow just above Heiligenblut. There
is. a crypt under the choir, entered by a flight of steps descending from the nave; a grand Sakramentshaus north of
the chancel where the holy blood is kept (not over the altàr);
and there is a lofty gabled tower and spire on the north
side of the chancel, whose pretty outline adds not a little to
the picturesqueness of the village.

From Heiligenblut, looking at churches by the same
hands on the way at S. Martin Pockhorn and Winklern, we
made our way back to Lienz, and thence, crossing the

mountains, descended on Kötschach in the Gail Thal, passing
a good church on the road at S. Daniel.

Kötschach is in one of the most charming situations for
any one who can enjoy mountains of extreme beauty of
outline, even though they are not covered with snow to their
base, nor are more than some nine thousand feet in height.
To me this pastoral Gail Thal, with its green fields, green
mountain sides, wholesome air, and occasional grand views of
Dolomite crags, among which the Polinik and Kollin Kofel are
the finest peaks, is one of the most delightful bits of country
I have ever seen. At Kötschach the architectural feature is a
fine lofty gabled steeple with an octagonal spire. It is very
remarkable how German these Germans are! Here, close
to the Italian Alps, we have a design identical with those
of the fine steeples of Lübeck, and as vigorously Teutonic
and unlike Italian work as anything can possibly be.

From Kötschach a pleasant road runs down the valley to
Hermagor, another charming little town beautifully placed,
and with—no small attraction—a capital hostelry. On the
road, at Kirchbach, the drivers of the country waggons in
which we were travelling pulled up their horses, to my no
small delight, in front of a most interesting mediæval
churchyard-gate; this is a simple archway overshadowed
by a shingled pent-house roof, to whose kindly guardianship
we owe it that a fifteenth-century painting of S. Martin
dividing his cloak with the beggar, and several saints under
craftily-painted canopies, are still in fair preservation on the
wayside gate, making one of the most lovely pictures possible
on the road.

At Hermagor, where the grand and massive mountain
range of the Dobratsch to the east, and the Gartner Kogel to
the west, give never-failing pleasure to the eyes whichever
way they turn, there is another fine church, very much of the
same character as that at Heiligenblut, but without galleries.

Between Hermagor and Ober Tarvis the churches are not important, but one in the village of S. Paul has the unusual feature of a cornice under the external eaves effectively painted in the fifteenth century, with elaborate and very German traceries in red and buff, which are still fairly perfect.

At Ober Tarvis the Predil Pass is reached ; and starting from thence in the morning, passing on the ascent the pretty Raibl See, and on the descent some of the most stupendous and aweful rocky precipices I have ever seen, we reached Flitsch to sleep, and on the following afternoon emerged from the mountains at Gorizia, not far from the head of the Adriatic, after a long and beautiful drive down the valley of the Isonzo.

I found absolutely nothing old to see here. It is a smart town, in which the hand of the improver has been particularly busy in the work of destruction; but it is the most convenient starting-place for a visit to Aquileja and Grado, and provides good horses and vehicles.

It is a drive of about a couple of hours from Gorizia to Aquileja. The country is perfectly flat, but teeming with vegetation, and it is not until the end of the journey is reached that one realizes under what baleful conditions life or existence is endured here. A Roman capital and a fragment or two of Roman columns or mouldings are all that one sees at first to show that one is driving into one of the greatest of the old Roman seaports. Here, where before its destruction by Attila in A.D. 452 the population is said to have been about a hundred thousand in number, there are now only a few poor houses, and a sparse population, pauperized and invalided by fever and swamps on every side, whilst the sea has retreated some three miles, and left the place to its misery without any of the compensating gains of commerce. Certainly Torcello is a degree more wretched and deserted,

but these two old cities have few compeers in misery, and I
advise no one but an antiquary to make the pilgrimage to
Aquileja, who is not quite prepared to tolerate dirt, misery,
and wretchedness with nothing to redeem them.

The one great interest in the city now is the cathedral.
This is a great cruciform basilica, with a central and two small

PATRIARCH'S THRONE—AQUILEJA.

apses east of the transept, and eleven arches between the nave
and aisles. The arrangements of the apse are interesting;
two flights of steps lead up to it from the nave, and in the
centre of the east wall is the patriarch's throne of white
marble, well raised on a platform above the seat which goes
round the apse. The whole arrangement is singularly well
preserved, and looks very well in spite of the destruction of

most of the mosaic pavement with which originally no doubt
the floor was laid, of which only a few tesseræ now remain, and
in spite also of the modernization of the rest of the apse. This
throne appeared to me to be not earlier than circa 1150, though
the church is said to have been built between 1019 and 1042.
These dates must, I think, be taken with large allowance for
alterations. With the exception of the apse and the crypt
under it, I believe the greater part of the church was
rebuilt in the fourteenth century; for though the Roman
capitals (which were everywhere ready to the hand) were
used on the ancient columns, the arches carried by them are
pointed, and the clerestory is evidently of the same age. This
combination of Classic columns and sculpture with pointed
arches is so very unusual, that it is quite worth while to
give an illustration of the interior. The columns, capitals,
and bases are of varied shapes and sizes, and evidently a
mere collection of old materials which happened to be handy
for the builder's use; the arches are rudely moulded, and the
clerestory of cinquefoiled windows, each of a single light, is
as insignificant as possible, and yet withal there is so grand
an area inclosed that the effect is good and impressive. The
nave is divided from its aisles by eleven arches on each side,
and measures about one hundred and fifty feet in length, by
one hundred and five in width. The aisle roofs are modern,
but the nave still retains its old roof, a fine example of a
cusped ceiling, boarded and panelled in small square panels.
The whole of this ceiling is painted, and with extremely
good effect, though the only colours used are black, white, and
brownish yellow. Each panel is filled with a small painted
hexagon filled with tracery painted in black and white, and
all the ribs and leading lines are yellow and black. The
purlines, which are arranged so as to form the points of the
cusps, are very decidedly marked with black. Simple as the
treatment is, the effect is admirable, and it appeared to me

35. DUOMO. AQUILEJA

to be owing to the large amount of white in the panels. Near the west end of the north aisle is a singular circular erection, which is said by the cicerone to be the receptacle for the holy oil, but which without this information I should have taken for the baptistery. It is a perfectly plain circular mass of stonework about fifteen feet across, with a doorway on the west side, a moulded base and cornice, and above the latter a series of detached shafts carrying a second cornice of marble. A square projection on the north side abuts against the aisle wall, and seems to have been the special receptacle for the vessel which held the oil. At present it seems to be as little used and understood by the people of Aquileja as it would probably be if it were in some country beyond the Roman pale; a remark by the way on old church arrangements which one finds oneself making almost everywhere, when one contrasts the intentions of the old builders with the uses to which more modern ideas—reformed or deformed, whichever they may be—are in the habit of applying them.

At Aquileja the appropriation of pagan fragments was carried so far that we found Classic capitals doing service as holy-water stoups.

The interior of the eastern part of the church is more interesting than that of the nave. It is all probably of the original foundation, and retains most of the old arrangements. The floor of the choir is raised some ten or twelve steps, with two flights of steps on each side of the centre. At the top of these steps, projecting sideways into the transepts, are tribunes with open balustrades which seem to have served as ambons. The apse has two rows of seats, with the patriarch's seat raised in the centre, and the altar stands in front of this on the chord of the apse. It is curious that this, which is an apse internally, is a square projection from the transept externally.

A descent on each side under the tribunes leads to the

crypt under the raised choir. This is very small, but is
divided into three aisles in width, and four bays in length.
The central space is screened round jealously with close grilles
reaching from floor to vault, so as to protect the shrine of
S. Hermacora, which occupies the centre. But little light
steals into this crypt, and that little has to find its way
between rank weeds which grow up round the windows ; but
there is quite enough to reveal vaults covered with paintings
of subjects, and to show as picturesque and beautiful an
ensemble as one need wish to see. Kneeling desks were
placed round the shrine, but the cultus of S. Hermacora
seems to be no longer popular, and the only pilgrims are
curious visitors like ourselves. The paintings on the
groining appeared to me to be of not earlier date than
the fourteenth century, and are very cleverly contrived to
suit the early vaults.

The transepts remain to be mentioned. Each has a small
eastern apse near the extreme end, and a tomb or shrine
between this apse and the choir tribune. These are of the
thirteenth century, and are enormous blocks of stone, panelled
and carved in front, and supported on four detached shafts.
In the south transept there are fragments of a Byzantine
screen round the altar in the small apse, which are of rare
beauty and intricacy. The screen consisted of a solid base,
breast-high, covered with carving, and upon which columns
stood originally at intervals of six feet, just as in the screen
at Torcello, of which I have given a view.

There is an early painting of Our Lord, seated on a throne
in the semi dome of this apse, and there are remains of an
early wall-painting in the choir-apse, partly covered by a
fifteenth-century picture in a good frame. The choir stalls
are of elaborate intarsiatura work, and date from the end
of the sixteenth century.

A little way to the north of the church stands its campanile, a tall plain mass of masonry, with the date MDXLVIIII. on the upper stage, and the inscription " *Tadeus Luranus hoc o. fecit.*" It is worth the climb to the top to get the view over the flat surrounding country, which reveals what one fails to see from the dead level of the road, that the Adriatic is not far off—far enough, it is true, to have ruined the port of Aquileja—but so near as to be a very important element in the fine prospect. From here we saw through the haze the island of Grado, on which I cast longing eyes in vain. My information as to the distance had been all at fault, and I thought that in a long day from Gorizia, I might see both Aquileja and Grado. This is, however, quite impossible, as the boatmen required, they said, three hours for the *trajet* each way. It was a misfortune to miss the church at Grado, which contains much that is worth seeing, and has considerable historical interest, as the seat of a patriarch, whose jurisdiction included Malamocco, Venice, Torcello, and Chioggia—and whose importance is vouched for by its old titles, " Venetæ oræ Istriæque Ecclesiarum caput et mater," and " Aquileja nova."

The patriarch's throne and the ambon or pulpit, which still remain in the church at Grado, are evidently extremely fine examples of Byzantine furniture. The former corresponds with that of Aquileja, but has the rare addition of a flat canopy or tester supported in front by two columns, which rest on the side walls of the steps leading up to the seat. Probably there was a similar canopy at Aquileja. The dignity of the patriarchal throne is not a little increased by the addition, simple as it is in its decorative features. The pulpit is even more striking; it is six-sided, all the sides being arranged in a series of bold circular projections, with sculptures of the Evangelistic emblems on their face. The pulpit is supported by a central shaft, and six smaller columns alternately plain and spiral, and above the pulpit a series of octagonal shafts are provided to support a canopy or dome over the head of the preacher. These columns carry arches which are of the common Venetian ogee trefoil outline, and, there can be little doubt, are later than the pulpit. The combination is, however, very picturesque, and not the less interesting in that it has a most strangely Eastern look.[1]

The rest of my party went, whilst I was sketching in the cathedral at Aquileja, to look at the baptistery. They reported it to be as completely modernized inside as it certainly is outside, and so I failed to enter it. I believe I lost nothing, though at one time it was well worthy of a visit.

A rapid drive back to Gorizia was made with the advantage of a view of the mountains before us all the way; and we arrived in time to avail ourselves of the last train to Udine, which we did not reach until after dark.

I arrived here in entire ignorance of what might be in store for me in the way of my art. I had seen no drawings of any of its buildings, and I suspect that most of my readers are in the same state of ignorance. It was with no little pleasure, therefore, that my earliest stroll in the morning brought me to a Palazzo Publico, which if not exactly magnificent in scale is at least very important, and has the special merit in my eyes of being all Gothic, and almost unaltered on the outside since its erection. It stands in a piazza which some sixteenth or seventeenth century scenic architect has treated with considerable skill. One or two public buildings and a steep hill behind them have been dealt with in such a way as to call to mind such a disposition of buildings as one sees, e.g., on the Capitol at Rome, and no doubt so as to increase very much the apparent importance

---

[1] I take these notes of Grado from ' Mittelalterliche Kunstdenkmale des Oesterreichischen Kaiserstaates.' Stuttgart, 1858.

GES. 1872.

Whitman & Bass, Photo-Litho to the Queen.

36. PALAZZO PUBLICO. UDINE.

37. PALAZZO PUBLICO. UDINE.

of this little city. The Palazzo Publico is a building of two
stages in height, the lower entirely open with pointed arches
resting on columns, and the upper presenting on its principal front a large balconied window, or Ringhiera, in the
centre, and smaller windows on each side of it, and at the
ends. The cornice and roof are modern, otherwise the whole
design is intact, and exactly in the state in which its architect
left it. The character of the design is clearly Venetian, and
the date about the beginning of the fifteenth century, but
still it is not slavishly Venetian as the houses of Vicenza are,
but on the face of it the work of a local architect who knew
enough of what was being done in Venice to profit by it
without absolutely copying.

The lower or ground story is open on three sides, and
has ten arches in front, and five at each end. The space
inclosed is irregularly divided by a longitudinal line of
columns, carrying semicircular arches, which support the
walls of the rooms above, the access to which is by a modernized staircase in the rear. The materials of the walls are
generally red and white marble. The balustrades between
the columns and the staircases leading to them are so good
and complete as well to deserve illustration. The upper
part of these, including the cusped heads to the openings, is
of white marble, whilst the shafts are alternately of the same
material and of serpentine. The upper story is modernized
within; but one learns to be grateful for small mercies, and
it was certainly with every feeling of gratitude to later
architects that I sketched this really beautiful building,
which they have been good enough to leave so nearly unaltered on the outside.

The state of the cathedral is less a subject for thankfulness!
The whole building has been completely modernized within
and without, with the exception of the west front and the
tower. The former was the façade to a nave with two aisles

on either side, or perhaps with one aisle and chapels beyond. All the roofs are of the same flat pitch, and stepped regularly so as to give a broken and bad outline to the mass. The work is mainly of brick, with some good detail in the windows of the outer aisles, of which I give an illustration. The west doorway is of the fourteenth century, with a very steep crocketed gable between pinnacles, and a badly

AISLE WINDOWS—DUOMO, UDINE.

sculptured tympanum with a curious assortment of subjects; in the centre the Crucifixion, right and left of this the Resurrection and an Agnus Dei, and above it the Nativity. Three circular windows light the three centre divisions of the front, and the two lower are connected by a broad band of brick arches which crosses the entire front just below the central circular window. There is not a word to be said in favour of such a design. It *is* old, and that is its only virtue!

38. DUOMO. UDINE.

The tower is more interesting, though it is only an incomplete fragment. The lower stage is of stone built in dark and
light courses, with a large sunk recess on each side: On the
west side is a fine doorway built of alternate courses of white
marble and serpentine, and there are small circular windows
in the cardinal sides just above the lowest stage. Above these
the whole is a plain mass of brickwork, of which a very small
portion only seems to be original. This tower is no less than
fifty-two feet in outside diameter, and its lowest stage is
finely groined, with no provision for the passage of bells.
It might almost as well have been intended for a baptistery
as for a tower! It stands close to the north side of the choir,
and by its side is a rather fine doorway leading into the
transept, with a good deal of late Gothic sculpture and architectural detail. There are niches and figures in the jambs and
round the arch, the Coronation of the Virgin under the latter,
and figures of the Annunciation stuck against the wall on
either side in a very haphazard fashion. The strange contrast in style between these two doorways will be seen in the
illustration which I give. Here we have, side by side, examples of the most pronounced kind of two national styles
of Gothic; the door into the tower being as clearly Italian
in its beautiful colour and refined simplicity, as that into the
church is German in its cleverness, want of repose, and hard
angularity of detail.

The only other old churches I could find in Udine were
San Giacomo and that of the Ospidale. The former is
modernized, but retains an early square brick belfry, arcaded
below, and with simple pointed windows of two lights above.
The church of the Ospidale is also modernized. The façade
has a gable with an old brick eaves-arcade, and the only too
common feature of a large circular window inclosed within
a square border.

A picturesque Renaissance well-canopy (dated 1487) over

the Fonte di San Giovanni was the only other feature I
could find worth sketching or making a note of; and having
seen everything, I took the railway on again to Venice.

The views of the Friulan Alps, under which one travels
for some distance, are very exquisite. We passed Conegliano,
where I once left the railway for a journey through the heart
of the Dolomite country to Cortina d'Ampezzo, and, to my
regret, hurried past Pordenone, having forgotten that at
any rate a tall brick campanile was there, which seemed
to promise some reward to the visitor. It is of plain arcaded
brickwork below, and the upper stage is slightly battered
out with very tall machicoulis, from within the parapet of
which a smaller octagonal stage rises, covered with a low
spire. The whole composition as one sees it from the railway
is unusual and very good, and recalls just a little the campanile of the Palazzo Publico at Siena.

CHAPTER X.

" With all its sinful doings, I must say
  That Italy's a pleasant place to me,
 Who love to see the sun shine every day,
  And vines (not nail'd to walls) from tree to tree
Festoon'd."   *Beppo.*

Venice to Verona — Verona to Mantua — Villa Franca — Mantua : its Churches and Palaces — The Theatre — Montenara — Campitello — Casalmaggiore — Longadore — Cremona : the Cathedral — Churches and Public Buildings — Lodi — Pavia : its Churches — Castle of the Visconti — The Certosa — Drive to Milan.

OUR gondolier, anxious not to be too late for us in the morning, slept in his gondola beneath our windows, and did his best, when the sun rose, to rouse the sleepy porter of our hotel, but in vain; and at last, when I awoke, I found we should have a very narrow escape, if indeed we did not absolutely lose our train. The thing was, however, to be done, and was done. We shot rapidly—only too rapidly for the last time—along the smooth waters on which we had been so pleasantly loitering before, and soon found ourselves at the railway station. Our journey was much like what such journeys usually are : as far as Verona we were only retracing our steps, but now the hot sun had quite cleared away the clouds which, when we passed before, hid the Tyrolese Alps from our sight, and these, whenever the high acacia hedges which line the railway allowed us a sight of them, made the journey so far beautiful.

The names of the engines on this railway are very unlike
the kind of nomenclature indulged in at home; we were
drawn to Verona, I believe, by the Titian, and saw, as we
rushed along, engines named after Dante, Sansovino, and
other artistic and literary celebrities.

We reached Verona at ten o'clock; the station, however,
is so much out of the town, and the day was so intensely
hot, that we gave up the idea of again going into it, and,
contenting ourselves with the general view of its quaint and
picturesque walls rising over the rugged hills which girt the
city on its northern side, we sat down to a breakfast of iced
lemonade and some of those deliciously light cakes which are
never had in such perfection as in Italy, and amused ourselves by watching the way in which the guards and drivers
of the train by which we had travelled proceeded to solace
themselves with a game at billiards, upon a table provided,
I suppose, by the very considerate directors of the railway
company.

The railway from Verona to Mantua crosses a country
which is thoroughly uninteresting in point of scenery; it
carried us on well into the great plain of Lombardy, rich,
teemingly rich, in its produce, but flat, arid, and sultry to a
degree. This was altogether one of our hottest days, and
took us fairly into a kind of district in which the heat is
most oppressively felt.

On the road we passed Villa Franca, a small town which
has a rather striking castle, with battlemented walls and a
good many square towers, still very fairly perfect; the whole
built in brick, and with battlements finished square at the
top, and not forked like those at Verona.

We reached the station at Mantua by twelve o'clock, but,
as this was very far from the city, it was nearly an hour
later before we were fairly landed at one—I forget which—
of the abominably dirty and bad inns to which sojourners

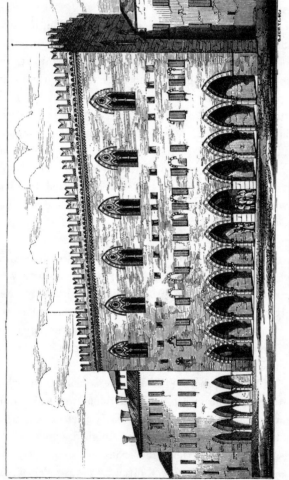

39.—DUCAL PALACE, MANTUA

within its walls have to submit with the best grace that
they can.

Mantua is nearly surrounded by water ; two large shallow
and unwholesome-looking lakes giving it this far from
pleasant kind of isolation. Over a long mediæval bridge
between these waters the way into the city from the terminus
lies. One of the lakes is higher than the other, and accordingly twelve mills, each adorned with a statue of an apostle,
are formed upon the bridge, and give it its name of Ponte
Mulina.

The general aspect of Mantua is very dreary and unpleasing, not less forlorn in its appearance than Padua, and
possessing but little attraction for an architect. The chief
architectural feature of the city is the Ducal Palace, which
contains, in the midst of a mass of Renaissance work of the
poorest and most unsatisfactory kind, some very good remains
of pointed architecture.

The finest portion is a long building of vast height, and
retaining more or less of Gothic work throughout, but
especially remarkable for the range of windows in its upper
stage. Its front faces on one side towards the Piazza di San
Pietro, and on the other with a very nearly similar elevation
towards the Piazza del Pallone, one of the courts in the vast
palace of the Gonzagas, of which it forms a part. This building is said to have been commenced about A.D. 1302 by Guido
Buonacolsi, surnamed Bottigella, third sovereign of Mantua,
and this date quite agrees with the character of all the
detail. The interior has been completely modernized, mainly
by Giulio Romano, who carried out very extensive works in
other parts of the palace. The windows in the upper stage
of this portion of the palace deserve notice as being about the
most exquisite examples of their class that I anywhere met
with, though those in the campanile of Sant' Andrea, hard
by, are only second to them. The main arch is of pure

pointed form, and executed in brick with occasional voussoirs of stone—one of which forms a key-stone—and over it there is a label of brick effectively notched into a kind of nail-head. The same kind of label is carried round the arches of the window-openings, and down the jamb as a portion of the jamb-mould, and again round a pierced and cusped circle of brick in the tympanum. In the sub-arches the key-stones and cusps are formed of stone. The whole of the jambs are of brick, but instead of a monial there is a circular stone shaft, with square capital and band and base. The whole is so exceedingly simple as to be constructed with ease of ordinary materials, and it is quite equal in effect to any stone window of the same size that I have ever seen.

The accompanying drawings will, I trust, sufficiently explain the merit of this magnificent piece of brickwork. The arcading upon which it rests, and the perfectly unbroken face of the whole, are very characteristic of Italian work.

On the opposite side of the Piazza di San Pietro is the cathedral, the only ancient portion of which is a small part of the south aisle. It is of very elaborate character, entirely built in brick, and so far as it remains appears to have been part of an aisle finished with a succession of gables, one to each bay, a common arrangement in German and French churches, where additional aisles are so frequently met with, but uncommon in Italy, where, as in England, churches have seldom more than one aisle on either side of the nave.[1] The brickwork in this small fragment of the cathedral, though elaborate, was not pleasing, being of rather late date.

On the same side of the Piazza as the cathedral is the Vescovato, a large pile of ancient building, but very much modernized. There still remain, however, some good three-light windows in the upper stage, inclosed within a circular arch, without tracery, and divided by marble shafts. Some

---

[1] It is to be seen, however, in the church of San Petronio, Bologna.

41.—CASTELLO DI CORTE, MANTUA.

old arches remain also in the lowest stage, which, though
now built up, are still valuable as examples of the best mode
of treating brickwork. They consist of three orders—the
two inner formed of alternate voussoirs of brick and stone,
carefully and regularly counterchanged, and the outer of a
moulded terra-cotta ornament. Between each of these lines
a brick of deep red colour is set edgeways, shewing a dark
line of little more than an inch and a half in width, and
valuable as very clearly defining the lines of the arch. All
these courses are on the same plane ; and probably another
rim of the arch is concealed by the walling which has been
filled in underneath.[1]

Going on from the Piazza San Pietro, and passing under
an archway, we came upon the Castello di Corte, also a part
of the ancient palace of the Gonzaga family, who were for a
long time lords of Mantua. It is certainly a very remarkable
piece of mediæval fortification, but its effect is much damaged
by the erection of walls between the battlements, which in
my view I have thought it much better to shew in their
original state, which is evident enough upon careful inspection. The heavy machicolations which run round the main
building have a peculiar and rather grand effect, particularly
in the flanking towers. This portion of the palace is said to
have been erected just at the close of the fourteenth century.

Close to the Castello di Corte is the Ponte di San Giorgio,
one of the entrances to the city, and built between the Lago
di Mezzo and the Lago Inferiore.

Retracing our steps, we soon found ourselves at the
great Palazzo della Ragione, or town-hall. It has been very
much altered, but one gateway remains in a very perfect
state, and is quite worthy of illustration. The marble
shafts in the upper stage of the building are coupled one
behind the other with very beautiful effect. Brick and stone

---

[1] See for an engraving of this archivolt, Chapter XIV. p. 451.

are used alternately in the main arch of this gateway, with thin dividing lines of brick, as in the Vescovato. In a wall close to the gate is a sitting figure, intended, it is said, to represent Virgil, of whom the Mantuans are still, as in duty bound, very proud. I cannot say much for the figure or its canopy, both of which are, however, mediæval.

We found nothing else worthy of notice in this building;

BRICK WINDOW—SANT' ANDREA, MANTUA.

but close to it stands the church of Sant' Andrea, a hideous Renaissance edifice tacked on to a most beautiful brick campanile.

The detail of this is throughout very fine. The tracery

42.—GATEWAY, PALAZZO DELLA RAGIONE, MANTUA.

O. JEWITT Sc.

43.—CAMPANILE, S. ANDREA, MANTUA.

is all of a kind of plate-tracery, consisting, that is to say, of cusped circles pierced in a tympanum within an inclosing arch; the shafts between the lights are of polished marble, and coupled one behind the other. The relative proportion of the cusps in this and in most other Italian buildings is very good. In trefoils, for instance, the upper cusp is usually smaller than the lower; and in all good cusping it must be so. Modern men generally reverse the order, and, at the present day, so little is the subject really understood that at least ninety-nine out of every hundred cusped window-openings are designed without feeling, and quite unlike the best old examples; and this, though apparently a point of very small importance, is really of great consequence to the perfection of any pointed work.

The faulty portions of this campanile are the elaborate arcadings in brick beneath the string-courses, and the awkward and abrupt manner in which the octagonal stage and the round tile spire are set upon the square tower. The present appreciation of the building by the good people of Mantua is shewn by the opening pierced in its lower stage, in front of which the modestly with-drawn folds of a green cur-tain disclose the interior

BRICK WINDOW—SANT' ANDREA, MANTUA.

devoted to a barber's shop, and in which the patient, seated in the middle of the shop, and looking into the Piazza, submits to the painful operation of shaving—a common picture in almost every street of an Italian town, but not pleasant when the place is a portion of a church.

The guide-books speak of the church of Sant' Andrea as " among the finest existing specimens of an interior in the revived Roman style." If it really is so, I advise all architects interested in the failure of the said style to venture, notwithstanding the forbidding west front, into the nave, when they will perhaps find comfort in seeing how miserable a building " one of the finest" of its class may nevertheless be!

The people at Mantua seemed to be excessively disturbed by my attempts at sketching, and at Sant' Andrea they mobbed me so thoroughly that I was really beginning to think of giving up the attempt in despair, when a kindly-disposed hatmaker, seeing my distress, came down to the rescue, and gave me and my party seats in a balcony on the first floor of his house, in which, sitting at my ease above my persecutors and listening to the good man's wife and daughters, I finished my sketch with great comfort.

In Mantua there are two or three other churches with brick campanili, but they are very inferior in their character to that of Sant' Andrea, and hardly worth special notice. We owe it to the French that there are not more interesting churches, for, having succeeded in capturing the city after a very prolonged siege, they sacked it, and are said to have destroyed no less than about fifty of them.

Here, as elsewhere in this part of Italy, most of the streets are arcaded on either side, affording pleasant shelter from the hot sun, but every twenty yards we come upon one of an unpleasant class of shops, in which cheese, oil, and the like comestibles are sold, with most objectionable effects on all people blessed with noses.

In the evening we found an Italian performance going on at the theatre, and so thither we went, anxious to see how far Italian comedy might be amusing. I fear our inquiry was not much to our edification, for the favourite

performers were mainly remarkable for the prodigious
rapidity with which they uttered their facetious sayings,
and so we lost more than half the dialogue. The theatre
was almost entirely filled with Austrians, but still there was
a sprinkling of Italians among them, which did away with
the absurdly martial appearance of the only other theatre
we had been into—that at Verona.

The next day was Sunday, but we were obliged to push
on; and so, resigning ourselves to the diligence which left
Mantua at about nine, we booked ourselves for Cremona,
under the promise that we should be delivered there
punctually by five o'clock.

We lost sight of Mantua almost immediately, for,
travelling along a dead flat and by roads whose sides are
lined with high hedges of acacia or orchards thickly planted,
you never see any place or building until you have absolutely
arrived at it. There was not much to interest me on the
road, and the weather, at first cloudy only and sultry,
gradually became worse, and, before we had gone far, settled
into a steady pouring rain; so we read, wrote, and occupied
the many hours in the rumbling diligence as best we might.

At Montenara, which we passed on our road, the church
has a brick campanile, with pilasters at the angles, and in
the belfry two-light windows, with marble central shafts
and round arches. It has one of the usual brick conical
spires, with small angle-pinnacles—a finish to these campanili which certainly does not improve upon acquaintance. They are constructed of bricks with semicircular
ends laid side by side, the joints being broken in each
course, and so making a very jagged kind of cone.

The only noticeable point about the church at Montenara
is that it has been lately rebuilt in the very worst taste, and
at an angle of forty-five degrees with the old steeple !

At Campitello there are several remains of interest.

There is a small domestic building, with four pointed windows of two lights at the side; the windows have

BRICK WINDOW—CAMPITELLO.

central shafts of stone, but are otherwise entirely of rough brickwork. The church has a kind of double belfry-stage, arcaded similarly in each stage with round arches. There are also here the remains of a castle by the river, with a fine tower of the same type as the angle-towers of the Castello di Corte at Mantua, and covered with a very flat-pitched roof.

At Casalmaggiore, a town of some importance on the Po, we stopped for dinner; but it was too wet to attempt to look at the river, and the only note I made was of a large new church now in course of erection, Renaissance in style, and with a large dome, and a choir and transepts, all

BRICK WINDOW—NEAR CASALMAGGIORE.

terminated with circular ends. The redeeming feature about it was that it was entirely constructed in brick with considerable care, though probably ere long this will be covered with a coat of plaster, of which modern Italians are not one whit less enamoured than are modern Englishmen.

At a village, the name of which I did not learn, between Casalmaggiore and Cremona, the church had a remarkably good simple brick campanile. The belfry windows were

pointed, of two lights, with a small pierced circle in the
head, the shafts being of stone of course. Beneath the
string-courses there was arcading, and the tower was finished
with three forked battlements of the Veronese type on
each face, and behind these rose a circular brick spire.
This tower was to the south-east of the church.

At Longadore we saw another church with a good early
campanile, of which I made a sketch. This was Romanesque,
with angle pilasters, and a central pilaster carried up as
high as the belfry-stage. The belfry windows were of three
lights and shafted. The battlement was most peculiar—a
quarter circle at each angle and a half circle in the centre of
each side, with a narrow space between them; the whole
executed in brick and covered in with a flat modern roof.
The angle pilasters finished under arcaded string-courses.
Generally speaking, in these churches the only ancient
features seem to be the campanili, and these are always of
brick and nearly similar in their general design, with pilasters at the angles, a succession of string-courses—generally
arcaded underneath—and windows in the belfry-stage only.

It was quite six by the time we reached Cremona, and,
depositing our passports at the gate, we trotted on along
the smooth granite (which in these towns is always laid in
strips between the rough ordinary paving for the wheels to
travel on), and after traversing a long tortuous street, and
getting a glimpse only of the cathedral as we passed near its
east end, we were soon deposited at the Albergo del Capello, a
comfortable hostelry, which we enjoyed the more by contrast
with the miserable quarters with which we had to put up at
Mantua.

Cremona is a city full of interest. The piazza in front
of the cathedral is equal in effect to almost any small piazza
I know of. On one side is the great marble west front of
the Duomo, backed by its immense brick campanile, whose

wide fame is proved by the old rhyme, of which the Cremonese are still so proud—

"Unus Petrus est in Roma,
Una turris in Cremona."

On another side is the Lombard baptistery, a grand polygonal building; on the third, a most interesting domestic building—the palace of the Jurisconsults—and the Gothic Palazzo Publico; whilst on the fourth, a narrow, busy street makes up, by the diversity of colour and costume of the crowd which is always passing along it, for what it wants in architectural beauty.

The cathedral must be first described, and it is rather difficult to do this clearly; but so far as can now be made out it seems much as though it had at first been built upon a simple plan, with nave, north and south aisles, and three semicircular eastern apses; and that then to this, in the fourteenth century, had been added, with hardly any disturbance of the original fabric, immense transepts, loftier even than the nave, and so long and large as to give the impression now that two naves have been placed by some mistake across each other. The groining of the nave is original in its outline, but barbarously painted in sham panelling so as entirely to spoil its effect, but otherwise there is little to notice in the interior, the whole of the church having been converted with the plasterers' help into Renaissance in the most approved manner. The walls are covered with painting, and round the columns, when we were there, were hung great tapestries, all of which gave the building a rich though rather gloomy colour.

The west front (if you can forget that it is a great mask only to the real structure) is rather grand from its large plain surface of arcaded wall; it has been grievously damaged by alterations, but the old design is still not difficult to trace. The doorway is very noble, and the open porch in front of it is carried up with a second stage, in which, under open arches, stand a very fine figure of the Blessed Virgin, and figures of other saints of more modern character on either side of her; above this is a great circular window, whilst the wall on either side of the porch and window is nearly covered with small arcading. The marbles in the wall, where the arcading does not occur, are arranged very regularly in horizontal lines alternately of red and white, each course being about ten inches or a foot high, and divided from the next by a strip of white marble about two or three inches in height. The great rose window is all of red marble, with the exception of one line of moulding which looks like green serpentine. There are some round windows in the lower stage on each side of the entrance, but they are quite modern.

On the north side of the nave rises the Torrazzo, as the campanile is called here—the "una turris in Cremona"—rising about four hundred feet from the pavement of the piazza. Its design is much like that of all the other brick campanili in this district—a succession of stages of nearly equal height, divided by arcaded string-courses, and marked with perpendicular lines by small pilasters, and almost without windows until near the summit. The dark red outline of this magnificent tower tells well against the deep blue Italian sky, which shone brightly behind it when we saw it; and the effect of its immense and almost unbroken outline, rising to such an extraordinary height, is so utterly unlike that of any of our Northern steeples that we need not trouble ourselves to compare them. Both are fine in their way; but the Italian campanili are made up of the reiteration of features so simple and so generally similar that we cannot fairly class their builders with the men who raised in England such a multitude of steeples, all varying one from another, and yet all so lovely.

A door in the east wall of the north transept leads into a small courtyard, sacred now to the cathedral clergy, from which the original scheme of the eastern part of the church may be fairly well seen. It appears to have been a stone building treated in the common fashion of Lombard churches, but with buttresses and a passage through them round the apse in front of the windows. There is a modernized crypt under the choir. The side walls of the north transept are seen very well from the same courtyard; they are well arcaded in brick, and entirely concealed from sight elsewhere by the enormous false transept-fronts, the backs of which as seen from here are certainly among the most ungainly works ever erected for the mere sake of being beautiful.

The rest of the exterior of the Duomo is almost all of brick. The most remarkable features are the two transept fronts, which are certainly magnificent in their detail, though most unreal and preposterous as wholes; they are, both of them, vast sham fronts, like the west front, in that they entirely conceal the structure of the church behind them, and pierced with numbers of windows which from the very first must have been built but to be blocked up. They have in fact absolutely nothing to do with the build-ing against which they are placed, and in themselves, irrespective of this very grave fault, are, I think, posi-tively ugly in their outline and mass. And yet there is a breadth and grandeur of scale about them which does somewhat to redeem their faults, and a beauty about much of their detail which I cannot but admire extremely. Both transepts are almost entirely built of brick and very similar in their general idea; but, whilst only the round arch is used in the south transept, nothing but the pointed arch is used in the northern, and it is quite curious to notice how very much more beautiful the latter looks than does the

44.—NORTH TRANSEPT, CATHEDRAL, CREMONA.

former.   The filling-in of stilted round-arched windows with
ogee pointed tracery and much delicate cusping gives the
south transept a singularly Eastern look, and it is impossible
not to feel that some such influence has been exercized
throughout its design.   It would indeed be most interesting
to find out what this was, but I am not aware that there is
likely to be any clue to it.   The date of the work is in all
probability somewhere about the latter part of the fourteenth century.   The detail and management of the whole
of the brickwork are exceedingly delicate and effective, surpassing in their way anything I have yet seen.

The putlog-holes are left unfilled, as they almost always
are in Italy.   The only stone used is in the doorway and
the window-shafts, and these last are almost always coupled
in depth.   The windows are elaborately moulded, and courses
of chevrons, quatrefoils, and
other ornaments are introduced occasionally as a relief
to what might otherwise be
the tedious succession of
mouldings which are necessarily rather similar.   The
cusping of brick arches is
always managed in the same
way ; the bricks all radiate
with the arch (not from the
centre of the cusp), and look
as though they might have

BRICK WINDOW—CREMONA CATHEDRAL.

been built, allowing plenty of length of brick for the cusps,
and then cut to the proper outline, the edges of the
cusps being almost invariably left square.   Some of the
terra-cotta arch ornaments and diapers are exceedingly good
of their kind.   The most remarkable feature, however,
about these transepts is the prodigiously heavy open arcade

which runs up the gables under the eaves-cornice—so heavy
and so rude-looking, that, taken by itself, it would probably
be put down as being of much earlier date than it really is.
The façade finishes with three heavy pinnacles arcaded all
round, and finished with conical caps.

To the north transept very nearly the same description
would apply, save that the doorway is much finer, and
entirely of marble.[1] It is part of the original Lombard
church, and has no doubt been taken down and rebuilt where
we now see it. The tracery of the rose windows is all

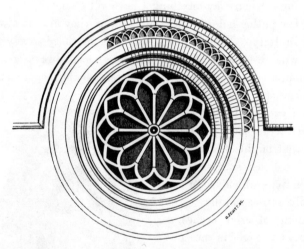

ROSE WINDOW—CREMONA CATHEDRAL.

finished in brick, and the detail generally is better and more
delicate in its character than that of the south transept. In
both the bricks are all of a pale red colour, and no dark
bricks are anywhere used.

The baptistery—which, as has been said, stands south-
west of the Duomo—is entered by a doorway with a projecting porch, whose shafts rest on the backs of animals. It is

---

[1] The two transepts are so very similar, that it seemed unnecessary to
engrave my sketches of both.

45.—PALACE OF THE JURISTCONSULTS, CREMONA.

octagonal in its plan, built of brick with the exception of the
side in which the door is placed, this being of marble, and is
very simple in all its detail.   There are three altars in it,
and an immense erection of masonry in the centre, which,
though not open, is evidently a font, amply large for im-
mersion.   Each side has three recessed arches on marble
columns, above which the whole is of red brick with stone
string-courses between the stages.   These have corbel-tables
under them, which are the only enrichments in the building.
All the brickwork is left to view inside, and the light is
admitted by a pierced arcade very high up in the walls.
The whole is domed over with an octagonal vault of brick,
in the centre of which is a small lantern, and the effect is
exceedingly fine and solemn, and enhanced very much by
the grave sombre colour of the bricks.

Close to the baptistery is a building, called in Murray's
Handbook the Palace of the Jurisconsults, turned when I

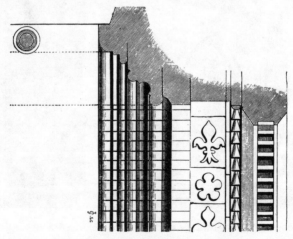

WINDOW-JAMB—PALACE OF JURISCONSULTS, CREMONA.

first saw it into a school for a not very polite set of children
and teachers, who all apparently felt the most lively interest

in my architectural pursuits. It was originally open
below, but the arches on which it stood are now filled up.
This upper stage is very simple and beautiful, and the whole
is finished at the top with a cornice and parapet, with
battlements pointed at the top like those in the Torrazzo,
and not forked as we have been lately so accustomed to see
them. At one end of this parapet a chimney rises above

CHIMNEY AND BATTLEMENT—CREMONA.

the battlement, which is, so far as I have seen, a unique
example of the ancient Italian contrivance for this very
necessary appendage.[1] It is exceedingly good in its detail,
and coeval with the rest of the work. There is a simplicity
and truthfulness of construction about this little building

---

[1] The chimneys so common in Venice are ancient, but yet hardly
redeemed from ugliness. They are cylindrical, with heads sloping out in a
strange fashion, and in the form of inverted truncated cones. See p. 253.

which make it especially pleasing after the unreal treatment
of the great transept-fronts of the Duomo.[1] By its side
stands the Palazzo Publico, out of one side of which rises
one of those singular and very tall brick towers, without
any openings whatever in its walls, which give such peculiar
character to some Italian cities, and of which we afterwards
saw good store at Pavia. The whole of the building shews
either traces of arcades or perfect arcades upon which the
upper walls are supported; they are, however, so much
modernized as to be comparatively uninteresting, though
enough remains to shew that their detail was once very
good. The building incloses a quadrangle, which is rather
small, but arcaded on three sides, and opens from the piazza
by open arches under the principal façade, and probably
dates from the middle of the thirteenth century, the date
1245 being given in an inscription in the courtyard.

There are many churches in Cremona, all more or less
appearing to be founded upon the work in the transepts
of the cathedral, but generally very inferior to them in
merit.

San Domenico has a west front singularly like theirs, but
debased in its detail. It has, however, a very fine campanile,
lofty, very simple, and pierced with pointed windows in each
stage, one above the other. The interior is completely
modernized, and not worth notice.

SS. Agostino and Giacomo in Breda is another church
of the same class, with a west front which is again a very
bad second edition of the cathedral, and which has been
horribly mutilated and modernized inside. It is, however,
to be remembered gratefully for a most lovely picture by
Perugino, representing the Blessed Virgin with Our Lord

---

[1] This building has recently (1872) been restored, and with not much
gain, though the barber's shop which used to occupy the ground-floor has
been removed.

seated, with SS. Augustine and James on either side. The
Virgin is very calm, dignified, unearthly, and very simple
and stately. Our Blessed Lord, in her arms, has perhaps
rather too much the character of an ordinary infant; and
the two saints have more than is quite pleasant of the
bend in their figures of which he was so fond; the heads
stooping forward, and the knees considerably bent, are a
little too evidently straining towards a reverential posture.
Such a criticism is a bold one to venture upon with the
recollection of so glorious a picture fresh in my mind—one
from which I really derived intense pleasure. The date of
this very fine work is A.D. 1494.

Sta. Agata is another church which still has its old
campanile intact, with round-arched windows, very simple
and not large. The church which has been built against it
tells its story so well, that at first we all mistook it for a
theatre! So much for Classic symbolism.

Another church, dedicated in honour of Sta. Margherita,
is a very poor erection of brick, with a simple campanile.
One or two other churches we saw with fair brick campanili, which were not otherwise remarkable; and one
there was, San Luca, close to the Milan gate, which seemed
to be very singular in its arrangements. It had a projecting western porch, with its columns supported on
beasts; and at the north-west angle an octagonal building
of brick, of exceedingly late date, which appeared to be a
baptistery.

I enjoyed the architectural remains in Cremona very
much indeed: its rich array of buildings in elaborate brickwork is very striking; and the campanile of the cathedral,
towering up high above the many other steeples, combines
well with them in the general views, and helps to convert
into a fine-looking city what is, perhaps, in its streets
and houses generally, very far from being anything of the

kind. The way in which the old walls and towers of the
Palazzo Publico combine with the steeple of the cathedral is
extremely fine, a large piazza a short distance to the west
of the palazzo affording perhaps the best point of view.

From Cremona we went to Lodi, on our way to Pavia,
and had a very pleasant drive. The heat was intense when
we started, and the drivers of all the carts we passed were
prudently ensconcing themselves in the baskets swung beneath their carts, to escape its effects. Throughout the
Lombardo-Venetian territory there is a great traffic always
going on, and there is a much nearer approach to English
arrangements, in the way of harness and tackle, than it
is at all usual to see on the Continent; though, indeed,
it ought in fairness to be said, that their carts are much
more scientific than ours generally are. Any vehicle with
more than two wheels is rarely if ever seen; and these two
wheels are sometimes of prodigious size—I should say quite
ten feet in diameter—whilst the length of the cart from end
to end is immense. The extent to which they are loaded
is almost incredible, and of course it requires great care in
order to make the trim exact; but when loaded, the draught
must be light for the weight. It is impossible to talk about
horses and carts without thinking of the magnificent cream-
coloured oxen which are everywhere doing hard work on
the roads and in the fields. They have most magnificent,
large, calm eyes; and this, with their great size and slow
and rather dignified motion, makes them look very grand.
They are always yoked to a pole, which rises up above
their heads at the end, and has a carved crosspiece attached
to it, against which they press their foreheads.

At Pizzighettone we crossed the Adda, here a very
fine and full stream, and then, changing horses, went on
rapidly towards Lodi. Leaving the main road, we travelled
along a less frequented byroad, infinitely more pleasant,

and in many places very pretty indeed. We followed the
course of a small river, which was turned to good account
for irrigation ; its stream being at times divided into no less
than three channels, in order to water the pasture-land on
which are fed the cows whose milk is to produce the far-
famed Parmesan cheese. Some part of the road reminded
us pleasantly of English lanes and English scenery, but here
and there a distant glimpse of the Apennines far behind us,
and of the Alps beyond Milan before us, made us aware that
we were indeed in Italy.

There is little to be seen in Lodi. It has a large
and rather shabby-looking piazza, at one corner of which
is the cathedral, whose only good feature is its doorway,
which is, however, very inferior to the western doorway
of the cathedral at Cremona, to which it bears some little
resemblance.

Another church has a Gothic brick front. The real roof
is one of flat pitch, spanning nave and aisles; but in the
façade the central portion is considerably higher than the
sides, so as to give the idea of a clerestory. This is a foolish
sham, and unhappily only too common in late Gothic work
in Italy. The centre division of the front is divided into
three by pilasters, which are semicircular in plan. In the
central division are a door and a circular window, in each
side division is a pointed window, and a brick cornice finishes
the gable, crowned with five circular brick pinnacles.

Another church in Lodi has a very beautifully painted
ceiling; this has been engraved by Mr. Grüner, but unluckily I did not know of its existence until I returned
home ; it seems to be an admirable piece of colour, and to be
well worth careful study.

There seemed to be nothing else worthy of notice in
Lodi ; but, as in duty, bound we walked down to the bridge,
—a rough, unstable-looking wooden erection over the broad

rapid Adda, with nothing about it to recall to mind the
great event in its history, its passage by Napoleon in 1796.

We left very early in the morning for Pavia: our way
led us through a country most elaborately cultivated, and
irrigated with a great display of science and labour; every
field seemed to have some two or three streams running
rapidly in different directions, and the grass everywhere
was most luxuriant. No view, however, was to be had on
either side, as the road found its way through a very flat
line of country, and all the hedges were lined with interminable rows of Lombardy poplars. It was a country which
would have done more good to the heart of a Lincolnshire
farmer than to that of an architect!

The only remarkable building passed on the road was
a castle at Sant' Angelo; a great brick building, with square
towers set diagonally at the angles. The walls were finished
with a battlement of the Veronese kind, and there were
several very good early pointed brick windows with brick
monials in place of shafts. A campanile, detached near
one angle, has fine machicolations in stone, now, however,
partly destroyed. The effect of the whole building was
very grand.

We soon reached Pavia, and were, as we expected to
be, well rewarded by its churches. The general aspect of
the city is singular, owing to the number of tall slender
brick towers which seem to have formed a necessary appendage to almost every house in the Middle Ages. They are
entirely without openings or ornaments of any kind beyond
the scaffold-holes, and one can compare them to nothing
that I know so well as to the great shot-tower at Waterloo
Bridge, save that they are always square and not circular.

We did our best to see the cathedral, but were unsuccessful; it was being repaired, and was so full of scaffolding
that we could see nothing. It contains a shrine said to

contain the body of S. Augustine, which I much wanted to see, but seemed in most respects to be an unprepossessing church.

From the cathedral we found our way to San Michele, a very celebrated church, and as interesting to an antiquary in search of curiosities as to an architect in search of the beautiful. The west end is very curious, and has a succession of sculptures, introduced in the most eccentric manner, and with but little method in their arrangement. There are three western doorways, and all of them are elaborately ornamented with carvings, the central door having above it a very singular figure of S. Michael.

San Michele, together with San Teodoro and San Pietro, seem all to be of about the same date, and are of the same character; the most remarkable feature being in each case the octagonal cupola, which rises above the crossing of the nave, choir, and transepts : externally these cupolas are arcaded all round under the eaves, and roofed with flat-pitched roofs, and are far from being graceful; open arcades are introduced under the eaves and up the gables, and everywhere there is a profusion of carving. It is likely enough that this Lombard-Romanesque style, as we see it at Pavia and elsewhere, did, as has been supposed, set the example which was very soon after followed in the great churches at Köln and elsewhere along the borders of the Rhine. In size, however, the children far exceeded their parents, for San Michele is not remarkable for its dimensions, except in the width of the transept.

The church consists of a nave and aisles of four bays, a transept of great length, a central lantern, and a short choir with circular eastern apse ; small apses are also built in the east walls of the transepts. A fine crypt is formed under the whole of the eastern arm of the cross, and is entered by steps on each side of the thirteen steps which lead up to

G.E.S. 1869

Whiteman & Bass, Photo-Litho to the Queen.

46. SAN MICHELE, PAVIA

47. CASTLE. PAVIA.

S.S. 1800

Waterman & Bann, Photo Litho to the Queen

the choir. The nave aisles have a second stage or triforium, groined throughout; and the whole of the church is vaulted, the transepts having barrel vaults and the three apses semi-domes. The internal effect of the lantern is extremely good; the pendentives under the angles are very simple, and low windows are introduced in a stage between them and the octagonal cupola or vault. The whole church is still left in its original state with red brick walls and stone piers and arches, save where, as in the eastern apse, the vault is painted with a Coronation of the Blessed Virgin, executed in the fifteenth century. It is very seldom, consequently, that a church of this age is seen to so much advantage; and undoubtedly the fine, simple, but well-ordered arrangement of the plan, and the dignified character of the raised choir and the central lantern, would, even if the colour were not as picturesque and agreeable as it is, make this interior one of extreme interest. One of the best portions of the exterior is the east end. Its extreme loftiness is enhanced by the groups of shafts which divide it into bays, and rise from the plinth to the cornice. This part of the building is mainly of stone, except in the fine gallery below the eaves-cornice, where brick and stone are used together. In addition to the west door already mentioned, there are two very elaborate doorways north and south of the nave in the bay next to the transepts.

San Michele is, on the whole, the most interesting building in the town, but is hardly superior to the grand remains of the old fortified castle of the Visconti, which stands just on the outskirts of the city, close to the Milan gate. This is only a portion of the original erection, only three sides of a great quadrangle which is inclosed by the building now remaining. The plan originally was a vast square with lofty square towers projecting at the angles, and of these only two remain. The whole front is still very nearly perfect, and

is not far from five hundred feet in length, the main building
of two stories in height and the towers of four, and all the old
windows more or less intact. The whole is crowned with a
forked battlement, and the old bridge still remains opposite
the entrance with its outer gate, though the drawbridge has
given way to a fixture. This grand pile is now used as a
barrack ; its most valuable architectural features are all
towards the internal quadrangle, which is of grand dimensions, more than three hundred feet in the clear. Towards
this court there is the same sort of arrangement throughout
(though many modifications of detail)—an open arcade of
pointed arches below, and a series of fine windows lighting
a corridor above. The lower arches are of stone, everything
else of brick, and the details everywhere are refined and
delicate almost beyond those of any brickwork that I know
elsewhere. The original scheme is best seen on the south
side of the quadrangle, of which I give an illustration. This
work dates, I suppose, from about A.D. 1300, but it was soon
found to be inconvenient to have open traceries for the upper
corridor, and the arches on the other two sides were filled in
before the middle of the fourteenth century with very good
two-light windows. Fortunately the whole of this work is
still in very excellent preservation, and deserves much more
notice and study than it has ever, I believe, received.[1] The
ordinary bricks used here measure $10\frac{1}{2}$ in. × 5 in. and are 3 in.
high, whilst in San Pantaleone they are $3\frac{1}{2}$ in. high and as
much as 15 in. long. Here (as generally in the centre of Italy)
the bricks have all been dressed with a chisel, with which
diagonal lines have been marked all over the face. I can
only assume that this has been done to improve the texture

---

[1] Mr. Grüner has published some very careful drawings of these details, in
which he has restored the painted decorations with which the coloured construction of the walls was enriched. The style of decoration was much like
that of Sta. Anastasia, Verona.

ᏀᎬᏚ. 1869

48. CASTLE. PAVIA.

49.—WEST FRONT, S. PANTALEONE, PAVIA.

of the bricks in appearance, and, perhaps where two bricks
are side by side on the same plane, to make a little distinction between them by tooling the bricks in opposite
directions. Two other features of Pavian brickwork may
also here be mentioned : one, that the depth of the arch-
bricks is almost always increased from the springing line to
the centre—the intrados and extrados not being concentric ;
the other, that the arch-bricks do not radiate from a centre,
but are arranged so as to obtain a vertical joint in the centre.
The first is a very defensible practice, the second seems to
me to be the contrary.

There are several other churches to be noticed here.
The most interesting to me after San Michele is that of
Sta. Maria del Carmine, or San Pantaleone (for it seems
to rejoice in a double dedication), which, in some respects,
is more akin to our northern Gothic work than any other
Italian church I have as yet described. The plan and all
the details of the interior are exceedingly simple. The
nave is divided into four groining bays, each of which has
two arches into the aisles ; the transept takes one bay and
the choir one, and there are an aisle and a row of chapels
on either side of the nave, and chapels on the east side
of the transept. The only openings between the arches
and the groining are small circles by way of clerestory,
ludicrously small as compared with the immense space of
blank wall below them, which seems to call loudly for
decorative painting. The whole of the interior is executed
in red brick, which has, however, been much daubed with a
coloured wash ; its effect is, notwithstanding, very fine and
well worthy of imitation. As in Italian churches generally,
the choir is very short as compared to the length of the
nave. The exterior is even better worth examination than
the interior ; the design of the west end is an exaggerated
example of the mode of finishing west fronts not uncommon

in Italian Gothic; it is to some extent a sham, and therefore bad, but there is much which is of value in its detail, as it is even more than usually elaborate; and apart from the general outline of the mass, which pinnacles and pilasters cannot redeem from ugliness, there is considerable beauty in the group of windows and doors arranged so as to rise gradually to the centre. The cornices are very heavy and elaborate, and the whole front may be looked at as a master-piece of terra-cotta and brick architecture. It is purely Italian in its great breadth and general arrangement, and, I confess, very far from being to my taste, though I could wish that we had more often some of the same breadth and simplicity in our own elevations.

It is very curious that this west end is the only elevation in this church which is at all distinctly Italian in its design; for those of the transepts and choir might much more reasonably be put down as imitations of Northern work; they are very similar, and a description of the latter will therefore suffice. It is flanked by massive buttresses, and has two large and lofty trefoiled lancets, surmounted by a circular window of great size; the whole is very richly moulded and executed entirely in brick. The buttresses and roof finish at the top in a rude temporary-looking manner, and it is therefore impossible to solve the interest-ing question of their original terminations, which must, I imagine, have been pinnacles. The ordinary bricks used here are about 10 in. × 3 in. in size, and laid with very wide joints of mortar; those used for window-jambs and arches are of much deeper colour and finer clay than the others. There is something quite refreshing in coming suddenly and unexpectedly upon such a simple and English-looking elevation, after the multitude of thoroughly Italian fronts it has been our fate to see lately.

On the north side of the nave there seems to have been a

60.—WEST END, S. FRANCESCO, PAVIA.

fine row of pointed windows, but they have been all destroyed to make way for Renaissance improvements.   There
are very large buttresses dividing the bays in this aisle—a
feature which is unusual in Italy, and which, in addition to
the design of the choir and transepts, would seem to show
that this church was not entirely the work of an Italian.
In the plan, too, it is remarkable that, though the general
arrangement is quite that of the large Italian churches,
such as the Frari at Venice and Sta. Anastasia at Verona, in
one particular it is unlike them.   The groining bays of the
aisles are square, and not oblong; and as two of the aisle
arches make one bay of the nave, the groining compartments
in both are as nearly as possible square.   This is an
arrangement which occurs often in German Romanesque,
but is not seen so often in Italy.

There is a fine campanile between the south transept and
the choir; it has four stages above the roof of the church,
and scarcely any opening below the belfry windows: these are
exceedingly good, of three trefoiled lights under an inclosing
arch, with two plain circles pierced in the tympanum, the
monials being shafts of white marble.   A low spire of
circular bricks finishes, but does not improve, this very
beautiful belfry.

There is another brick pointed church at Pavia—San
Francesco—which has a fine west front redeemed from the
common Italian character by the grand window-arch in its
central division; and though this has been filled in with
later and barbarous work, to the entire concealment of the
tracery, its effect upon the whole front is astonishingly
good.   The detail is very elaborate, and in the arch a great
number of terra-cotta ornaments are introduced.   The
front is divided by large pilasters into a centre and wings
corresponding with the nave and aisles, but these are again
subdivided by smaller pilasters, each of which is composed of

three circles on plan, and finished rather nicely with a kind
of finial at the top.

San Francesco is lighted by a succession of small
clerestory windows, and the aisles have large buttresses,
the greater part of the upper portion of the west front
being a mere mask to make out the desired outline. I
begin really to wonder whether I shall see a west front
before I leave Italy which is not a purely unnecessary and
unprepossessing sham!

Pavia is a busy and a pleasant city, and one that
improves on acquaintance; it is true that it was very
hot and sultry, but to this I have been fairly acclimatized,
and so rather enjoyed it, except when a piazza had to be
crossed in the sun, or a walk to be taken along a street
unprotected by arcading, which by the way is much rarer
here than in Padua, Mantua, and other cities which I have
been describing. The main street of the city is very
picturesque, with somewhat of a fall towards the south, so
that just a glimpse is obtained between the houses of the
distant Apennines.

From Pavia we went, on our road to Milan, to pay a
visit to the renowned Certosa. The road thither, which is
also that to Milan, pursues a monotonously straight course
by the side of a canal, or canalized river, and between rows
of stiff trees, until, about four miles from Pavia, a turning at
right angles out of the main road soon leads to the gateway of the monastery, and through this—which stands
open apparently rather through carelessness than out of
hospitality—we drove into the courtyard in front of the
church. This, grown all over with weeds, looked certainly
very desolate and wretched, and but a poor preface to the
polished marbles of the west front, and the riches and
paintings of the interior of the church.

The west front is of great magnificence of material,

though of a kind of design which seems to have proceeded upon the principle of setting all established architectural styles and customs entirely at defiance. This indeed may be said of the whole church, which is a kind of mixture of Lombard-Romanesque features with some Gothic, and no slight dash of the Renaissance spirit; altogether a most magnificent hybrid, but certainly a hybrid. The doors stand wide open, and from the decaying and desolate court in front of the church we enter into the nave, full of every-thing that is magnificent in material, and all preserved with jealous care and in admirable order; we look up to the lofty vault which spans the grand width of the nave, and find the groining ribs arched overhead in pure pointed form, and cannot help marvelling how far this one pointed feature harmonizes—I had almost said sanctifies—the whole interior, though in fact, save this one point, there is scarcely a single detail throughout the church which would ever pass muster as really being of Gothic character.

I think it is hardly possible to scan or criticize the architecture of such a building; it is better to follow the guidance of the cicerone, and look at the pictures behind the many altars set around with precious stones, and inclosed within reredoses made of such an infinite variety of marbles, that, with some degree of envy, one thinks how precious such an array would be on this side of the Alps, even if spread through fifty churches.

The nave and aisles are divided from the side chapels and from the transepts by high metal grilles, and the transept is again divided by another screen from the choir: this produces a very singular and unusual effect, and makes the transept appear somewhat like a nave placed at right angles to the choir. All the chapels on either side of the nave communicate with one another, so that the monks are able, without entering the nave, to obtain access to all

of them, whilst females are carefully excluded both from
the chapels and from the transepts and choir. Except a
Perugino in one of the chapels on the north side of the
nave, and one picture in the sacristy, there seemed to be no
pictures of any very great value; in fact, travellers are
asked rather to admire the value of the stones which are
used in the altars, and the marbles in the reredoses behind
them, than the paintings which they inclose. The groining
of the church, enhanced as it is in effect by the way in
which it is painted—with a blue ground, powdered very
richly with gold stars—conduces more than anything else
to the very fine effect of colour which the nave produces;
and the beautiful pavements, composed mainly of red and
white marbles, laid in elaborate geometrical patterns, increase not a little the general effect. This is an instance
of the superiority of decorative painting over pictures as
far as improvement of architectural effect is concerned.

South of the church are two cloisters; that nearest to the
church of ordinary size, but the other, to which it leads,
prodigious in its dimensions, and very singular in its effect,
being surrounded at regular intervals by the houses of the
monks rising out of and above the regular line of the cloister
roof.   I went into one of these houses, and found its accommodation exceedingly ample; three rooms, closets, and a garden being provided for each monk. The arches of the cloisters
are exceedingly rich in terra-cotta ornaments, and throughout
the exterior of the church and other buildings it is remarkable
how very elaborate these ornamental mouldings are ; they
are left in the natural reddish colour, and, as the walls are
whitewashed, they have a very singular effect. We found
here, as at other places, men busily engaged in making casts
for the Crystal Palace at Sydenham, whose managers certainly
seemed to have ordered casts of everything that could be
modelled throughout Europe !

31.—THE CERTOSA OF PAVIA.

There are now[1] twenty-five monks at the Certosa, and the
number appears to have been gradually on the increase
since the reconstitution of the monastery in 1844 ; it was
certainly very gratifying to see that, whilst all the rest of
the buildings looked forlorn and dilapidated, the church
itself was most scrupulously well preserved, presenting in
this respect a great contrast to the fate of monastic churches
generally in the North of Italy.

A tedious drive by the side of a long straight canal,
passing on our way large well-managed farms and other
signs of uncommon agricultural activity, took us from the
Certosa to Milan ; and long before we arrived there the
white pinnacles of the Duomo, with the Alps in the far
distance, came in sight ; certainly, seen thus, the Duomo is
one of the least satisfactory or imposing great churches I
have ever seen, and does but little in the way of imparting
character—as most cathedrals do—to the city which lies at
its foot.   At last we reached Milan, and entering through a
triumphal arch—the Ticinese Gate—and passing the front
of Sant' Eustorgio, we threaded our way down a very long
narrow street, by the side in one place of a row of Roman
columns, still standing tolerably perfect in the midst of the
crowded highway, until at last we found ourselves housed in
a more luxurious hotel than it has been our fortune to meet
with for some days.

---

[1] This was written in 1855.

CHAPTER XI.

"In the elder days of art,
    Builders wrought with greatest care
Each minute and unseen part,
    For the gods are everywhere."

Longfellow.

———◆———

ANY one who has followed the route from Venice to Milan
described in the last chapter will do well, instead of following it on a subsequent visit, to make a *détour* from Padua
to Ferrara and Bologna and thence by Parma, Modena, and
Piacenza to Milan. I shall give some notes of such a journey
in this chapter, the .towns visited on the·road completing
the subject which I have set before me in this volume, and
leaving no important city north of the Apennines, save
Ravenna, undescribed. This exception is serious; but the
omission will be remedied naturally when, as I hope I soon
shall, I ask my readers to go with me to the towns on the
east coast of Italy.

The journey from Padua to Bologna is now, and I suppose
always was, extremely uninteresting. The only objects on
the road which possess much attraction for the artist are the

towns I have mentioned, and these certainly much more repay a visit than do those on the parallel line of road which we have just travelled. Scenery there is none to speak of, and fortunately a railway makes the journey a quick one now; but when I first travelled it I retained no recollection at the end of the route save of long straight and dusty roads lined on either side with tall poplars, and wearisome to the last degree. At Monselice we found a picturesque town domineered over by the ruins of a large castle, whose walls climb the steep sides of the hill on which it stands. Here I saw a good and little altered Romanesque church, with pilasters in place of buttresses, and walls crowned with the usual eaves-arcade. At Rovigo, further on, there is one of the tall brick towers so common here, with its Ghibelline battlement perfect. Just before reaching Ferrara we crossed the Po—here a large, unbridged, and dreary-looking river, flowing rapidly between high artificial banks to the sea. Its bed is, I suppose, now quite above the level of the plain, and year by year the question becomes more urgent and yet more difficult of answer, what is to be done with it? Certainly there are rivers and rivers; and this great stream left none but painful and disagreeable impressions on my mind. At length, after ten hours and a half of the slowest of drivers and worst of vehicles, we reached Ferrara—a *trajet* now performed by railway in about an hour and a half, with advantage to every one's time and temper, and no counter-balancing loss.

The entrance to the city through a dirty suburb of tumble-down houses was not prepossessing. I knew nothing of what I had to see, and my delight was therefore all the greater when we drove into the piazza in front of the Duomo, and I found myself gazing at a building which at first sight looked as though it had been brought straight from the North of Europe, and planted here in the thirteenth century as a warning against Italian fashions! Further examination proved that I was not far wrong in my first estimate of the west front; but it revealed also, I am sorry to say, that this and part of the south side were the only parts of the old cathedral which had been spared, when in the seventeenth century the whole of the church was gutted and converted into about as bad a Renaissance building as one could wish not to see.

The west front is a great screen, and does not and never did follow the line of the roofs. It has three gables of about equal height covered with arcading, which increases in depth and richness of moulding and shadow to the top, where there are very fine open arched galleries, stepped up to suit the raking lines of the gables. I know no Italian work which imitates so closely as this does the extreme richness which some of the Norman and English churches of the same period exhibit. The arches of the arcades are carried upon clusters of columns which are set with extraordinary profusion one behind the other. The centre of the three divisions of the west front is almost wholly filled with a very fine porch of three stages in height, and finished with gables on its front and sides. The lower stage of this porch, as indeed of the whole church, is round-arched, and belongs probably to the church consecrated here in 1135. The knotted shafts which carry the front wall rest on figures sitting on lions. The doorway is deeply recessed, and has figures of saints with scrolls.[1] The tympanum of the arch has a sculpture of S. George and the Dragon, and the lintel below it eight subjects, beginning with the Salutation, and ending with the Baptism, of Our Lord. At the top of this stage is an inscription which contains the date given above.

---

[1] Said to have been carved by Nicolò, who is supposed to be the same man who wrought on the west door of San Zenone, Verona. This does not appear to me to be likely; the work at Verona being, I think, earlier than that at Ferrara.

52. DUOMO. FERRARA

Whiteman & Bass, Photo-Litho to the Queen

G.E.S. 1867.

The next stage is later, and has three arches with traceries
carried upon chevroned and twisted shafts, with a statue of
the Virgin and Child in the centre.   This stage forms a sort
of balcony.   The upper stages are covered with sculpture.
In the gable is Our Lord as Judge in a vesica-shaped aureole ;
around and above Him are saints and angels, and below a
group of angels dividing the good from the bad.   The subject
is continued on to the wall on each side of the porch, where
on one side are represented the souls of the just in the lap of
God, and on the other the descent of the wicked into the jaws
of Hell.   The whole scheme is a picturesque and unusually
disposed treatment of the Last Judgment.   There is, however, not much merit in the sculpture as a work of art,
though as an enrichment of the buildings it is most effective.
The statue in the centre is said to be by Nicola Pisano.
The south front of the cathedral has a long range of arcading
carried on engaged columns, each arch inclosing a small
arcade of three divisions.   Above this, below the eaves, is a
very fine arcade of later date all carried on groups of shafts,
and treated in the Venetian manner with ogee-arched labels
above round arches.   This stage is built of red marble ; the
lower part of the wall, of brick and stone.

A large font of white marble is the only relic of the
original church which is still to be seen inside.

There is not much more to see here.   The castle is
remarkable as standing surrounded by its moat in the very
midst of the city.   The old portions of it are much like the
castle at Mantua, and present the same boldly battered base,
and the same heavy machicoulis and battlements.   I saw
also two or three old churches here, but of no interest ; they
were of the latest phase of Gothic—bordering on Renaissance
—and very poor in their detail.

The picture-gallery is in a rather magnificent palace of
the D'Este family.   Garofalo—the best of Ferrarese painters

—is represented by a fine Adoration of the Magi, and other
works. But the collection generally is not interesting.
There are also in the churches a great number of works of
other Ferrarese painters, and most travellers go also to see
the house of Ariosto and the prison of Tasso. But on the
whole the attractions of the city are not great. The streets
are grass-grown and deserted, lined with palaces of coarse
and bold but uninteresting design, and I was in no way
sorry to leave it for Bologna, expecting to find there much
more to interest and occupy me.

The drive from one city to the other was very wearisome.
The land was rich with vines, mulberry-trees, and rice-fields.
The grapes were being gathered, and everywhere along the
road we met vast casks borne in grand waggons drawn by
white oxen, carrying home the grapes to the wine-press.
These waggons have an elaborately carved tree from back to
front, and the wheels and casks are also similarly adorned.
They are really very handsome, and quite carry one back
to those old times when even in utilitarian England the
adornment of a carriage was not thought beneath the
notice of an artist.

On the road we changed horses at Altedo, where I
sketched the good brick campanile of the church, which has
windows much like the example figured at page 299.

Bologna is, I fear, only known to many Englishmen at
the present day as the one station in Italy at which you
may always depend on getting some food, and not less as a
station which seems to be on the road to and from every
part of the peninsula. There is no excuse, therefore, for not
visiting it; and if the general feeling is not one of enthusiasm
for what one sees, there is still very much that is worth
seeing, and in San Petronio a fragment of a church which, had
it been completed on the scale intended, would have been one
of the finest and, I suppose, almost the largest in Italy.

GES 1857

W. Rushworth del.

53. SAN PETRONIO. BOLOGNA.

The streets are not of the best. They are very narrow, and often arcaded with pointed arches supported on circular columns, but contain few houses of any interest, whilst the churches have been a good deal altered and damaged in modern times.

The cathedral is a recent building of no beauty. Two lions which once supported the columns of a Lombard doorway now carry the holy-water stoups; and in a passage near the sacristy is a carved, painted, and gilded rood of the twelfth century—a piece of furniture which is rarely found remaining in Italian churches. The grandest church in Bologna is undoubtedly San Petronio, which is well placed on one side of the Piazza Maggiore. It was not commenced until 1390, so that we must not be surprized to find the faults in detail which mark the period. But the general scheme of the church is so magnificent that these faults do not strike the eye at all offensively. As it stands even now, with only its nave and aisles finished, it gives a vast idea of size and space, though this is hardly appreciated at first, owing to the enormous dimensions, the fewness of the parts, and the extreme simplicity of all the details. The west front is of immense size and width, but its only finished parts are the plinth and doorways, the whole of the rest being left in rough brick. The detail of this finished part is of poor character, and later than the fabric. It is rather richly carved with figures, which are sometimes much praised, but which seemed to me (with the exception of a Pietà over the south-west doorway) to be of poor style and character. Going round to the side of the building, the design is of earlier date and much more interesting. The aisle-windows are noble designs of four-lights in each bay, separated by buttresses and surmounted by steep-pitched gables. The detail is an extremely good combination of brick and stone, whilst a magnificent plinth of stone and

marble gives great force to the work. The transept was
never built; but at the point where it was intended to be
connected with the aisle, there is a curious conceit—a window
at a projecting corner with half its arch and tracery facing
south, and the other half facing west. It is, so far as I

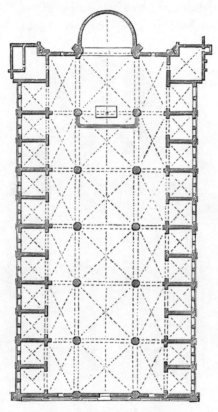

PLAN—SAN PETRONIO, BOLOGNA.

remember, a unique example in a church, but is just a little
like the angle-windows in some of the Venetian palaces,
though these never indulge in such an absurdity as is the
construction of two halves of pointed arches over such an
opening.

The interior is very magnificent. The columns, arches,
and walls generally are of brick, now coloured and whitewashed (but originally intended to be seen, as is evident
from parts of the incomplete work where the internal
brickwork is still exposed and is executed with the greatest
care), the capitals and bases being all of stone. The columns
of the nave are bold clusters; they are about sixty feet from

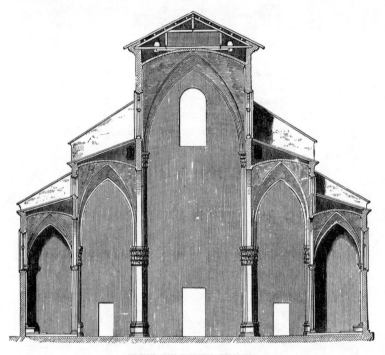

SECTION—SAN PETRONIO, BOLOGNA.

centre to centre, rather short in proportion to the height of
their capitals, which are carved with stiff foliage. Above
these is a large pier running up to carry the groining, and
there are pointed arches opening to the aisles of very lofty
pitch, but which, owing to their great size, certainly look very
attenuated. Two chapels open into each bay of the aisles:

these are lighted by the large four-light windows already
mentioned, whilst both nave and aisles have no windows
except cusped circular ones of no great size, placed as
near as possible to the groining, which is very simple
throughout the church. There is scarcely a horizontal string-
course or a label to be seen, and the mouldings are few and
simple ; yet, nevertheless, the effect is grand. Such a church
may well trouble the mind of the English student who thinks
that no building is complete which has not its arcade, its
triforium, and its clerestory. One of our puny churches would
stand—nave, aisles, chancel, tower, and spire and all—within
one of the bays of the nave and aisles here ; and there is a
grand sense of restraint and simplicity about this work which
impresses me more each time I see it. At the same time the
interest is of this grand kind—there is a sense of the immense and infinite, but no condescension to the love of detail
and delight in dainty variety which undoubtedly strikes us
in most good Gothic works, and makes them so enjoyable.

The church which inspired the design of this was, no
doubt, the cathedral at Florence. But of the two the design
of San Petronio seems to me to be the more beautiful.
The addition of chapels beyond the aisles and the traceries
in their windows make the design a little less bald and insipid, and also give a somewhat truer impression of the real
scale than one has at Florence. But at the best such work
does not create enthusiasm. The principal effort of the
architect was to build something very big, and he succeeded ;
unfortunately he so contrived as very nearly to prevent one
from quite realizing how vast his work is, and I hardly know
a more serious charge that can be made against an architect
than this.[1]

---

[1] The complete church was to have been 800 feet long, and 525 feet across
the transepts, with a central dome 130 feet in diameter.—Fergusson's ' History
of Architecture,' ii. 210.

Whiteman & Bass Photo Litho to the Queen.

54. SAN PETRONIO. BOLOGNA.

From this church I went to San Domenico, famous for a
very elaborate tomb or shrine of the saint by Nicola Pisano.
This is not a work that entirely pleases me. It is a high
coped tomb covered with sculpture on the sides, erected
behind the altar. The history of its erection by Nicola
Pisano in 1265 gives it value as a dated work by a great
artist. He seems to have been a good deal assisted by his
scholar, Fra Guglielmo Agnelli, whose work is by no means
equal to his master's. The tomb alone is the work of these
artists, the rest of the work about the altar having been frequently added to and altered in later days, and each sculptor
employed having done his best to glorify his own skill and
dexterity instead of thinking, as Nicola Pisano evidently did,
simply of telling his story in the most straightforward way.

The stories represented in the bas-reliefs had more than
common value for a sculptor of original power. In the
centre is the Madonna ; on one side the resuscitation by
S. Dominic of a youth who had been thrown from his horse,
and on the other the saint disputing with heretics and
burning their books. At the angles are the four Doctors,
and at the back two more subjects from the Life of S.
Dominic, probably designed but certainly not executed by
Nicola Pisano.

The church which contains this tomb has been ruthlessly
modernized ; but in the open piazza on the north side of it
are two monuments of much interest. One of these has a
square basement of brick, supporting detached shafts, above
which are round arches, the whole being finished with a brick
pyramid. Under the canopy thus formed is placed the
sarcophagus, marked with a cross at the end, and finished at
the top with a steep gabled covering. The detail of this is all
of late Romanesque style. The other monument is of later
date and much finer design, though keeping to the same
general outline. In place of the brick basement of the first

this has three rows of three shafts, which support a large
slab. On this are arcades of pointed arches, three at the sides
and two at the ends, carried on coupled shafts, and within
this upper arcade is seen the stone coffin carved at the top,
and with a stiff effigy of the deceased carved as if lying on
one of the perpendicular sides. This monument is also
finished with a brick pyramid. The whole design is certainly
striking; it has none of the exquisite skill that marks the
best Veronese monuments, but it is a very good example of
the considerable success which may be achieved by an architectural design without any help from the sculptor, without
the use of any costly materials, and with only moderate
dimensions. The upper tier of arches is kept in position by
an iron tie, and, in spite of its slender look, still stands after
five hundred years' exposure, in perfect condition.

San Giacomo is another example of a modernized church,
which has, however, some interesting features. On the
exterior there is a rather good treatment of the polygonal
apse, with steep gables and pinnacles over the windows on
each side. This is somewhat like the apse of San Fermo,
at Verona. The campanile on the south-east of the nave
is a very lofty late Gothic erection, finished with an incomplete Renaissance belfry-stage. The old portion is divided
into a succession of stages of equal height, and is mainly
striking on account of its good colour—being all of red
brick—and simple outline. The west front is, as is usual
here, a great gable divided into three parts by pilasters and
half columns; the doorway is of the thirteenth century, and
its columns rest on lions' backs. The detail of the windows
at the ends of the aisles is extremely good, and seemed to me
to be of the same date. The windows are of two-lights,
with shafts for monials, and a broad transome of plate tracery;
the tympanum of the arch at the top is similarly filled: here,
though the jambs are of brick, the whole of the rest of the

J.S.S. 1857

Whiteman & Bass, Photo Litho to the Queen.

55. MONUMENT. BOLOGNA.

design is executed in stone, and the likeness to some of the later Venetian church windows in the Madonna dell' Orto and SS. Giovanni e Paolo is too great not to be observed. The cornices here are very good. I noticed not only bricks of unusual shapes, very well arranged for effect, but also disks of earthenware, set with the convex side in view, and of brilliant glazed colour, generally blue or green. Their effect is extremely good.

The church of Sta. Maria Maggiore is less altered internally than the rest. It is of great length, groined throughout, and in general effect and proportions seemed to me to have a somewhat less Italian air than the other churches. The apse has an aisle and chapels round it of which the brick detail externally is effective. Here there are large tiles cut to a trefoil shape placed flat against the wall-face as an ornament. They are good-looking, but have not stood well.

In front of this church there is a court or atrium, surrounded with a perfectly open arcade, which is continued all along the north side of the church next the road and over the public footpath. The columns are very slender and of marble; and though the arches which they carry are segments of circles (not an agreeable form), the whole effect is extremely light and graceful.

San Francesco *was* one of the finest churches in the city. It is now so shabby and decayed outside, and so covered with painters' and decorators' work inside, that all its good effect is ruined. Its interior was the victim of what was, I daresay, a very well-meant restoration some years ago, and little of it has been left in its original condition. It has a chevet with aisles and chapels, and externally the rare feature (in Italy) of flying buttresses to support the choir vault. They were built by men who had never seen one before, I suppose, and are as crude and misshapen as they well could be.

Two campanili close to each other, south of the choir,

group strangely with it in the perspective view. They are unlike in size and design, and illustrate the perfect indifference with which all mediæval architects viewed the gravest departures from laws of symmetry. The larger of the two has rather rich Gothic details, the belfry-stage having traceried windows of three lights with spiral shafts for

CLOISTER—SAN STEFANO, BOLOGNA.

monials. The gables in this church have large white marble crosses let into them; these are rounded at the ends, and each end has a bright green tile disk inserted. The west front is of the usual description—a great sham front of hideous outline. Most of its windows are lancets, new, but probably copied from old examples, and the doorway under a canopy is of good character.

I have left to the last what, I suppose, is in fact the oldest of the Bolognese churches—San Stefano. It is a collection of seven churches, rather than one church, and, in spite of modernization without end, it is still a most curious and interesting jumble of old buildings. The churches are dedicated to—1, San Stefano; 2, San Lorenzo; 3, San Sepolcro (a circular church); 4, The Corte di Pilato (a cloister); 5, Sta. Trinità; 6, SS. Pietro e Paolo (with three Romanesque apses); and 7, San Giovanni. No. 3 has an aisle round the circular portion, and was probably a baptistery, and there is still an old ambon in it. One gets fairly puzzled in this nest of queer little churches or parts of churches, and I found but little of architectural—as distinguished from antiquarian—interest in them. The brickwork in the cloister and in some of the external walls is extremely good. Some of the latter are diapered or reticulated on the face with square yellow tiles with dividing lines of red brick, and the cornices are of the same two colours also. In the cloister the columns and inner order of the arches are of stone, the rest of the walls and cornices being of red and yellow bricks, and in one part there is a course of red, green, and yellow tiles alternated. The effect of this work is extremely pretty.

Probably travellers remember Bologna more by its two leaning towers than by any other feature. One comes here however, from either side, after rather a surfeit of this sort of thing. On the one side is Pisa, with its leaning tower, and on the other we may see them at Rovigo, Ferrara, and elsewhere. The soil here is generally bad for foundations, I suppose, and these plain brick towers without any projection at the base are the most ill-contrived constructions for such

foundations that one can conceive. In this case it is possible
to get views of the two towers which shew an apparently
impossible amount of overhanging on the part of the smaller
one, and I confess to a strong preference for walking to what
one may call the windward side of such an erection ! There is
no beauty in these towers, their only features being the vast
array of putlog holes in their walls, and the machicolated
battlement of the higher of the two.

Of domestic buildings of the Middle Ages there are not
many remains. The Casa dei Mercanti, though it dates
from the end of the fourteenth century, is not pleasing.
The front has two lofty pointed arches on the ground story,
and a canopied Ringhiera of very poor design above. But as
the whole front has been restored, the bricks painted bright
red, and the stonework cleaned and repaired, I am disposed
to believe very little in the antiquity of any of the details.
Certainly I found it not worth sketching, which was the more
disappointing as I had heard of it always as a fine building.
The Pepoli Palace has some old brickwork and a Ghibelline
battlement of unusually picturesque outline.   The Piazza
Maggiore in front of San Petronio is certainly the best
feature in this not very striking city. As always in Italian
towns, it must be visited early in the day if it is to be seen to
advantage. In the morning it is crowded with fruit and
vegetable dealers, sitting under bright-coloured umbrellas;
in the afternoon it is *triste* and deserted, save by the cabmen,
who pursue the stranger with their importunities.   One side
of this piazza is occupied by the Palazzo Publico—a large pile
of building altogether Gothic in its inclosing walls, I fancy,
but they have been so much altered from time to time that
not much detail remains.   It seems, however, to have been
much like the Castle at Mantua in its character, with bold
machicoulis at the top of the walls, and a well battered-
out base to the whole building.   In a tower here there is a

window which I engrave, because it shews well how good an effect may be produced by the skilful use of the very simplest materials. The combination of stone with brick adds much to the effect; and though this is in itself a very small and unimportant work, it appears to me to be exceedingly suggestive.

BRICK WINDOW—PALAZZO PUBLICO, BOLOGNA.

The Academy of the Fine Arts will be visited by every one who cares for Francia, and by many who fancy they care for the Caracci. As one of the former class, I recommend it very heartily. It contains a large collection, gathered in papal times from convents and churches, and mainly by painters of the Bolognese school. This school has the redeeming virtue of counting Francia on its list of painters, which may atone for much. He is seen here to advantage; and one trio, consisting of two of his pictures on either side of one of Perugino's, forms the noblest group in the gallery. Here one

sees how much in common the two men had in spite of
Francia's more forcible character. The same love of pure
and rich colour, the same well-defined grouping, the same
religious feeling mark them both. And never, I think, has
the Madonna—pensive, lowly, and simple—been more
beautifully represented than here by Francia. It is a face
that one hopes to remember. Here, too, is Raffaelle's S.
Cecilia, no doubt a very great work, but not great quite in
the sense one wishes to understand the word at his hand.
S. Cecilia and S. John are very fine, but S. Paul is a sort
of burly ruffian. The heavenly choir is very mundane, and the
whole work somewhat academical in its design and treatment.
The earlier pictures here are very disappointing. The early
Bolognese painters seem to have painted coarsely and
heavily, and to have drawn badly, and there is no comparison for a moment between their work and that of the
early Sienese and Florentine painters on the one hand, and
those of Padua and Verona on the other. One has indeed
in their works a sort of foretaste of what one has from their
followers—the Caracci, Domenichino, Bagna-Cavallo, and to
some extent Guido. Dismal colour, great striving after
chiaroscuro, violent and distorted attitudes, and a purely
conventional and academical style, are not great recom-
mendations of any school, but they are things which must be
accepted if one is to enjoy these works at all heartily.

A very short railway journey takes one from Bologna to
Modena. The one object of interest here is the cathedral,
but this is a building of extreme historical and architectural
value, and has fortunately been left with so few alterations
that we can make out its history with fair certainty. At
Bologna everything was built of brick—here at a short
distance we find our eyes rejoicing again in the sight of
stone and marble.

The ground-plan of the cathedral consists of a nave with

aisles terminated at the east end by three semicircular
apses. There are a sacristy on the north of the choir-aisle,
and a tower to the north of this. There are two doorways
on the south side, three at the west end, and one on the
north side. A grand crypt with arches on slender shafts
occupies the whole space under the eastern part of the
church. The access to the choir from the nave is by stairs
against the aisle walls in the same position as at San Zenone,
Verona. Here the stairs and their handrails are not later
than the thirteenth century, and the choir is divided from
the aisles by screens of the same age; solid below, and with
a continuous cornice carried on coupled shafts above. The
cathedral is said to have been founded in 1099, but an
inscription on the south wall gives the date of the consecration
of the building by Pope Lucius III. in July 1184. I believe
that the former date represents the age of the plan, and of
most of the interior columns and arches still remaining, but
that before the later date the whole exterior of the cathedral
had been modified, and the groining added inside. The
work of both periods is extremely good and characteristic.
The columns of the nave are alternately great piers and
smaller circular columns of red marble. The great piers
carry cross arches between the groining bays, and each of
these in the nave is equal to two of those in the aisles. The
capitals here are very close imitations of Classical work, with
the abaci frequently concave on plan. The main arches
and the triforium openings of three lights above them are
seen both in the nave and aisle, the vaulting of the latter
being unusually raised. There is also a plain clerestory,
and the vaults are now everywhere quadripartite. The
outside elevation of the side walls is very interesting. Here
we seem to have the old aisle wall with its eaves-arcade
added to and raised in the twelfth century, and adorned with
a fine deep arcade in each bay, inclosed under round arches,

which are carried on half columns in front of the buttresses or pilasters. These arches shew exactly what the original intention was at Ferrara, where it will be recollected they still in part remain. Certainly they would have made the side walls very rich in their effect, even if there had not also been two porches, a projecting pulpit, and various bas-reliefs inserted in them.

All the doorways deserve special mention. The eastern of the two on the south side, with the porch of two stages in front of it, is remarkable for the extreme skill and delicacy of its enrichment. The shafts are of white marble, and the mouldings which separate them of red, while the former are all carved in the most delicate manner. The porch is mainly built of red marble, and is carried on detached shafts, cut out of one block knotted together and resting on lions. The whole of this work is evidently an addition to the aisle, and dates from about A.D. 1180. The other doorway on the same side may probably be a work of the original foundation in 1099. It has the twelve Apostles on the jambs, and rude shafts carrying a canopy in front of it. The west doorway has also a porch, and sculptures of the twelve months on its jambs. It is covered with carving of foliage and figures executed by the same Wiligelmus who was employed on the western doorway of San Zenone, Verona. Among other figures are those of King Arthur and his knights, inscribed with his name,[1] "Artus de Bretania," above his head. The west front is very remarkable. The ends of the aisles have two arches inclosing small arcades similar to those in the bays of the side walls, and the end of the nave has the same arcade on each side of a porch of two stages in height, the lower of which is carried on detached

---

[1] Mr. Perkins, 'Italian Sculptors,' p. 251, says that the nationality of Wiligelmus has been much disputed. Kreuser says that he came from Nürnberg; and the representation of King Arthur's victories over the Visigoths is adduced as a proof that he was not an Italian.

56. DUOMO. MODENA.

shafts resting on lions' backs. The upper part of the porch was altered in order that a great wheel window might be inserted, sometime in the fourteenth century.

This rose window fills the whole upper part of the western gable, and is, like many Italian examples, very unskilful in its design. The vast number of divisions or spokes, and the very slight prominence of the arcuated part of the filling-in, make it look in very truth a wheel window and nothing better. Above it are an insignificant figure of Our Lord and the Emblems of the four Evangelists sculptured in low relief. The lower portion of the walls is covered in the most promiscuous manner with bas-reliefs, and a medley of mural tablets, the number of which would delight the eyes of an English parish clerk ; but nevertheless the rich character given to the work by the fine shadows of the arcades in the lower half of the front, is worthy of special notice and recollection. The tower and spire are very lofty. The former has six stages of nearly equal height, all round-arched, and on the top of this two octagonal stages crowned with a modern spire. The lower stage of the octagon is old, and was finished in 1317 by Enrico da Campione, one of the family of architects of whom I have before spoken. The tower has pilasters at the angles, and two intermediate on each face, so that there is a triple division in elevation, and all the horizontal string-courses are marked by arched corbel-tables. The repetition of these very simple features, and the absence of all openings in the lower part of the steeple, shew how simple the elements of a good work may be.

I found nothing else of any interest in Modena, and made my way from thence to Parma, impatient to see not only the cathedral and the baptistery, but also Correggio's treatment of the decoration of the former. In spite of the great fame of these works, I fear I must at once confess that they took away most of the pleasure which I had anticipated

from my visit to the cathedral at Parma. This is a grand
Lombard church, fairly perfect in its architectural details
and arrangements, but entirely ruined in its architectural
effect by the frescoes with which most of its walls and roof
have been covered. These have been painted without the
slightest thought of the requirements of the building, and
as a matter of course they have entirely ruined its effect.
The frescoes in the dome are by Correggio, and are amongst
his most celebrated works. Like all the rest of the paintings
here, they present, when regarded from below without the
assistance of a glass, a confused mass of distorted figures
and limbs, not at all relieved by the dark and dismal colouring in which they are executed, and which doubtless is not
what it once was. It is true that when examined in detail,
and still more when examined in Toschi's careful engravings,
they are full of beautiful drawing and skilful chiaroscuro,
but the impression they have left on my mind is mainly one
of the extreme risk of attempting to decorate a building
without previous training in and knowledge of the requirements of architecture. As an example of Lombard architecture the cathedral at Parma is almost ruined, whilst it
would be difficult to conceive a worse-fitted building for the
display of Correggio's fancy and skill. The ill-assorted
union, in itself ruinous to both, has been aggravated by the
bad state of repair which has damaged and no doubt altered
the colour of the frescoes; and the impression now produced
is that of simply the gloomiest interior in Italy.

The church is cruciform, with a central cupola and apses
to the three eastern arms of the cross. The nave and aisles
of seven bays are vaulted, and there is a large and striking
crypt under the whole eastern part of the church which goes
far to redeem its otherwise barren character. The effect here
is remarkable, owing to the complex perspective and great
number of single slender marble shafts carrying the vaulted

roofs, and in part also to its unusual height.   The capitals
are all carved—frequently with coarse volutes; the church
was founded in 1058, and no doubt this
crypt is of about that age.

Very near to the cathedral on the
south-west is the now much more interesting baptistery. This is on the
exterior a large and lofty octangular   plan of baptistery.
building, adorned in a succession of stages by small detached shafts carrying the cornices and strings which divide
the elevation.   Internally the scheme is very different.
The eight-sided interior is subdivided, so that sixteen shal-

low apses are set around
the inside face of the walls.
These are separated by columns,. and above them on
each side are two stages in
height, each subdivided into
three divisions, which are
again subdivided by smaller
columns. A great vault or
cupola covers the whole, and
from its height gives an air
of solemnity to the interior.
It seems never to have been
treated as a real dome, being
covered with a flat roof,
resting on the external walls,

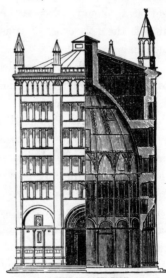

SECTION OF BAPTISTERY.

which are carried up far above the vault. The paintings
with which the walls are covered are arranged without any
order or general scheme of design. They seem to have been
given by various donors, and each gave what best pleased his
fancy; but owing to the early date of most of the work, there
is in parts—especially in the vault—a fine effect of colour.

This baptistery is said to have been commenced by the
architect Benedetto di Antelamo in A.D. 1196,[1] who is also
credited with many other works here, and specially with
much of the early sculpture in the Duomo and baptistery ;
it was not completed until 1260.

There are three great doors to the baptistery.   On the
northern is sculptured the Tree of Life, and over this twelve
prophets carrying medallions with half figures of the Apostles.
Below are subjects from the lives of Our Lord and S. John
Baptist.   The western door has a sculpture of the Last
Judgment, and the southern a not very intelligible, though
no doubt symbolical, figure of a man seated in a tree and
gathering honey.   Inside there are various sculptures, and
among them a series of illustrations of the labours of the
months.

My day in Parma was pleasantly concluded with a visit
to the Gallery, and then, finding no more mediæval remains,
I pushed on to Piacenza.

This is a city of no small interest, and remarkable above
everything else in the possession of a Palazzo Publico of
unusual and striking design—a building of special value and
interest to me, since it is a capital example of the use of
brick and marble together.   Before looking at any of the
churches I devoted myself to this building with the more
satisfaction when I found that it was really, in some respects,
one of the very best works of the sort that I had ever seen.

An inscription carved under a banner on a square stone,
in the front, records the commencement of the work in
1281, and I think we may assume that no part of it is of
much later date than this.   It consists, as do most of these
buildings, of a lofty open ground story, and a principal story

---

[1] The inscription on the north door is as follows :—

"Bis binis demptis.   Annis de mille ducentis
Incepit dictus, opus hoc sculptor Benedictus."

G.G.S. 1869

57. PALAZZO PUBLICO. PIACENZA.

above this. The façade is very dignified in effect. On the
ground level are five lofty arches, very slightly moulded, and
resting on square piers just rounded at the corners. The
material of this stage is marble, mainly white, but with just
a line of red and another of grey near the string-course
which divides this from the next stage. From this point up
almost the whole work is executed in brickwork of very
elaborate and delicate detail. The two stages have no kind
of uniformity or connection with each other, six windows
being arranged above the five arches. In the centre of the
first floor is the old doorway to the Ringhiera (which was
altered in the seventeenth century); the windows on each
side are of three lights, inclosed under a round arch with a
deep archivolt very slightly recessed—all the enrichments
being on very nearly the same face as the wall. These
windows agree in size, but vary very much in all their
details. Some of the subordinate arches are pointed, some
round, and the tympana are everywhere filled with fine
brick diapers. Above this stage the walls finish with a
good marble cornice of intersecting arches, and then with a
forked battlement. At the four angles of this are raised
turrets, and the ends are finished with battlemented gables,
very quaint and picturesque, as will be seen by the illustration which I give. The niches between the two arches in
the principal story seem to have been intended for paintings.
The marbles used here are red and white. Red is used for
the arcades under the cornices, for the middle order of the
rose window, and the inner order of the main arches.
Elsewhere the marble is white, except the one grey course
below the principal string. The whole of the lower stage is
open below on all sides and groined—in brick, I think—
though it is now plastered; indeed, save the parts already
described as being of marble in the principal fronts, the
whole of this building is built of red brick. Behind the

open ground story there remains a portion of an internal
quadrangle, which, incomplete as it is, shews, nevertheless,
the same delicate attention to detail which is conspicuous on
the façades. I know hardly any detail of Italian brickwork
which is so refined and good as that in the arches and some
cusped circles between them in this quadrangle.

I have seen this building, full as it is of eccentric
departures from ordinary rules and customs—piers being

BRICKWORK—PALAZZO PUBLICO, PIACENZA.

placed over openings, and round and pointed arches used
indifferently—quoted for our benefit as a remarkable example
of a public building erected in the Middle Ages in the most
regular and formal fashion! It is, on the contrary, if the
plain truth is to be spoken, an example of a very bold
disregard of such fashions indulged in without any detrimental effect.

Piacenza cannot boast of any very fine churches. They
have been much ruined internally by modern alterations, and

externally they do not seem ever to have been very attractive.
The cathedral is a Lombard church of fine size, and with
some good points.   There are three western porches of two
stages in height, according to the usual Lombard fashion.
The doors are rudely sculptured; that in the centre with the
signs of the Zodiac, and the northern door with the Annunciation, Salutation, and other subjects on its lintel.   The
columns rest on monsters, griffins, and men.   The whole
front is now finished with one large low-pitched gable,
which has an arcade stepped up to suit its cornice.   This is,
however, a fourteenth-century alteration of the older church,
as is also a rose window in the centre.   A brick tower of
late date rises at the north-west angle of the church, and
is finished with a circular spire built of round-ended bricks.
The external walls of the Lombard church were all built of
stone or marble with shallow buttresses; the windows were
very simple, and the effect was mainly due to the fine open
arcade below the eaves, carried now on shafts, now on
figures.   The north-east view is very picturesque, owing to
the number of angles and apsidal terminations which are
seen together.   These are produced by a plan of most
unusual character, the transepts as well as the choir being
finished with three apses, and an octagonal brick lantern
rising out of the centre.   Internally the cathedral, in spite
of alterations, is still very interesting.   The nave opens
with eight arches to the aisles and transepts; but the three
arches which open to the latter are much loftier than the
five western arches, so as to allow of the transepts opening
to the nave to nearly its full height.   The groining of the
nave is divided into three bays of sexpartite vaults—each
bay being equal to two bays of the aisles, and there is a
lantern over the two eastern bays.   The transepts and aisles
have quadripartite vaulting.

  Under the choir is a crypt of great interest and beauty,

owing to the vast number of delicate columns which carry
the vault. It is planned on a cruciform arrangement, with
the principal altar in an octagonal central compartment.
Here the priest celebrates on the eastern side with his back
to the choir stalls in the apse, and his face toward the west.
The access to this crypt is by two staircases at its south-
west and north-west angles.

The large brick church of San Francesco is of the fourteenth century ; it is very simple, but not striking in effect.
The east end has been planned irregularly—to suit the site,

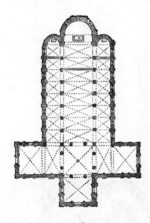

no doubt—with an apse and aisle
round it, and irregularly shaped
chapels beyond the apse. The
effect is bad, owing to the unskilful way in which the work
has been done. The west front
has the favourite sham gable
adorned with circular windows,
some of which are absolutely
above the roofs of the aisles !
San Giovanni in Canale is another church which has nothing
of interest, save a few remnants
of old brickwork.

PLAN—SANT' ANTONINO.

Sant' Antonino is a remarkable church, hopelessly modernized with plaster enrichments. Like the cathedral, it has
a lantern in the centre crossing, carried on eight columns
from the ground, which produce internally a very new and
really striking effect. The lantern is finished above the roof
with three stages, each of which is lighted with a two-light
window in each face. There is a fine early marble doorway
to the north transept, with men and monsters supporting
the shafts, and some delicate carving. In front of this, at
the end of the fourteenth century, was built a lofty porch

with a great open archway to the north. It is finished with brick pinnacles and cornices, and is higher than the transept. The hinges on the west door here are very good, and the windows in the aisles—lancets with seven cusps in the head —are quite worth notice. Piacenza struck me, both in its churches and Palazzo Publico, as a town which had possessed a very distinctly developed school of architecture of its own. The churches are peculiar, not to say eccentric, in their planning, and the Palazzo Publico is quite unique in its design and general treatment.

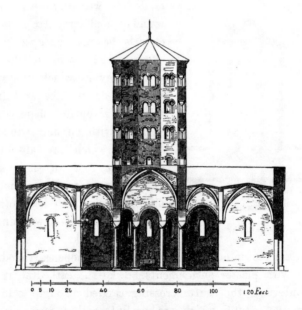

SECTION—SANT' ANTONINO, PIACENZA.

The only other old work I noticed here was a house in the Strada San Marco. This is all of brick, and has arches of slightly horse-shoe shape. The bricks are all axed on the face, and are of large size —$11\frac{1}{4}$ inches long by about $2\frac{3}{4}$ inches high.

Not very far to the east of Piacenza is Asti, a dull city, distinguished, however, by some remarkable features in its churches. The most important of these are the Cathedral and San Secondo. They are extremely similar in general design : they have naves with short choirs, transepts, low octagonal vaulted lanterns over the crossing, and apsidal chapels in front of the transept gables, and at San Secondo to the several bays of the aisle. Their towers are on the east side of the transepts. The peculiar feature of their detail is the very elaborate way in which brick and stone are counterchanged in the jambs and arches of windows and doorways. The moulded members of a jamb are alternately of brick and stone, and in each course stone comes above the brick of the courses below. San Secondo cannot, I think, be earlier than circa 1400, but at first sight looks like a building of 1200. The cathedral is probably somewhat though not very much earlier. Its plan was evidently derived from that of the cathedral at Piacenza. Its proportions are bad, and it is only redeemed by the picturesqueness of some of its details. Another church has an octagonal campanile ; and another, one of sixteen sides. This is of brick, except the upper stage, which is coursed in brick and stone. Its sixteen sides have alternately a window and a shaft running up to the cornice, and in the stage below it there are eight windows below the shafted sides of the belfry. The composition of this tower is certainly very good. Another fine lofty tower with bold cornice and Ghibelline parapet recalls the Veronese towers to mind, and there are besides not a few remains of mediæval domestic work, so that a day may be well spent at Asti by an architect.

CHAPTER XII.

" Launce ! by mine honesty, welcome to Milan."
Two Gentlemen of Verona, act ii. sc. 5.

———◆———

Milan: the Cathedral—Sant' Ambrogio—Sant' Eustorgio—Sta. Maria delle
Grazie — Certosa of Chiaravalle — Novara — Vercelli — Monza : the Ca-
thedral — The Broletto — Sta. Maria in Strada — Como : the Broletto —
The Cathedral.

Milan is better known to the generality of English travellers
than, perhaps, any other city south of the Alps; and its
older portions afford a fair idea of some of the most salient
points of Italian manners and customs, whilst its new and
much-vaunted arcades and streets seem to be not only so
cosmopolitan as to be un-Italian, but so bald and poor in
design as to be repulsive wherever they are! Its narrow
busy streets, though they are wanting indeed in the arcading
so characteristic of very many other towns we had passed
through, have that peculiar charm which life and bustle
always give to strange places; the crowds of foot-passengers
threading the narrow ways, with no protection from the
omnibuses and carts which jostle against them, are full of
animation, and lively and picturesque in their costumes.
Elbowing our way between them, we soon found ourselves
in a piazza, with the Duomo rising before us in all the
magnificence of its white marble walls. If it be indeed true

that it was designed by a German,[1] there is on the outside
even more cause for astonishment at his work than if it had
been the work of an Italian. The west front is quite modern,
but the rest of the exterior, all in its original state, is as
little German in its character as any building I have ever
seen, and—shall I add it?—as little really grand as a work
of art. I had just caught a glimpse of its general outline
and effect by the bright moonlight, on the evening of my
arrival, with the music of an Austrian band sounding pleasantly in my ears, and, thus seen, there was certainly
something wild and striking in its effect. I saw the
brilliantly light colour of the white marble in the full
brightness of the moon, and little of the poverty of moulding, or the heaviness of traceries, or the preposterous
tenuity of pinnacles, which daylight revealed, to the destruction of any belief I might still have in its beauty ; and
the more I examined it in detail the less satisfactory did it
appear ; for neither in its general mass, nor in its detail,
does it bear examination. Its walls are panelled all over,
the panelling having a peculiarly painful kind of pendulous,
unsupported, and unconstructional character, and the string-
courses are marked by a continuous trefoil arcading on their
under side, which recalls the frequent Italian string-courses

---

[1] It is commonly said to have been designed by Heinrich von Gmünden
in 1387 ; but in a most interesting note at p. 116 of ʻItalian Sculptors,ʼ
Mr. Perkins gives the evidence for and against the claim of a German to be
the architect of this cathedral. He believes that there is no longer any
reasonable doubt that the first architect was Marco Frisone da Campione.
Heinrich Adler von Gmünden, who has commonly been stated to be the
architect, did not come to Milan until five years after the foundation of the
church. Marco da Campione died in 1390 ; and the church was ready for
divine service in 1395. The criticisms I have made in the text appear to me
to be equally applicable to an Italian architect trained in Germany, or to a
German working in Italy ; and if Marco da Campione was the architect, one
is compelled, by the logic of the building itself, to say that either he had
studied north of the Alps with a view to perfecting his design, or that he
depended very largely on the help given him by such men as Henry of
Gmünden, whom he had called in to his assistance.

in brick. The buttresses are bold in their formation and
scale, but poor and weak-looking in their design, and finish

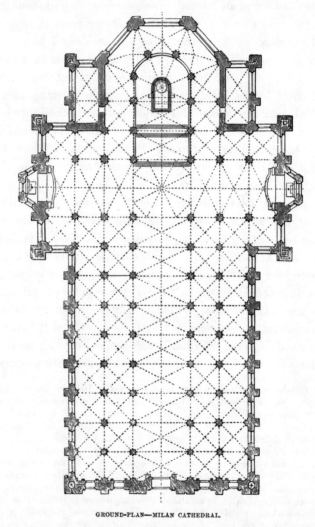

GROUND-PLAN—MILAN CATHEDRAL.

at the top with pinnacles, whose thin outline, seen against
the deep blue sky, is painfully bad and unsatisfying. The

panelling of the walls is continued up to their whole height without any decided line of parapet or cornice, and finishes in a rough serrated line of small gables, which is particularly restless and wanting in repose. Great flying buttresses span the aisles, and then in the clerestory is repeated exactly what we have already seen below, the same panelling, the same parapet, and the same light pinnacles; the windows, however, are here very small and insignificant, whilst those in the aisles are remarkable for their large size and for the singular traceries with which they are filled. All the lower windows are transomed with a line of tracery, surmounted in each light by a crocketed canopy running up into the light above.· In the apse this tracery fills the four outer lights only on each side of the two centre lights, the others being continued without interruption to the sill; and in these windows it is remarkable that each light is subdivided with a small monial below this band of tracery.

Altogether, an effect of a prodigious number and repetition of vertical lines is produced, and yet, notwithstanding this, the effect of the entire building is decidedly rather horizontal and depressing than the contrary; this is not more owing to the absence of all visible roofing than to the way in which the parapets, with their irregular gabled outline, attract the eye to a markedly horizontal feature.

Upon the whole, therefore, the exterior is in no respect more Italian than it is German in its style; it belongs to no school, and has no fellows: from the beginning it has been an exotic, and to the end of time will probably remain so, without a follower or an imitator in the singular development of which it is the only example; and there does appear, if we consider the matter, to be some intrinsic probability that such a building must have been designed by a foreigner rather than by a native. It has, in fact, all

the appearance of having been the work of a stranger who
was but imperfectly acquainted with the wants or customs
of Italian architecture, working to some extent with the
traditions of his national school before him, but, at the
same time, impressed with a strong sense of the necessity
under which he lay, of doing something quite unlike what he
had been taught to consider necessary for buildings in his
native land. It will be found upon examination that there
is absolutely hardly one point in which this vast building
follows the traditions of Italian pointed work. Its plan
has not any Italian characteristics in its arrangement or
proportions. Its windows have moulded monials instead of
shafts ; its walls are buttressed instead of being marked with
pilasters here and there ; its pinnacles are Northern in their
idea, for strength rather than (as Italian pinnacles were)
only for ornament ; its walls have no cornices, and there are
no sham fronts or attempts at concealing the necessary
features of construction ; the walls are panelled instead of
being arcaded, and there is a constant endeavour to break up
plain surfaces of wall, unlike the predilection for smooth
broad surfaces so usual in thoroughly Italian work, and destructive of the kind of breadth and dignity which this last
generally has ; finally, if rest and life may be taken—as by
some they are—to be respectively the distinguishing features
of Italian and Northern pointed work, then, assuredly, the
lack of repose in Milan Cathedral—caused mainly by the
degree to which the system of panelling is carried over the
whole building, and the extent to which the use of the
simple horizontal line is carefully excluded—goes far to
consign its exterior to some school of life and restlessness of
the most unsatisfactory character. The one point in which
an Italian model has been at all followed is the section,
where the proportions of the aisles to the nave and the
pitch of their roofs certainly shew a knowledge of San

Petronio, Bologna. But its architect appears to me to have
been shocked at the necessity under which he lay of sacrific-
ing the steep lines of roof so dear to him in his native land,
and to have striven with all his might to provide a substitute·
for their effect by the vertical lines of his panelled buttresses
and walls, by the gabled outline of his parapets, and by
the removal even of such a slight horizontal mark as the
commencement of the traceries of his windows on one line.
And his work is a most remarkable standing proof of the
failure of such an attempt; for, despite all these precautions,
and I incline to believe in consequence of them, the general
effect is, after all, entirely horizontal. Extremes meet, and
so the attempt to avoid absolute horizontal lines has completely failed, because in their place we have a succession
of vertical members placed side by side in such endless
numbers that we really think more of the horizontal arrangement of these members, slight though they are, than
we should of the simplest defined horizontal line.

And the same consequence followed the same kind of
work in England. I know no building in which the horizontal line is more painfully predominant than in Henry the
Seventh's Chapel at Westminster, where, nevertheless, it is
broken endlessly by vertical lines of pinnacles, and where
the walls are covered in all parts with perpendicular lines of
panelling.

Indeed, I should have but little respect for such a
building as this exterior of Milan were it not for its rare
material (used though it is in a prodigal manner, and
without particular reference to its nature) and its immense
size – though this is far less in appearance than in reality.
But my detraction and harsh criticisms must end here; for
if, having first made the circuit of the entire church, the
flight of steps which leads up to the west door is last of all
mounted, the first feeling must be one of perfect amazement

and delight—amazement that the same mind which conceived the exterior should have been able also to achieve anything so diverse from it as is the interior, and delight that anything so magnificent and so perfect should ever have been reared on the southern slope of the Alps, to exhibit, to the eyes as it were of enemies, the full majesty and power of the pointed architecture of the North. And mark, upon consideration, how very natural this was. Its architect had been tied down in his exterior by the wants, or supposed wants, of a climate unlike his own, and a material to which he was unused; his genius had thus been fettered and kept under; but here all shackles were undone, and he was free to carry out to its very greatest perfection what he had learnt or dreamt of in his Northern home. And what a result has he not achieved!—absolutely and without doubt one of the grandest interiors in the world is, I do believe, this noble work of his; its grandeur amazes one at first, and delights all the more afterwards as one becomes on more intimate terms with it, and can look at it with less emotion than at first. And how shall I describe it?—for to say that it has so many bays in length or in width is not sufficient; all this, and even the detail of its design, were familiar enough to me before I saw it, but still the reality was so very far beyond any description, that I felt, and feel still, averse from attempting it.

A few only of the most noticeable points, therefore, shall be touched; and, as it seems to me to teach less of Italian art or architecture than of Northern, I shall feel myself acquitted of neglect, inasmuch as the main, if not the sole, object of my Italian notes is as to the development of really Italian work. I was struck at first by the prodigious width and height of the building. The nave is enormously wide, and has two aisles on either side, those next to it being also of great size and height, and having clerestories

in their outer walls.　The outer aisles are lighted with large
traceried windows, filled with stained glass, which gives the
church a character very unlike that of the generality of
Italian Gothic churches, in which coloured glass is so rarely
seen in large masses.

There is, therefore, a regular gradation in the heights
of the five main divisions of the church, which are well
proportioned to their respective widths; and, resting as
these divisions do upon four rows of clustered columns of
immense size and height, a more magnificent internal effect
is produced than I can recollect even any approach to in any
other church; for not even in Köln or in Amiens is there
any effect so magnificent as that of this forest of prodigious
piers.　They are finished at the top with capitals peculiar
to this building, and quite unlike anything I have before
seen—I suppose at least twelve feet deep, with a kind of
arcade of tracery surmounted by a crocketed gable on each
side, and finished above and below with courses of foliage, and
with figures standing in the niche-like panels of the arcade.

Such a contrivance would be clumsy and absurd if
attempted on a small scale, but here, at the summit of these
immense columns, it is thoroughly successful, and, I believe,
the only contrivance which could have been successfully
adopted.　The capitals vary very much in detail and in
merit; but one of the finest is seen close to the west entrance,
and recalls forcibly the best Northern pointed work, having
indeed, neither in detail nor in design, one single trace of an
Italian influence.

So grand are the columns that the excessive poverty and
lightness of the arches which divide the nave from the aisles,
which is perhaps the greatest defect of the interior of the
church, is not for a long time noticed; they have, however,
but little apparent work to do, and so their lightness may
perhaps be a virtue.

Throughout the interior there is a very remarkable love shewn everywhere for a moulding which was never used by Italians, but was so much used among ourselves—the wave-mould. Then, again, all the shafts are filleted, and the fillet turning off gradually into the round line of the shaft, produces the same moulding; a fulness and richness are consequently very noticeable in all the interior, very different indeed from anything else that I saw in Italy. The solitary blot upon this otherwise noble work is one for which its architect is in no way responsible—the cells of the groining are all filled in with painted imitations of elaborate traceries in brown colour, an abominable device, which never ceases to offend and annoy the eye more and more every time it is observed.[1] The window tracery throughout is meagre, confused, and unmeaning, and the traceries introduced at mid-height most unsatisfactory; but the glass with which it is filled, though poor and late in its character, contains much rich colour, and gives the entire building a very grand and warm tone.

Compared with other foreign churches, there is in this—the largest of them all—a singular absence of side altars There are indeed some three or four; but so great is the prominence given to the high altar in the choir, that one scarcely thinks of the possibility of the existence of any others, and has to look about a good deal before discovering where they are to be found.

In common with so many of the Italian churches the pavements here are very fine, and impart no small degree of additional magnificence to the interior.

Many are the works which might be catalogued in this

---

[1] When I first saw this I thought it was an entirely modern device. In 1871, however, in passing through France, I found at La Fère a church of flamboyant character, with all the cells of its groining covered with sunk traceries; and at Chambéry the painting on the roof of the Sainte Chapelle is said to be old.

great church, but I must content myself with noticing one only—the great bronze candelabrum. This is, I suppose, the most precious work of its kind in Europe. It was placed in the cathedral in 1557, a date too late for its execution by some three hundred years. The supports are four winged dragons, heads downwards, and with tails intertwined. The shaft has bosses in the centre, and branches out above into a profusion of branches full of exquisite leafage. This is all conventional in character, and entirely like thirteenth-century work. In spaces formed for the purpose and on the bosses are various figures and subjects all wrought with singular skill, and a lavish profusion of ingenuity which cannot be too much admired. Among these are the Temptation and the Expulsion from Paradise, the signs of the zodiac, figures illustrating architecture and music, and a variety of others.

After I had seen the cathedral I had, by way of enjoying the pleasures of a contrast, to devote myself patiently to all the troubles attendant upon personally procuring my passport. At Milan personal application was absolutely enforced; and there, in a small room crowded by vetturini and other Italians of the lower order, relieved by one or two unfortunate travellers like myself, I had for nearly two hours to endure heat, noise, and all the other annoyances of such a work, before I succeeded in getting my passport *visé*, with permission to abide three days only within the walls. This system is certainly most vexatious to an Englishman; but at the same time, if people will make a point of keeping the rulers of a city constantly on the *qui vive* with plots, or rumours of plots, I do not see what other resource their rulers can have. Some idea of the state of the population may be drawn from the way in which the soldiers patrol the streets, in companies of three or four, during the whole day, giving an impression of a place where men keeping guard singly would be in danger; and then again the great number of the troops at the gates and elsewhere throughout the city certainly presents very much the impression of a place whose normal condition is one perpetual state of siege.[1]

Next to the cathedral the great architectural attraction of Milan is the famous church of Sant' Ambrogio, which has equally as great claims upon the antiquary and upon the ecclesiologist as upon the architect.

Entering from the west, it presented a most striking and, to me, most novel effect. In advance of the church is an open atrium, surrounded by a cloister of Lombard-Romanesque character, the columns having quaintly and stiffly carved capitals of stone, and the wall and arches being built of mixed bricks and stone. Three arches, open from the atrium to the west end of the church, and above them three other arches of similar plan, and arranged in triplet fashion, that in the centre being the highest and widest, nearly fill up the great flat pediment of the church, on either side of which rise towers—that on the north divided into stages by means of arcaded strings, like most Lombard belfries; that on the south perfectly plain and rude, and perhaps therefore of the very early date at which some antiquaries appear to place the building of the main structure of this portion of the existing church.[2]

This arrangement, borrowed though it may be from heathen days and civil buildings, is nevertheless uncommonly satisfactory; it serves to prepare the mind for the entrance to the church itself, and, instead of the abrupt transition commonly made from the world to the holy places, here the intermediate atrium gives time and space to throw off all worldly thoughts, and to enter entirely into the religious feelings proper in such a place.

[1] I leave this passage as it was written in 1855. Such troubles are now all passed and gone; but we run some risk of forgetting how much we have gained in this way by the political changes that have occurred since then.

[2] The atrium was added, it is said, in the ninth century.

The entrance by the west doorway is of great interest, for in its very ancient doors are inserted some still more ancient fragments, said by tradition—and there is every reason to believe it to be true—to be portions of the gates which S. Ambrose shut against the Emperor Theodosius.

The interior has suffered much at various times, either by repairs or alterations; and as most of the groining is of pointed character, the first impression is that of a very low, simple, and solemn-looking pointed church of early date. Upon more close examination, however, it is found that the main walls throughout are Romanesque, and that this groining was subsequently inserted, and again in later times strengthened and supported by great piers and arches of Classic character.

The plan, after passing the atrium, is a nave of three bays, each subdivided into two by arches into the aisles, a lantern over the altar, and three eastern apses. There are no transepts. The most striking object in the interior is the magnificent Romanesque baldachin above the high altar. This is supported on four marble shafts, and has a semi-circular arch on each face, with figures and foliage in the four flat pediments or gables which finish it above. Three flights of five steps lead up to the altar from the north, south, and west, and the whole is protected both on the east and the west by high metal screens. Here is a splendid shrine for the relics of the tutelar saint, of the same age as the early church, which is however so jealously concealed that I have never seen it.[1] The front of the altar itself is very magnificent, executed entirely in metal, and containing subjects from the life of Our Blessed Lord and from that of S. Ambrose. A modernized dome rises above the baldachin; and behind this an apse decorated in mosaic upon a gold ground very grandly finishes the interior of this interesting church.

[1] See, for description of it, Hemans' ' Mediæval Christianity,' &c., p. 305.

Whiteman & Bass. Photo Litho to the Queen.

58. BALDACHIN. S. AMBROGIO. MILAN.

On the north side of the nave is a very curious pulpit, coeval with the church and remarkable for its carvings, and for a Roman sarcophagus which occupies the space between the columns which support it.

From Sant' Ambrogio I made my way under a burning sun to what I expected to find a very interesting church, that of Sant' Eustorgio. I was, however, very much disappointed; the interior is abominably modernized, though still retaining enough of its old Romanesque features to be intelligible if carefully studied, and remarkable for many ancient monuments on its walls. It has nave, aisles, and chapels beyond the aisles, the whole groined, and there is a prodigious ascent to the choir, which is raised upon a crypt.

That for which it ought to be visited is the exquisite monument to S. Peter Martyr, executed by G. Balduccio da Pisa, in 1339. It consists of a sarcophagus supported on pilasters, in front of which are statues representing virtues. Few works of the kind have ever been executed, in which the skill of the sculptor has been more happily united with that of the architect than in this. It deserves all praise.

Sta. Maria delle Grazie, which I next visited, is a church known generally as that in the refectory attached to which is to be seen all that remains of L. da Vinci's painting of the Last Supper. I know not how much this may have suffered within the last few years, but really, when I read the kind of remarks which I so frequently see about it, I cannot help fancying, rather strongly, that they have perhaps been written before instead of after seeing the veritable picture. It is in fact in the last stage of decay, with scarcely any of its colouring or drawing intelligible; and has probably been entirely repainted since Leonardo's death. Visitors who go to admire and do admire the Leonardo, might do worse than in examining and admiring the extremely fine and fairly well-preserved earlier fresco or distemper painting by Montorfano

which covers the opposite wall of the refectory, and contains a good and busy painting of the Crucifixion, painted
in 1495. The church is of very late pointed date, entirely
of brick, with a large and ugly dome added by Bramante.
The nave arcades are pretty good—pointed arches springing from the square Classical-looking capitals of equally
Classical-looking columns; very much as in the church of
San Francesco at Venice. Elaborate brick cornices and the
usual sham front leave the same kind of impression on my
mind in respect to this church that it has of all late Italian
pointed work in brick—one of a tasteless, unreal, and
unsatisfactory school of art.

South of the cathedral there is a fine late brick campanile attached to the church of San Gottardo, which rises
from behind some of the great public buildings in which
the city abounds. This is a very elaborate work, octagonal
in plan and covered with arcades one above the other, and
finished with a low spire. It is a fourteenth-century building at the earliest, but in spite of this most of its arches are
semicircular. It is certainly a rich and picturesque tower,
and well deserves inspection.

The remaining churches in Milan seemed to be all
Classical, of different grades of merit and size. There were
indeed some very late examples of brickwork of some value,
but really, save the cathedral, there is not much architectural art to be studied or dwelt upon in Milan. The
cathedral, too, teaches little; its main office is, rather, to
prove the consummate beauty and magnificence attainable
by the pointed style, carried out severely and simply on the
very grandest scale, and this its interior does triumphantly
beyond all cavil.

A visit to Milan had always been looked forward to by me
with great interest: first, from curiosity as to the real effect
and merits of the Duomo; and, secondly, from a longing

Walmsan & Ross. Photo Litho to the Queen.

59. PIAZZA DEI MERCANTI, MILAN

to see the magnificent Sposalizio of Raffaelle, which is the
gem of the collection in the Brera; and this famous gallery
was therefore one of the first objects of my curiosity. The
careful examination of the pictures which adorn its walls
was, however, when we were there, much hindered by an
exhibition of modern Italian pictures, hung in the same
rooms as, and in most cases in front of, the old works. We
were able, fortunately, to get a fair view of what I believe to
be not far from the greatest work of one of the greatest
painters in the world—the Sposalizio being in a room un-
occupied by other pictures and unmolested by the modern
exhibitors. The man who could so paint at the age of
twenty one must, assuredly, have been almost matchless, for
never have I seen a painting more thoroughly noble and
delightful, in every way recalling to mind, it is true, in
every figure the manner of his master, the great Perugino,
but not the less enjoyable on that account.

The modern pictures were almost invariably worthless,
and shewed no sign of any revival parallel to that which I
trust I am not too sanguine in believing that one sees at the
present day in England.

In the Piazza dei Mercanti is a much-altered building of
the thirteenth century (its date is said to be 1228), which
looks in its arrangements like a Palazzo Publico, and which
in its original state must have been very charming. On the
lower stage are five open arches, which have been modernized,
I believe; above this a line of square panels, inclosing
shields, forms a bold string-course, the central portion being
brought forward on corbels for a Ringhiera. The *piano
nobile* consists of five pointed arches carried on delicate
shafts, and above was a deeply sunk line of arcading, each
division garnished with a statue. There was once evidently
a canopy over the Ringhiera. The materials of this front are
black and white stone, but they are used with such mode-

ration that there is nothing at all bizarre in the general effect of the façade.

In addition to these buildings there is still to be described another very grand brick domestic building of late date—the Ospidale Maggiore—which contains a great deal of very rich detail, half Renaissance and half Gothic in its character, though the general scheme of the building is wholly Renaissance. This building has been much extolled, but I think those who have praised it so much have mistaken clever manipulation of detail for good architectural design. The terra-cotta enrichments with which it is so richly set are hardly surpassed in their way by any of the same period in Italy, but I cannot admire the building as a whole.

With this building my architectural notes in Milan must end, but I should advise all students of architecture to include in their visits one of about half an hour's drive to the Certosa of Chiaravalle just outside Milan. The church here has been much modernized, but over the centre of the crossing still rises a brick lantern and steeple of singular interest. My engraving will explain what the character of this work is, better than any words. The construction is singular. Behind the base of the second stage of the great octagon a spire is constructed which carries the upper steeple, and the whole of the walls pierced with the second, third, and fourth series of windows are really only screen-walls or parapets in front of the spire. The height of the whole lantern from the ridge to the base of the spire is about ninety feet, and the effect of the complicated brickwork is not bad. It is somewhat difficult to say exactly when it was built. The Certosa itself was founded in 1135, and consecrated in 1228, but my impression is decidedly that though the whole steeple is built with round arches, it is not really a work of earlier date than about A. D. 1370 to 1400. The steeple of San Gottardo in Milan, which also has round arches everywhere, and is in some other

60. CERTOSA OF CHIARAVALLE.

respects somewhat similar in detail to this, dates from 1339,
and it would be a great mistake to argue for an earlier date
in either case from the mere use of the round arch.   If I
recollect right, the low third stage in height at Chiaravalle
is modern.

Milan was on the whole rather disappointing to me in
my architectural capacity, though pleasant enough in every
other; and after I had lounged and driven about, first in one
direction and then in another, and had really enjoyed my last
great Italian city very much, finding that little more was to
be done but to eat ices, look at smart carriages on the Corso,
and long for more chance of a clear view of the Alps than the
hazy sultry weather afforded, I made up my mind to leave
earlier than I had originally intended.

No architectural student should turn his feet homeward
from Milan without having first of all visited Vercelli.   It is
easily reached by railway, passing on the road Novara, where
there was only a few years back a fine Lombard cathedral,
which has unfortunately been lately supplanted by a modern
Italian fabric, even more than usually vapid and uninteresting,
and where there is still an old baptistery so plastered and
painted as to have lost almost all its old interest.   The
traveller has therefore to content himself with the views—
which become better as he proceeds—of the snow-capped
Alps (including their noblest peak, Monte Rosa) to the north
of the railway, which, in clear weather, are most glorious in
their effect.

The cathedral at Vercelli is modernized, and I believe not
worth visiting; I confined myself to the remarkable church
of Sant' Andrea, which is fortunately close to the railway
station, and of unusual beauty and interest.   The interest is
historical as well as architectural.   The church was built by
Cardinal Guala de' Bicchieri, who had been in England as
legate from the Pope at the very beginning of the thirteenth

century, and is said to have brought back with him to Vercelli
a French or English architect. The evidence of the building
itself is in favour of a French rather than an English influence, but neither is felt anywhere save in the interior, and
the outside views shew to my eyes no trace of any but an
Italian hand. It is the square-ended choir probably which
has made some writers say that it was designed by an English
architect. This choir is short, and on the east side of each
transept are two chapels, which are apsidal. The whole
church is groined; the columns between the nave and aisles
are well clustered, and all the mouldings and details are
well and skilfully drawn. The church is well designed to
suit the climate, all the windows being small except at
the east end, where there is a fine triplet, with a circular
window filled with well-designed tracery above. Over the
crossing of nave and transepts is a raised lantern, groined,
and lighted by very small windows high up. The angles
under it have extremely well-designed pendentives with
carvings of the Evangelistic emblems in the centre. Brick
is used for the main portion of the work, counter-changed
in many parts with stone, and the proportions and details
of the interior are so good that I found myself in the rare
state of mind (in an Italian church) of admiring without
grumbling! The dimensions are good without being imposing, the total length being a little over two hundred
feet, and the width across the transepts about a hundred
and twenty feet.

The exterior has a great bald west front with three
round arched doorways, and a false gable between two small
but lofty flanking towers. The walls are arcaded under the
eaves, and over the crossing rises an octagonal lantern, which
is gathered in after a rather ungainly manner above the
lowest stage. This steeple is finished with a low circular
brick spire adorned in the most curious fashion with small

G.E.S. 1869.

Whiteman & Bass, Photo Litho to the Queen.

61. SANT' ANDREA. VERCELLI.

circular brick pinnacles—one over each side of the tower—
which look extremely like a collection of chimneys.

Detached from the church, and standing at an angle to
it, is a simple campanile of later date (1399), and of four
stages in height. The combination of this eccentrically
placed tower with the rest of the church is very remarkable,
and appears to have been simply a caprice. Its effect certainly
does not warrant the sort of admiration which should lead
any modern architect engaged in studying the church to
recommend the copying of the relative positions of it and its
bell-tower. I ought not to forget one feature—the buttress
—which is treated here in quite the French or English
fashion, with bold projection and good steep sloped weather-
ings instead of in the usual Italian fashion as a mere pilaster.

North of the nave of the church is a good cloister, on the
east side of which is a fine square chapter-house, divided by
groining piers into nine bays. The original triple entrance
to the chapter-house—a door with window on each side—still
remains, and there is a communication also through a groined
sacristy with the north transept. I know few churches
which shew more just sense of the best treatment of a good
Gothic interior than this does. In its original state, when
the brickwork was exposed in its natural colour, the effect
was of course much better than it is now ; but the effect
is still so good that I may safely assert that, were the exterior
equal to the interior, there would be few more beautiful
churches in Northern Italy.[1]

There is an interesting monument in the south-east chapel,
corbelled out from the wall and decorated with sculpture and
painting. In the gable is the Coronation of the Blessed

---

[1] It is worth notice that the regular-looking bays of the nave are of very
various widths. The two eastern are 21 feet; the next two, four feet less;
and the fifth still narrower. The bricks here measure 1 ft. $\frac{1}{2}$ in. × 5 in., and
are $3\frac{1}{4}$ in. high, and have all been chiselled on the face.

Virgin, below a figure kneeling before her, and said to represent the architect of the church, who died in 1246, being
Abbat as well as architect. Immediately opposite the church
is a hospital founded by the same cardinal. It has been
much altered, but there are still some ancient portions,
which I could not get leave to see.

From Vercelli we retraced our steps to Milan, and halted
no longer than was necessary before going on to Monza on
our way to Como. Here we were well rewarded and most
agreeably surprized. We found a very curious and good
Broletto, a cathedral of fine and elaborate brickwork with a
great west front of marble, and another brick church of most
elaborate detail. The west front of the Duomo is a very
fine example of Italian Gothic in marble; it is divided into
five divisions in width, those in the centre and at the sides
being the widest, and is constructed in yellow and dark grey
marbles in alternate courses, the former very deep, the latter
generally shallow, but varying without much rule.

All the roofs are flat, but finish at the west at different
levels, and not in one continuous slope. The eaves have
heavy cornices, and under these, all the way up, is an arcade
resting upon shafts supported on corbels. The windows are
all filled with traceries which are certainly not at all equal
to English tracery, as they are very flat in their effect, and
have no proper subordination of parts. There is a large rose
window in the centre division treated in a better manner
than is usual, and set within a square line of moulding, with
small circles in the spandrels, and a line of square panels on
each side continued in the most unpleasing way above; five
other smaller circular windows are similarly treated. In some
parts of the wall the courses of black marble are continuations
of the black arch-stones of the windows, which, though not
uncommon in Italian pointed work, is never satisfactory in its
effect. In the upper part of the front this is not the case.

The central division has a porch resting upon detached shafts, and with a semicircular arch, which is, however, richly cusped; and throughout the front semicircular and pointed arches seem to have been used quite indiscriminately. The buttresses which divide the front were originally finished

CATHEDRAL—MONZA.

with pinnacles, of which one only now remains; this is certainly very beautiful, of precisely the same type as the pinnacles on some of the tombs of the Scaligers at Verona, standing on detached shafts, with gables on either side, supported on trefoiled arches, and with small pinnacles between the gables, all of which are crocketed; the mouldings are

very flat, but in the pure white marble seen against the
deep blue sky of Italy this flatness is as much a virtue and a
beauty as its counterpart executed in stone in chilly England
would be poverty-stricken and tame. All the remainder of
the exterior of the Duomo is of red brick, with some particularly good detail. I give one window from the south side of
the choir as an example.

There is a large low cloister on the north side, and from
this the central tower is best seen; it is an octagon of two
stages in brick and stone, a good deal arcaded, and has a
pyramidal tiled roof, with a square turret in the centre.
This forms a dome internally, which is however (as is the
whole of the church) miserably modernized.

The cornices under the eaves here are of brick of good
detail, but of the common arcaded character. I noticed
an inscription on the east end, referring to the erection
of the church in 1390, a date which tallies very well with
the character of most of the external detail. Internally
there is a rather remarkable pulpit or ambon on the north
side of the nave. It is a gallery measuring some twenty
feet east and west, supported on detached shafts with a
projection in the centre, and of combined Gothic and Renaissance detail; so large a pulpit certainly suggests rambling
discourses.

On the whole, such a church as this is very interesting,
and to some extent striking; but, much as I admired the
conjunction of the two marbles, and the more than usually
Gothic character of some of the details, there was yet
enough in the ungainly outline of the sham front, and in
the capricious use of round and pointed arches indifferently,
to damp my pleasure, and make me cease to admire the
work very decidedly. There is a difference in construction
which ought to be noted between this marble front and
the marble work at Venice; for, whilst the latter is not at

62.—BROLETTO, MONZA.

all constructional, this is entirely so, the marbles not being veneered on to the wall, but forming a portion of its substance. I need not say that in this respect, when we wish to use marble in England, the paucity of our supplies will probably always compel us to imitate the Venetians rather than the architects of Monza, Como, or Milan.

The sacristy here is worth visiting. Among other relics are two fifteenth-century chalices of unusually good workmanship. They appeared to me to be by a German rather than an Italian hand.

BROLETTO—MONZA.

The Broletto, which stands near the cathedral in the centre of the city, is very interesting. It is raised upon open arches of stone, two at either end and five at the sides. In my sketch of it the southern end is shewn with the projecting Ringhiera in the second stage; the northern end is very singular, the tower rising out of one side, with the steep-pitched roof of the other half abutting against it. The detail of the windows is very good, the arch-stones in some of them increasing in depth towards the centre, with an effect of very great strength. All the windows are shafted. The dimensions of this building are forty-two feet from east to west, and sixty-four feet from north to south.

The only other ancient building which I could find was the church of Sta. Maria in Strada; the most elaborate example of late work in brick and terra-cotta that I have anywhere seen. The effect is not satisfactory; for when, as here, carvings are imitated and repeated in terra-cotta, and traceries entirely executed in it, one begins, I confess, to long much for a little of the fire and spirit which some mark of the individual artist might have given such an amount of elaborate decoration in stone. The west front is the only part of the church of any interest, the interior having been thoroughly modernized, and retaining no traces of its original character.

The door and windows in the lower stage have been interpolated, and besides this there is a strangely ugly window above them, about which—as this is the last of its class we shall see—I wish to say a word. In starting on a continental journey, between London and Croydon on the South-Eastern Railway you used to pass under several great semicircular arched bridges. When first built, the engineer chose, in order to gratify some odd fancy, to prop these up by two piers of brickwork, dividing the arch into three, and putting the whole in great jeopardy. It is curious that this singularly supported and divided arch finds a counterpart in almost every large church in the North of Italy. It was the one great idea of the Renaissance builders, and, until they had taken out one of the old windows and inserted in its place one of these hideous contrivances, they were never satisfied. In Venice every church, even the noble church of the Frari, has them, and I believe scarcely a large church in the North of Italy is without at least this one evidence of the delicacy of taste which characterizes the Renaissance age!

The skill which is shewn in making and fitting together

brickwork such as that in the front of this church is very great indeed, but, after all, I fear, rather mistaken, for the effect is most unsatisfactory, and every one must see that throughout the façade there is an evident attempt to satisfy the eye by the exceedingly elaborate character of the detail, rather than by the fitness of the thing itself, or by the beauty of the proportions. The insufficiency of the windows for the extent of wall is an obvious fault, and not less so is the fact which I am almost tired of referring to, that the whole front is sham and designed without any reference whatever to the wants of the building, to which it forms the street-front.

In the evening we left Monza for Camerlata, a village within about a mile of Como, availing ourselves again of the Milan and Como railway.

The Camerlata station was soon reached, and after some little delay we found ourselves ensconced in one of those long omnibuses so fashionable in Italy, and driving down a long hill, planted on either side with trees, towards Como. Above us, to the right and to the left, we could see, by the bright moonlight, the shapes of the mountains which hem in this arm of the fairest of lakes; whilst just above us, proudly perched upon a crag, were the ruins of a castle, which lent, when we saw it by daylight, an additional charm to the otherwise beautiful view.

Soon we were in the outskirts of the town; but it was long before we reached the borders of the lake, after following the windings of an almost interminable street, passing the guardhouse, and, to our sorrow, parting again for the last time with our passports, then crossing the piazza in which stand the Duomo and the Broletto side by side—for me the main attraction of the place—until at last we were fairly discharged at an hotel on the very edge of the water.

We had heard an Austrian band as we rolled across the

piazza, and so without delay thither we returned in time to
hear the last of Austrian music, and to revel by moonlight
in the beauty of the many-coloured marble front of the fair
Broletto. We stood listening to the music for about a
quarter of an hour, when suddenly a word of command was
given, the men who held the lanterns marched to the front,
the band formed behind them four abreast, the lights were
extinguished, and, suddenly breaking into a lively march,
the band disappeared, and the crowd soon left us in quiet
possession of the piazza, whose old houses still rang with
the wild and clamorous echoes of the beautiful music.

We returned to our inn, and had infinite trouble in the
attempt to find a voiturier to take us to the Lago Maggiore
in time for the steamer on the morrow. The route by which
I had fully intended to return was to go by the lake to
Menaggio, thence to cross to Porlezza and by the Lake of
Lugano, and then from Lugano across the Monte Cenere to
Bellinzona; to my great annoyance I found, however, at
Milan that, owing to the long-standing quarrel between the
Emperor and the Confederation, no travellers were allowed
to pass immediately from the Austrian into the Ticinese
territory, or *vice versâ*, and we were obliged, therefore, to
defer seeing the beautiful Lake of Lugano, to go instead
to Laveno, and thence to Bellinzona, by the Lago Maggiore;
and our difficulty at Como was to find any true account of
the time that it would take us to reach Laveno, or of the
time at which we were likely to find the steamer to
Magadino. In the end it was decided that we should start
at seven the next morning, and accordingly soon after five I
was out in the piazza taking notes and sketches of my last
Italian building, the Broletto of Como.

In general character this is somewhat similar to the
Broletto at Bergamo, but in real beauty it is scarcely inferior
to any one building I have seen in Italy. Towards the

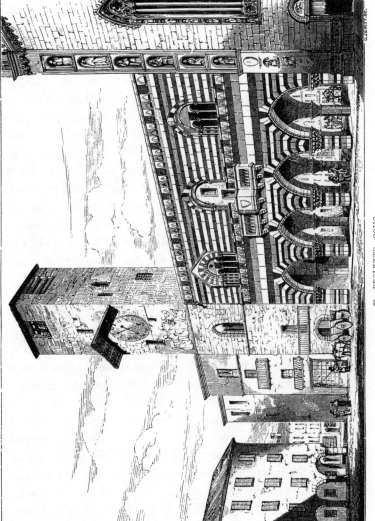

68.—BROLETTO, COMO.

piazza it has four arches on the ground story, which is
divided from the next stage by an arcaded string-course.
This second stage has three windows only over the four
arches below; and another very noticeable irregularity is,
that one of these windows, and that not the central, has a
pedimental canopy above its arch, and has more shafts than
the others. The central window has been modernized to
some extent, but this was the Ringhiera, and the balcony
still remains, though looking more modern than the rest of
the front. Some of the arches of these windows are very
noticeable; for though they are semicircular, the back of the
stones which form them is cut with a different sweep, so
as to produce an outer pointed line, and thus to leave
an impression on the eye of absolutely pointed windows.
Another arcaded corbel-table finishes the façade, or rather
ought to finish it, for above this some barbarian has added
another stage, nearly to the destruction of the effect of the
building.[1] North of this façade a great plain tower of rough
stone recalls to recollection those of Bergamo and Brescia;
it boasts of an immense clock and some faint traces of
painting, and is left unfinished at the top. The whole of
this façade (with the exception of the campanile) is built of
red, white, and dark grey marbles, which are very carefully
and effectively contrasted in their arrangement; the courses
are very irregular in their widths, and apparently arranged
upon no systematic rule. The opposite (east) side of the
Broletto is very similar, but one of its windows is remarkable for the way in which the shafts are knotted
together in the centre. This is not at all an uncommon
feature in Italian pointed, and I have often wondered how
it is that the eye is not at once disgusted with it, instead
of being, as it usually is, pleased. I take it to be a justifiable

---

[1] I think no apology is necessary for the omission of this modern stage in
my view of the Broletto.

device on some such ground as this: it takes much labour
and skill to cut several shafts out of one block of marble,
but all this labour and skill is unthought of, if they are
entirely separated, or held together by a band which might
perchance be made of some other material; this knot therefore is devised as the only means of explaining to us that
the shafts so carved have really been accomplished with a
very great expenditure of time and patience and skill, and
do not depend upon any artificial band for the firmness with
which they are all united in one. The capitals of all the
columns in this Broletto are very well carved.

By the side of the Broletto stands the Duomo, the bad
character of whose west front, even though it is of late
Gothic, hardly tempted me to go in to see the effect of the
interior. I did so, however, and found a large but uninteresting church, with groining of pointed section, which
gives considerable character to an otherwise insipid work.
The west front has doorways of Lombard character, and
above them a large rose window; but every part of the
exterior and interior seems to have been so much altered
that little remains of the original work.

Internally works of restoration were going on, and these
permitted me to see that the whole church had a great deal
of colour introduced on the walls and over the groining,
though I was unable to ascertain anything satisfactorily as
to its age or character.

About ten minutes' walk from the cathedral is the fine
Lombard church of Sta. Maria. This has unfortunately been
much modernized, but its east end with an apse arcaded
outside, and finished with a fine eaves-cornice rich in shadow,
is still extremely striking and almost unaltered. It is built
of black and white stone. Here, alas! I remember that I
thought at the time of my first visit, ends my hurried study
of Gothic architecture in Italy. But if at that day it was

G.E.S. 1867.

64. STᵃ MARIA. COMO.

somewhat sad to leave Como after an all too rapid journey, it has been my happiness to revisit the quaint old town again and again since, and each time with increased pleasure. Italian scenery, Italian art, Italian travel, afford some of the happiest recollections of well-spent days of travel, which, if they have never been able to exceed in pleasure or to approach in profit the remembrances of travels in my own and other lands, undertaken for the same purpose, are nevertheless full to overflowing with lessons in art which no true architect could afford to despise or wish to forget.

CHAPTER XIII.

"And now farewell to Italy—perhaps
For ever !   Yet, methinks, I could not go,
I could not leave it, were it mine to say
' Farewell for ever ! ' "
                                        Rogers.

———◆———

Departure from Como — Varese — Lake of Varese — Italian Boatmen —
Intra — Laveno — Lago Maggiore — Magadino — Road to Hospenthal —
The Dazio Grande — Airolo — Hospenthal — Ascent of the Furca — Valley
of the Reuss — Lake of Luzern — Luzern — The Unter Hauenstein —
Strasburg.

THERE was great delay in leaving Como; the passport officer
was asleep, and no one dared to awaken him for our convenience; at last we determined to start, and went off to the
passport office, and, after waiting nearly half an hour, the
dilatory clerk arrived, and our passport having been stamped
with the "Buon per partire," so uncivilly glad to get rid of
you as it seems to be, I mounted the carriage, and we were
soon on our way.

All Como was astir, and bedecking the houses and
churches, and building triumphal arches across the roads,
for some religious fête whose nature we did not discover;
but we soon left its streets and hills behind, and began to
look out anxiously for our first view of Monte Rosa and its
attendant Alps; but, alas! the weather, instead of clearing,
rapidly became more and more cloudy, and ere long we felt
that we must give up all hope of getting even the most

distant glimpse of the monarch of this portion of the Alpine chain.

Without this view, from which we had promised ourselves so much pleasure, the road is tame and uninteresting all the way to Varese, where we changed our horses and carriage. It is an uninteresting town, with a good many villas and gardens, belonging, I believe, to inhabitants of Milan, who come out here for the mountain air. None of their houses are free from that general look of dreariness and lack of care which seem to afflict most Italian villas. Passing through Varese, we soon saw on our right a very famous pilgrimage church crowning the summit of a considerable hill, and approached by a succession of chapels, somewhat as in the still more famous pilgrimage church of Varallo, and so popular that round it there seems to have grown up a small town for the accommodation of the pilgrims.

Farther on we passed the lake of Varese, and from one point in the road had a view of no less than about five different lakes, one of which was Lago Maggiore. The Lago di Varese is a tame, uninteresting sheet of water, surrounded by low flat woody country, except at one point on the north, but even there the hills do not rise immediately from the lake.

The only approach to old buildings that we saw were one or two brick campanili of early date, and the remains of a castle, near Varese, finished at the top with the favourite forked battlement.

We had much ado to make our driver understand our desire to reach Lago Maggiore without delay, and, to say the truth, there was something too much like cruelty in the attempt to compel our poor steeds to any such feat of speed and strength as the performance of some six miles an hour really appeared to be. As we neared the lake the scenery improved; and woody hills, with here and there a dashing streamlet finding its way down the hill-side, and a glimpse now and then of the blue water of the lake, made the way pleasant. At last we reached the outskirts of the village of Laveno, and were immediately chased by all the male population of the place, who explained their eager pursuit when at last we stopped on the beach, by vying with one another for the privilege of conveying us across the lake to Intra, where we had to join the steamer. I asked their charge, and they rather astonished me by demanding twelve francs and a buono-mano; of course I blandly offered them five francs, much to their disgust, and with shrugs of their shoulders and grand looks of contempt they turned away. However, I was determined not to submit to so palpable an imposition, so, when I was having my passport *visé*, I asked the courteous passport-officer what the fair charge might be? "Four and a half lire," was the answer. "But how am I to compel the rascals to take me?"—"Oh! bring them up to me," he replied; so down I went to where all the boatmen were discussing together the atrocity of my offer, and, taking two of them by the arm, I quietly walked them up to the friendly officer; the rest followed, and then commenced one of the most amusing scenes I ever witnessed. The passport-officer told them to take me for the four and a half lire, upon which, they all, standing with their right arms extended towards him, answered with a furious volley of Italian ejaculations, quite unintelligible to me, but sufficiently absurd when contrasted with the quiescent state of their antagonist. Their eloquence was, however, all in vain; for, after a short attempt to reason them into submission, my friend sent them off, and threatened to send a soldier with us if they did not start at once. Before I could reach the beach again the luggage was all in the boat, and in another minute we were afloat, propelled by three sturdy fellows, who, after having tried in vain to make me pay fourteen lire and a buono-mano, were really not apparently much annoyed when I paid them the legal fare, being about one-fourth less than at a guess I had first of all offered! They were evidently true philosophers.

I fear that my experience of travelling in Italy obliged me to look upon the proceedings of these men as by no means unusual or peculiar to boatmen; wherever you go it is the same, and, unless you wish to pay much more than the rest of the world ever thinks of paying, you must make a point of disputing hotel accounts, shop charges, and voiturier's charges; the result always is, that you pay about twenty per cent. less than you otherwise would, and are evidently looked up to with infinitely more respect.

About half an hour sufficed to take us to Intra, the Sardinian port opposite to Laveno, just a glimpse being obtained of the famous Isola Bella as we crossed. A Sardinian soldier welcomed us to his liberal Majesty's dominions, and, as we told him that we were going on by the steamer, allowed us to go into the town without shewing our passports. There was, however, nothing to see, except the pretty view of the opposite hills—they are scarcely mountains—and of the long sheet of water stretching up and down for many a mile, and commanded almost more completely hence than from any other place in its whole extent.

We dined at a very miserable inn, with a pretty lookout, and, as it happened to be a *jour maigre*, could get nothing fit to eat; the landlord took, however, a convenient view of the matter, and, assuring us that he never made any difference on this account, charged us as though we had eaten all the delicacies of the season. Here, again, as I had time on my hands, I amused myself with lowering my host's demands, and finally paid him a fair valuation for a very *maigre* dinner.

This business was no sooner satisfactorily finished, a sketch of the opposite coast having been secured during the argument, than the steamer arrived, and in a few minutes we were ploughing our way along the fair expanse of water, leaving the not very honest people of Laveno and Intra behind us and forgotten, all our attention being devoted to the gradually developing beauties of the upper end of the lake.

We were amused at Laveno by the warlike demonstrations of the Austrians, who had there a very smart little war-steamer for the protection of their interests on the lake, besides a small fort. They had, in fact, less territory on the lake than either Sardinia or Switzerland; luckily, however, for the peace of the water, these two last states seemed not to think it necessary to keep up a rival force, and so the little war-steamer at Laveno remained, untouched and uncared for, and her officers passed their lives in smoking cigars and longing for some change of place and duty, which was provided for them at last by the abrupt conclusion of Austrian rule in these parts a few years after the time of this visit.

Our steamer kept very much to the Sardinian shore of the lake, and, as there are two or three great bends in its course, a view of one small portion only of the lake is obtained, until, upon reaching a promontory, and rounding it, as it were a new lake and new scenery are disclosed; and happily, as the water is ascended towards Magadino, each turn brings more beautiful scenery than the last, until, as the head of the lake is neared, the view is very grand—not equal, certainly, to the head of Lake Como—but still exceedingly beautiful. The sun was just setting as we reached Locarno, and then our steamer, skirting along the sedgy shores of the lake— where the Ticino, at its entry, brings down a continually increasing deposit of mountain refuse—brought us in a few minutes to Magadino.

Our principal companions on the steamer were a large party of English, whose travelling-carriage and horses blocked up half the boat, and a very pleasant old Italian woman, whose elaborately neat hair and magnificent array of pins, each filigreed at the end, and all radiating like arrows from a central knot of hair, through which two larger and more magnificent pins were passed horizontally, forced upon our notice—but not more strongly than it had been forced before—this wonderful smartness and elaborate treatment and get-up of the hair, so common among the middle and lower classes in the North of Italy, and so unlike the customs of a similar class in England: I am bound to say, though, that the result of the elaborate straining and dressing of the hair seems generally to be, that, by the time women are fifty, they have no hair at all, or, at best, some two or three stray locks, which are then brought carefully together, and tied up, with a bold disregard of effect, in a knot at the top of the head.

When we landed at Magadino we found a diligence waiting, and, securing the *coupé*, jumped in, and were soon trotting off rapidly on the road to Bellinzona; in little more than an hour we passed through its gateway without having our passports demanded (how pleasant a change after Italy!), and were soon comfortably ensconced at the very respectable Albergo dell' Angelo.

We started from Bellinzona very early the next morning, determined, if possible, to surmount the worst part of the road and to sleep at Hospenthal, on the northern side of the pass. The view of Bellinzona on leaving it is very striking; three old castles perched on crags above give it an air of picturesque antiquity, and these, with the mountains rising grandly on either side of the Ticino, and sloping down in the distance to the bosom of Lago Maggiore, make a most beautiful picture. The situation is not, however, to be compared

to that of Chiavenna, whose wall of mountains, clothed with
Italian luxuriance of foliage, is pierced here and there with a
chasm only, for the passage of some headlong river dashing
down into the broad valley below the town; here the valley
continues to be of considerable width for some miles above
the town, whilst there one scarcely sees in what way any
road is to escape across the mountains.

The first portion of the road is not very interesting.
The pass of the Bernardino soon turns off to the right up a
valley which allows a partial view, and from this point the
S. Gothard road is sole possessor of the valley. Our first
change of horses was at Bodio; and from thence the road
gradually became much more beautiful. Many churches are
seen scattered here and there on the summits of the inac-
cessible-looking mountains on either side of the valley, all of
them whitewashed and generally distinguished by their tall
campanili, and sometimes by the small cluster of houses
and the patches of cultivated ground around them, betoken-
ing man's labour as well as man's religious love, on the
summit of these forbidding-looking steeps. And whilst the
distant prospect was so fair, the scenery close to the road was
embellished by vineyards and magnificent chestnuts, growing
in some places among great rocks shivered from the mountain-
side above, and, in others, in groves on either side of some
beautiful stream descending in a silver fall over the grey
precipices which overhang the road.

The villages through which we passed were pretty and
picturesque, and the villagers all very busy in the fields
bringing in their hay, and gathering their grapes, which are
always trained here over rocks and roofs in the most picturesquely irregular way ; and altogether the valley, rife with
so many signs of industry and activity, bore thoroughly the
appearance rather of a Swiss than of an Italian district.
The upper slopes of the mountains, on either side, were

clustered with fir-trees, and the deep blue water of the
Ticino, here gently murmuring, there hastily dashing over
some rocky impediment, made grateful music in our ears
and imparted additional beauty to the way.

At Biasca and Giornico there are ancient churches, the
exteriors of which are, however, of no interest; though the
interior of the latter, with its crypt and curious paintings,
well deserves a passing visit; but besides these all seemed
new, and the houses as well as the people and the scenery
soon began to remind us of Switzerland. There were those
particularly large well-to-do looking inns in every village,
with white walls and windows resplendent with green
wooden shutter-blinds which are so common throughout this
country; and here and there were to be seen houses with a
display of well-carved or craftily-framed woodwork, which
gave proof of our rapid approach to the land *par excellence*
of carpentry.

But it was not till Faido had been passed, and the
increasing barrenness of the hills, the entire absence of
vineyards, and the only occasional appearance of some grand
old chestnut-tree, weatherbeaten and rugged from conflict
with many a storm, or, may be, some frightful inundation
such as the Ticino loves at times to indulge in, shewed
how rapidly we were rising into mountain regions, that
the scenery became really striking. Then the road seems
suddenly to arrive at the end of the valley, but presently as
we advance, a narrow gorge in the mountain is perceived,
and we enter this, the most magnificent portion of the Val
Levantina, called Dazio Grande. The road is admirably
engineered, carried through two or three short tunnels, and
in excavations in the rocks above the torrent; the dark blue
water leaps from rock to rock, and here and there dashes
down in a fine waterfall; and the scenery is altogether so
striking that, on the whole, I am much inclined to give the

preference to this portion of the valley—that is to say, from
the commencement of Dazio Grande to within a short distance
of Airolo—over any portion of similar length in the whole
course of the Splügen. The first narrow defile passed, the
valley opens out again, and, with occasional glimpses all the
way of the old road winding below near the margin of the
stream, and destroyed some years since in a storm, ere very
long we reach another defile as beautiful as the last, but
much shorter; for here, after crossing the stream and
mounting a short distance, a projecting rock is pierced, the
river finds its outlet beneath through a chasm not twenty
feet in width, and then, the valley opening out again, Airolo
is seen just before us, and beyond the little cluster of houses
which marks the village rise the mountains, so grandly and
abruptly closing in the head of the Val Bedretto, up which
our course now lies, whilst every here and there on their
rugged sides or summits some snowy peak or glacier edge
tells not uncertainly of their grand elevation.

We arrived at Airolo by about two o'clock, and here we
had a rest of an hour and a half for dinner, followed by a
ransacking of a collection of Swiss woodwork, ending—as
such an operation always does—much to the advantage of
its proprietor.

With fresh horses we were soon on the road again, and
now the weather, which had been unpromising and occasionally wet, seemed inclined to improve, and we commenced the
real ascent of the mountain under rather more promising
circumstances than we had at first anticipated. The road
soon leaves the river, and, turning to the right, winds and
twists about in the serpentine fashion known only to Alpine
roads, and quite incomprehensible until one has seen them,
keeping the church and village of Airolo in view, first on the
right, then on the left, for hours. Here and there a straight
bit of road gives hopes that the zig-zagging is over, but the

thought is no sooner expressed than it is contradicted by another ascent worse than before, and one begins to envy the electric telegraph carried here in straight lines from point to point, where one would have thought it impossible to gain footing for its supports, and giving fair idea of the directness and speed of the communications of which it is the channel. The head of the Val Tremola, as the valley along which the road finds its way is called, is nearly reached, and the last glimpse of the mountains, at the head of Val Bedretto, is caught, when a stream is crossed and the last flight of zig-zags is commenced; these are both numerous and intricate, and as one looks down upon them from above, their interlacings produce a most singular effect. At last, however, these are surmounted, greatcoats and plaids are in requisition, and we all begin to feel uncomfortably cold. The cold grey colour of the wild mountains of granite, great blocks from whose sides strew the ground thickly on either side, seems to harmonize well with the scene, and when presently we pass the Capuchin hospice our driver tells us that we are at the summit. Two or three dark deep-looking pools or tarns stand close to the hospice, and reminded me in their gloomy and cold aspect of the tarn which gives so much character to the hospice of the Grimsel. The same kind of scenery accompanied us on the now rapid descent; the sun went down, and the stars were soon out shining brilliantly upon the mountain road, when at last a sudden turn brought us in sight of lights, and then, descending a few zig-zags, we saw below us the roofs of the houses of Hospenthal, and, in less time than it takes to describe, were standing on the steps of one of the best inns even in Switzerland, the Goldner Löwe, and superintending the unpacking of our goods.

In such an inn as this everything proves forcibly that one is in Switzerland; the rooms are all very clean and very

small, and there is a certain homely air about everybody
and everything which is the especial charm of the better
class of Swiss country inns, and in which they excel, perhaps,
all but the very best English inns of the same kind.[1]

We spent an amusing evening, having for companions a
Frenchman with his wife and two daughters, all very lively
and exceedingly loquacious: the walls of the modest *salle à
manger* rang with hearty laughter until after the time at
which early travellers generally go to bed, and so we
paved the way doubtless for a hearty night's rest.

The first thing to be done in the morning, after the
discussion of the excellent trout and honey put before us,
was to take a stroll up to the old castle which lends so much
picturesque character to the village. The weather was
glorious; the perfectly blue sky overhead, the bright green
of the valley, the luxuriance of the lower slopes of the
mountains, and the view up the pass of the Furca closed in
with a white line of snow, combined together to make us
all regret our determination to push on rapidly for Luzern ;
and no sooner was the regret felt than—like idle school-
children enjoying themselves while they may—we made up
our minds to ascend the Furca, sleep on the summit of the
pass, and return early the next morning. No sooner said than
done ; our horses were taken out of the carriage, and in half
an hour, with a guide and horses for the ladies, we were on
our way for a mountain excursion, full of that elastic feeling
which the treading of a Swiss mountain-path always gives,
and bent upon enjoying ourselves to the full.

The contrast with the flat dusty roads and the sultry
weather to which you are so often forced to submit in Italy
made the walk especially pleasant; and though, compared to

---

[1] This old inn is a thing of the past. A large, bustling, and much smarter
hotel has taken its place; and a magnificent carriage-road has put a stop to
all need for walking by pleasant field-paths to the Furca.

many other mountain excursions, it was of slight interest,
under the circumstances it presented more than common
attraction to us.   The path was one of those pleasant ways
so common in Switzerland—a paved narrow road between
banks of fields or low walls, gradually rising and falling,
now crossing the dry bed of some glacier torrent, and now
bridging the stream which descends the valley to feed the
Reuss.   The fields were rich in colour, and bright with
various and lovely flowers, and the lower slopes of the
mountain were tinted a rich purple with the bloom of herbs,
cropped gratefully here and there by small and melancholy
looking sheep.

The small village of Realp is soon reached, and then
the ascent begins ; this is rather stiff, and it has taken us,
when, we reach the summit, just four hours and a half of
hard walking from Hospenthal.   We found dinner going on
at the little hostelry at the top, and, after partaking of it,
started again to ascend the Furca-Horn, a mountain rising
above the summit of the pass, and, as we had been told,
quite worth the trouble of the ascent.   There was no
kind of path, and in places the mountain-side was so
steep that I began to think it was no place for ladies to
scramble up ; however, they thought otherwise, and after
divers tumbles in the snow, and surmounting rather for-
midable-looking obstacles, we reached the summit at last,
and, sitting down on the edge of a great rock, spent a long
time in enjoying the glorious view.

Just under us was the vast glacier of the Rhone, and then
beyond it we looked down the long valley of the same river
until its shape was obscured by mist, and traced the path by
which we had walked in a previous journey up the steep
Meyenwand to the Grimsel.   Immediately in front of us
were the vast peaked mass of the Schreckhorn, the whole
course of the glaciers of the Aar, and the peaks of the

Finster-Aarhorn, the Jungfrau, and the Mönch; above our heads rose the Galenstock, and opposite us the Mutthorn and Monte Fiudo; whilst the summit of Monte Rosa, discerned with difficulty among a marvellous array of distant peaks, completed one of the finest views of snow-covered mountains which it has ever been my good fortune to behold.

Long time did we keep our elevated seats, scanning again and again the glorious panorama, and at last, most unwillingly, commenced the descent; this was more difficult, though much more speedy, than the ascent, as the side of the mountain was both steep and slippery. We reached the summit of the pass, itself about eight thousand three hundred feet above the sea, in little more than an hour, the ascent to the Horn having occupied about two hours and a half; and here we found our French friends of the previous evening, who had in vain endeavoured to follow us in our ascent, but had been one and all obliged to give up the attempt.

Late at night we all went out again to look at the most glorious moonlight effect it is possible to imagine; the peaks of the mountains and the vast fields of snow or glacier lighted up by the bright light of the moon had a charm about them peculiarly fascinating.

Very early the next morning we started again on our way back to Hospenthal, and got down to the inn in good time, had breakfast, and then, mounting our carriage, we were soon off again down the valley of the Reuss. The Devil's Bridge was ere long reached, and the glorious scenery with which it is surrounded amply redeemed the expectations I had always formed of its extreme beauty; indeed for grandeur, combined with luxuriant cultivation of the lower slopes of the mountains, and for the wild beauty of the course of the river itself, nothing even in Switzerland surpasses the narrow valley through which the turbulent Reuss finds its way from Andermatt to Amsteg.

Here the valley widens considerably, and orchards full of fruit-trees, covered with bright-looking apples, spread half over the valley, on each side of which the mountains are very grand in their outline. Before long Altdorf is reached, and all the scenes so dear to Swiss freemen are rapidly passed, until at last our carriage sets us down on the very edge of the lovely Lake of Luzern, where the half-hour which we have to wait for the departure of the steamer is spent in attempting a sketch of the rocks which descend so precipitously into the deep recesses of the lake.

Much harm is done by overpraising beautiful scenery, and even the Lake of the Four Cantons suffers from this; for so much has been said and written about its unmatched loveliness and grandeur, that the result is perhaps a slight disappointment with the reality. One great beauty, no doubt, is the succession of entirely distinct views which different portions of the lake afford, though at the same time the irregular outline of the water very much diminishes its apparent scale; I doubt, too, whether there is any one view so grand as that at the head of Lake Como, though otherwise I know no lake which can be preferred to it.

On the voyage down the lake, Tell's Chapel and the famous Grütli were of course seen; a distant view was caught of the old cradle of Switzerland, the little town of Schwytz, with the grand peaks of the Mythenberg rising proudly behind it; the Righi, and the black-looking Pilatus, were each in turn passed; and as evening drew on, the flat shores of the lower part of the lake were neared, and presently the spires and turrets of Luzern came in sight. In a few minutes the bustle of landing being over, the immense Schweizer Hof received us within its capacious walls, just in

time for one of those accommodating late tables-d'hôte so
acceptable after a long day's travel.

Three or four hours spent the next morning in strolling
about served only to convince us that there was not very
much of architectural interest in the city itself. A line of
old wall, broken at short intervals by picturesque and
irregular towers, and a very long covered bridge across the
lake just where the Reuss runs out of it, are the only
noticeable features. The bridge is ornamented with an
immense number of oil-paintings—two to each principal
rafter—illustrative of the history of the place and country,
not valuable as works of art, but curious in themselves, and
giving much additional interest to the structure.

The principal church has two western towers and spires;
the latter are of metal and managed in the way so common
in this part of the world, though never, so far as I know,
attempted in England,[1] with the angles of the spire over the
centre of the cardinal sides of the tower. The whole of the
rest of the church is modernized; and there is a singular
modern cloister, which nearly surrounds the churchyard,
and contains an immense array of graves and grave-crosses.

We left Luzern at eleven for Basel, in the diligence,
and had a very pleasant ride over often-travelled ground, of
which, therefore, the less said perhaps the better. The
rich luxuriance of the crops, the careful farming, the vast
barns, and the great loads of produce which are constantly
met upon the road, remind the traveller more of England than
any other portion of the Continent ever does. The Lake of
Sempach was soon passed on our right, and at last a pause
was made in the good old-fashioned way, for a very comfortable dinner at the little old town of Zofingen. At Aarberg

---

[1] The famous steeple of Antwerp is arranged in the same way. The
spires of S. Elizabeth at Marburg, and the metal spires of the churches at
Lübeck and Lüneburg, are also somewhat similarly treated.

the dashing Aar was crossed, and soon the ascent of the Unter
Hauenstein range was commenced; and here we enjoyed
the most extensive of all the day's views of the Alps—the
last and grandest. Gradually as the summit is reached
peak after peak is seen rising up above the mist which
shrouds the lower slopes of the mountains, their white outlines tenderly relieved against the blue sky: we recognized
one after the other almost the entire range of the grandest
mountains in Europe, seen before nearer but not in fairer
guise, but wherever seen leaving the same lasting impression
upon the mind. Suddenly we overpassed the summit, and
began rapidly to descend the northern slope of the hills;
but the last link that bound us to the land in which we had
been voyaging, as we hope, not for the last time, is never
to be remembered but with affectionate regard, touched, as
every one must be, in viewing such a panorama, with the
extreme glory of the scene.

We had now done with mountains and with mountain
scenery, though the road was still interesting and very
pretty, and at last late in the evening we reached Basel. The
moon was shining brightly on the Rhine as we went to our
beds for the last time, in this journey at least, in Switzerland.

We were amused, on our way to Strasburg, by the
comparative insignificance in our minds of the chain of the
Vosges, which, on our outward journey, had impressed us as
really very striking in their outline. So much for the effect
of a recent acquaintance with grander mountains!

Strasburg Cathedral was visited, not for the first time
and with a consequent increase of pleasure. Such magnificent architecture as that of its most exquisite nave is
truly refreshing after Italian work, and, small as its scale is
compared to that of Milan, it in no way lost its effect upon
my mind. I was particularly struck by the vast difference between the delicate art shewn in the design of the traceries,

in the softly rounded contour and dark recesses of the mouldings, and in the vigour and beauty of the carving of all the
capitals, heightened as they are by the flood of coloured
light let into the interior by its immense windows filled
with some of the noblest stained glass in Europe, compared
with that shewn in the rude traceries, heavy carving,
and plainness or absence of moulding, which characterize
almost all Italian Gothic work. No more strong or decided
example need be desired of nearly all the points of contrast between the best work, north and south of the Alps,
than this, the first great northern Gothic church seen
on the homeward way, presents, when compared with all
the work which has nevertheless been studied with so much
pleasure and advantage on the southern side of the Alps.

It is only fair to say that the first impression produced
by the west front of Strasburg was one—felt, indeed, before,
but much more strongly now—of the smallness of scale and
narrowness of the whole. I have not at any time had
any especial love for this front, but, just after seeing
the simple unbroken façades of Italian churches, with
their grand porches and their simple breadth of effect,
there is something so entirely destructive to all repose in
a front covered as this is with lines of tracery, panelling,
niches, and canopies in every direction, that it leaves, I
confess, a painful feeling upon the mind, of the restless
nature of its designer's thoughts. But this is true only of
the west front, for, on entering by the door into the nave, all
such thoughts are banished on the instant, and you stand
awestruck at the beauty and solemnity of the art in which
hitherto Northern architects alone have ever approached at
all nearly to perfection, and convinced at the same time
that, with such a work to refer to, we need never doubt,
between the comparative merits of Gothic architecture north
and south of the Alps.

CHAPTER XIV.

"Alas! of thousand bosoms kind,
    That daily court you and caress,
How few the happy secret find
    Of your calm loveliness!"
                        Christian Year.

———◆———

Concluding Summary—Classic and Gothic Architecture—Italian Gothic—
Shafts—Cornices—Monuments — Cloisters—Windows—Brickwork—Colour
in Construction—Truth in Architectural Design and Construction.

I PROPOSE in this chapter to sum up, as shortly as I can, the
information which I have gathered in the course of my tours
in the North of Italy, on the subject of mediæval art. In
doing this I shall have to remark, not only on the beauties,
but also on the failings of Italian Gothic architecture, and
to give expression to the thoughts which arise in examining
its remains as to developments which are possible to us in
the same direction, as well as to suggest some of the
lessons which may be learnt from them.

I think it may be gathered, from what has been already
said, that it will be useless to look for anything like the com-
pleteness in the development of the style in Italy which our
ancestors attained to in England; and this is easily accounted for. In England there were no Classic buildings to
find here and there an admirer, or perhaps a cluster of
disciples, as in Italy; and men worked, therefore, when the

Gothic style was thoroughly established, freely, and in their own way, and apparently quite untrammelled with a suspicion even that there had ever been another style brought to perfection by people above most others civilized and refined in their habits and tastes, and one moreover which was distinguished by certain broad and strongly marked lines of separation from the style which they inherited from their fathers, and practised and brought, as nearly as they could, to perfection. In England, therefore, in the Middle Ages, we may look in vain for any evidence of active sympathy with a more ancient and venerable style than that which was then in the fulness of vigour, life, and constant development; and consequently, if it be likely that any infusion of the art practised by the ancients could have aided the Northern architects in their work, we must not expect to find here any trace of such assistance or such advantages. But in Italy the case was far different: the love for the remains of earlier ages was never dead, but only slept, ever and anon to break forth in some new appropriation of ancient materials, or some imitation and reproduction of an ancient form or idea. So in Venice, in the thirteenth century, whilst pointed arches were being reared by some to support the walls, not only of the churches, but of the houses also, other hands were busy with the task of raising aloft those two Classic shafts, with their antique capitals and detail, which, even to the present day, stand peculiar and well-remembered features of the Piazzetta of S. Mark; standing proofs, if such are indeed wanted, that there had been artists in earlier days whose art was noble and well worthy of the emulation of men in all ages.

And this Classic seed fell into not ungrateful soil; for though there, as elsewhere throughout Europe, the value of the pointed arch as a feature in construction—independently, that is, of its intrinsic beauty—must have been well known, and was boldly recognized where it could not be avoided, there were nevertheless in a hundred ways proofs that men still remembered the lessons and traditions of the past, and used it with a certain degree of caution and unwillingness, and associated with features which, rightly or wrongly, were at the time eschewed by all Northern architects, either as being contrary to its spirit, or through ignorance of their existence. This fact would seem, therefore, to place the Italian works of the Middle Ages in the ranks of hybrid and mixed styles, and to debar them from competition with the more pure contemporary works of Northern Europe.

There will, however, always be much profit in the careful examination of such works as these in Italy, because their authors stood in the same position that we do now, and, conversant to some extent with the beauties of the best Gothic architecture of the North and the best Classic examples of Italy, took what they deemed best from each, and endeavoured to unite the perfections of both.

Classic architecture is that of the lintel and impost, involving the idea of rest: Gothic is that of the arch and the flying buttress, involving the idea of life and motion. The two ideas are absolutely opposed to each other. Classic architecture, directly it admits the arch, ceases to be true to itself in any real artistic sense; yet if it refuses to use, and to exhibit the use of the arch, it denies itself wilfully the use of the best known mode of construction. Gothic architects may still, on the other hand, as they always have done, gain much from the teachings of Classic buildings. And if sometimes there is too great liveliness and want of repose in their works, they may usefully study those of their predecessors who undoubtedly obtained more breadth and repose in them by some knowledge of Classic examples, than they would have had if they had not known them.

Gothic architecture was essentially the work of scientific

men; the most consummate skill being displayed in arranging thousands of small blocks of stones, any one of which might be carried upon a strong man's shoulders, into walls rising far in height above anything ever dreamt of by the Greek, bridging great openings, and providing by the exactest counterpoise of various parts for the perfect security of works whose airiness and life would seem to have lifted them out of the region of constructive skill; and yet all these wonderful works were executed in materials as ponderous in their nature as those which the Greek had handled so rudely in construction, and so delicately in ornamentation.

The natural result of this excess of science was, perhaps, that less delicacy and beauty of detail became necessary; for when the plain rough walls, without carving and without ornament, were nevertheless of necessity so beautiful in their intricacy of outline and delicacy of structure; and when, too, so little (comparatively) plain surface remained to be looked at or dwelt upon, men cared less for the choicest examples of the sculptor's art, and were less obliged to satisfy the eye with them. Much, therefore, as Art gained in most ways by the invention of the arch, she at the same time lost something which had been until then possessed, and which, too, was essential in the highest order of work.

This was the case, speaking generally; but, as need hardly, I suppose, be said, there are examples scattered here and there throughout the North of Europe, and particularly in France and England, which shew distinctly enough that their artists had grasped this necessity in its very fullest extent; and were in no degree satisfied with anything less than the greatest perfection in the sculpture, and other decorations with which they adorned their works.

Italian architects stood, in the thirteenth and fourteenth centuries, in a position in many respects very different from that held by their Northern contemporaries, and the marks of this difference are everywhere to be seen. It was natural to them to reconcile in their works, so far as they could, the principles of two styles which we are too prone to deem irreconcilable; and where they have achieved a real success, it ought to be a lesson that the course which they pursued is still open to us, though with larger opportunities and greater knowledge. At the same time they committed faults which we ought especially to beware of imitating in any respect.

They ignored, as much as possible, the clear exhibition of the pointed arch, and, even when they did use it, not unfrequently introduced it in such a way as to shew their contempt for it as a feature of construction; employing it often only for ornament, and never hesitating to construct it in so faulty a manner, that it required to be held together with iron rods from the very first day of its erection. This fault they often found it absolutely necessary to commit, because they scarcely ever brought themselves to allow the use of the buttress; and this reluctance was a remarkable proof of their Classic sympathies. Classic architecture was as distinctly symbolic of rest as Gothic was of life; the column and lintel of the one were as still and symbolical of perfect repose, as the arch of the other, sustained by the strong arm of the flying buttress, was of life, vigour, and motion. Italian Gothic architects then, in never resorting to the buttress, avowed their feeling that a state of perfect rest was the only allowable state for a perfect building, and they preferred almost always to use the arch for its beauty only, and avowedly not for its constructional value, which they evidenced by tying it together with iron bars at its base, which there was no intention of disguising, and therefore no shamefacedness in the use of. From this, I believe, at least one beauty arose. It is obvious that the pointed arch, descending upon the capital of a shaft without any visible stay or buttress to retain it in its place, would look weak and thin; and it was soon perceived that, in order to overcome this difficulty, the only course was to add to its substance by cusping it on the under side. Thence came the trefoiled arches so frequent in Italy, and always so very lovely. As so much depended upon them, no pains were spared in bringing their outline into the very purest form. To this we owe the absolute perfection which characterizes some of the trefoiled arches in early Italian work; of this we have an example (to take one instance among many) in the tombs of the Scaligers, at Verona, in which the mass of the trefoil descending from the arch conveys to the eye the impression of a firmness which, in part, it certainly gives, but which would nevertheless be insufficient in reality for the stability of the work, without the aid of the connecting rod of iron below.

In northern Gothic architecture, arches invariably tell their own story, and do their own work, avowedly and without any disguise; in Italy this is the exception, not the rule, and the commonest exception is seen in the arcades dividing the aisles from the naves of churches, and in the large open arches forming the arcades upon which public and private buildings so often stand, though even these are sometimes (as in the second stage of the Ducal Palace at Venice) formed of continuous traceries in place of arches, and are dependent for their stability, like the single arches of tombs and monuments, upon the assistance of iron ties.

Another proof of the reverence for ancient tradition in art is furnished by the extent to which, throughout the time of the prevalence of pointed architecture in Italy, the round arch was also used. Examples of this are very frequent, and of the most capricious kind. At Cremona, e.g., the south transept has semicircular arches throughout, and the north transept pointed arches; the date of both being, however, as nearly as possible the same.   At Verona, in the old house given in plate 14, some of the bearing arches are pointed, some round; and again, in some buildings the main arches are round, and the ornamental pointed.   Again, one of the most common cornices in all the mediæval brickwork of Italy is a continuous arcade of round arches intersecting one another, and forming at their intersections pointed arches; and in the Ca' d'Oro, one of the most elaborately ornate late Gothic buildings in Venice, some of the entrance arches are pointed and some round.   It needs not, however, that examples should be multiplied, for almost every building exhibits some trace of this kind of confusion.

The Venetian love for the ogee arch, which spread thence to Verona, Vicenza, and Ferrara, has been already mentioned; no doubt we must look to the East for the very early introduction of this feature in Venice, and I only incidentally refer to it here as proving, from the way in which it was perpetually used, that its adopters had no peculiar love for the form of the pure pointed arch, of which it is certainly a most vitiated perversion.

With this, by way of preface, let us now go on to look at the features of these Italian works in detail.   We shall find that we have two influences brought out, even more strongly than in most mediæval works, in Italian buildings.   These are, first, local, and next, personal influences.   The Venetian, the Bolognese, and the Veronese, for instance, are all distinctly local styles, in which early traditions were preserved, to some extent, from first to last; and to these might be added the Florentine, the Genoese, and the Pisan.   On the other hand it is impossible not to notice the very great personal influence exercized over their descendants, as well as over their contemporaries, by some of the greater Italian architects, of whom I may adduce Nicola Pisano as the most eminent example.

There is a third influence which must not be overlooked
—that of foreign architects. Milan Cathedral, designed by a
German, is very unlike any other Italian building in style;
San Francesco at Assisi was also the work of a foreigner;
and the western front of Genoa Cathedral owes much of its
peculiar and extremely beautiful character to contact with,
and knowledge of, French art; whilst Vercelli is another
instance, as far as its interior is concerned, which may be
included in this list. Generally speaking, however, the influence of the foreigner seems to have been confined pretty
much to the particular church designed by him.

In the Middle Ages the Italians led a life more akin to
our own, at the present day, than other people. The country
was populous, the cities numerous and rich, and the people
full of emulation and individuality. This was precisely the
condition of things that would lead, most certainly, to the
employment of artists from a distance, and to the establish-
ment of a professional practice of the art earlier than elsewhere. It led to the employment of the family of the Pisani,
of the Campione clan, the sculptors of Como, the Cosmati in
Rome, and many others. In England and in France it is
much more difficult to point to any facts proving the employment of the same architects in various parts of the country,
and there is, at first sight, therefore, less of what is obviously
personal in their art in the Middle Ages.

The history of our old architects in England and France
is very peculiar; they were, as a rule, each confined to a
certain district, in which they wrought in what was in fact a
merely local variety of their national style. In point of artistic
talent, they were very equally matched, so that it is difficult
to assign the pre-eminence to any one over the rest, though
in England we may point to our Yorkshire abbeys, and in
France to the buildings in the Isle de France as being on
the whole the finest examples. We have had no Nicola Pisano

here; our old architects' work is singularly equal in its
character in each period; and whether it was displayed in the
little village church lying concealed on the banks of a rippling
stream, or in the vast abbey of some sequestered valley, or in
the cathedral church of the busy city, there seems to be matter
for equal admiration in all. In Italy, on the other hand,
we see a number of individual architects exercizing each
his peculiar influence, varying very much in their skill and
power, and having, moreover, the doubtful advantage of a
constant recollection of the works of a different style of art,
from whose traditions they never escaped.   Placed, in short,
very much in the position that we are at the present day,
they never wrought with the same absolute and joyous
freedom that marks their contemporaries' work in France and
England; and thus, though their architecture may be inferior,
it is of very special value to us; for we may, perhaps, see better
the cause of some of our own shortcomings, when we inves-
tigate theirs, and so we may hope to excel the works which
they executed under conditions so similar to those under
which we labour, even if we cannot quite rival the complete perfection of the greater mediæval architects of the
North. And, seeing that all the faults of Italian Gothic
artists arose from their incomplete devotion to the new
art, and their lingering fondness for the old Classic forms,
we shall be led probably to recognize the paramount importance of throwing ourselves heartily and entirely into
the study and practice of the one great and national division
of our art, and then, not venturing to attempt to design in
some base imitation of Classic one day, or in a pretended
Gothic the next, as is only too much the custom, we shall
make our sense of art so completely a portion of our inmost
selves, as never to do anything new in any but our own one
special style.   We shall, in short, recognize, as the greatest
danger to the progress of real art, that eclectic spirit

which the Italians never escaped from, and which, in our own day, leads men to design their work in the style which they or their clients fancy for the moment, and not in that which is the truest result of previous experience, and most fitted to the country in which it is to be executed.

In examining the features of any national school of architecture, it is worthy of notice how distinctly some of its peculiarities and prejudices are marked from the very first, even in the ground-plans of the buildings it produced. This is notably the case in the ecclesiastical edifices of France, England, and Germany. Each country, after the art had become settled and, so to speak, acclimatized, had its special arrangement of plan, which was seldom departed from and was handed on from age to age as a precious heirloom. And, going to Italy, we shall find that the same feature strikes us there in almost all the buildings of the pointed style, and that the buildings from which they were directly derived are the same as those from which we indirectly derived our own. Their plans are all derived from two ancient types, both of which are of venerable antiquity. It was from the basilica, converted into a church, with its nave and aisles terminated at the end, by an apsidal projection from a sort of transept, that all of one class of the Italian Gothic churches with transepts were copied. Indeed, if we look at the ground-plan of S. Paul without the walls, at Rome, and compare it with the fully developed church of Sta. Anastasia, at Verona, we shall see that absolutely the only difference is the addition of small chapels on the east side of the transept; so that in place of the one apse, which marks the former, we have the central apse and subsidiary chapels on each side of it. The church of San Clemente, at Rome, with its three aisles ended with parallel apses at the east end, is a variety of this type, followed in such churches as the Cathedral of Torcello, and indeed in all later Italian

Gothic churches without transepts. And even when, as in the thirteenth and fourteenth centuries, the Italian architects endeavoured to secure an immensely wide unbroken area of nave, they still looked back fondly to these old precedents, and finished them at the east, with three parallel apsidal chapels.

The other model was the Byzantine plan of S. Mark's at Venice, itself imported from the East, which was copied closely in the south-west of France, and produced no slight effect in modifying the simple Romanesque plan, until it assumed all the characteristics of the complete Lombard style, and from the North of Italy sent out vigorous off-shoots, of which the most important were those which we trace all along the valley of the Rhine, and throughout the centre of France.

Thus, the ground-plans of Italian Gothic buildings were simply a natural development from those of earlier date, and adhering, as they always did, very closely to the older plan and arrangements, afford us scarcely an example of those later developments of prolonged choirs, of which our English cathedrals and abbeys afford perhaps the most magnificent examples, or of the splendid French *chevet* with its surrounding aisle and chapels. The traces of Classic influence on the plan are indeed so many and so clear, that it is hardly speaking too strongly to say that Gothic planning was never developed by Italian architects, so shackled were they by the ever-present influence of buildings in another style. Hence, the more we study their peculiarities, the more we see how curious a mixture there is in them of the character of Classic and Gothic buildings, and how essentially clumsy all their planning is when compared with the scientific work of the more thoroughly Gothic architects of the North. If we compare an ordinary Italian groined church with a French or English example, we shall find one very marked difference in them. In the former each

bay of the nave is square, and hence each bay of the
narrower side aisles is oblong, with the greatest width
towards the nave; in the latter, on the contrary, the aisle
compartment is square, and that of the nave oblong, with its
narrowest side towards the aisle. Hence, in the former, the
points of support are farther apart, and the plan loses much
of its intricacy, and at the same time, no doubt, the whole
building loses much of its apparent scale. The enormous
church of San Petronio at Bologna, for instance, has but six
bays in the length of its vast nave, and the eye refuses to be
convinced by the practical measurement of the foot of the real
dimensions of the building. The object of the Italian architect always was to obtain as few points of support as possible
in a given area; but there is little if any real gain in this.
The points of support in the Italian churches were larger,
and the cost in the end was probably much greater than in
the apparently more intricate and complex plans of the
French and English architects. The science displayed in
their planning was therefore of a superficial and mistaken
description, and not really equal to that which marks the
work of their Northern competitors.[1]

The same absence of subdivision is seen in the elevation
of each bay of an Italian church, where in place of the triple
division in height of our great Northern churches, with their
well-accentuated proportions and beautiful variety of detail,
we have a singularly meagre design perpetually repeated, and
consisting generally of simple broad arches, with a small
circular clerestory window above them, and no other kind of
decoration, save where the painter has come with his ever-

---

[1] The usual plan is sometimes deviated from and improved by having two
bays of aisle opening with two arches into each bay of the nave, so that every
bay of groining throughout the church is very nearly square. This is a
common plan in early German churches, and is one of the many indications of
similarity between German and Italian work, which might be adduced were
we to enter on this interesting question.

ready art to the rescue of the apparently incompetent
architect.

How this plainness and severity was corrected we have
already seen in the interior of Sta. Anastasia, at Verona—
a church which, though it is simple and unadorned in its
construction almost beyond any large church with which I
am acquainted, has been made remarkable, owing to the
skill of its decorator, for being more than usually ornate
and magnificent.

The invariable simplicity of Italian groining has been often
noticed in these pages, and need only be referred to here as
illustrating the love of simplicity upon which I have dwelt.
No one feature gains so much by it as this, and I can fancy
the horror with which an Italian, or indeed any other architect, in the thirteenth century, would have viewed such fine
works in their way, as our own examples of complicated fan-
traceried groinings. The painting of this simple groining
at Verona, at Lodi, and still more at Assisi, proves how it
ought always to be treated; and happily in England we have
still more than one example of the same kind, as, for instance, two chapels in the Cathedral at Winchester.

So far for the plan. When we look at single features of the
building we shall find another peculiarity meeting us at every
turn, and of the good effect of which it is impossible to speak
too warmly. This is the constant use of the detached shaft or
column. This is the one great and lasting beauty which was
derived from Classic examples. The Italians, finding it used
with luxurious profusion in their Classic and Byzantine buildings, persevered in its use throughout the whole Gothic period.
It is true that, as time wore on, there was a somewhat less free
use of it than at first, but it was never altogether ignored. We
cannot say as much for our own ancestors: so long as the influence of Lombard and Romanesque art is visible in French,
German, and English Gothic, so long the detached shaft was

used, and just in proportion as in course of time that influence
decreased, so did the frequency of its use decrease.   Our fourteenth and fifteenth century buildings present nothing in
its place but combinations of mouldings, in themselves very
beautiful, but by no means so beautiful as to reconcile us
to the loss of that which they so entirely supplanted.   One
consequence of their introduction, to the exclusion of the
detached shaft, was, that the art of sculpture deteriorated just
in proportion as the art of moulding was developed.   There
is no place in which architectural sculpture can be more
fittingly displayed than in the capital of a column.   It is the
most convenient, and at the same time the most conspicuous,
position for it.   It is, too, the most important feature in
every design in which the detached column is used.   The
gathering together of all the arch mouldings into one above
the capital, in order that their forces may be collected before
being transmitted to the ground, leads naturally to the laying
of a special emphasis on this point above all others; and it is
one of the strongest among the many reasons in favour of
earliest Gothic, and against the later varieties of the style,
that in the former the use of shafts involved the use of
forcible and elaborately-cut capitals, so that this point might
be most distinctly marked, whilst in the latter, by the disuse
of the shaft and the constant practice of carrying the mouldings of the arch down to the ground without any interruption,
it was made as little of as was possible.

In this respect, therefore, above all others, Italian Gothic
artists—having given way to change less than their contemporaries—are worthy of our highest admiration.   The
love of variety, which is characteristic of all good Gothic
art, is conspicuous in the Italian treatment of the shaft just
as much as in the northern Gothic variation of mouldings.
When they are plain cylinders, and not banded (and the
band occurs but seldom in Italian work), they often taper

slightly, and with very beautiful effect. This was distinctly
a relic of the Classic entasis, and the examples given in
a note will suffice to shew the extent to which the shaft is
reduced in proportion to its height.[1] Wherever, however,
the shaft is spiral or decorated with carving, or when the
occurrence of a band destroys the idea of its continuity
from base to capital, its monolithic character needs not to
be marked, and the shaft is then always made of the same
diameter throughout. The ornamentation is of various
kinds. Circular shafts are inlaid, carved, diapered, or made
of marbles selected for their beauty of colour. Lucca
Cathedral affords, perhaps, the best examples of decoration
by inlaying: there the shafts are of white marble inlaid
with dark green; some have a diaper, others are girt with a
succession of simple chevrons, others with spiral lines, others
with crosses, flowers, fleurs-de-lis, or foliated circles; and
one, at least, with a succession of imitations of arcades one
over the other; but I remember no example of the same kind
in the buildings described in these pages. At Lucca these
inlaid shafts are frequently alternated with sculptured shafts,
of which examples are common all over Italy. They are
deeply cut with spiral lines of mouldings, occasionally
adorned with sculpture of flowers, as in the doorways at
Bergamo and Modena, and are often also inlaid richly with
mosaic.

The best examples of the richer kinds of shafts are seen
frequently in Italian Gothic buildings and monuments south
of the Apennines. Such, for instance, as those which, with
rich iron work between them, form the screen round the altar

	Height of Shaft.	Diameter at Base.	Diameter at Neck.
	Ft. in.	In.	In.
[1] Cloister, San Zenone, Verona . . .	3 $11\frac{1}{2}$	$5\frac{1}{8}$	$4\frac{1}{4}$
Cloister, Genoa Cathedral	4 5	6	$5\frac{1}{4}$
Cloister, San Stefano, Bologna . .	2 $8\frac{1}{2}$	$4\frac{3}{8}$	$4\frac{1}{8}$

under the "crossing" of Sta. Chiara at Assisi, or in the
monument of Pope Benedict X. at Perugia, where the shafts
are of white marble, the spiral lines formed with a bead and
fillets, and at the base and neck of the shaft the beads are all
connected together with small arches, in the spandrels of
which vine leaves are delicately carved; whilst to add to the
extraordinary richness of the work, small figures are carved
in the marble creeping round the shaft in the hollow formed
by the spiral construction, and the spaces between the
mouldings are filled in with glass mosaic patterns in red,
green, and blue on a gold ground. The shafts of Orcagna's
shrine in Or' San Michele, Florence, are of the same character, but these extraordinary decorations occur generally
only in the best and richest internal work, executed under the
direct influence of Florentine, Neapolitan, or Roman artists.[1]

The arrangement of spiral shafts was generally, but not
always, symmetrical. In the Campanile of Florence, where
they occur in pairs on each side of a window, they are
always arranged with the spiral lines curving in opposite
directions. In the porch of Sta. Maria Maggiore, Bergamo,
the three shafts in each jamb are all different: the first
spiral and carved, but not moulded; the second moulded
with chevrons; the third spiral and moulded only, and the
central shaft is red whilst the others are all white. In the
spirally designed string-courses of the Venetian palaces the
spiral lines are always worked in opposite directions right
and left of the centre.

Another bold variety is seen in the beautiful coupled
shafts at the entrance to the crypt of San Zenone, Verona,
where both the shafts are quatrefoil in section, but entirely
different in character, one of them being quite straight, the

---

[1] The shafts used in the shrine of S. Edward at Westminster are of the
same description, and shew that in one of the most exquisite works in England
our early architects saw no incongruity between their beautiful but foreign
character and the otherwise, at that time, purely national architecture.

other slightly, but yet conspicuously, spiral.   In a monument in the south aisle of the same church, four shafts are cut out of one block of marble; and in order that this may be realized they are knotted together in the centre; and a similar example exists in the porch, of which I have given a view, at Trent, and in one of the windows of the Broletto at Como. The shafts round the lower basin of Nicola Pisano's beautiful fountain at Perugia are in clusters of three, chevroned, spiral, and fluted in the greatest possible variety; and in later works, in which we find that the error of continuing arch mouldings to the ground, instead of stopping them on the capital, was occasionally committed—as, e.g., in the archway to the baptistery in the church of the Frari, at Venice— we see an instance of a moulded imitation of such a cluster of shafts as these of Nicola Pisano's, chevroned and spiral, forming jamb and arch alike.   In the later doorways, such as those of the western front of the cathedral of Como, and many of those at Monza, Pavia, and in most of the Venetian churches and buildings, the jambs and arches are identical in section; but even in these cases there is always a capital interposed, and I hardly remember an example of a continuous moulding without an impost, which at least marked—if often in an incomplete manner—the line of the springing of the arch.

I must not forget that which is, after all, the most charming of all arrangements of shafts, viz. the use of them in couples, set generally one behind the other, so that, in elevation, extreme delicacy is secured, whilst, in perspective, there is beautiful light and shade, and ample effect of strength. This is a favourite arrangement in cloisters and in belfries; and, wherever it occurs, one regrets, as one looks at it, that though in old days French, Spanish, German, and even Irish [1] architects gladly followed the Italian

---

[1] Jerpoint and Cong Abbeys are Irish examples.

example, it was so seldom that an Englishman condescended
to do the same.[1]

In the treatment of mouldings the Italian Gothic work is
quite peculiar. An Italian architect would have been surprized,
could he have seen the dark and piquant recesses of the mouldings in which his Northern brethren in the thirteenth and
fourteenth centuries so much delighted. He rarely, if ever,
indulged in a deep hollow, but made a point rather of shewing the hard sharp outline of the square edges of his stones
or bricks, relieved only by the interposition of simple round
members, alternated with flat hollows ; his mouldings, even
when designed for such grand works as the Ducal Palace, being
bald and crude in design, though they conduced no doubt to
that breadth of effect to which he always desired that everything should be sacrificed. There is but little skill shewn
in the way in which their contours are drawn, and the
carelessness with which they are fitted to the size of the
capital that carries them is a constant source of disgust to
any one who has been trained by the study of the exquisite
English mouldings of the same period. The architectural
carving was designed with the same idea ; for when it was
introduced elsewhere than in the capitals of columns, it was
always very flat and delicate, severe in outline, and not
much relieved, and often very decided in its direct imitation of nature. This, however, is mainly seen in the earliest
examples, for I am bound to say that later Italians never
rivalled the Byzantine capitals of S. Mark's, or some of
those in the early church of San Zenone, Verona. Indeed,
as time wore on, the carving in Italian buildings became
steadily worse and worse. Most of the later Venetian
capitals are bad in their outline, confused and purposeless

---

[1] English examples may be seen in the western porch of Fountains Abbey,
and among the extensive fragments of Egglestone Abbey, near Barnard
Castle.

in all their lines, and shew no sense of that vigorous petrifaction of the elements of natural growth and form, which
was so sensitively felt and expressed by French and English
artists.

CORNICE—SAN FRANCESCO, BRESCIA.

And, next, we come to the cornice, the feature which
above all others must most startle men who, for the first
time, make acquaintance with Italian work, and which most
recalls in its idea its Classic prototype; for, though its
treatment in detail is as unlike that of the ancients as it
can well be, it is, nevertheless, so decidedly marked and so
prominent a feature (crowning not only the summits of walls,
but even running up the gables, and returning round buttresses), that it is impossible not to regard it as another
evidence of admiration for, and imitation of, earlier work.

The ordinary northern parapet is never used, the eaves almost always finishing with the common Italian tiles projecting slightly over the deep cornice of the walls.   We have nothing at all parallel to these cornices in England, and I remember but few examples of anything of the same kind in the North of Europe, save in the transept of Lübeck Cathedral, and such churches as those of Bamberg and the Rhine country; which last seem to be derived from the Lombard churches of Pavia, and to have nothing in common with later pointed work, and to have exerted little, if any, influence on its development.

I have said enough, I hope, to explain the grounds for my opinion that, with the single exception of their use of shafts, we never find the same kind of perfection in Italian Gothic buildings as in French or English works of the same date; but I am not slow to allow, nevertheless, that they do contain features of extreme beauty and purity; and many of them peculiar to themselves.   There is perhaps no country in the world which excels Italy in the buildings which were erected for civic and domestic purposes.   The Doge's Palace, and many of the other palaces at Venice, the Broletto of Como, the other houses or palaces of which I have given illustrations throughout this volume, are some only among many which might be enumerated, any one of which would have not only an advantage over very many of our own buildings, as a model of good architecture, but at the same time the merit of fitness for the purposes for which our domestic buildings in towns are at the present day required.   Then again, there are, as I have shewn, the exquisite porches; the peculiar, and generally noble, campanili; the many-shafted cloisters; the perfect monuments; the use of brickwork of the best kind; and, finally, that in which Italian architecture of the Middle Ages teaches us more than any other architecture since the commencement of the world—the introduction of colour in construction—which is managed generally with such consummate beauty, refinement, and modesty, that even where it accompanies faulty construction and unworthily sham expedients, it is impossible to avoid giving oneself up altogether to admiration of the result.

It will be seen that I am not by any means a blind enthusiast about Italian architecture. Who, indeed, that has studied on the spot, as I have done, not only a vast number of buildings in England, but also nearly all of the best examples in France, Spain, and Germany, could do otherwise than profess his truest allegiance to be due to the truthful beauties of his own national variety of the style ? I should think that most students would agree with me, if they found themselves able to institute such a comparison.

The first view of an Italian Gothic church, whatever its date, is startlingly and, I think, disagreeably unlike anything that we are accustomed to in our own old buildings. You may go to a great English cathedral and find that from every point of view, inside and outside, every feature is well proportioned to its place, and beautiful in itself, whilst the *tout ensemble* is also perfect in proportion and mass. This can never be said of Italian work. It never produced anything perfect both in detail and in mass ; and one always finds it necessary to make excuses for even the best works, such as one never finds necessary, or allows oneself to think of making, for English works. There is something really absurd in comparing even the best of the Italian churches with such cathedrals as those of Canterbury or Lincoln, so superior are the latter from almost every point of view. The Italian church is usually a long, broad, rather low building, lighted with but few windows, having but a small, if any, clerestory, and with scarcely any irregularity in shape or plan ; it has scarcely ever more than one tower, and this is never combined with the rest of the design

in the manner common to us in England or France.
There is no approach, therefore, to such combinations of
steeples as are familiar to us at Canterbury, Wells, Laon,
Reims, or Rouen, and undoubtedly there is very much
less external grandeur. The steeple, when it does occur, is
often detached; and when it is engaged, it does not open
into the church, but is placed in some irregular and abnor-
mal position, where it is at once felt that it is purposely not
intended to be looked at in conjunction with the main façade
of the building. There is no attempt even to secure a
tolerable sky-line. The only relief to the monotonous outline of the main building is at the crossing, where something
in the way of a low, mean dome is occasionally introduced,
but this is always of but slight elevation, and not intended to
produce any good external effect, such as was aimed at in our
own central steeples. So also if we look at their façades,
we have a feature on which, in common with ourselves,
they often lavished considerable expense, and probably the
greatest pains. The treatment is very similar in its idea
throughout the whole period during which the style pre-
vailed; and the effect produced is undoubtedly oftener very
disappointing than attractive. The commonest type of
façade is one in which the cornice, which is generally of
slight projection, but deep and marked in character, is carried
up the flat gable of the building, whilst the whole front,
divided by vertical pilasters into three or five divisions in
width, is lighted either by a series of circular windows, or
by one large and important rose in the centre. This class of
front is common to most of the Gothic churches in Lombardy.

At Ferrara, we see another and very different design in
the grand front to the cathedral, which, save that it is
entirely and shamelessly a sham front, might vie even with
that of a Northern cathedral in beauty, intricacy, and
richness of character; but this design is not really very

Italian in style, and is a solitary example. When an Englishman sees the tympanum of the principal doorway of such a church filled with a sculpture of S. George and the Dragon, he may be pardoned for recollecting that our royal family have sprung from the same stock as the D'Estes, once Lords of Ferrara, the front of whose cathedral is almost the finest in Italy.

Other portions of Italian churches are even less satisfactory than their façades. I have already explained that the clerestory is rarely lighted by anything more elaborate than a succession of circular windows of small size. The church of Sta. Anastasia, Verona, gives us the best example of these, the windows there being of brick, filled in with very good early plate tracery in stone. The east end is often more picturesque than the west; and that of the church of San Fermo Maggiore, Verona, affords a good example. The east ends of the churches of the Frari and SS. Giovanni e Paolo, at Venice, are perhaps the two finest examples of this portion of the building to be seen in Italy, and are worthy of very high praise.

If we descend from generals to details, we shall find much more to admire, and altogether much more to interest us. The doorways and the porches, which protect without concealing them, are often especially beautiful. I have already mentioned the doorways of Sta. Anastasia and San Zenone at Verona, of S. Mark's, Venice, the cathedral at Modena, and the north porch of Sta. Maria Maggiore, at Bergamo, all of which are full of beauty and full of national character. Another favourite and beautiful type is that of the porch on the north side of San Fermo, at Verona, which is arched on each face, and roofed with a flat-pitched roof, gabled both ways. In the doorways, inclosed within these porches, we shall hardly find so much to admire, and must not expect anything like our own or the great French examples.

Generally the opening is square-headed, with a lintel often formed by an ingenious dovetailing of stone together,[1] and the mouldings of the jambs are too often continuous and very small and badly marked in their sections.

The exquisite monuments which so often occur against the walls or by the sides of Italian churches are somewhat similar in idea to these porches. Of these I have said so much that I only refer to them here, as among the most charming features of Italian art. I think that our own monuments, rich as our country is in them, will only be considered much superior to the best of these by those whose patriotism warps their judgment! One of the most perfect examples of the class is to be seen in the Castelbarco monument close to the church of Sta. Anastasia, Verona. Here the pointed trefoiled arch, on each face of the canopy over the tomb, springs from four detached shafts, and fits very closely under flat gables or pediments, above and from between which rises a perfectly plain pyramidal mass of stone. The very simplicity of the design of these monuments is their greatest charm; and so conscious were their designers of this, that they seem to me to have lavished all their care and refinement upon them. There are of necessity iron ties at the springing of the arch; but it was felt necessary to give the eye a sense of security beyond what the existence of these ties could afford, and this was accomplished by adding on the under side of the arch a simple and rather heavy cusp, generally proportioned with a degree of delicate skill of which modern architects appear to me (if I may dare to say it) never to dream. I believe that good architecture may generally be detected at once, by the excellence of such apparently small matters as the shape of a cusp.

---

[1] Numerous examples of masonry arranged in the same way occur in old English examples. The openings of fireplaces in particular are often so constructed.

I am certain that good Italian architecture invariably has cusping, which is both nervous in its curve and yet delicate ; and I believe that most modern cusps are drawn by the hundred as a mere matter of routine, without care and without pleasure, and consequently without good effect.

Not less beautiful than the porches and monuments is another feature which occurs in Italy, as often as, and perhaps more perfectly than, anywhere else—the cloister. This consists generally of an open arcade supported on detached shafts, and is very frequently of two stages in height. Notwithstanding their extreme simplicity and moderate amount of enrichment, these Italian cloisters are always capital in their effect. They owe this very much to the number of shafts which support their arches ; these are generally of marble, coupled together except at the angles, where there are usually four. Some of the cloisters which still remain in Verona, are among the most beautiful examples. Nor are those of San Stefano, Bologna, nor at a later date those of the church of Sant' Antonio at Padua and at Brescia, less worthy of study. They never have the beautiful traceries of our Northern cloisters, for the sufficient reason, that the climate rendered less protection from the weather necessary ; and the consequence of this is, that their arcades, being always severely simple in design, no effort was ever spared to make them as perfect as possible in their proportions.

The cloisters of the cathedral at Aosta are interesting as affording an instance of the lavish richness of illustration which some of the mediæval sculptors bestowed on their work ; the capitals throughout being sculptured with illustrations of subjects, all of which are made fully intelligible by inscriptions incised in the stone—a favourite practice not only of early Italian sculptors, but of their brethren in Germany and France. In the cloister of San Gregorio, Venice, we have

another variety in which the shafts support the woodwork of
the roof in a very picturesque fashion, without any arches.
This is a type of cloister which might often be most useful in
modern work, and is an evidence of the extent to which a
Gothic artist may, when necessity requires it, trench boldly
on what is ordinarily supposed to be the exclusive province of
Classic art—the use of the shaft and lintel; but here the
Gothic artist with his usual reality made his lintel of wood
in place of stone.

The Italian treatment of windows is especially worthy
of note. The drawings which I have given will shew how
generally the tracery, commonly called plate-tracery, was
used. It is, indeed, a very beautiful mode of treatment, but
quite distinct from all fully-developed systems, inasmuch as
it deals only with the piercings here and there in the block
of stone which forms the window-head, and not with the
intricate combinations of lines which mark out the outlines
of the spaces to be pierced. The difference is great—the one
kind giving that exquisite depth and mystery and admitting
of the infinite variety so characteristic of northern Gothic, the
other giving breadth and flatness of effect, and leaving space
on its broad surfaces for the play of the brilliant sunshine,
save where the black piercing of some simple form—quatrefoil
or trefoil—gives life to the otherwise monotonous window-
head. Of the two the former admits of infinitely more
variety and display of fancy and ingenuity; though the
latter, perhaps, when seen at its best, is really the more
beautiful. Both of them are, however, so good as to be
equally usable, and neither of them to the exclusion of
the other.

In Italian Gothic traceries, it is difficult to shew the pro-
gression or regular development which marks every stage of
northern Gothic. There are numerous examples of simple
lancet windows, of cusped lancets, of combinations of lancets

cusped or uncusped, and oftentimes of windows of plate-tracery, and then of more developed tracery which, however, was still treated as plate tracery with the addition of mouldings. In the later windows an unsightly effect is produced by the wide and bald plain splay or reveal which is usually formed round the window, outside as well as inside, and also by the placing of glazing behind the traceries in a separate wooden frame, so that they are completely concealed from view on the interior. The tracery of the second stage of the Doge's Palace at Venice is probably equal to any that has ever been executed, and may well be the pride of the country. It has also the special peculiarity, common to all Venetian domestic work, of being sufficiently strong in its section and construction to bear an enormous weight of wall without the aid of any discharging arch above it. There is another class of traceries which seems to have been essentially an Italian invention, and which is as objectionable as any tracery that I know. Examples of this may be seen in the south transept of SS. Giovanni e Paolo, at Venice. They give the idea of having been cut out to order, from an enormous mass of ready-made tracery, kept in slab, sold by the superficial yard, and cut to fit any opening required. There is no attempt to finish the tracery where it meets the inclosing arch, and the effect is consequently always rude and unskilful.[1]

Another feature is, the constant use at all dates of shafts in place of moulded window monials; and another,

---

[1] There is a very curious example of Italian tracery in the church of San Giacomo, in Bologna. This is a two-light window, composed of a series of slabs of stones, pierced with geometrical figures and supported by shafts. It has, beginning at the sill and reckoning upwards—1, two lights divided by a shafted monial ; 2, a slab pierced with two trefoiled heads to the lights; 3, a large transome panel of stone pierced with a quatrefoil and two trefoils ; 4, same as 1st ; 5, same as 2nd ; 6, the arch, whose tympanum is filled in with another pierced slab of stone. It will be seen that the construction of such a window as this is altogether unlike that of any English window.

the very frequent insertion of a transome of tracery, across the middle of the height of the window. The use of the shaft instead of the moulded monial does not seem to be so admirable in ecclesiastical as in domestic work. It generally accompanied the system already mentioned of fixing the glazing in wooden frames, behind the stone-work, and hence seldom looks well in church-windows except on the outside. The deep transomes pierced with tracery are of common occurrence. They are seen in almost all the Venetian Gothic churches, but their utility and beauty are alike doubtful.

No country affords more frequent examples of circular windows than Italy. They occur in almost every church, and are of stone, marble, and brick. The best example I know, of very early pointed character, and one which is unsurpassed anywhere, is in the west front of the church of Sta. Maria, Toscanella. Here there is an inner wheel, and the space between the two wheels is divided by shafts, between each ' of which is pierced a quatrefoil. The little window in the gable of the oratory of San Zenone, Verona, is a favourable example of a smaller window. It is of eight lights divided by shafts, and well moulded and proportioned in all its parts. Other circular windows as at S. Mark's, Venice, and in the church of Sant' Antonio, Padua, are of the class already described, where the tracery seems to have been inserted, without reference to, or connection with, the inclosing circular line.

I have now, I think, exhausted the distinguishing features of an Italian church, with the exception of its campanile. This, as I have said before, is always a single steeple (with the perhaps unique exception of Genoa Cathedral, which has two), generally detached from the main fabric, planted wherever it happened to be most convenient; sometimes as at Ver-

celli, not even at right angles to the building to which it is
attached, and with but little reference to its effect upon the
remainder of the building. There are no features of Italian
buildings which are so universally remembered with pleasure;
and similar as they are in their general scheme, there is
nevertheless a considerable variety in their treatment in
detail. The first thing to be noted is, that they are never
supported by buttresses, and that the usual mode of ascent
was by a staircase in the thickness of the wall, and not by
any such excrescence as a staircase turret. The outline
is severely square and simple, and, unlike as it is to most
of our English steeples, generally exceedingly striking.
No doubt the apparent height of these towers is enormously
increased by the absence of buttresses. The originals of
all Italian campanili seem to be the early steeples of the
Roman churches, divided into a series of stages of equal
height, pierced with windows not varying much in design
throughout. The most exact reproductions of these steeples
may be found so far from the centre of Italy as at Susa
at the foot of the Mont Cenis, and in other very similar
erections all over the North of Italy. With certain broad
general features of resemblance there are, however, several
local variations, which may be divided roughly into the
following separate classes or schools :—(1) The Pisan : (2)
the Venetian and Veronese : (3) the Genoese : and (4)
the Florentine : of which I need here only speak of the
Venetian and Veronese, which are undoubtedly among the
finest. In the Veronese there is a very distinct imitation of
the pure Romanesque examples, whilst in the Venetian there
is generally less subdivision into stages, the walls being
arcaded with very slightly recessed lofty arcades, and the
horizontal divisions being much fewer in number. Of these,
San Giacomo del Rialto is one of the best examples; it is
executed, as all the Venetian examples are, in brick. In

all these examples the pilasters at the angles are carefully marked. But there is another variety of distinctly Italian towers in which this is not the case. The finest example of this is the tower of the Scaliger Palace, at Verona, where the simple unbroken mass of masonry and brickwork shoots up into the sky all but unpierced until the belfry stage. Of this kind of tower the examples are not unfrequent in the smaller churches in Lombardy, and in the public halls and private houses of many of the cities described in these pages. The tower at Asti is one of the best of these.

There remain two other subjects which, more than any others, meet us at every stage of our study of Gothic architecture in Italy. These are, first, the use of brick; and secondly, the introduction of coloured materials in construction, of both of which, as we have seen, there are so many valuable examples.

It has been by far too much the fashion of late years to look upon brick as a very inferior material, fit only to be covered with compo, and never fit to be used in church-building, or indeed in any buildings of any architectural pretension, so that I suspect many people, trusting to their knowledge of pointed architecture in England, would be much surprized to find that, throughout large tracts of the Continent, brick was the natural, and indeed the popular material during the most palmy days of architecture in the Middle Ages. Yet so it was that in Holland, in the south-west of France, in Northern Germany, and the Low Countries, in large tracts in Spain, and throughout Northern Italy, stone was either scarce or not to be obtained, and brick was therefore everywhere and most fearlessly used.

In all these countries, just as in Italy, it was used without any concealment, but each country developed its practice in this matter for itself, and there is therefore considerable diversity in their work.   They are all unlike, and far superior to what remains to us of ancient brickwork in England, for I need hardly say that, with a rare exception here and there, and in comparatively small districts, brick was not used in England between the time of the Romans and the fifteenth century, and, when used afterwards, was seldom remarkable either for any singular beauty or originality of treatment. In this matter, therefore, we are obliged to go to the Continent for information.

Italian brickwork is remarkable as being almost always executed with nothing but red bricks, with occasional but rare use of stonework; the bricks for the ordinary walling are generally rather larger than ours, in no way superior in their quality, and always built coarsely with a wide joint of mortar.   Those used for windows, doorways, and generally where they were required to attract attention and to be ornamental, were made of much finer clay and moulded with

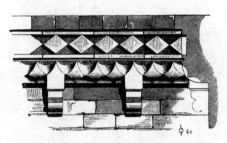

STRING-COURSE—PALACE OF JURISCONSULTS, CREMONA.

the greatest care and skill.   The transepts and campanile of Cremona Cathedral are instances of red brick used without any intermixture of stone save in the shafts of the windows, and their effect is certainly very grand.   The mouldings are elaborate, and the way in which cusping is formed singularly successful.   This, it must be observed, was not usually done

by means of bricks moulded in the form of a cusp, but with
ordinary bricks, built with the same radiating lines as those
of the arch to which they belonged, and cut and rubbed to
the necessary outline.   Sometimes, as, e.g., in the windows
at Mantua, which are some of the very best I have ever seen,
the points of the cusps and key-stones of the arches are
formed in pieces of stone, the alternation of which with the
deep-red hue of the bricks produces the most satisfactory
effect of colour.   This sort of treatment is common at
Brescia, Verona, Mantua, and Venice, but unknown at
Cremona.

In nearly all cases where brick is used for tracery, it is in
the shape of plate-tracery. The tympanum of the arch is filled

WINDOW IN NORTH TRANSEPT, CREMONA CATHEDRAL.

in with a mass of brickwork, through which are pierced the
arches over the several lights of the window, and these are supported on marble or stone shafts with carved capitals, instead

of monials :[1] and above these sometimes, as in the windows
of Sant' Andrea, Mantua, are three cusped circles; sometimes, as in the palace at Mantua, only one cusped circle;
or else, as in a beautiful example at Cremona, the plain
brick tympanum is relieved by the introduction of a panel

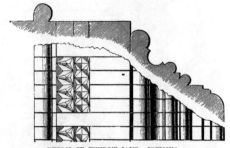

DETAIL OF WINDOW-JAMB—CREMONA.

of terra-cotta, bearing the cross on a shield, whilst round its
outer circumference delicately treated though large cusping
defines the outline of the arch.[2]

The windows at Coccaglio[3] and at Monza[4] are examples of
tympana left quite plain, or, as in the former case, pierced
only with a small opening of a few inches in diameter, which
nevertheless gives much effect to the design.   In the latter
case there is a feature which is well worth notice, because it
is remarkable in the best Italian brickwork, and always very
effective.   Labels are exceedingly rare, but their place is
usually supplied by a course of very narrow deep red bricks
which surrounds the back of the arch.   In the window in
Monza Cathedral there are two such courses—one about $4\frac{1}{2}$
inches wide, the other not more than $2\frac{1}{2}$.   They serve to
define the arch and keep it distinct in effect from the walling

---

[1] The windows in the Castle of S. Angelo, between Lodi and Pavia, are
the only examples I met with of the use of brick for monials. In Northern
Germany, on the contrary, where the shaft was almost unknown, brick
monials are universal, and generally unsatisfactory in their effect.

[2] See preceding page.   [3] See pp. 69, 71.   [4] See p. 390.

around it. Sometimes, as in the Vescovato at Mantua, and
in the houses at Asti, these narrow bricks are introduced

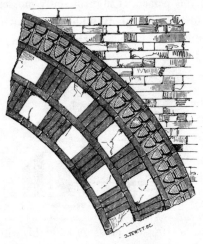

BRICK ARCHIVOLT, VESCOVATO—MANTUA.

between a succession of rims of brickwork on the same face,

ARCH-MOULD—CREMONA.

alternated very picturesquely
with squares of stone, and
sometimes, as in some beautiful
arcading outside San Fermo
Maggiore at Verona, to define
and enliven the lines of stonework; for in this case, though
the work is all in stone and no
brick was really required, so
great was the appreciation of
colour, that it was gladly and
most successfully introduced.
In the early cloister of San
Zenone we see it again, as also in all the very beautiful
arches which still remain in the Broletto of Brescia.

But beside this there was another way in which Italian architects produced a very beautiful effect : this was in the alternation of stone and brick. We have one of the first examples of this in the magnificent walls of San Zenone at Verona, in which a deep red brick is used in courses alternating with a very warm-coloured stone. The brick is used very irregularly : beginning at the base of the walls over the cloisters, we have alternately with courses of stone, first a band of three courses of brick, after this one course of brick, four courses, five courses, two courses, one course, and then the cornice, which is mainly of stone, but relieved by two courses of narrow bricks ; in spite of the variation in the height of the brick courses, those of stone in this case are nearly uniform in depth. In the west front of San Fermo Maggiore[1] we have brick and stone used in alternate and regular courses all the way up ; in this case the brick is used rather for colour than for any other reason, though the side walls of this church are entirely of brick and crowned with excessively deep brick cornices.

The churches at Asti afford examples of the worst kind of counterchanging of stone and brick ; in them the jamb of a window is treated like a chess-board, being chequered with alternate red and white both horizontally and vertically. To accomplish this the construction is ingeniously twisted, and it need hardly be said that the effect is not at all good.

The interior of San Zenone, Verona, is lined with brick and stone, arranged just as it is outside, and the effect is most satisfactory ; indeed, this and the interior of the baptistery at Cremona, still left in their original state, shew how noble an effect of colour may be given by brick internally, and how mistaken we are when we cover our walls with undecorated plaster. I have seen it maintained by men who possibly had never seen such old works as these in their old

[1] See plate 17, p. 133.

state, that such colour as this is savage and fit only for uncul-
tivated men.　If, however, there is refinement in whitewash
or plaster, I am unable to see it, and I can see no more incon-
sistency in honestly shewing the real materials of the wall
inside than in doing so outside.　This at any rate is beyond
all doubt what these old Italian architects did.

The east end of the church of the Frari at Venice is
another example of coursing with stone.[1]　There, however,
the courses are far apart, and seem to be intended to define
the lines of the springing of arches, of transomes, and the
like ; and this they do very satisfactorily.　But, perhaps, the
very best example of mixed stone and brick is that which we
have in the window-heads of the church by the side of the
Duomo at Verona, in which the arrangement of the two

colours is quite perfect.　In this
case the cusped head of the light
is executed in stone, not in
brick ; and this is, I think, as a
general rule, by far the better
plan ; for if an attempt is made
to execute tracery in brick, we
have the example of the Germans
before our eyes as a warning.
They rarely (S. Katharine, Lübeck, is almost a solitary exception) used stone in their window
tracery ; and as they never developed the kind of brick plate-
tracery which is so characteristic
of the best Italian work, they
built windows which were either

WINDOW—VERONA.

bald and ugly in their simplicity, or else, endeavouring to
execute elaborate traceries by the use of bricks, moulded into

[1] See plate 24, p. 199.

the forms of component parts of tracery, they produced what are even more distasteful than any other kind of window; in part because they consist of an endless repetition of small reticulations, and in part because they lead naturally to the constant reproduction of the same window for economy's sake.

BRICK WINDOW, SANT' ANDREA—MANTUA.

There can be no doubt that the best windows for brick churches are either those beautiful Italian developments of plate-tracery in which all the bricks are carefully cut and rubbed for their proper place, or those in which, within an inclosing arch of line upon line of brickwork, a small portion of stone is used for the traceries. And this last has the advantage of giving much more opportunity for variety of form and beauty of effect than any brick traceries can ever give.

There is one point in which a curious practical difference exists between our old work and most old Italian. Here it was not the custom to have keystones to pointed arches, whilst there it is quite the rule to have them; this may have been partly, perhaps, because it was a matter of convenience to mark the central stone in arches composed of alternate voussoirs of brick and stone, and it may have been partly some relic of Classic traditions: not only, however, is there a keystone, but sometimes, as in the Broletto at Brescia, this is additionally distinguished, above the rest of the stone voussoirs, by some small ornament carved upon it. With one more fact I think I may end what I have to say on this head: this is with reference to the mode in which some of the Italian brick arches very beautifully follow the fashion, not so uncommon in stone, of increasing in depth as they approach the centre. In this manner, one sometimes sees an arch whose outer circumference is pointed, whilst its inner line is a semicircle. This was a fashion most popular in Florence, and not so common in Northern Italy; still it is to be seen at Monza, Verona, and elsewhere. The effect is always very good, and, though quite unknown to our forefathers in England, may well be introduced in our works, as it gives great appearance of strength, and is no doubt, at the same time, the strongest possible form of arch.

No one can deny that the study of Italian brickwork must be useful to those who are compelled, as we so often are, to use the same material in buildings for whose good architectural effect and character we are anxious. But, far as it is in advance of most ancient brickwork in England, there are points in which we must refuse to follow it; we need not, for instance, in attempting to rival its beauties, confound them with faults which were essentially those of the whole Italian style, and not specially of Italian brickwork. We may with the greatest advantage emulate the Italian system of brick-window tracery, whilst we take care never to imitate the equally common custom in Italy of erecting sham fronts in order to display our traceries. Again, though they never used any but red bricks, there is no reason why we should not enliven our work with the contrast of other colours. Germany gives us examples of green and black bricks, and, indeed, Italy affords some (e.g., Sant' Antonio, in Padua, Murano, and Torcello) of a yellow-ish brick; and, no doubt, the effects producible by these contrasts of colour are such as Italian architects were always ready to avail themselves when they had the opportunity. This their parti-coloured works in marble sufficiently prove; but at the same time it was seldom that they ventured upon such works in brick; and as it must be admitted that there is no sort of work which so much requires skilful handling, or which is so liable to degenerate into vulgarity, as this, it is probable that they advisedly abstained from it.

As to the question whether it be desirable or not to introduce brick at all in ecclesiastical edifices, or generally in public buildings, one might, a few years ago, have been anxious to say somewhat. I trust, however, that the ignorant prejudice which made many good people regard stone as a sort of sacred material, and red brick as one fit only for the commonest and meanest purposes, is fast wearing out, and that what now mainly remains to be done is to shew how it may most effectively be used, not only in external, but also in internal works.

One word only as to its colour, for I think that we ought as much as possible to insist upon this being taken into consideration. We do not, as a general rule, I suppose, adopt any material in good works of architecture simply because it is the very cheapest that can be obtained ; sometimes, indeed, we must, and then I should be the last to contend against what is simply an act of necessity, not of choice ; but ordinarily, before, for economy's sake, we determine to sacrifice the colour of our work, and to use those detestable-looking dirty yellow bricks in which London so much indulges, we ought to consider whether, by some economy in other respects, we may not save enough to allow of the use of the best kind of red brick for the general face of our walls.[1]

At the present day there is, I think, absolutely no one point in which we fail so much, and about which the world in general has so little feeling, as that of colour. Our

[1] It would be difficult to give stronger evidence of the intrinsic effect of a good coloured material than is afforded by the fact that designs so really ignorant in their architectural detail as, e.g., most of the buildings of the time of William III. and Queen Anne should nevertheless have a certain charm for us, solely derived from the beautiful colour of the bricks with which they are built.

buildings are, in nine cases out of ten, cold, colourless, insipid, academical studies, and our people have no conception of the necessity of obtaining rich colour, and no sufficient love for it when successfully obtained. The task and duty of architects at the present day is mainly that of awakening and then satisfying this feeling; and one of the best and most ready vehicles for doing this exists, no doubt, in the rich-coloured brick so easily manufactured in this country, which, if properly used, may become so effective and admirable a material.

The other mode of introducing colour in construction, by means of the use of marbles, deserves also some notice. In my notes upon the buildings as they were passed in my journeys, I have described two modes in which this kind of work was treated: the first was that practised in Venice—the veneering of brick walls with thin layers or coats of marble; the other, that practised at Bergamo, Cremona, and Como —in which the marble formed portion of the substance of the wall.

These two modes led, as would naturally be expected, to two entirely different styles and modes of architecture.

The Venetian mode was rather likely to be destructive of good architecture, because it was sure to end in an entire concealment of the real construction of the work; the other mode, on the contrary, proceeded on true principles, and took pleasure in defining most carefully every line in the construction of the work. It might almost be said that one mode was devised with a view to the concealment, and the other with a view to the explanation, of the real mode of construction.

I have already described, at some length, the main features of these old works in marble, and I feel, therefore, that all that need now be done is to point out the degree to which they afford matter for our imitation with the coloured

materials and marbles which we fortunately have in Great
Britain fit for the purpose, though not in very great variety.

There appears to me to be a certain limited extent to
which we may safely go in the way of inlaying or incrustation: we may, for instance, so construct our buildings as
that there may be portions of the face of their walls in
which no strain will be felt, and in which this absence of
strain will be at once apparent; obviously, to instance a
particular place, the spaces inclosed within circles constructed in the spandrels of a line of arches can have no
strain of any kind. They are portions of wall without any
active function, and may safely be filled in with materials
the only object of which is to be ornamental. All kinds of
sunk panels inclosed within arches or tracery would come
under the same head; the spaces between string-courses
might also do so very frequently, if, as in old examples, the
string-courses were large slabs of stones bedded into the very
midst of the wall, and so capable of protecting the thin, weak
slabs of marbles incrusted between them.

In Venice we have some grand examples, at S. Mark's, of
this system of incrustation filling in the whole of the space
within large arches; here it is lawful, because there is no
weight upon it to thrust it out of its place or disjoint it, as
the least pressure most certainly always will. So far in
praise of the Venetian system. But in other parts of the
same building we have this system carried to a length which
I cannot but think most mistaken, and which, I most heartily
trust, may never find imitators here. In these the
arches were constructed in brick, and then entirely covered
with marble. Of course there was some difficulty in
doing this, and the way in which the difficulty was met was
extremely ingenious; a succession of thin slabs of marble
was placed round the soffeit of the arch, having perhaps
enough of the cohesion given by the form of the arch to

enable them to support their own weight, and further supported by metal staples let into the joints of the brickwork.
The edges of these thin slabs projected sufficiently in advance
of the face of the brickwork to allow of their being worked
with some kind of pattern—generally, as has before been said,
a sort of dentil—and of their giving some support to the thin
slices of marble with which the walls were then covered.
The whole system was excessively weak; and this can nowhere be better seen than in the Fondaco de Turchi, where
almost the whole of the marble facing and beautiful medallions, in which it was once so rich, have peeled off, and left
nothing but the plain and melancholy substratum of brick.
Few architects, I should think, would like to contemplate
their work perishing in this piecemeal manner, any more
than they would enjoy the thought of a west front left
unfinished, like that of Sta. Anastasia at Verona, and prepared only for marble with rough, irregular, and unsightly
brickwork.

It would be unjust not to say that often, very often, this
system of incrustation, even when carried to the extreme
limits of what seems to be lawful, wins upon our love by the
exquisite delicacy and taste of the sculptured patterns,
worked in low-relief, with which it is covered. The men
who did this work were, perhaps, more of sculptors than of
architects; and certainly it must be confessed that never in
buildings in which the construction is mainly thought of,
is there, so far as I know, so much elaborate thought and
skill exhibited in the decorative part of the work as in
buildings such as these.

Sometimes, the sculptured medallions set in the centre
of a plain surface of marble are of exquisite taste and
beauty; whilst here and there, as e.g. in S. Mark's and in
one or two spots in the water-front of the Ducal Palace,
are examples of great beauty, of medallions formed of marbles

of various colours, arranged with great refinement in some
kind of geometrical pattern, which shew another and equally
beautiful mode of relieving plain spaces of walling.

The plain surfaces of the walls in Venetian work were
commonly either entirely inlaid, or else inlaid within a square
inclosing border of projecting moulding. The inlaying was
composed of a number of rectangular slabs of marble, not by
any means always of the same size, supported to some extent
by the projections of the inclosing marbles or by those of the
archivolt, but always dependent mainly on metal cramps let
into the fabric of the wall; and, when possible, these marbles
were slabs cut out of the same block, and put side by side, so
as to produce a kind of regular pattern wherever the veining
of the marble was at all positively marked.

The other mode of introducing constructional colour in
marble commends itself to one's reason as that which is
most likely to endure for ages, and as that, therefore, which
ought, wherever it may be, to be adopted. The first idea of
the architects of these buildings seems to have been to
arrange their material with as much regard to strong contrasts of colour as was possible. The first thing they did,
therefore, was to alternate the colours of every course of
masonry, either simply as in the Broletto at Como[1] and in
Sta. Maria Maggiore at Bergamo,[2] or as in the west front of
the cathedral at Cremona, where very narrow layers of white
marble are laid between each of the other courses, which
are of course so much the more defined.

The description which I have already given of these
works, as well as of the porch at Bergamo, will shew how
regular is the way in which this system of counterchanging
the colours was carried out by the purely constructional
school; this is, in fact, the great mark of difference between
the constructional and the incrusting school of Italian archi-

---

[1] See plate 63, p. 397.   [2] See plate 1, frontispiece.

tects, the whole arrangement of coloured materials by the two schools being quite different, and producing singularly different results. The most common fault of the Venetian system of incrustation must have been that upon a general surface of plain wall you had here and there a square patch of marble surrounding a window opening; that of the other system would be, in the opinion of many, that you have too stripy an effect of colour, and that all the divisions, moreover, are horizontal.

The former must certainly have been the case wherever the incrustation did not extend over the whole surface of the walls, which was very frequently the case; but the latter is not really a fault; it was only an elaboration in a more beautiful material of the same system which we have seen pursued with such happy results by the builders of Verona in brick and stone,[1] and which we find adopted by the architects of Northern Germany in the frequent alternation of courses of red and black brick, and sometimes by our own forefathers in the coursing of flint work with stone, or in the counter-changing of red and white stones which we see in some of the Northamptonshire churches. The system was a thoroughly sound one, because it not only proceeded from and depended on the natural arrangement of the material, but afforded the best possible means for displaying the various colours which were to be used.

Probably all these systems are mainly useful now as shewing us certain principles which we may work out and apply to our own somewhat different circumstances; and surely one of our first objects ought to be the discovery of the extent of our means and opportunities, which in this matter are at the present day far beyond what is generally imagined.

It must never be forgotten by us that our forefathers had

___

[1] Some of the mediæval buildings in Greece have small patterns carved in low relief all round the walls in occasional courses, which are evidently intended to produce the kind of effect referred to above.

very limited means of obtaining materials from one locality and transporting them to another; and were moreover, to a great extent, unacquainted with the materials which might, if necessary, be obtained. We have not this excuse; we not only know what materials we may obtain, but we have at the same time marvellous facilities for their conveyance between all parts of the country; and we know also how much has been done of old in other countries by using them in a proper way.

No excuse therefore can be found for us if we continue to neglect to avail ourselves of them as though they were still undiscovered. We have alabaster, which may be wrought at a really trifling expense; large fields of marbles, of which those of Devonshire and Ireland are particularly valuable for architectural decoration, and those of Derbyshire and Purbeck for the formation of shafts and columns: we have, moreover, an exhaustless supply of granites of various colours; of serpentine; and, lastly, of building-stones of many tints, many of which may be very effective when contrasted. In addition to these natural materials we have every facility for making the most perfect bricks; and, owing to the excellence already achieved by our manufacturers of glass and pottery, we have no difficulty in making mosaics and tiles, either for roofing, flooring, or inlaying, of any degree of beauty, either of colour or form.

With such advantages we ought long since to have effected far more than we have ever attempted, or apparently ever thought of. Our buildings should, both outside and inside, have had some of that warmth which colour only can give; they should have enabled the educated eye to revel in bright tints of nature's own formation, whilst to the uneducated eye they would have afforded the best of all possible lessons, and, by familiarizing it with the proper combination of colour and form, would have enabled it to appreciate it.

And then, if ever the day shall come when our buildings thus do their duty and teach their proper lesson to the eye, we may hope that we shall see a feeling, more general and more natural, for colour of all kinds and for art of every variety in the bulk of our people. At present it is really saddening to converse with the majority of educated men on any question of colour. For them it has no charms and no delight. The puritanical uniformity of our coats and of all our garments is but a reflection from the prevailing lack of love of art or colour of any kind. A rich colour is thought vulgar, and that only is refined which is neutral, plain, and ugly.

Perhaps in all this there may be something more than art can ever grapple with; it may be ingrain, and part of the necessity of the present age; but if so, oh for the days when, as of yore, colour may be appreciated and beloved, when uniformity shall not be considered beauty, nor a hideous plainness be considered a fit substitute for severity! Oh too, for the days when men shall have cast off their dependence on other men's works, and the customs of their own days, and, like true men and faithful, shall honestly and with energy, each in his own sphere, set to work to do all that in them lies to increase the power of art and to advance its best interests. All these aims and objects are more or less bound up with the best interests of a people, however old and however powerful, because they depend for ultimate and real success upon the thorough belief, on the part of all its votaries, in certain great and eternal principles, which, if always acted upon, would beyond all doubt sometimes make great artists and always good men.

The principle which artists now have mainly to contend for is that of TRUTH; forgotten, trodden under foot, despised, if not hated for ages, this must be their watchword. If they be architects, let them remember how vitally necessary

truthfulness in construction, in design, and in decoration, is
to any permanent success in even the smallest of their works ;
or sculptors, let them recollect how vain and unsatisfactory
has been their abandonment of truth in their attempted
revival among us of what in Classic times were—what they
no longer are—real representations and natural works of art ;
if painters, let them remember how all-important a return
to first principles and truth in the delineation of nature and
natural forms is to them, if they are ever to create a school
of art by which they may be remembered in another age.

Finally, I wish that all artists would remember the one
great fact which separates by so wide a gap the architects,
sculptors, and painters of the best days of the Middle Ages
from us now—their earnestness and their thorough self-
sacrifice in the pursuit of art, and in the exaltation of their
religion.   They were men who had a faith, and hearts
earnestly bent on the propagation of that faith ; and were it
not for this, their works would never have had the life,
vigour, and freshness which even now they so remarkably
retain.   Why should we not be equally remembered three
centuries hence ?   Have we less to contend for, less faith to
exhibit, or less self-sacrifice to offer than they, because we
live in later days ?   Or is it true that the temper of men is
so much changed, and that the vocation of art has changed
with it ?   I believe not.   There have been evidences enough
that there is no lack of liberality on the part of our em-
ployers, where there is any evidence of skill and enthusiasm
for his work on the part of the artist. The English architect
of to-day has opportunities as great as those of any of his
predecessors, if he will but use them.   But he must use his
art as one who respects both himself and it.   There is no
real respect for an art when it is treated, as it always has
been by the Renaissance architects and their followers, as a
mere affair of display.   No good building was ever yet

erected in which the architect designed the front, and left the flanks or internal courts to take care of themselves. So also no good building was ever seen, in which the exterior only was thought of, and the internal decoration and design neglected. But this is almost universal now, except in the few buildings in which the Gothic style has been carefully revived. In such treatment of art as this, there is an ingrain falseness, which is as demoralizing as it is ruinous. If architecture is only an affair of outside display, no one will take any real interest in it, for from the first it is the evidence of the architect's love for his work which has given the human interest which is all in all to it.

It is this truthfulness only, in every line and every detail of every part of a building, which can ever make great architecture—it is this only which one would wish to extract from the works of our forefathers—and this only which I have desired to discover in the works of those Italian artists whose labours I have been considering, and whose efforts I have endeavoured to set before my readers; and it is this desire which can alone be my excuse for having undertaken the work which I have now brought to a conclusion.

KEY PLAN OF CAPITALS DUCAL PALACE VENICE.

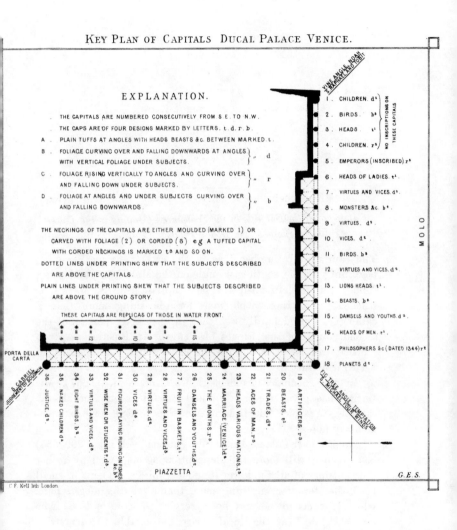

EXPLANATION.

THE CAPITALS ARE NUMBERED CONSECUTIVELY FROM S.E. TO N.W.

THE CAPS ARE OF FOUR DESIGNS MARKED BY LETTERS. t. d. r. b.

A . PLAIN TUFTS AT ANGLES WITH HEADS BEASTS &c. BETWEEN MARKED. t.

B . FOLIAGE CURVING OVER AND FALLING DOWNWARDS AT ANGLES } „ d
WITH VERTICAL FOLIAGE UNDER SUBJECTS.

C . FOLIAGE RISING VERTICALLY TO ANGLES AND CURVING OVER } „ r
AND FALLING DOWN UNDER SUBJECTS.

D . FOLIAGE AT ANGLES AND UNDER SUBJECTS CURVING OVER } „ b
AND FALLING DOWNWARDS.

THE NECKINGS OF THE CAPITALS ARE EITHER MOULDED (MARKED 1) OR
CARVED WITH FOLIAGE (2) OR CORDED (3) e.g. A TUFTED CAPITAL
WITH CORDED NECKINGS IS MARKED t3 AND SO ON.

DOTTED LINES UNDER PRINTING SHEW THAT THE SUBJECTS DESCRIBED
ARE ABOVE THE CAPITALS.

PLAIN LINES UNDER PRINTING SHEW THAT THE SUBJECTS DESCRIBED
ARE ABOVE THE GROUND STORY.

THESE CAPITALS ARE REPLICAS OF THOSE IN WATER FRONT.

VINE ANGLE NOAH & RAPHAEL AND LOBET

MOLO

1 . CHILDREN. d³
2 . BIRDS. b³
3 . HEADS. t¹
4 . CHILDREN. r³
5 . EMPERORS (INSCRIBED) r³
6 . HEADS OF LADIES. t¹.
7 . VIRTUES AND VICES. d³.
8 . MONSTERS &c. b³.
9 . VIRTUES. d³.
10 . VICES. d².
11 . BIRDS. b³
12 . VIRTUES AND VICES. d³.
13 . LIONS HEADS. t¹.
14 . BEASTS. b³.
15 . DAMSELS AND YOUTHS. d².
16 . HEADS OF MEN. r¹.
17 . PHILOSOPHERS &c (DATED 1344) r²
18 . PLANETS d³.

NO INSCRIPTIONS ON THESE CAPITALS

FIG TREE ANGLE TEMPTATION MICHAEL FOUR WINDS

36 . JUSTICE. d³.
35 . NAKED CHILDREN d³.
34 . EIGHT BIRDS. b³.
33 . VIRTUES AND VICES. d³.
32 . WISE MEN OR STUDENTS r². d³.
31 . FIGURES PLAYING RIDING ON FISHES &c. b².
30 . VICES. d³.
29 . VIRTUES. d³.
28 . VIRTUES AND VICES d³.
27 . FRUIT IN BASKETS. t¹.
26 . DAMSELS AND YOUTHS. d³.
25 . THE MONTHS. r³.
24 . MARRIAGE (VENICE) d³.
23 . HEADS VARIOUS NATIONS. t³.
22 . AGES OF MAN. r³.
21 . TRADES. d³.
20 . BEASTS. t¹.
19 . ARTIFICERS. r³.
18 . PLANETS d³.

PORTA DELLA CARTA

S. GABRIEL JUDGEMENT OF SOLOMON

PIAZZETTA

MOLO

G.E.S.

C. F. Kell lith London

APPENDIX.

Catalogue of the Subjects of the Sculptured Capitals in the Lower Stage of the Doge's Palace, Venice.

THE capitals are numbered as in the accompanying key-plan, beginning at the south-east angle on the Molo front, and going from right to left until the last capital, near S. Mark's, is reached. For those who wish for something more than a catalogue, I need hardly say that in the latter portion of the second volume of the 'Stones of Venice,' Mr. Ruskin has given all that can be desired, with his usual felicity and beauty of verbal illustration.

In the 'Annales Archéologiques,' vol. xvii. (1857), Mr. Burges has given a very full and careful account of all the capitals, to which M. Didron Aîné has added some supplementary notes.

Zanotto (' Il Palazzo Ducale di Venezia,' vol. i. pp. 209–355) has given a still more full description, accompanied by rather rude outlines of all the lower range of capitals. There is small need, therefore, for anything more than a mere catalogue here, which it seems to me may be of service to some of those who are able to look at the Ducal Palace, but unable to carry with them any of the weighty volumes to which I have referred.

South-east Angle.—Above the capital is the Drunkenness of Noah. Above this, on a level with the traceries of the upper arcade, the archangel Raphael, with Tobit, who bears a scroll with these words —

> EFICE Q̄
> SO̱ . FRE
> TV̄ . RAFA
> EL . REVE
> RENDE
> QUIETU̅.[1]

CAPITAL I. Partly built up. Has three figures of nude children, one with a comb and shears, another with a bird. The foliage is good ; but the nude figures have the appearance of semi-Renaissance work.

II. Partly built up. Large birds—one devouring a serpent, another a fish, and the third pluming its feathers. The foliage here is not very good, and the design of the capital in no way first-rate, the birds being treated in a very naturalesque way.

III. Partly built up. Large heads, male and female. The man has a helmet, partly of plate, but with chain mail round the neck.

IV. Partly built up. Children, nude, holding (1) a bird, and (2 and 3) fruit.

V. Partly built up. Emperors. This is the first capital which has inscriptions. Those visible are (1) TITUS VESPASIAN IPAT ; (2) TRAJANUS INPE ; and (3) (OCT)AVIANUS IPATO.

VI. Partly built up. Large heads, alternated with tufts of foliage, badly carved.

VII. Virtues and Vices. (1) Liberality ; inscribed LARGITAS. ME . ONORAT. (2) Constancy ; COSTANCIA . SU . NIL . TIMES. (3) Discord ; DISCORDIA . SU . - - - DISCORDANS. (4) Patience ; PATIENTIA . MANET . MECUM. (5) Despair ; DESPERACIO . MORS . CRUDELIS. (6) Obedience ; OBEDIENCIA.A.DNO.EXIBEO. (7) Infidelity ; INFIDELITATE.—ILI.GERO. (8) Modesty ; MODESTIA.ROBŪ OBTINEO. This capital should be compared with No. XXVIII. The foliage here is very beautiful ; but the execution of No. XXVIII. is best.

---

[1] "Oh, venerable Raphael, make thou the gulf calm, we beseech thee !". This figure looks towards the sea and the port.

VIII. Monsters, generally with musical instruments. A riding figure here wears chain armour. There are no inscriptions on this capital, and its intention is very obscure.

IX. Virtues. (1) Faith; FIDES.OPTIMA.IN.DEO. (2) Fortitude; FORTITUDO.'SUM.VIRILIS' (Mr. Ruskin), or 'INVINCIBILIS.' (3) Temperance; TEMPERANTIA.SUM.IN.OMIBU. (4) Humility; HUMILITAS.ABITAT.I.ME. (5) Charity; KARITAS.DEI.MECU.EST. (6) Justice; REX.SUM.JUSTICIE. (7) Prudence; PRUDENTIA.METIT. OIA. (8) Hope; SPE.HABE.IN.DNO. The differences between this capital and No. XXIX. are very slight. In the latter, Prudence has a book, which she has not here; and Temperance has a jug here in addition to the chalice which the other carries.

X. Vices. (1) Luxury; LUXURIA.SUM.IMENSA. (2) Gluttony; GULA.SINE.ORDINE.SU. (3) Pride; SUPERBIA.PREESSE. VOLO. (4) Anger; IRA.CRUDELIS.E.IN.ME. (5) Avarice; AVARITIA.ANPLECTOR. (6) Idleness; ACCIDIA.ME.STRIGIT. (7) Vanity; VANITAS.IN.ME.HABUNDAT. (8) Envy; INVIDIA.ME. COBVRIT. This capital is very finely sculptured.

XI. Birds. Some web-footed, some not so; and with no inscriptions.

XII. Virtues and Vices. (1) Misery; MISERIA. (2) Cheerfulness; ALACRITAS. (3) Folly; STULTICIA..E.REGNAT. (4) CASTITAS (CE)L(EST)IS.E. (5) HONESTY; (HO)NEST(ATEM. DILIGO). (6) Falsehood. (7) Injustice; INJUSTICIA.SEVA.SU. (8) Abstinence; ASTINECIA.OPTIMA.E.. This capital is so much damaged as to be hardly intelligible without comparison with No. XXXIII.

XIII. Lions' heads, large and coarse, and with very poorly carved tufts of foliage between them.

XIV. Wild animals. The whole of the beast, not the head only, is given. They are poorly carved and designed.

XV. Damsels and Youths. Considered by Selvatico, and after him by Mr. Ruskin, to represent Idleness. There are no inscriptions. More probably they represent the youth of the higher class with marks of their sportive occupations. This is an extremely well-carved capital.

XVI. Eight large heads alternately with tufts of foliage. The whole finely carved and designed. Supposed by Zanotto to

represent the foreigners who traded with Venice. Selvatico
describes it as representing Latins, Tartars, etc., and as being in
fact a repetition of No. XXIII. (*vide infra.*)

XVII. Philosophers. This is very much damaged, and the
inscriptions are nearly destroyed. (1) Solomon. (2) Priscian.
(3) Aristotle. (4) Tully. (5) Pythagoras. On a label carried
by this figure Mr. Burges reads the date 1344. Mons. Didron
interprets it 1399; this is a date, however, which he will not
admit, believing the real date to be 1299. Mr. Ruskin does not
appear to have seen these figures, and I have been unable to
satisfy myself about them.

XVIII. This is the angle capital. Above it is the Temptation of Adam and Eve; and on the second stage, the four winds
on the capital of the arcade, and the Archangel Michael above.
The whole is a perfectly beautiful group of sculpture, of an
equally beautiful and well-selected story.

Planets. (1) Creation of Man; DE.LIMO.DS.ADA.DE.COSTA
FORMAVIT.ET.EVA. (2) Saturn; ET.SATURNE.DOMUS.EGLOCERUNTIS.
ET.URNE. (3) Jupiter; INDE.JOVI.DOMA.PISCES.SIMUL.ATQ.CIRONA.
(4) Mars; E - - ARIES.MARTIS.ET.ACU - - E.SCORPIO.PARTIS. (5)
The Sun; EST . DOMU . SOLIS . TU . QUOQ.SIGNE.LEONI. (6) Venus;
LIBRA . CU . TAURO . VENUS . - - T . PURIOR . AURO. (7) Mercury;
OCCUPAT.ERIGONE.STILBONS.GEMIUQ.LACONE. (8) The Moon; LUNE
CANCER.DOMUT.PBET.I.ORBE SIGNORIO. The whole of the sculp-
ture of this capital deserves careful study. Mars is a figure in
chain mail. Venus, seated on a bull, and the Moon— a female
figure in a boat, with a crescent in one hand and a crab in the
other—are both of them exquisitely treated.

XIX. Artificers. Figures alternately crowned and uncrowned
working at parts of a building. The foliage is admirable. The
pieces of stone on which the artificers are at work are inlaid
with porphyry. Mr. Ruskin points out that all the architectural
details represented are such as would be found in the early part
of the fourteenth century. It is certainly very curious that
among the workers one has 'DISCIPULUS OPTIMUS;' another—
'DISIPULS INCREDUL,' over the head: a reference to S. John and
S. Thomas, which is not intelligible to me.

XX. Beasts. Eight large heads, well carved and set as

knops below masses of rather heavily treated leaves. The beasts have their names inscribed : LEO. LUPUS. URSUS. MUSIPUL. CHANIS.[1] APER. GRIFO. VULPUS.

XXI. Trades. Finely carved. Inscriptions over the heads of the workmen : (1) LAPICIDA SUM. (2) AURIFICES. (3) CERDO SUM. (4) CARPENTARIUS SUM. (5) MENSURATOR. (6) AGRICHOLA. (7) NOTARIUS SUM. (8) FABER SUM.

XXII. The Ages of Man. A very interesting capital. (1) + LUNA . DNAT . IFANCIE . P . ANO . IIII. (2) MECUREU . DNT . PUERICIE . P . ANO . X. (3) ADOLOSENCIE . (VEN)US . P . AN . VII. (4) INVENTUTI.DNT.SOL.P.AN.XIX. (5) SENECTUTI.DNT.MARS.P. AN . XV. (6) SENICIE.DNT.JUPITER.P.ANN.XII. (7) DECREPITE. DNT.SATN.UQ.AD.MOTE. (8) ULTIMA.E.MORS.PENA PECATI.

XXIII. Nations. This is treated in the same way exactly as No. XX. The heads are inscribed, LATINI. TARTARI. TURCHI. ONGARI. GRECI. GOTI. EGICY. PERSII. It will be found that, counting from the south-west angle, the second and fifth capitals on each front are of the same description, i.e. Nos. XIII. and XVI. on the west side, and XIX. and XXIII. on the Piazzetta-front. I think this militates against Mr. Ruskin's view that this capital is not old, as it shews how very regularly they are placed ; and I do not see much to choose between in these four capitals. It is worth notice here that this capital is, to a considerable extent, a replica of No. XVI. ; but the latter has no inscriptions.

XXIV. Love and Marriage. This is a much larger column than the others. It carries a cross wall above, so placed as to allow of rooms on the sea-front, about sixty-three feet in width. It is one of the most exquisite of all the series. The subjects are : (1) A young man with his hand on his heart, admiring a damsel. (2) They meet and converse. (3) She puts a crown on his head, and presents him with an apple. (4) They embrace. (5) The marriage bed. (6) They hold their bambino wrapped in swaddling clothes between them. (7) The child grows, and enjoys life. (8) The child is dead, and his parents mourn over his body. The change in character from the extreme smartness

---

[1] Mr. Ruskin founds an argument on the introduction of an H in this way in what he calls one of the Renaissance capitals of the Piazzetta (the 33rd). He omits to notice its use in this undoubtedly early capital.

of dress in the earliest subject to the carelessness about it in the last, should be observed.

Above this capital is a figure of Venice personified, in one of the divisions of the tracery. She is seated on lions' backs, with her feet above the sea.

XXV. Labours of the Months. This is not a replica. (1) March; MARCIUS . CORNATOR. (2) April and May; APRILIS + MAGIUS. (3) June; JUNIUS.CU.CERISIS. (4) July and August; JULIUS + AUGUSTU. (5) September; SEPTEBE . SUPEDITAT. (6) October and November; OCTOBE̅ + NOVEMBE. (7) December; DECEM - - - CAT SUUM. (8) January and February; JANVARIVS+ FEBRUARU.

XXVI. Sports and Employments of damsels and young men. This is a replica of No. XV. The foliage here is exquisitely carved. There are no inscriptions. The figures, as in the other, hold : (1) A horse. (2) A bird, and the leg of a larger bird (hawking?). (3) A distaff. (4) A dog. (5) A flower. &c. &c.

XXVII. Fruit in baskets. This is not a replica. It is the finest of the " knop " series of capitals. The fruit is admirably carved, and here the exact imitation of nature in the fruit, combined with foliage in the knops between the baskets, which is quite conventional and architectural in its character, is extremely interesting and instructive, as shewing how distinctly the sculptor knew the proper limits of conventional and realistic representation. The fruit are described : (1) Cherries; SEREXIS. (2) Pears; PIRI. (3) Cucumbers; CHOCUMERIS. (4) Peaches; PERSICI. (5) Gourds; CUCHE. (6) Melons; MOLONI. (7) Figs; FIGI. (8) Grapes; HUVA.

XXVIII. Virtues and Vices. This is a replica of No. VII. The differences are very small. Here H is prefixed to the " ONORAT " of the other capital.

XXIX. Virtues. A replica of No. IX.

XXX. Vices. A replica of No. X., but well deserving study.

XXXI. Monsters. A replica of No. VIII., but very rudely carved, and very inferior to the next.

XXXII. Students. This is *not* a replica of No. XVII. The figures are admirably treated, all looking thoughtful, and some holding foliage. It seems to represent the more thoughtful side of youth as compared with the idle side, represented in the

capitals XV. and XXVI. Zanotto supposes the figures to be
the Seven Wise Men of Greece; but the eighth figure—a woman
speaking—does not lend itself to this. Mr. Burges most ingeniously suggests that it refers to Nouvella d'Andrea, who, in
her father's last illness, lectured from behind a curtain to his
pupils; her father died in 1348.

XXXIII. Virtues and Vices. This is a replica of No. XII.

XXXIV. Eight birds. A replica of No. XI.

XXXV. Nude children. A replica of No. IV. They have
birds, fruit, etc., in their hands.

XXXVI. Justice and Lawgivers. This is the north-west
angle column. The capital has the following subjects: (1)
Justice; JUSTITIA.   (2) Aristotle; ARISTOTEL . CHE . DIE . LEGGE.
(3) Moses; - - - L. PUOLO.D.L.SUO.ISEL.RITA.[1]   (4) Solon; SAL.
UNO.DEI.SETE.SAVI.DI.GRECIA.CHE.DIE.LEGGE. (5) Scipio; ISIPIONE.
ACHASTITA.CHE - - E.LA.FIA.ARE.[2]   (6) Numa Pompilius; NUMA
POMPILIO.IPERADOR.EDIFICHADOR.DI.TEPI.E.CHIESE.   (7) Moses re-
ceiving the tables of the law; QUADO.MOISE.RICEVE.LA.LEGE.I.
SUL.MONTE.   (8) Trajan; TRAINO.IPERADORE.CHE.DIE.JUSTITIA.
A.LA.VEDOVA.

The carving of foliage in this capital is, I think, simpler,
and on the whole better than that on the other great angle,
capital No. XVIII., with which it invites comparison: but the
carving of the figures is quite inferior, and later in character.
The foliage above this capital, which supports the Judgment of
Solomon, is inferior to that on the capital itself, and is, I believe,
considerably later in date, being no doubt of the same age as
the figures in the Judgment, i.e. not earlier than 1430–1450.
Above this angle is the figure of the Archangel Gabriel.

---

[1] Unintelligible; but explained by Zanotto to be: "Mosè che die' legge al suo
popolo Israelita."

[2] Zanotto reads this: "Scipione a castita che rende la figlia al padre."

THE END